ORIGINAL RIGHT-TO-LEFT
BACK OF THE BOOK.

PAGES, PANELS, AND SPEECH BALLOONS READ FROM TOP RIGHT TO
BOTTOM LEFT, AS SHOWN ABOVE. TRANSLATIONS ARE PROVIDED
FOR THE SOUND EFFECTS.

COMING SOON...

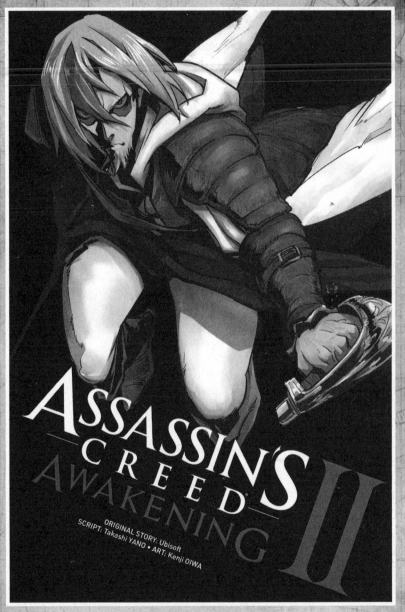

EDWARD AND MASATO'S ADVENTURES CONTINUE IN THIS STUNNING MANGA!

ON SALE IN OCTOBER!

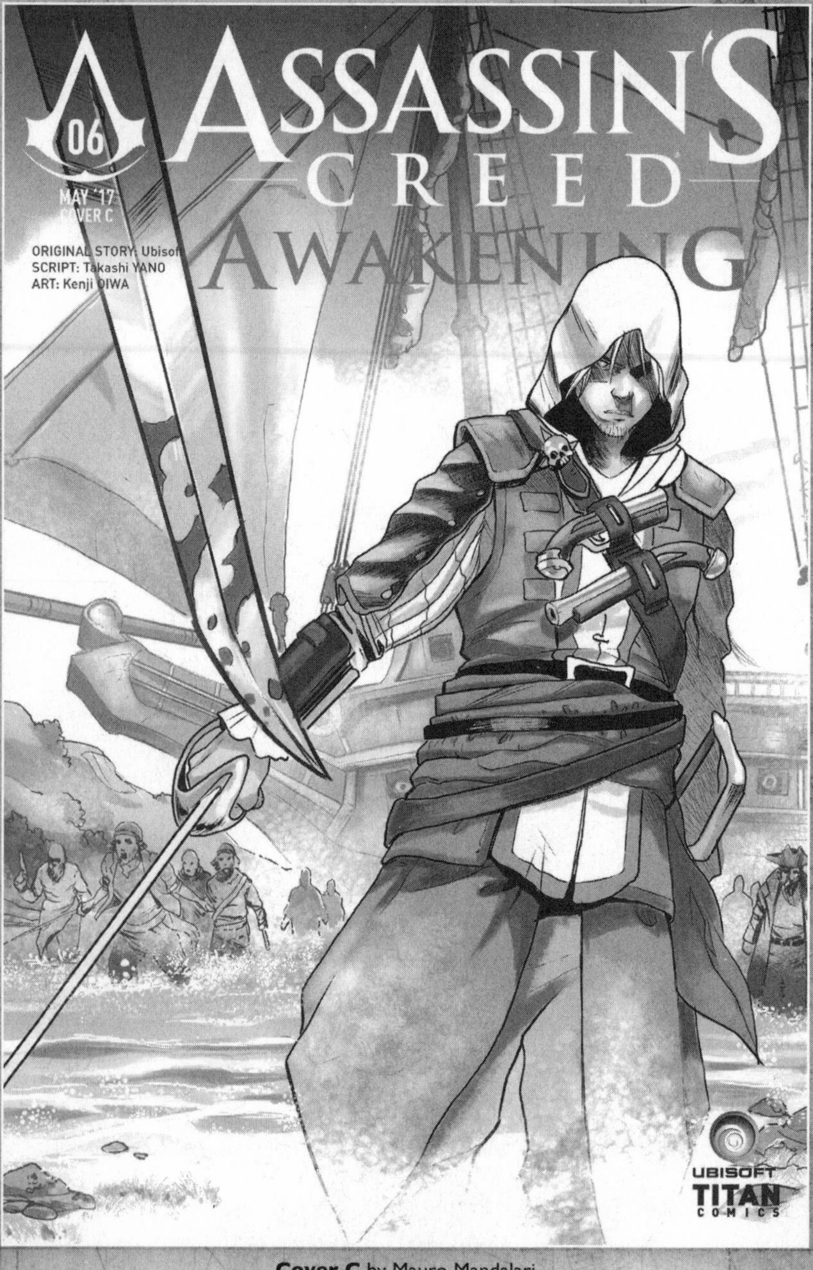
06
ASSASSIN'S CREED
AWAKENING
MAY '17
COVER C
ORIGINAL STORY: Ubisoft
SCRIPT: Takashi YANO
ART: Kenji OIWA
UBISOFT
TITAN COMICS

Cover C by Mauro Mandalari

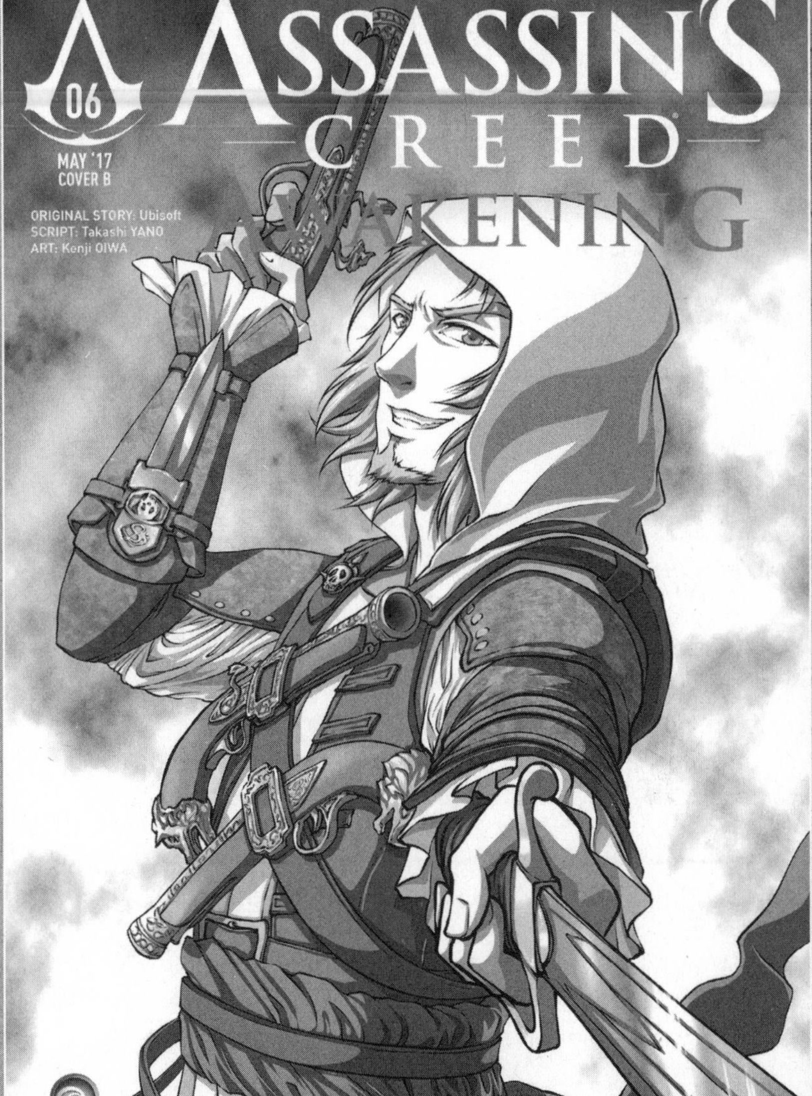
ASSASSIN'S CREED
06
MAY '17
COVER B
AWAKENING
ORIGINAL STORY: Ubisoft
SCRIPT: Takashi YANO
ART: Kenji OIWA

Cover B by Sonia Leong

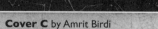

05

APRIL '17
COVER C

ASSASSIN'S CREED

AWAKENING

ORIGINAL STORY: Ubisoft
SCRIPT: Takashi YANO
ART: Kenji OIWA

UBISOFT

TITAN
COMICS

Cover C by Amrit Birdi

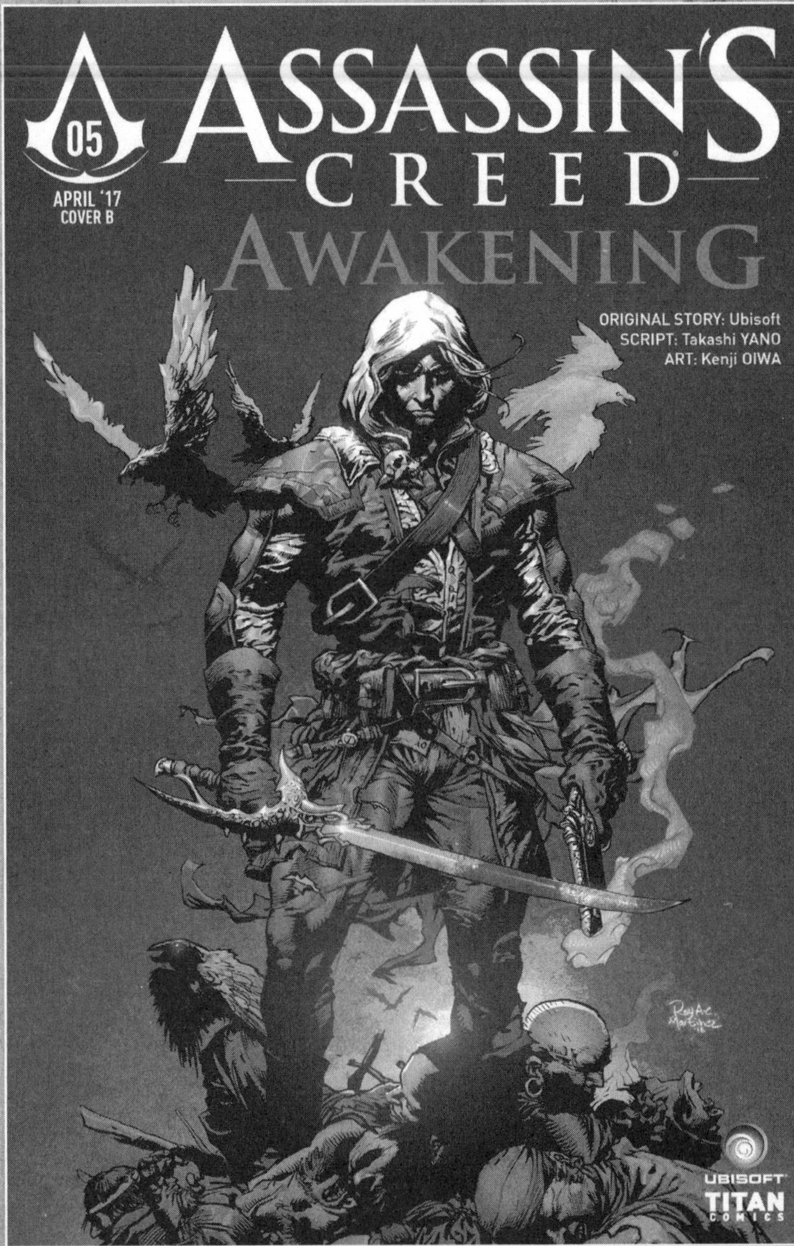
ASSASSIN'S CREED
AWAKENING
05
APRIL '17
COVER B
ORIGINAL STORY: Ubisoft
SCRIPT: Takashi YANO
ART: Kenji OIWA
UBISOFT
TITAN COMICS

Cover B by Roy Allan Martinez

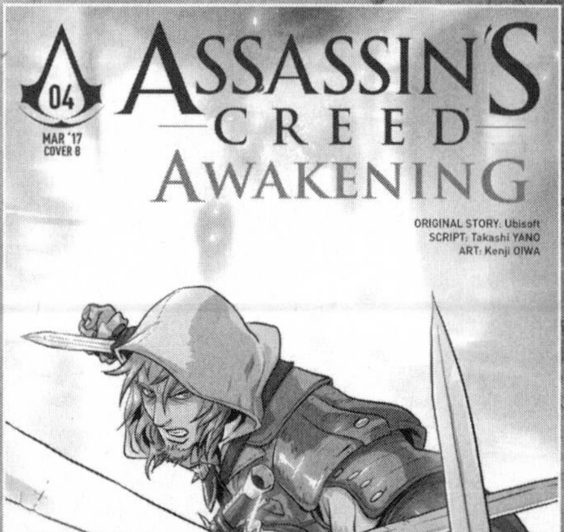
04
ASSASSIN'S
CREED
AWAKENING
MAR '17
COVER B
ORIGINAL STORY: Ubisoft
SCRIPT: Takashi YANO
ART: Kenji OIWA
UBISOFT
TITAN

Cover B by Andie Tong

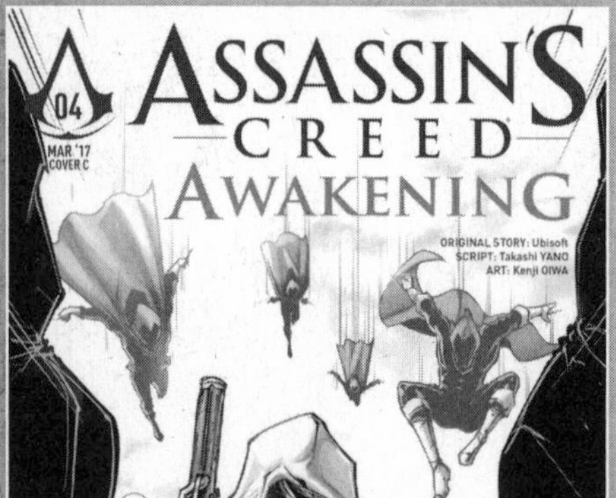
04
ASSASSIN'S
CREED
AWAKENING
MAR '17
COVER C
ORIGINAL STORY: Ubisoft
SCRIPT: Takashi YANO
ART: Kenji OIWA
UBISOFT
TITAN

Cover C by Amrit Birdi

03
ASSASSIN'S
CREED
AWAKENING
FEB '17
COVER B
UBISOFT
TITAN

Cover B by Andie Tong

03
ASSASSIN'S
CREED
AWAKENING
FEB '17
COVER C
ORIGINAL STORY: Ubisoft
SCRIPT: Takashi YANO
ART: Kenji OIWA
UBISOFT
TITAN
COMICS

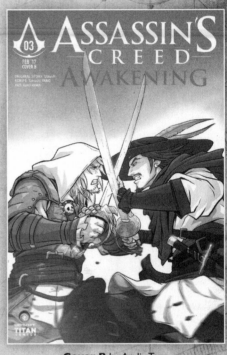

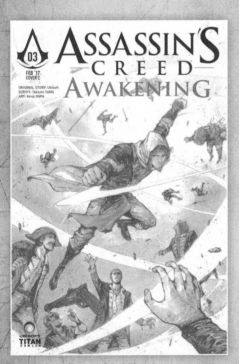

Cover C by Yifeng Jiang

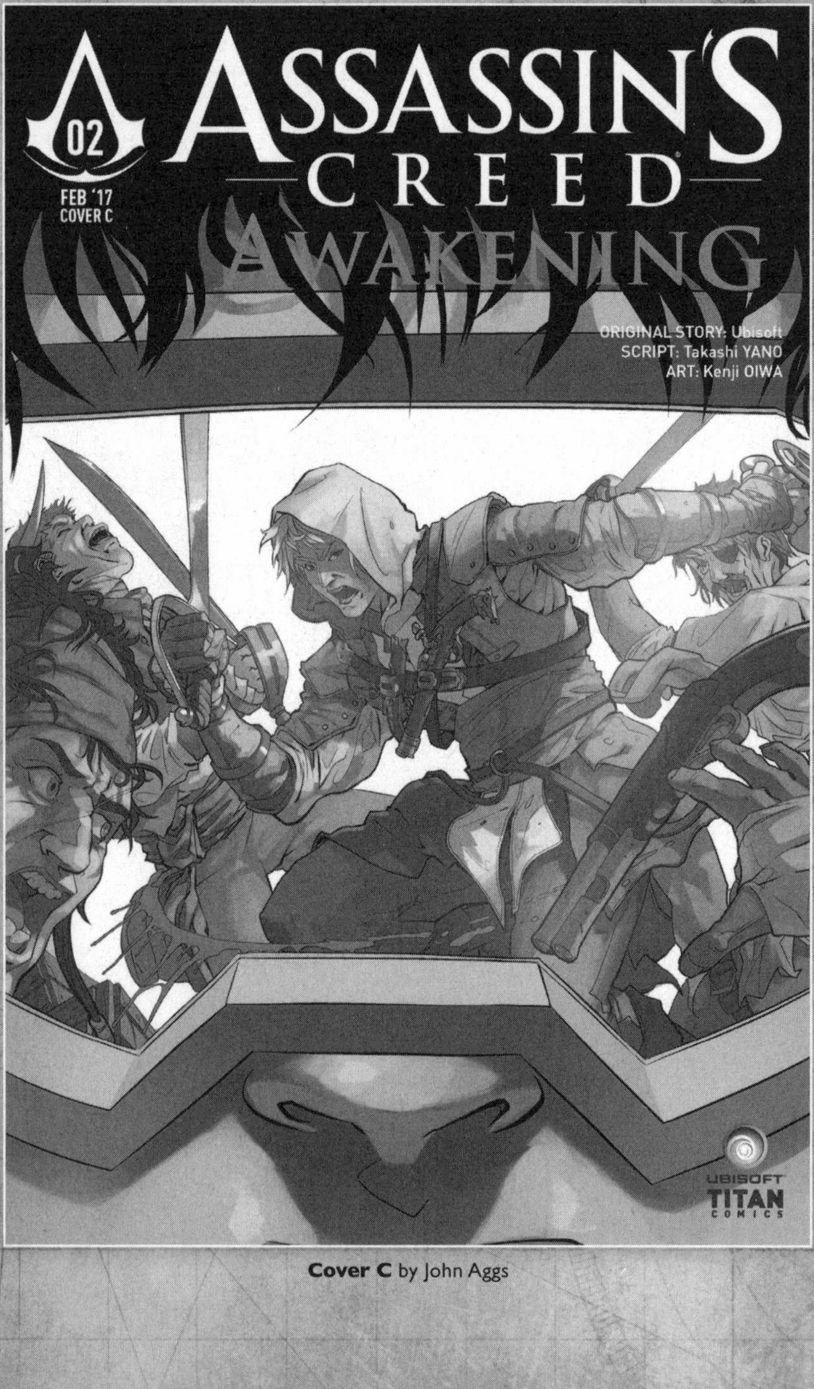
02
FEB '17
COVER C
ASSASSIN'S CREED
AWAKENING
ORIGINAL STORY: Ubisoft
SCRIPT: Takashi YANO
ART: Kenji OIWA
UBISOFT
TITAN COMICS

Cover C by John Aggs

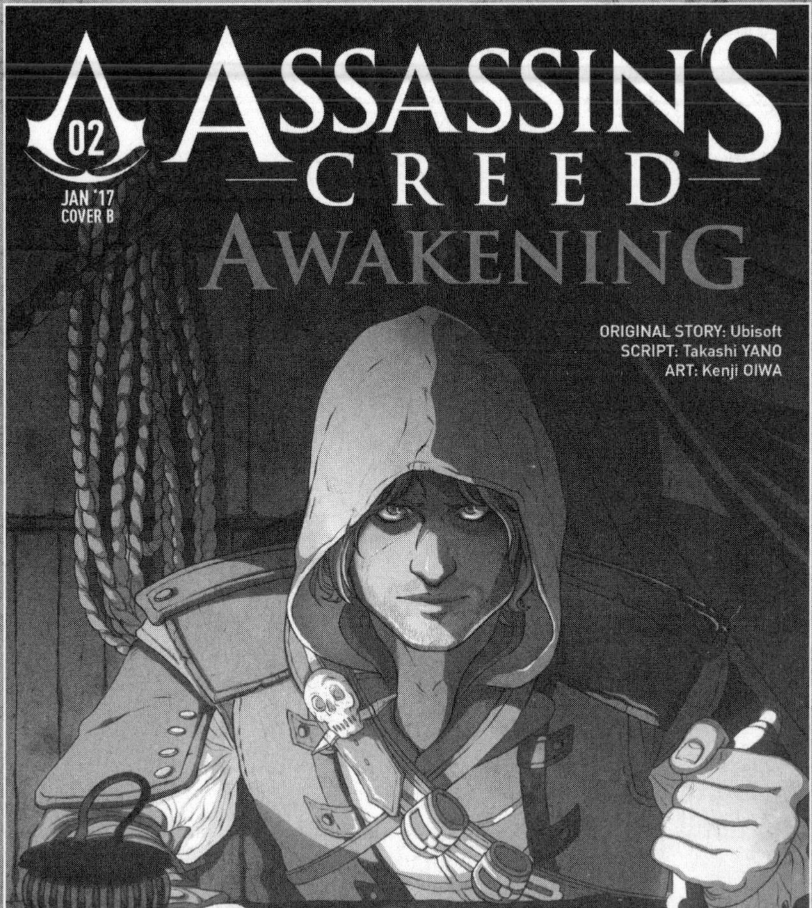
02
JAN '17
COVER B
ASSASSIN'S
CREED
AWAKENING
ORIGINAL STORY: Ubisoft
SCRIPT: Takashi YANO
ART: Kenji OIWA
UBISOFT
TITAN COMICS

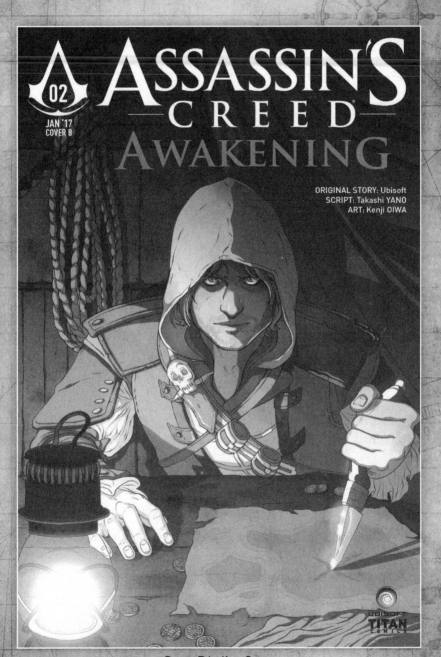

Cover B by Kate Brown

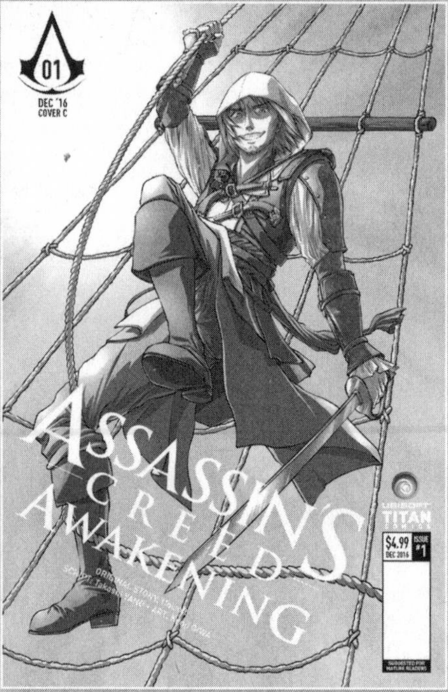
01
DEC '16
COVER C
ASSASSIN'S
CREED
AWAKENING
UBISOFT
TITAN
$4.99
DEC 2016
ISSUE
#1

Cover C by Sonia Leong

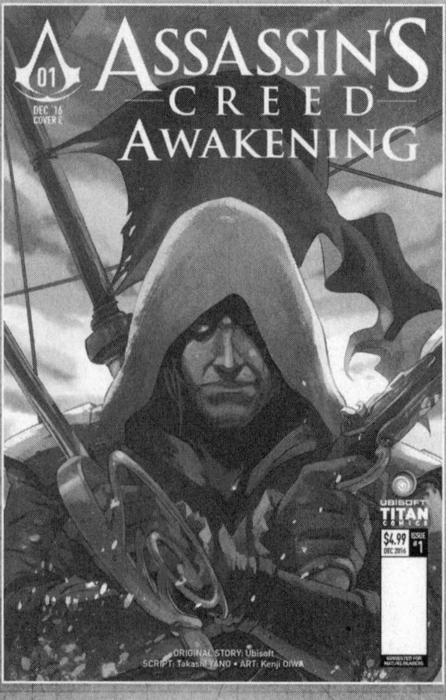
01
DEC '16
COVER E
ASSASSIN'S
CREED
AWAKENING
UBISOFT
TITAN
$4.99
DEC 2016
ISSUE
#1
ORIGINAL STORY: Ubisoft
SCRIPT: Takashi YANO • ART: Kenji OIWA

Cover E by Nana Lee & John Aggs

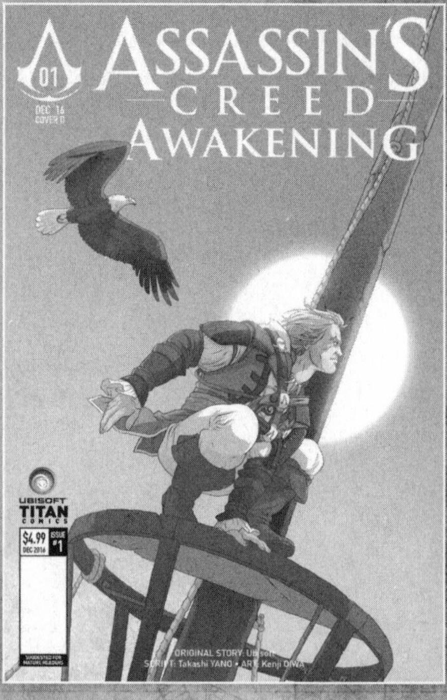
01
DEC '16
COVER D
ASSASSIN'S
CREED
AWAKENING
UBISOFT
TITAN
COMICS
$4.99
DEC 2016
ISSUE
#1
ORIGINAL STORY: Ubisoft
SCRIPT: Takashi YANO • ART: Kenji OIWA

Cover D by Kate Brown

COVER GALLERY

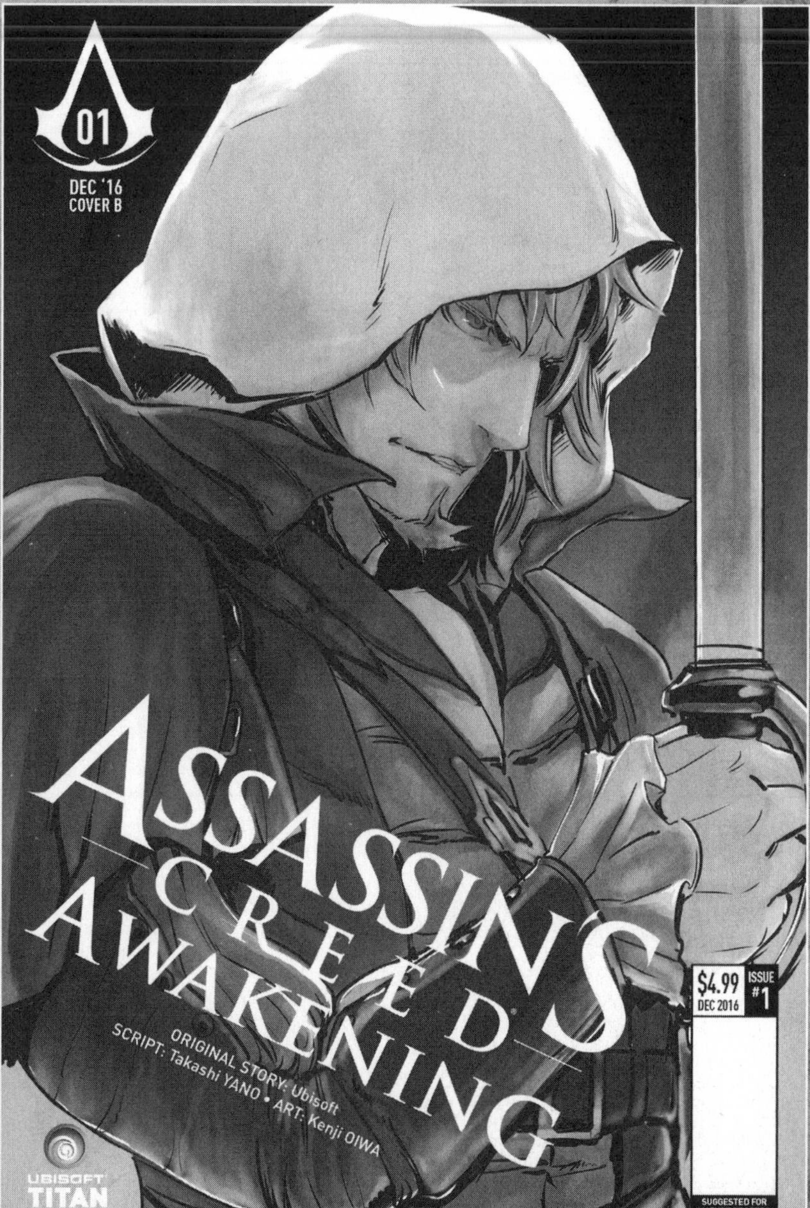

01
DEC '16
COVER B
ASSASSIN'S CREED AWAKENING
ORIGINAL STORY: Ubisoft
SCRIPT: Takashi YANO • ART: Kenji OIWA
UBISOFT
TITAN COMICS
$4.99
DEC 2016
ISSUE #1
SUGGESTED FOR MATURE READERS

Cover B by Kenji Oiwa

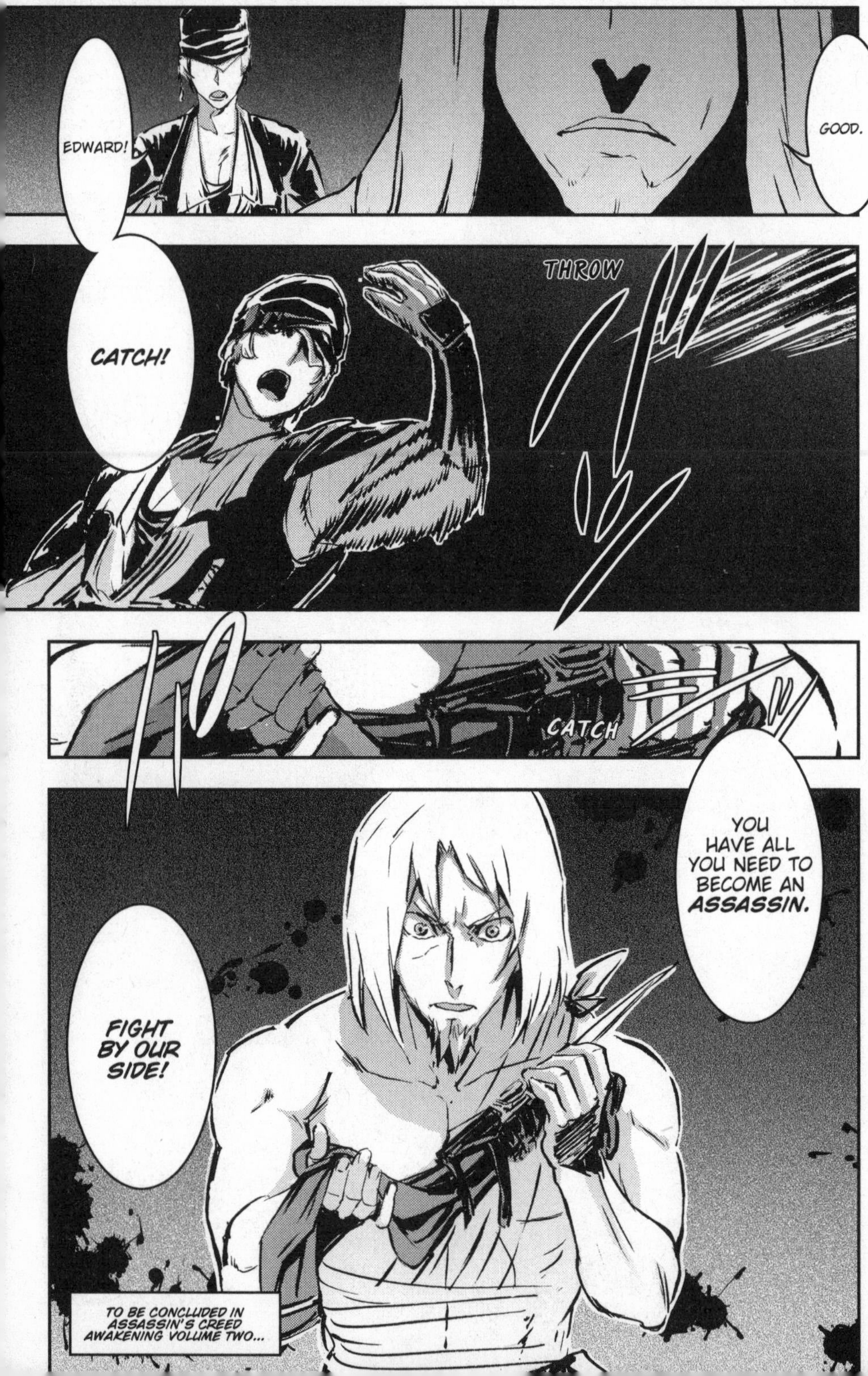
GOOD.
EDWARD!
THROW
CATCH!
CATCH
YOU HAVE ALL YOU NEED TO BECOME AN ASSASSIN.
FIGHT BY OUR SIDE!
TO BE CONCLUDED IN ASSASSIN'S CREED AWAKENING VOLUME TWO...

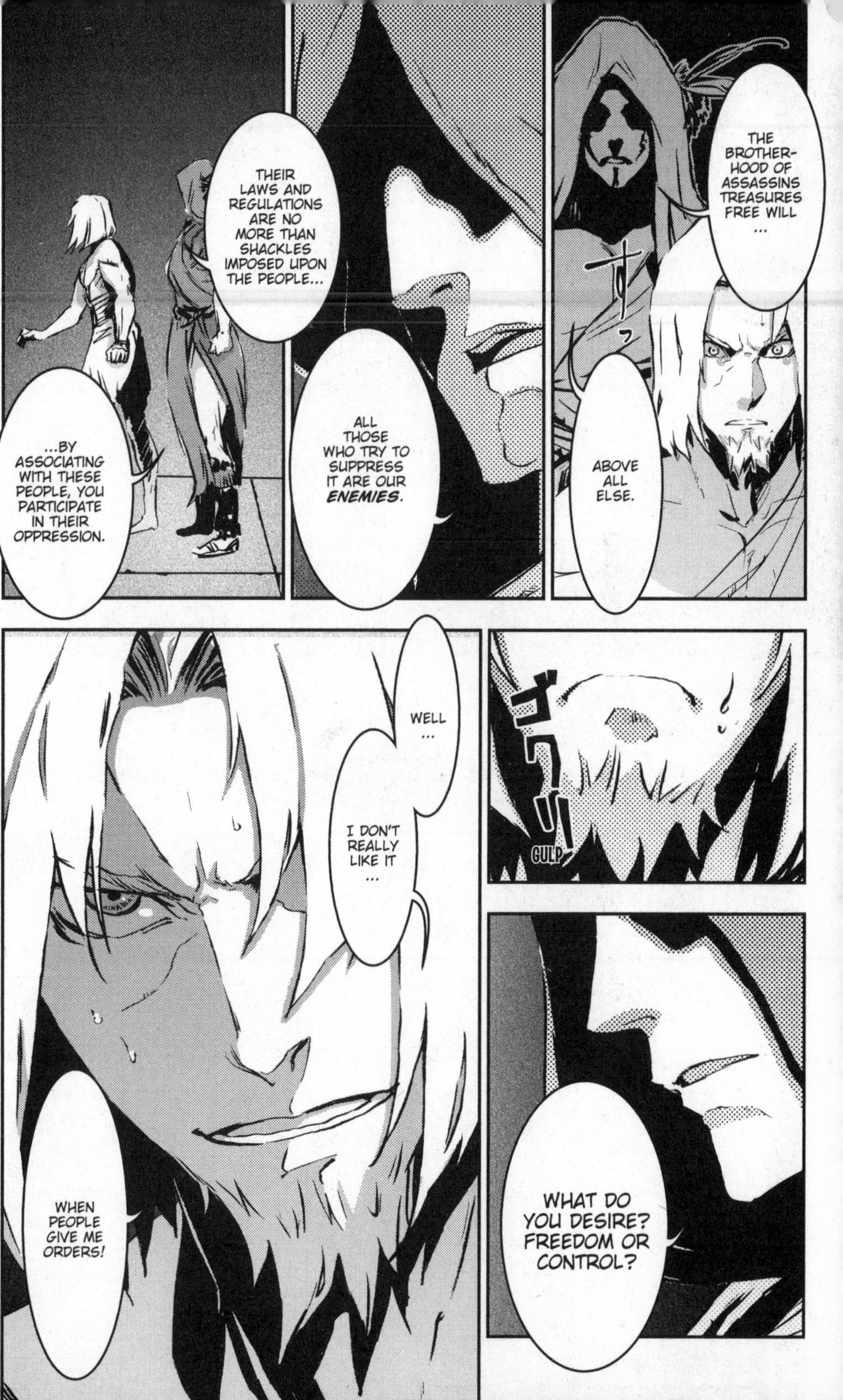
THE BROTHER-HOOD OF ASSASSINS TREASURES FREE WILL ...
ABOVE ALL ELSE.
ALL THOSE WHO TRY TO SUPPRESS IT ARE OUR ENEMIES.
THEIR LAWS AND REGULATIONS ARE NO MORE THAN SHACKLES IMPOSED UPON THE PEOPLE...
...BY ASSOCIATING WITH THESE PEOPLE, YOU PARTICIPATE IN THEIR OPPRESSION.
GULP
WHAT DO YOU DESIRE? FREEDOM OR CONTROL?
WELL ...
I DON'T REALLY LIKE IT ...
WHEN PEOPLE GIVE ME ORDERS!

DISAPPEAR

!!

ASSA-SSINS?

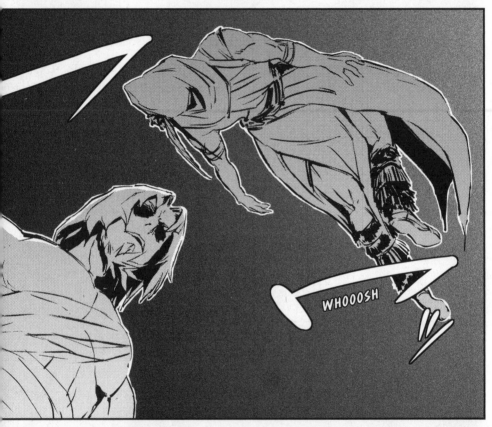

WHOOOSH

LAND

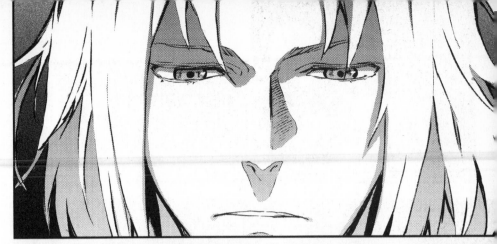

ARE YOU FINALLY AWAKE?

SNEAK

WHO... ARE *YOU* ...?

I AM A MEMBER OF THE BROTHERHOOD OF ASSASSINS

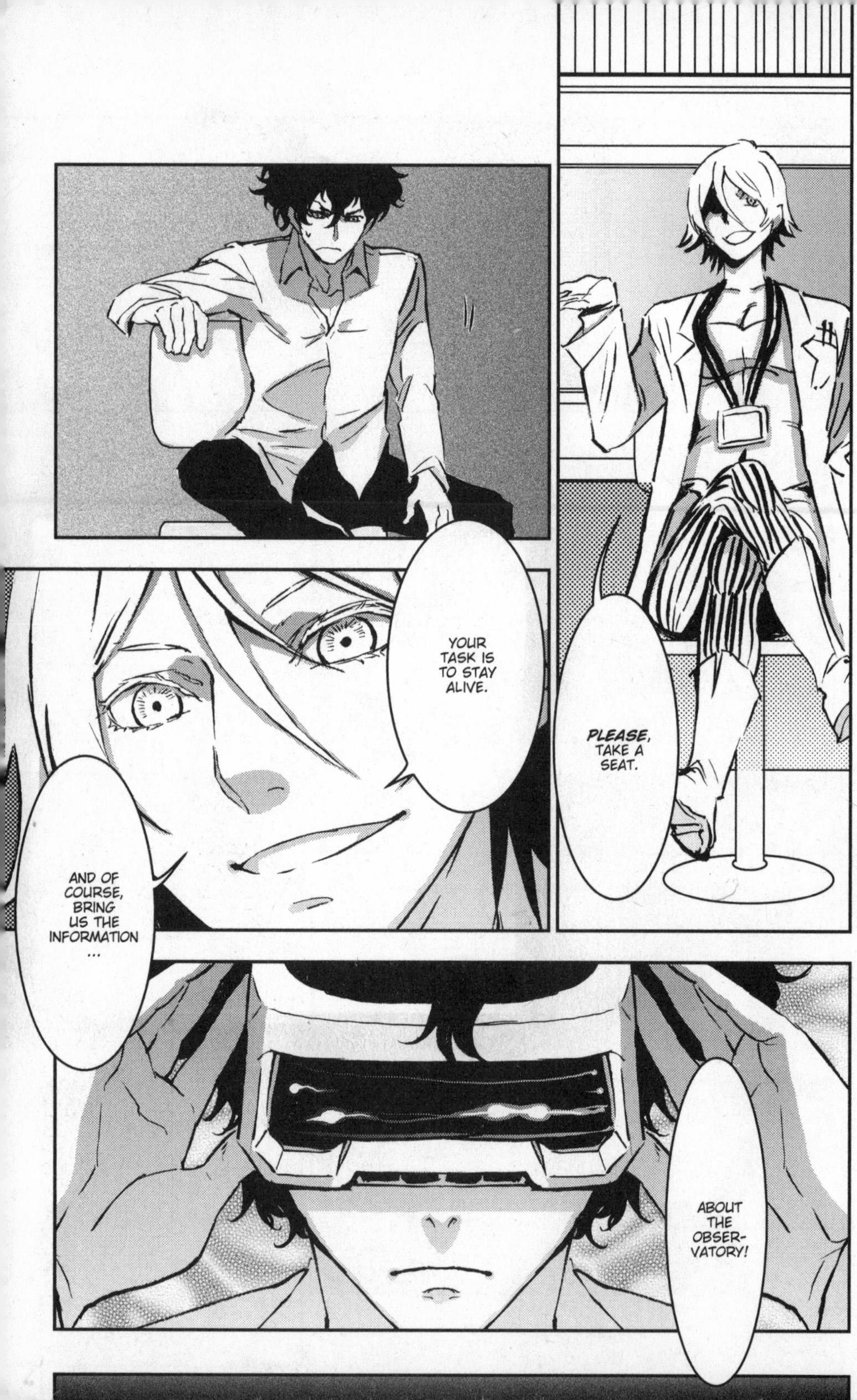
PLEASE, TAKE A SEAT.
YOUR TASK IS TO STAY ALIVE.
AND OF COURSE, BRING US THE INFORMATION ...
ABOUT THE OBSERVATORY!

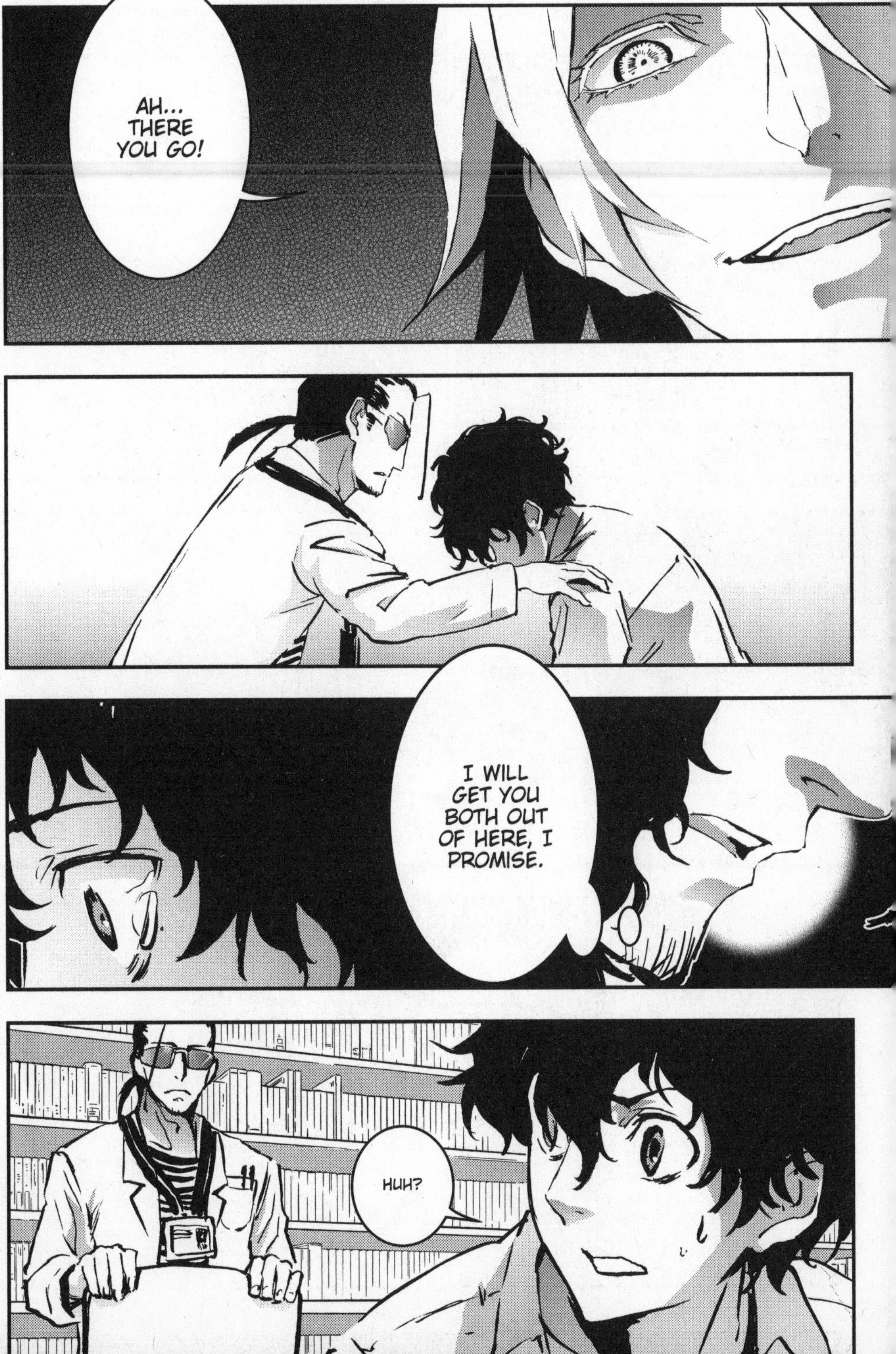
AH... THERE YOU GO!
I WILL GET YOU BOTH OUT OF HERE, I PROMISE.
HUH?

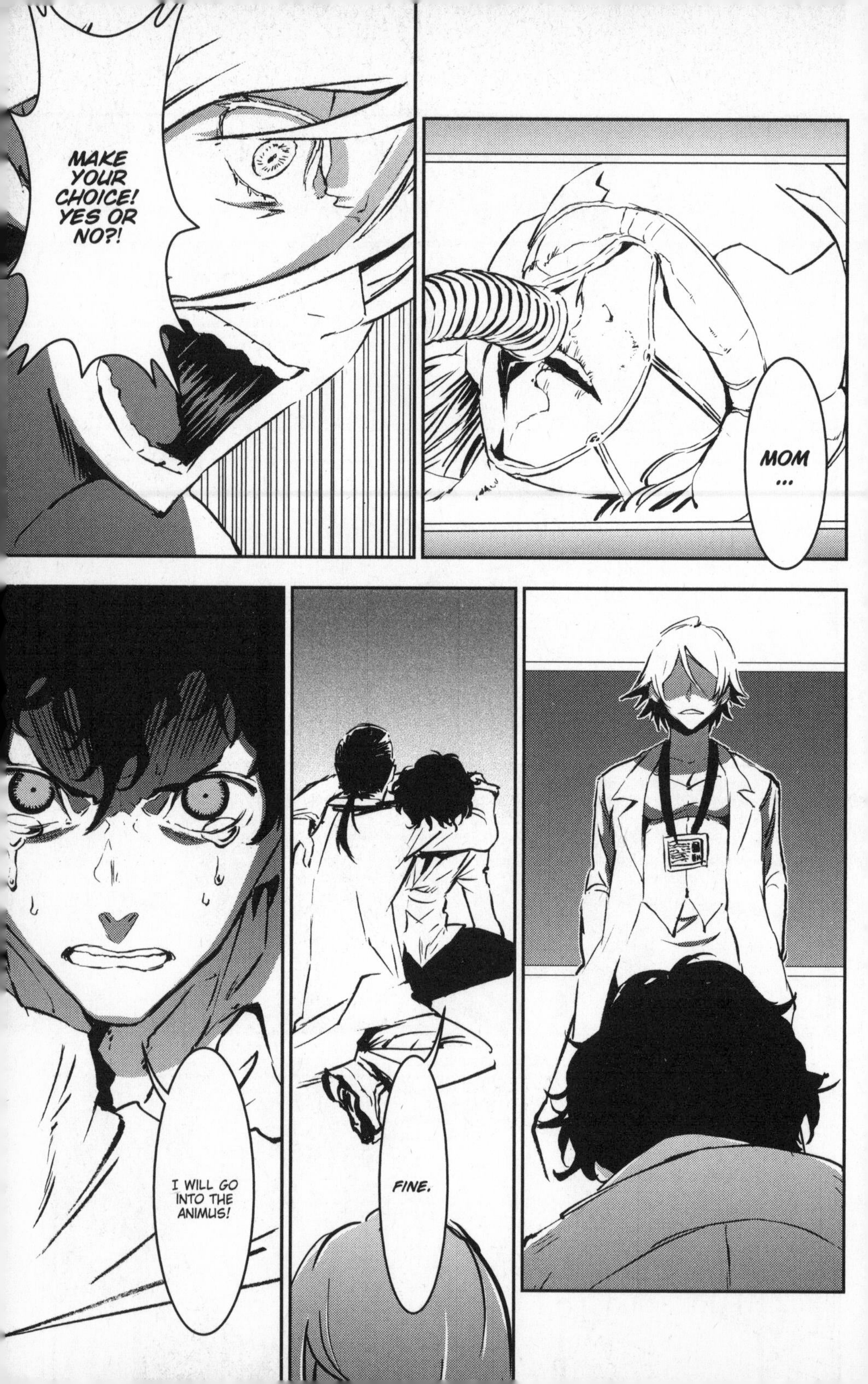
MOM ...
MAKE YOUR CHOICE! YES OR NO?!
FINE.
I WILL GO INTO THE ANIMUS!

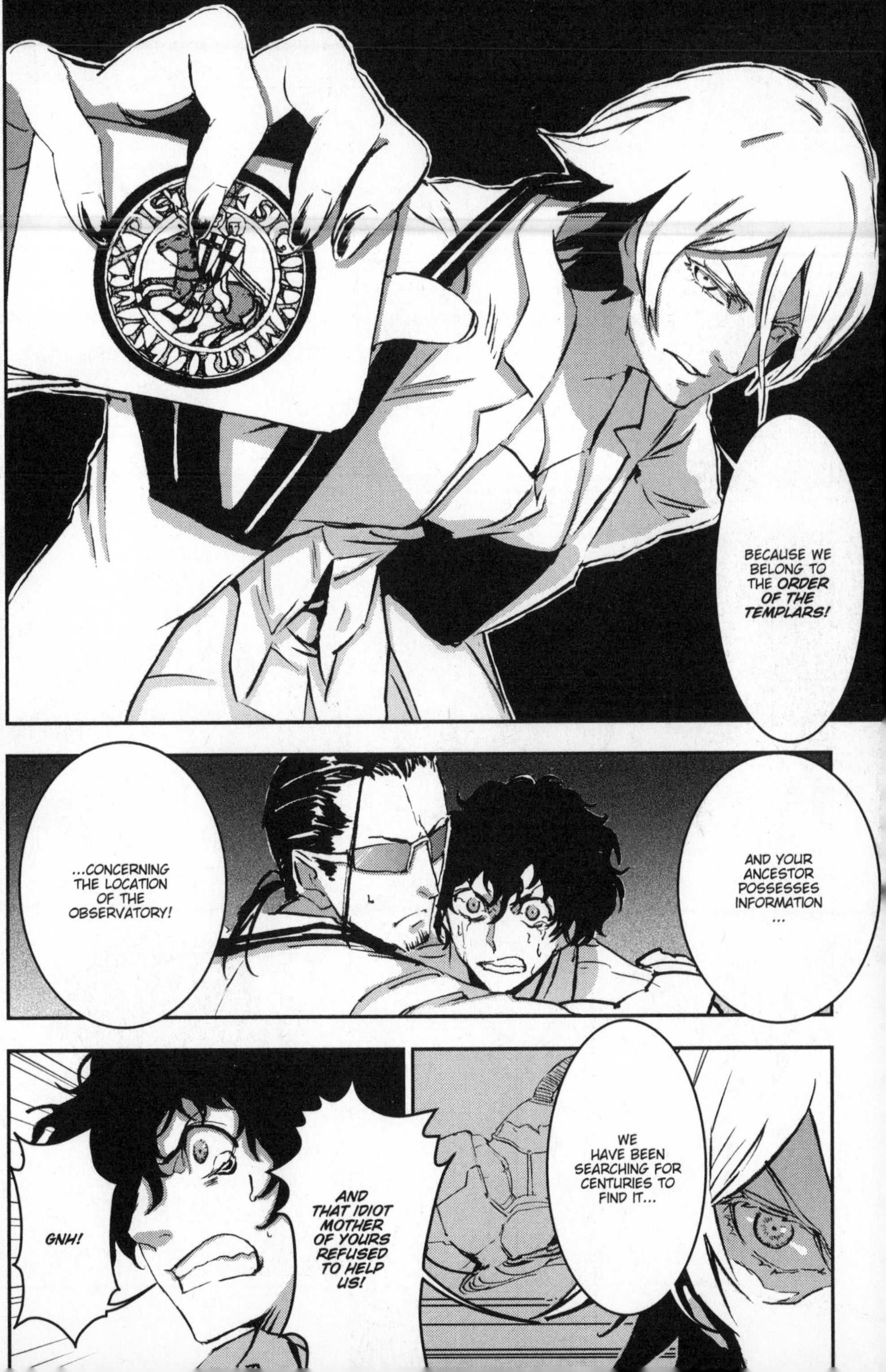
BECAUSE WE BELONG TO THE ORDER OF THE TEMPLARS!
AND YOUR ANCESTOR POSSESSES INFORMATION ...
...CONCERNING THE LOCATION OF THE OBSERVATORY!
WE HAVE BEEN SEARCHING FOR CENTURIES TO FIND IT...
AND THAT IDIOT MOTHER OF YOURS REFUSED TO HELP US!
GNH!

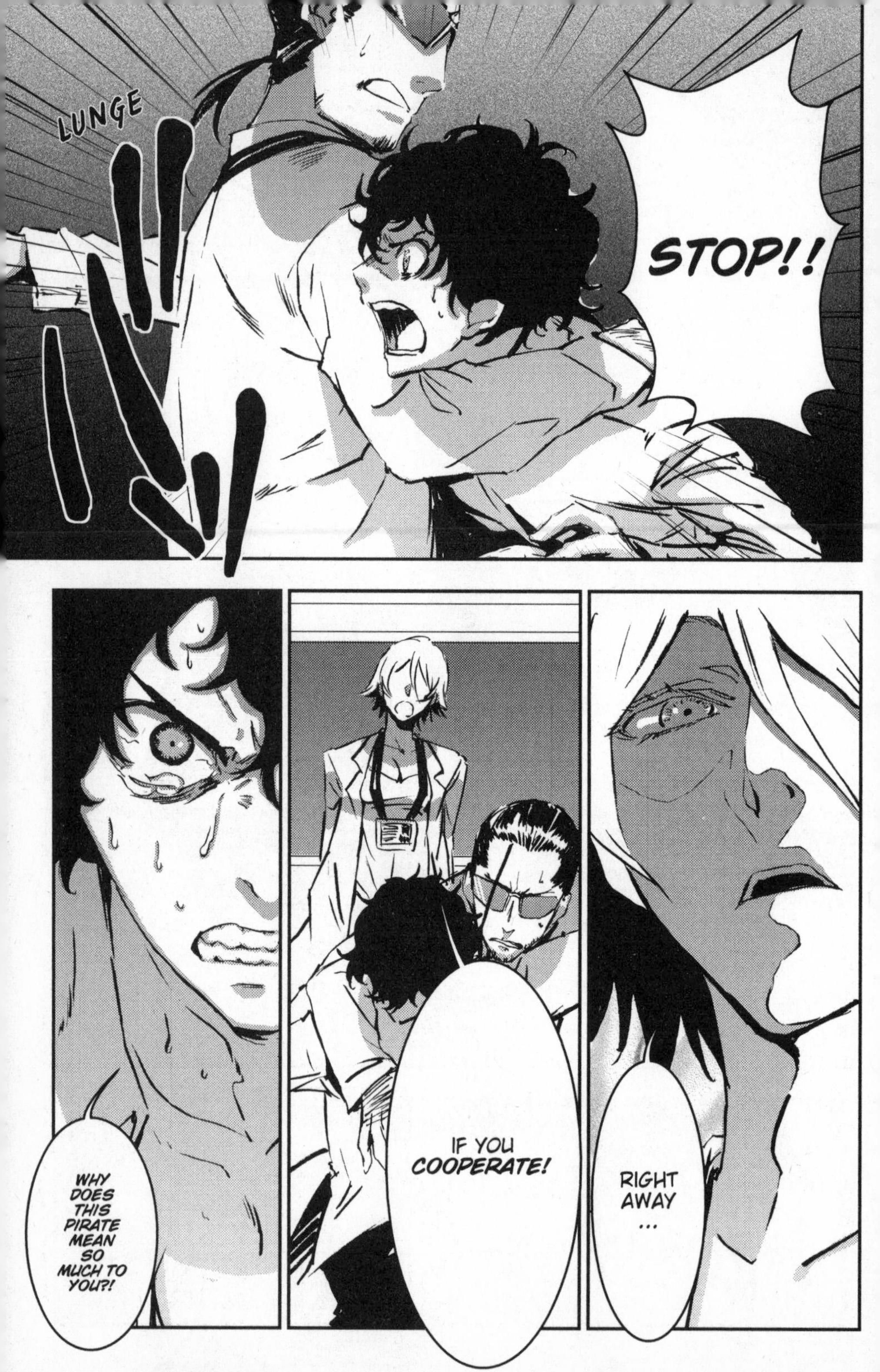
STOP!!
LUNGE
RIGHT AWAY ...
IF YOU COOPERATE!
WHY DOES THIS PIRATE MEAN SO MUCH TO YOU?!

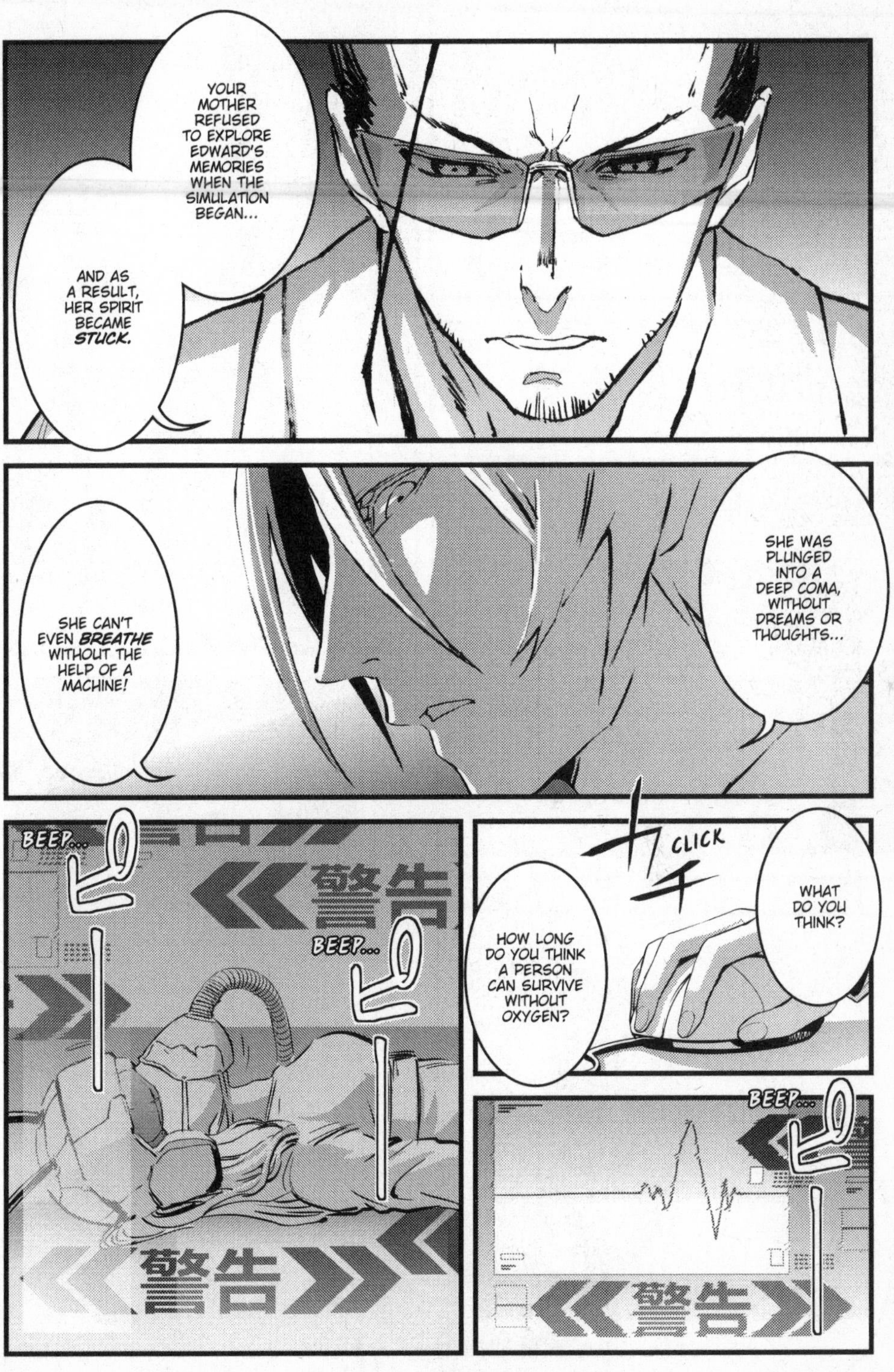
YOUR MOTHER REFUSED TO EXPLORE EDWARD'S MEMORIES WHEN THE SIMULATION BEGAN...
AND AS A RESULT, HER SPIRIT BECAME *STUCK.*
SHE WAS PLUNGED INTO A DEEP COMA, WITHOUT DREAMS OR THOUGHTS...
SHE CAN'T EVEN *BREATHE* WITHOUT THE HELP OF A MACHINE!
WHAT DO YOU THINK?
カチ
CLICK
HOW LONG DO YOU THINK A PERSON CAN SURVIVE WITHOUT OXYGEN?
ピー
BEEP...
警告
ピー
BEEP...
ピー
BEEP...
警告
警告

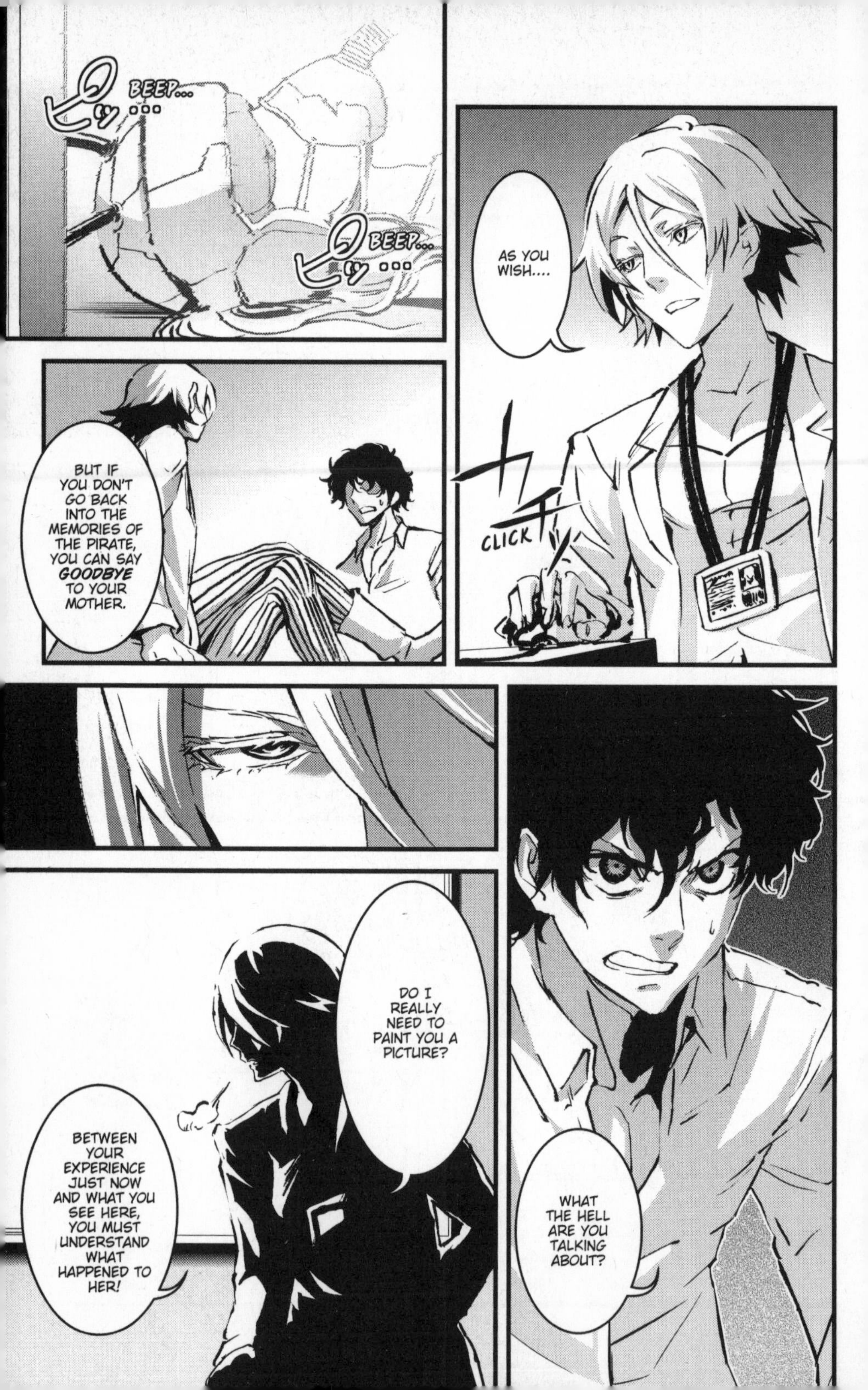
AS YOU WISH....
カチ
CLICK
ピッ...
BEEP...
ピッ...
BEEP...
BUT IF YOU DON'T GO BACK INTO THE MEMORIES OF THE PIRATE, YOU CAN SAY ***GOODBYE*** TO YOUR MOTHER.
WHAT THE HELL ARE YOU TALKING ABOUT?
DO I REALLY NEED TO PAINT YOU A PICTURE?
BETWEEN YOUR EXPERIENCE JUST NOW AND WHAT YOU SEE HERE, YOU MUST UNDERSTAND WHAT HAPPENED TO HER!

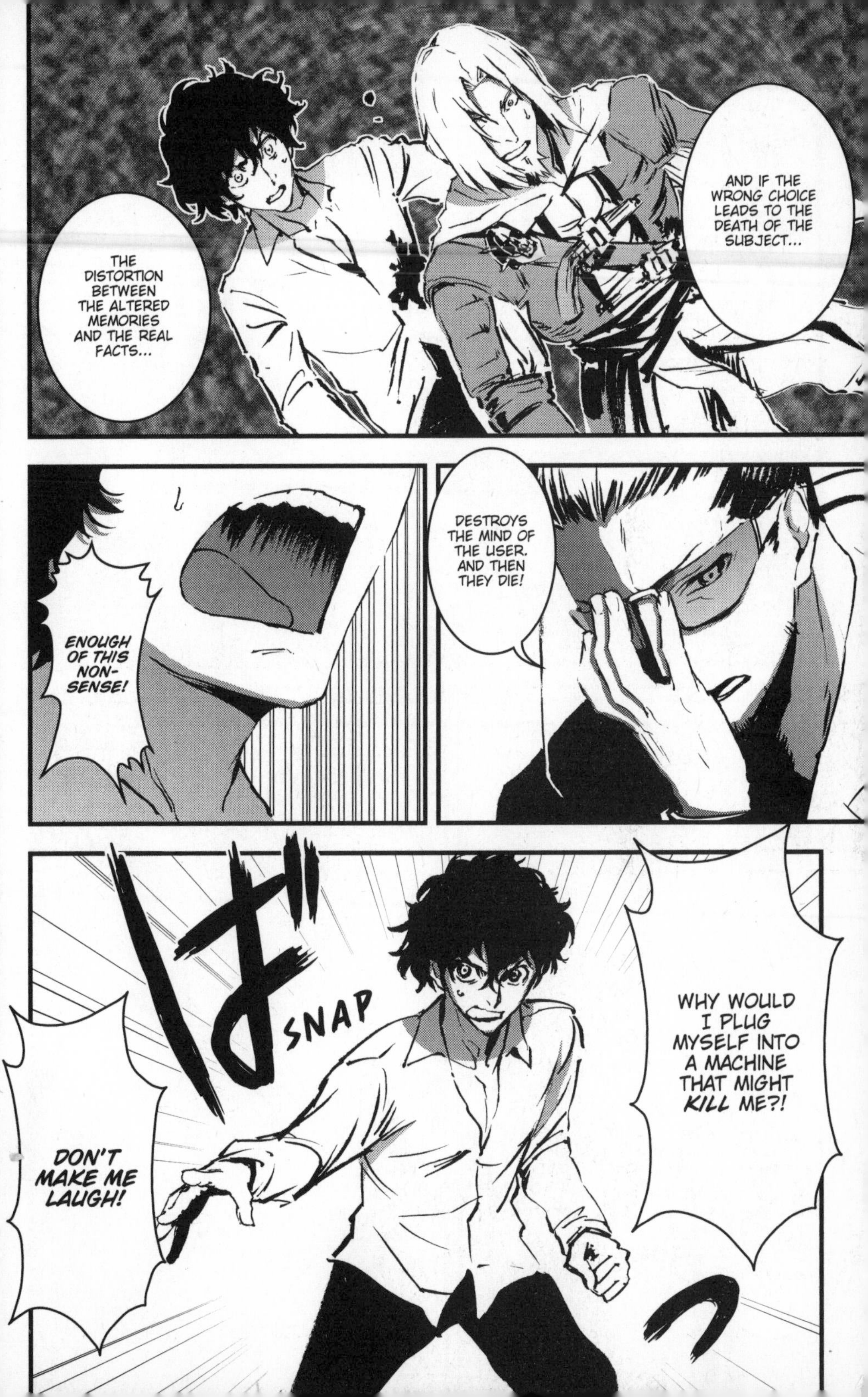
AND IF THE WRONG CHOICE LEADS TO THE DEATH OF THE SUBJECT...
THE DISTORTION BETWEEN THE ALTERED MEMORIES AND THE REAL FACTS...
DESTROYS THE MIND OF THE USER. AND THEN THEY DIE!
ENOUGH OF THIS NON-SENSE!
WHY WOULD I PLUG MYSELF INTO A MACHINE THAT MIGHT KILL ME?!
SNAP
DON'T MAKE ME LAUGH!

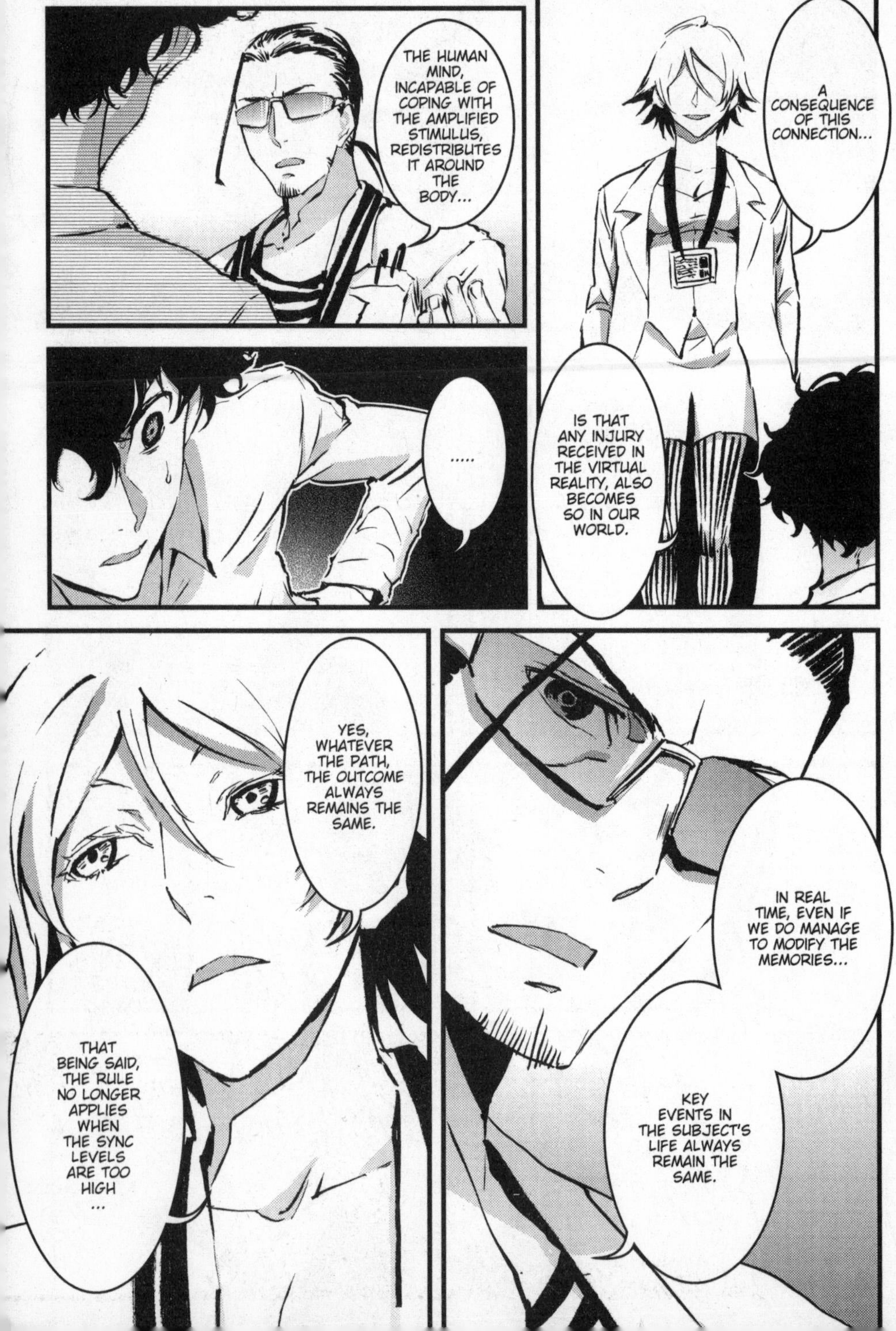
A CONSEQUENCE OF THIS CONNECTION...
IS THAT ANY INJURY RECEIVED IN THE VIRTUAL REALITY, ALSO BECOMES SO IN OUR WORLD.
THE HUMAN MIND, INCAPABLE OF COPING WITH THE AMPLIFIED STIMULUS, REDISTRIBUTES IT AROUND THE BODY...
.....
IN REAL TIME, EVEN IF WE DO MANAGE TO MODIFY THE MEMORIES...
KEY EVENTS IN THE SUBJECT'S LIFE ALWAYS REMAIN THE SAME.
YES, WHATEVER THE PATH, THE OUTCOME ALWAYS REMAINS THE SAME.
THAT BEING SAID, THE RULE NO LONGER APPLIES WHEN THE SYNC LEVELS ARE TOO HIGH ...

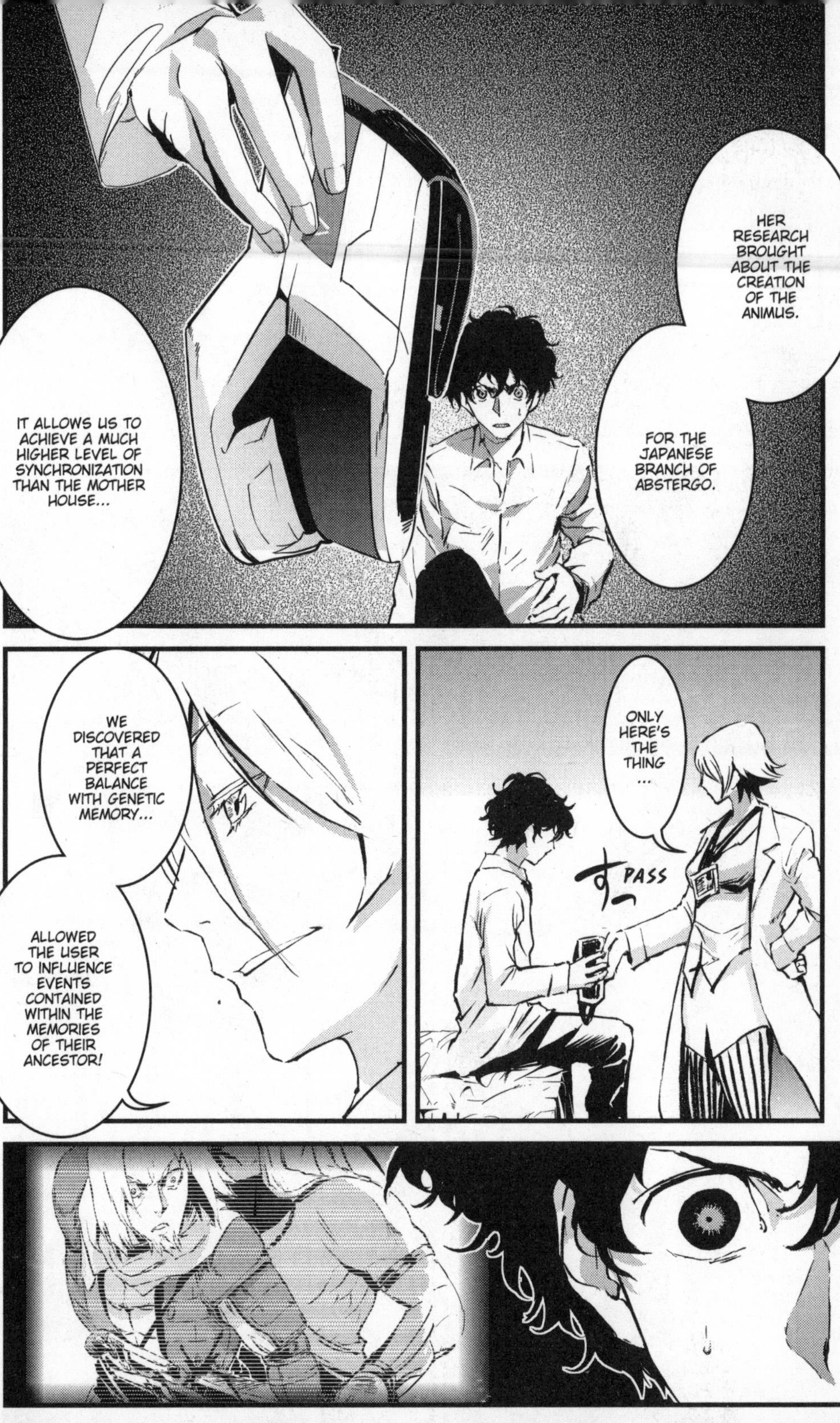
HER RESEARCH BROUGHT ABOUT THE CREATION OF THE ANIMUS.
FOR THE JAPANESE BRANCH OF ABSTERGO.
IT ALLOWS US TO ACHIEVE A MUCH HIGHER LEVEL OF SYNCHRONIZATION THAN THE MOTHER HOUSE...
ONLY HERE'S THE THING ...
すー PASS
WE DISCOVERED THAT A PERFECT BALANCE WITH GENETIC MEMORY...
ALLOWED THE USER TO INFLUENCE EVENTS CONTAINED WITHIN THE MEMORIES OF THEIR ANCESTOR!

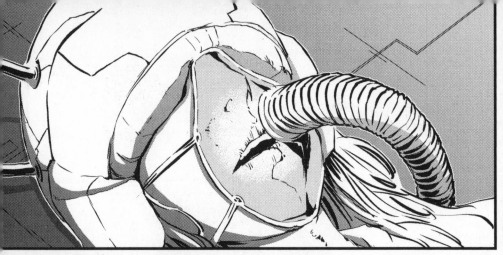

SHE WAS WORKING ON A WAY TO FACILITATE ACCESS TO THE MEMORIES...

...AND TO FIND A BETTER SYNCHRONIZATION WITH GENETIC MEMORY...

MOM?

CLICK   CLICK

?

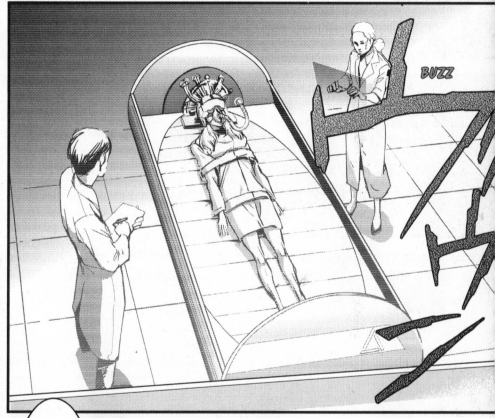

BUZZ

SAY HELLO TO YOUR MOTHER!

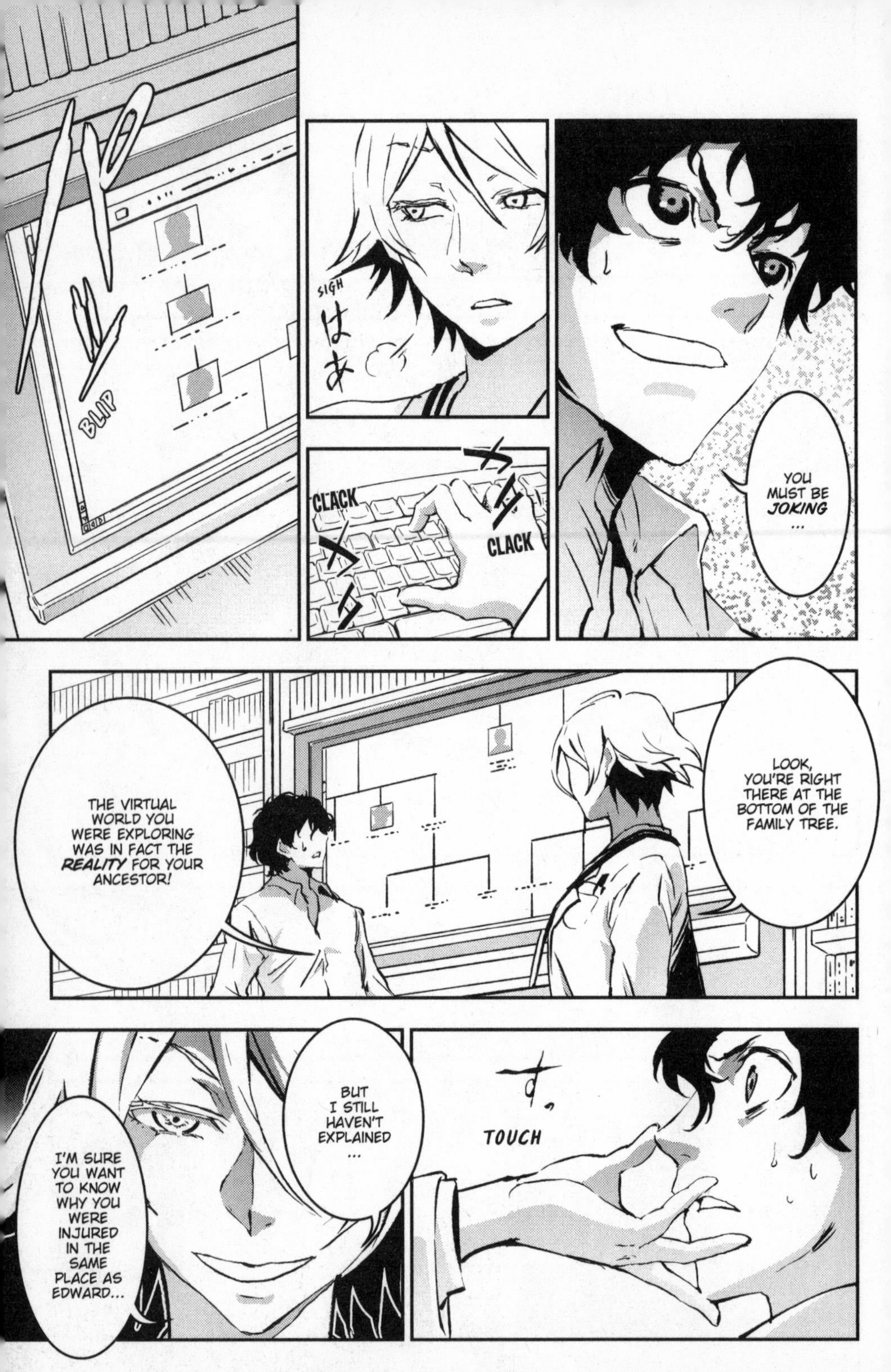

YOU MUST BE JOKING ...
SIGH
はあ
CLACK
CLACK
BLIP
LOOK, YOU'RE RIGHT THERE AT THE BOTTOM OF THE FAMILY TREE.
THE VIRTUAL WORLD YOU WERE EXPLORING WAS IN FACT THE REALITY FOR YOUR ANCESTOR!
TOUCH
BUT I STILL HAVEN'T EXPLAINED ...
I'M SURE YOU WANT TO KNOW WHY YOU WERE INJURED IN THE SAME PLACE AS EDWARD...

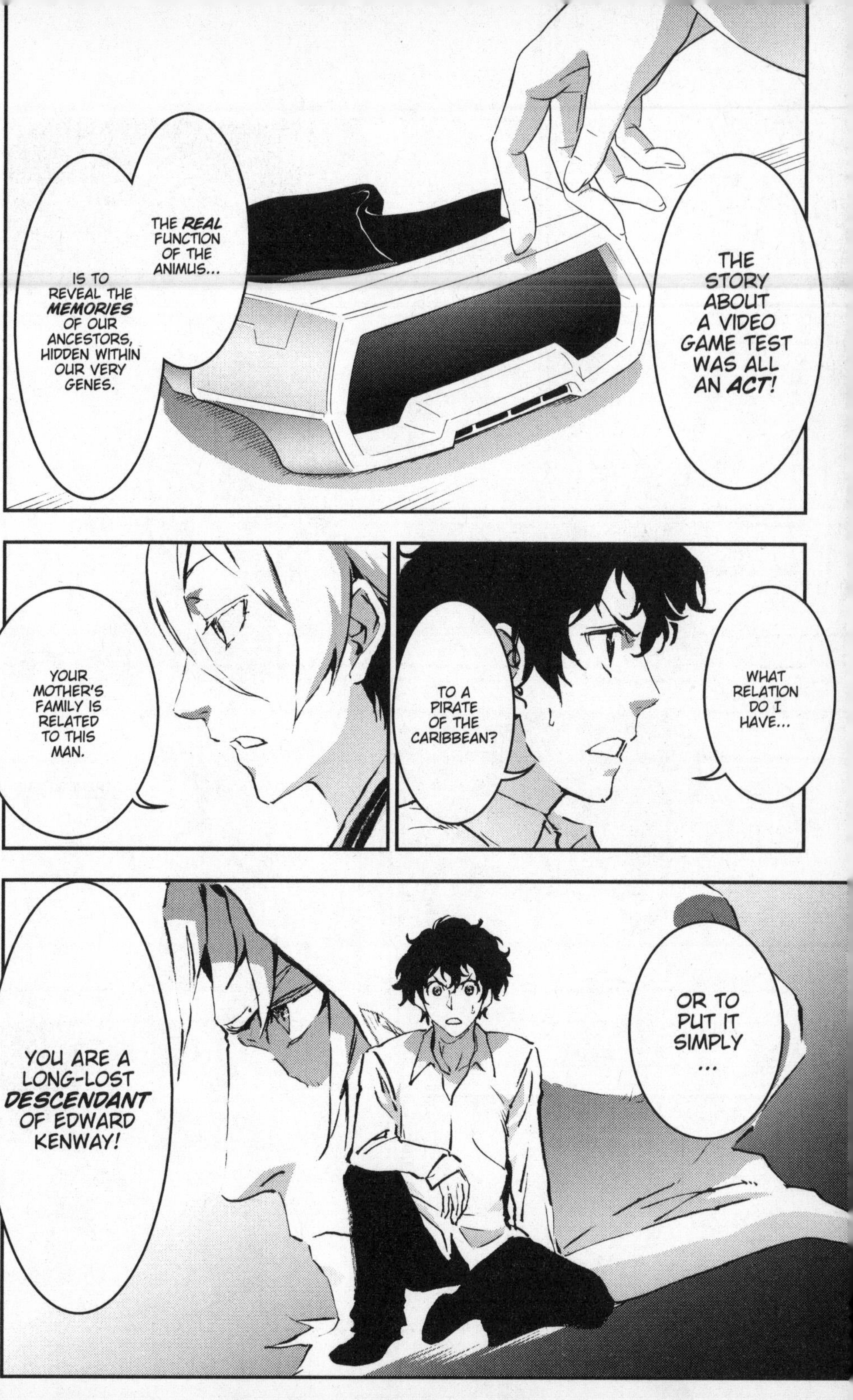
THE STORY ABOUT A VIDEO GAME TEST WAS ALL AN ACT!
THE REAL FUNCTION OF THE ANIMUS... IS TO REVEAL THE MEMORIES OF OUR ANCESTORS, HIDDEN WITHIN OUR VERY GENES.
WHAT RELATION DO I HAVE...
TO A PIRATE OF THE CARIBBEAN?
YOUR MOTHER'S FAMILY IS RELATED TO THIS MAN.
OR TO PUT IT SIMPLY...
YOU ARE A LONG-LOST DESCENDANT OF EDWARD KENWAY!

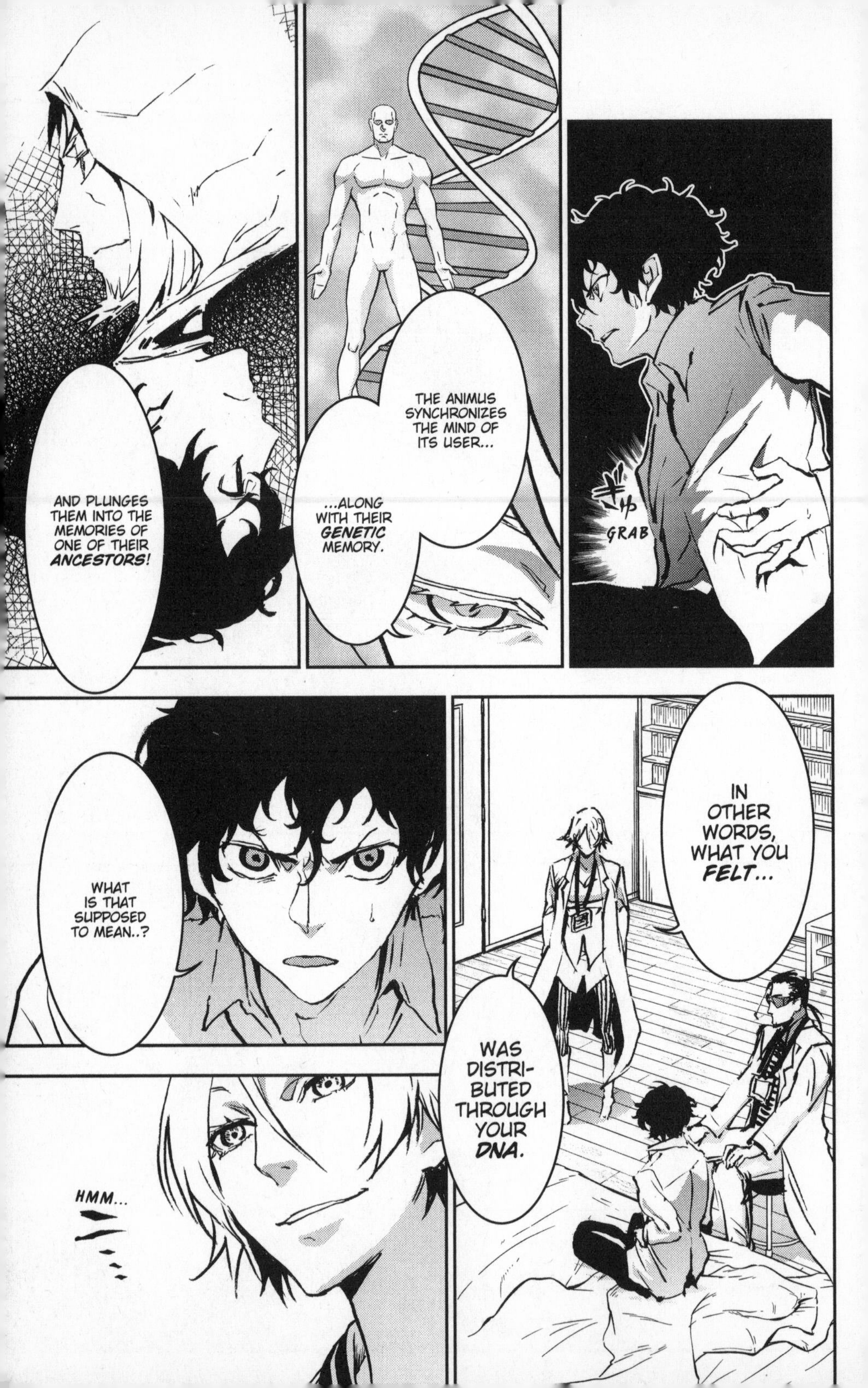
GRAB
THE ANIMUS SYNCHRONIZES THE MIND OF ITS USER...
...ALONG WITH THEIR GENETIC MEMORY.
AND PLUNGES THEM INTO THE MEMORIES OF ONE OF THEIR ANCESTORS!
IN OTHER WORDS, WHAT YOU FELT...
WAS DISTRI-BUTED THROUGH YOUR DNA.
WHAT IS THAT SUPPOSED TO MEAN..?
HMM...

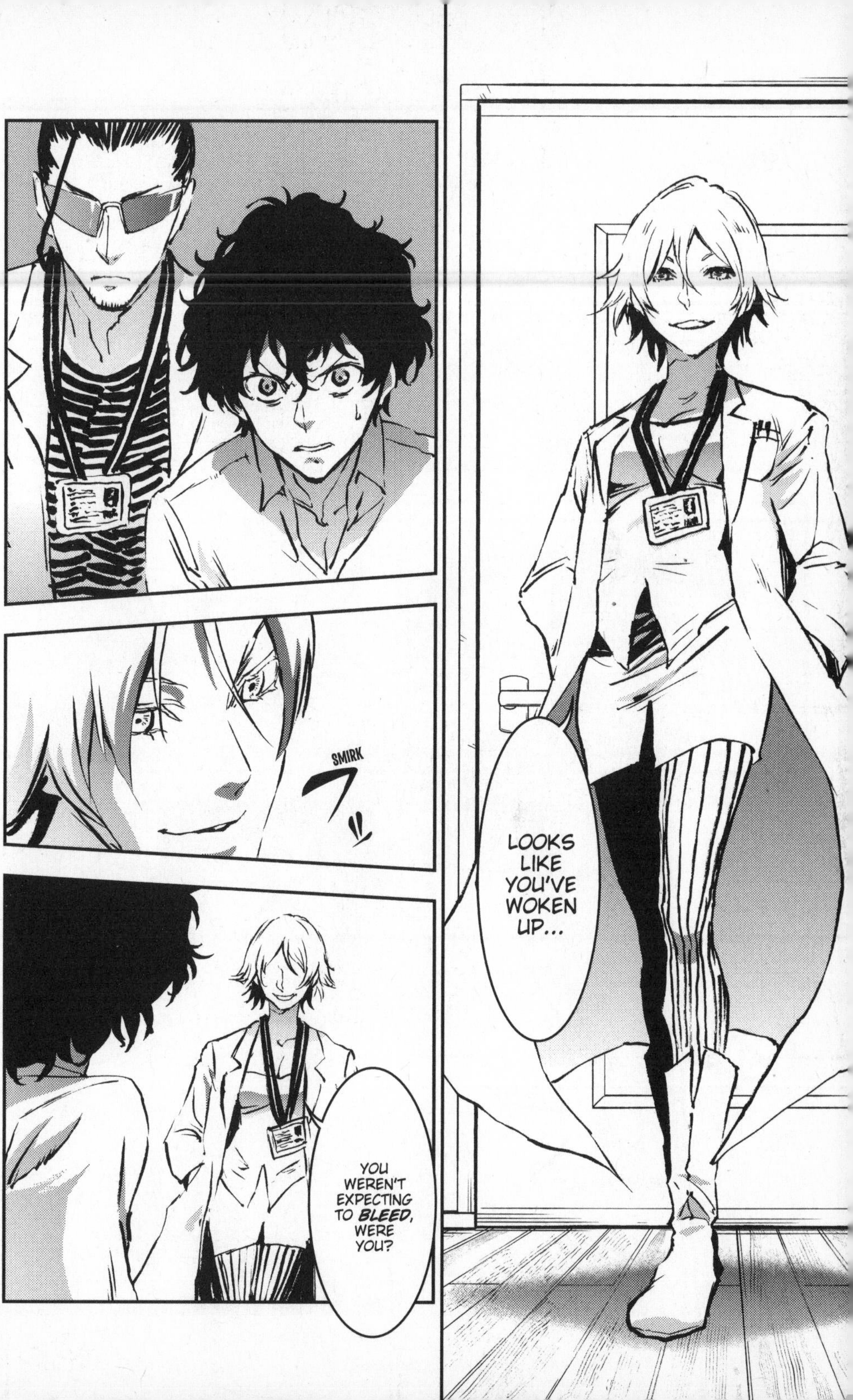
LOOKS LIKE YOU'VE WOKEN UP...
SMIRK
YOU WEREN'T EXPECTING TO *BLEED*, WERE YOU?

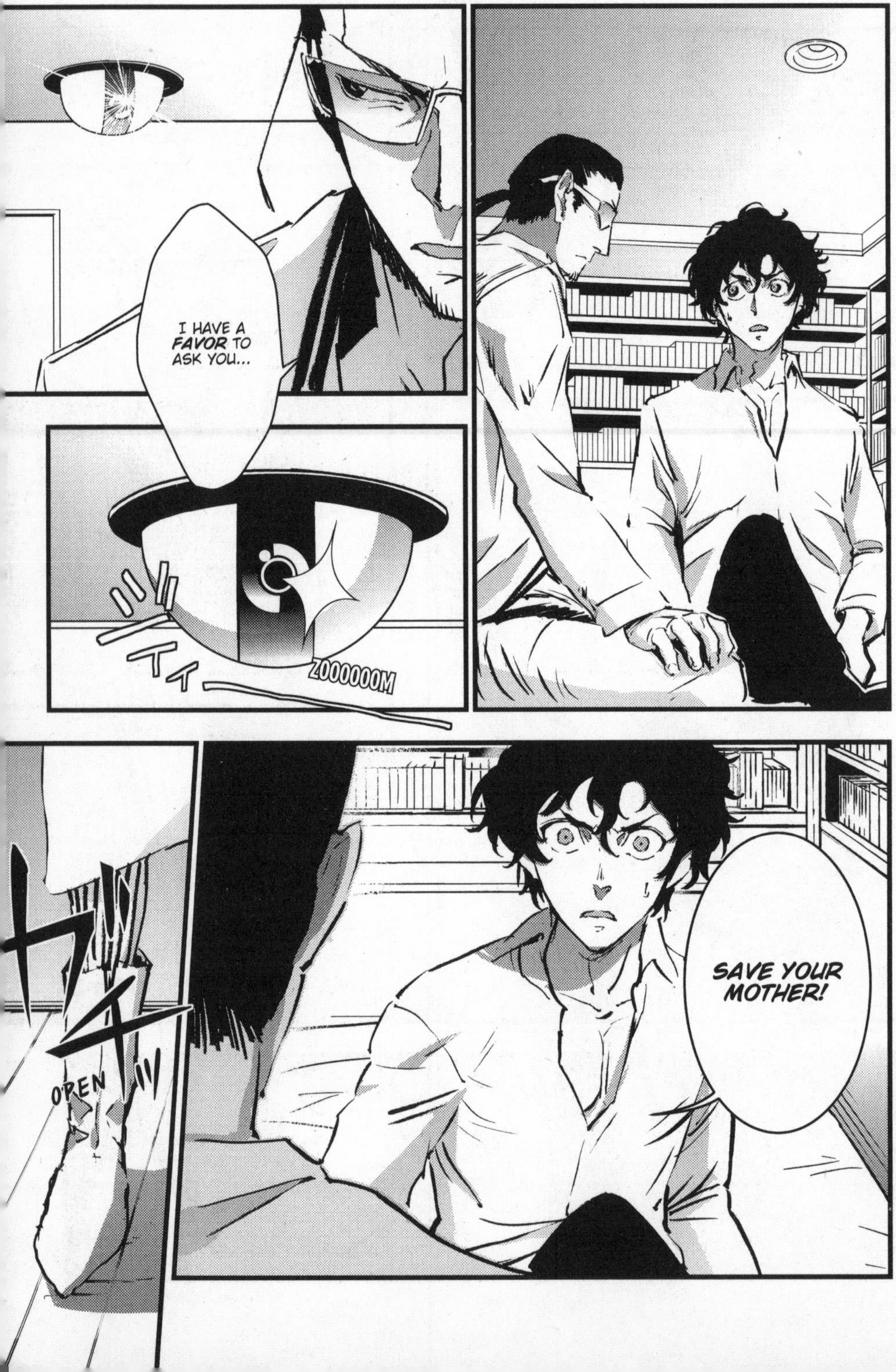
I HAVE A FAVOR TO ASK YOU...
ZOOOOOOM
SAVE YOUR MOTHER!
OPEN

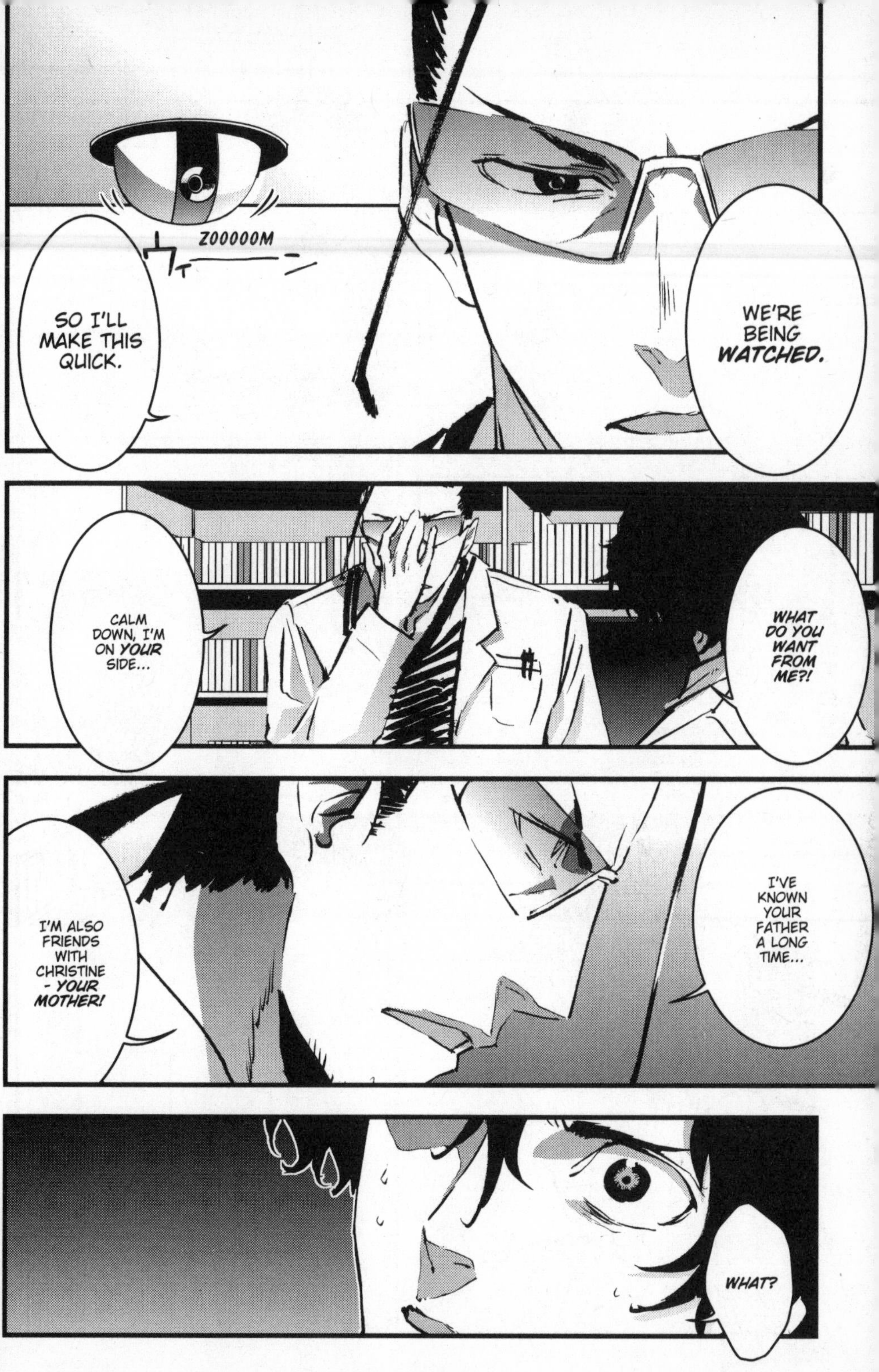
WE'RE BEING WATCHED.
ZOOOOOM
SO I'LL MAKE THIS QUICK.
WHAT DO YOU WANT FROM ME?!
CALM DOWN, I'M ON YOUR SIDE...
I'VE KNOWN YOUR FATHER A LONG TIME...
I'M ALSO FRIENDS WITH CHRISTINE - YOUR MOTHER!
WHAT?

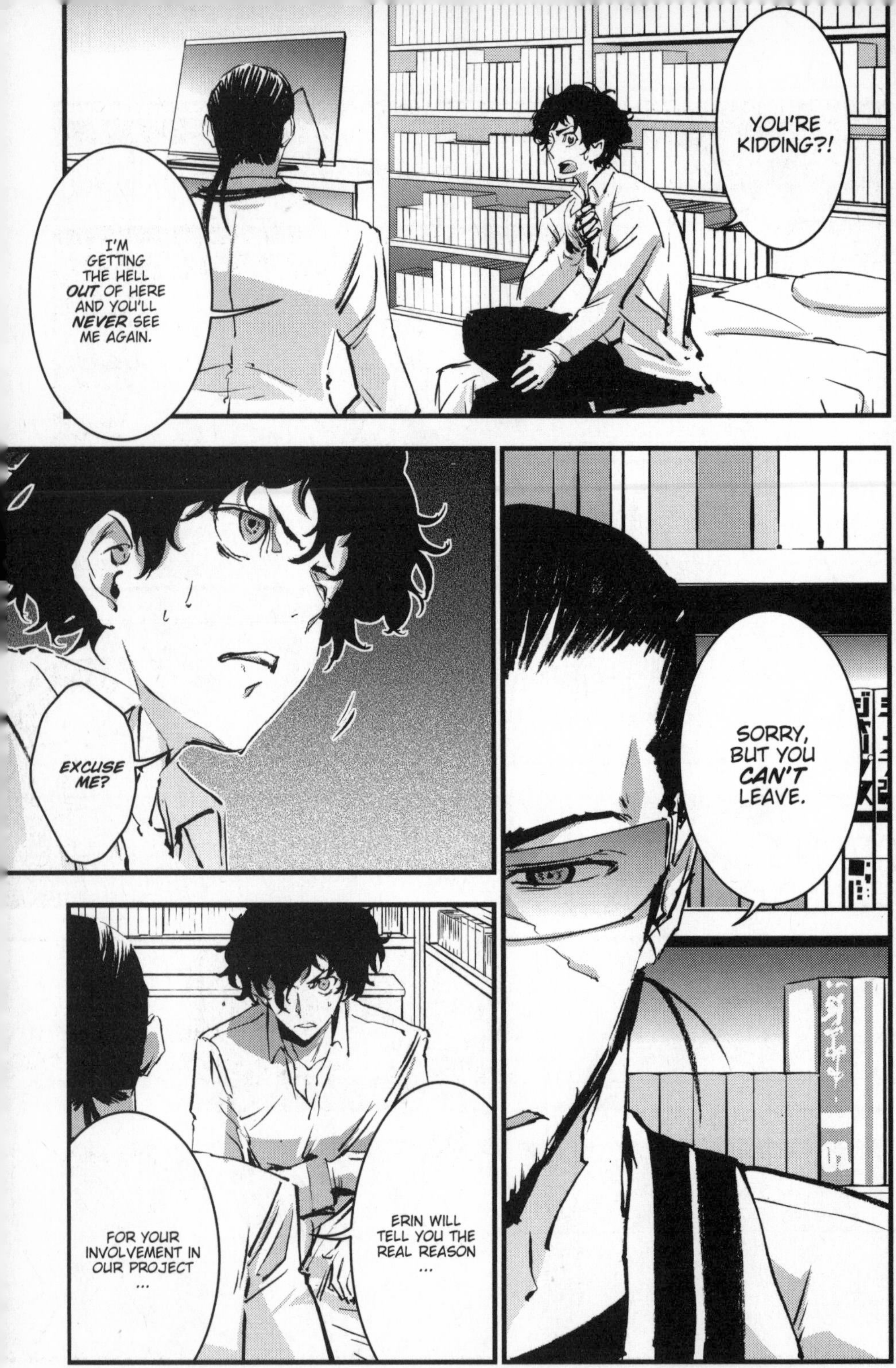
YOU'RE KIDDING?!
I'M GETTING THE HELL *OUT* OF HERE AND YOU'LL *NEVER* SEE ME AGAIN.
SORRY, BUT YOU *CAN'T* LEAVE.
EXCUSE ME?
ERIN WILL TELL YOU THE REAL REASON ...
FOR YOUR INVOLVEMENT IN OUR PROJECT ...

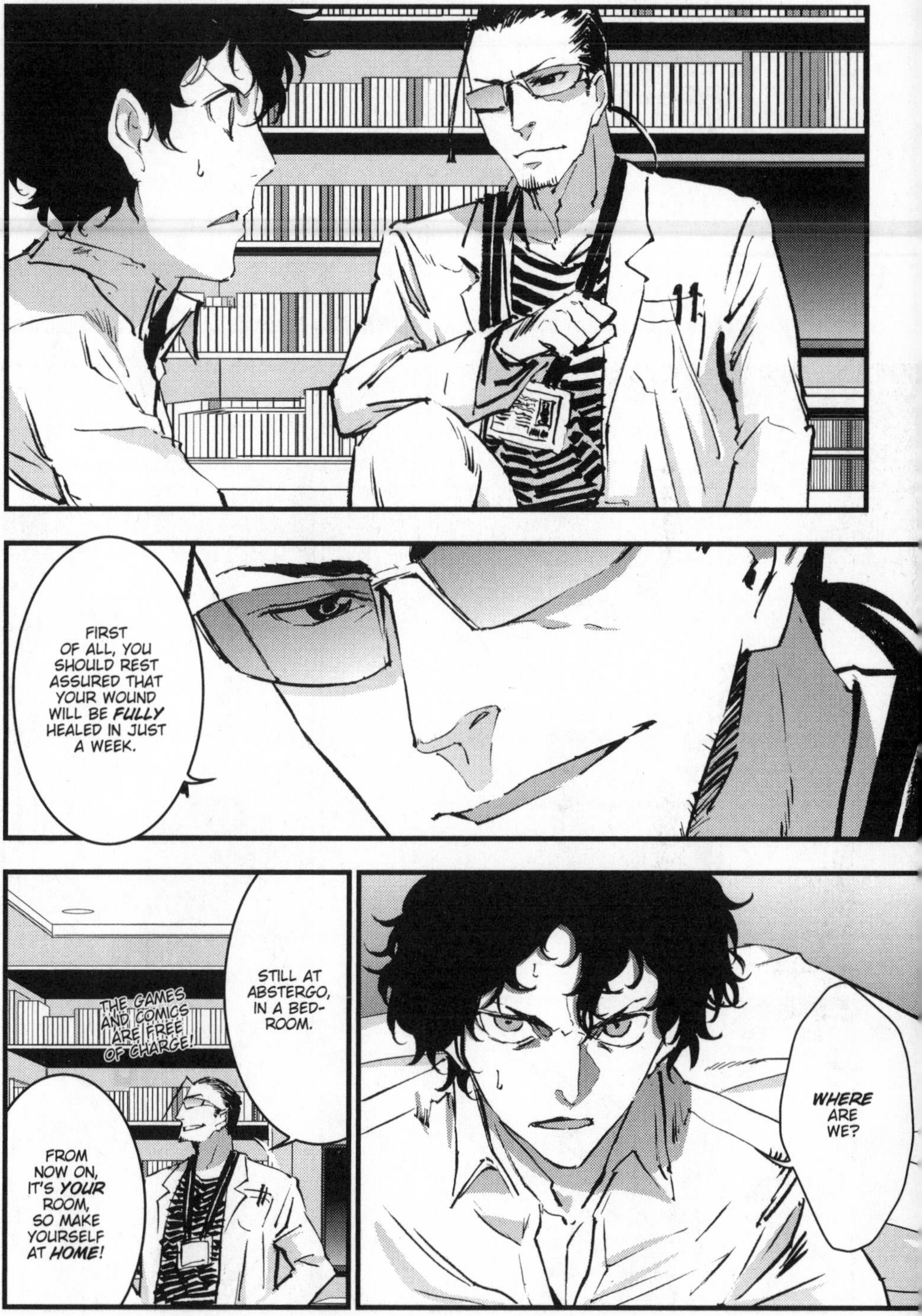
FIRST OF ALL, YOU SHOULD REST ASSURED THAT YOUR WOUND WILL BE ***FULLY*** HEALED IN JUST A WEEK.
WHERE ARE WE?
STILL AT ABSTERGO, IN A BED-ROOM.
THE GAMES AND COMICS ARE FREE OF CHARGE!
FROM NOW ON, IT'S ***YOUR*** ROOM, SO MAKE YOURSELF AT ***HOME***!

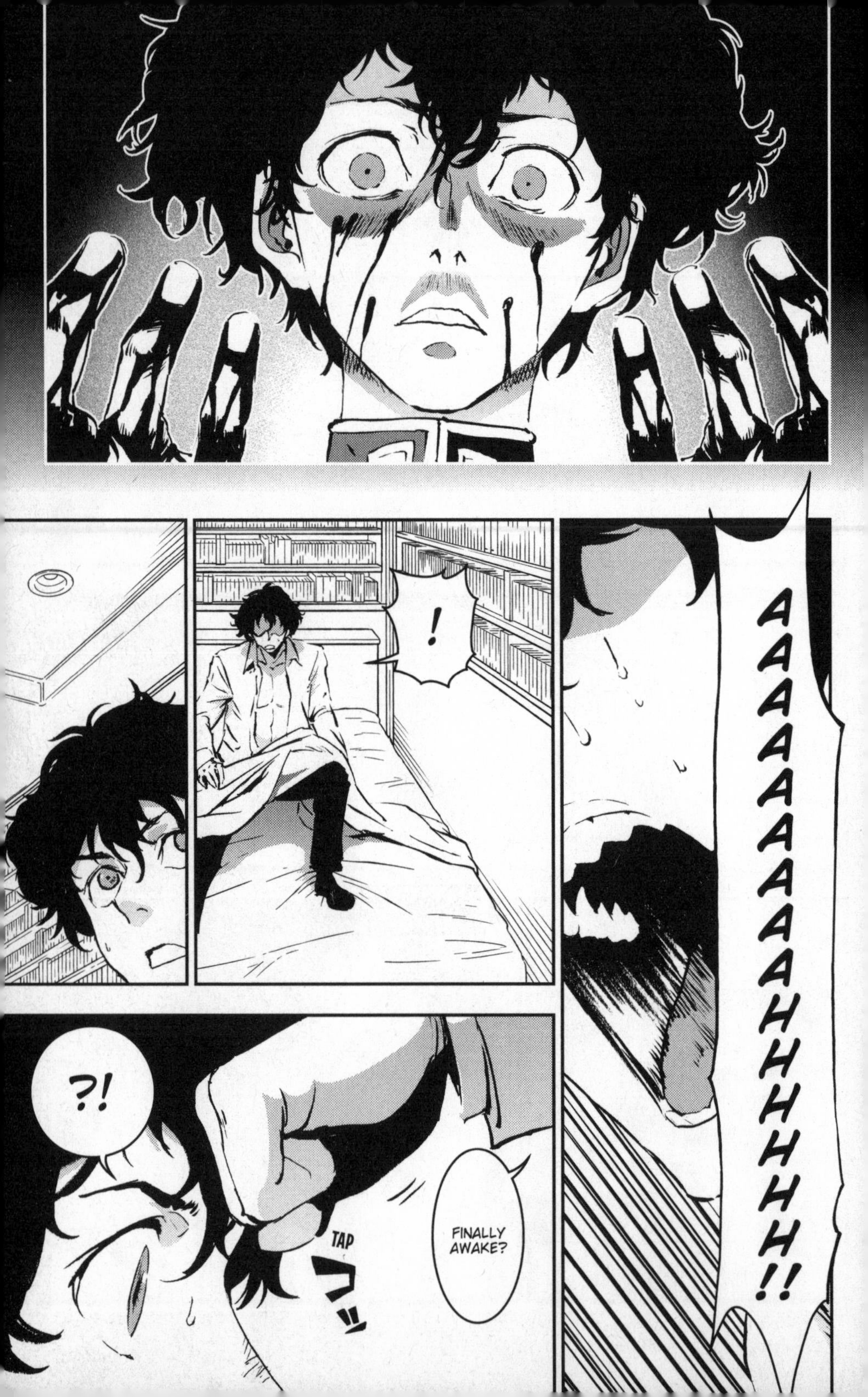
AAAAAAAAAHHHHHH!!
!
FINALLY AWAKE?
TAP
?!

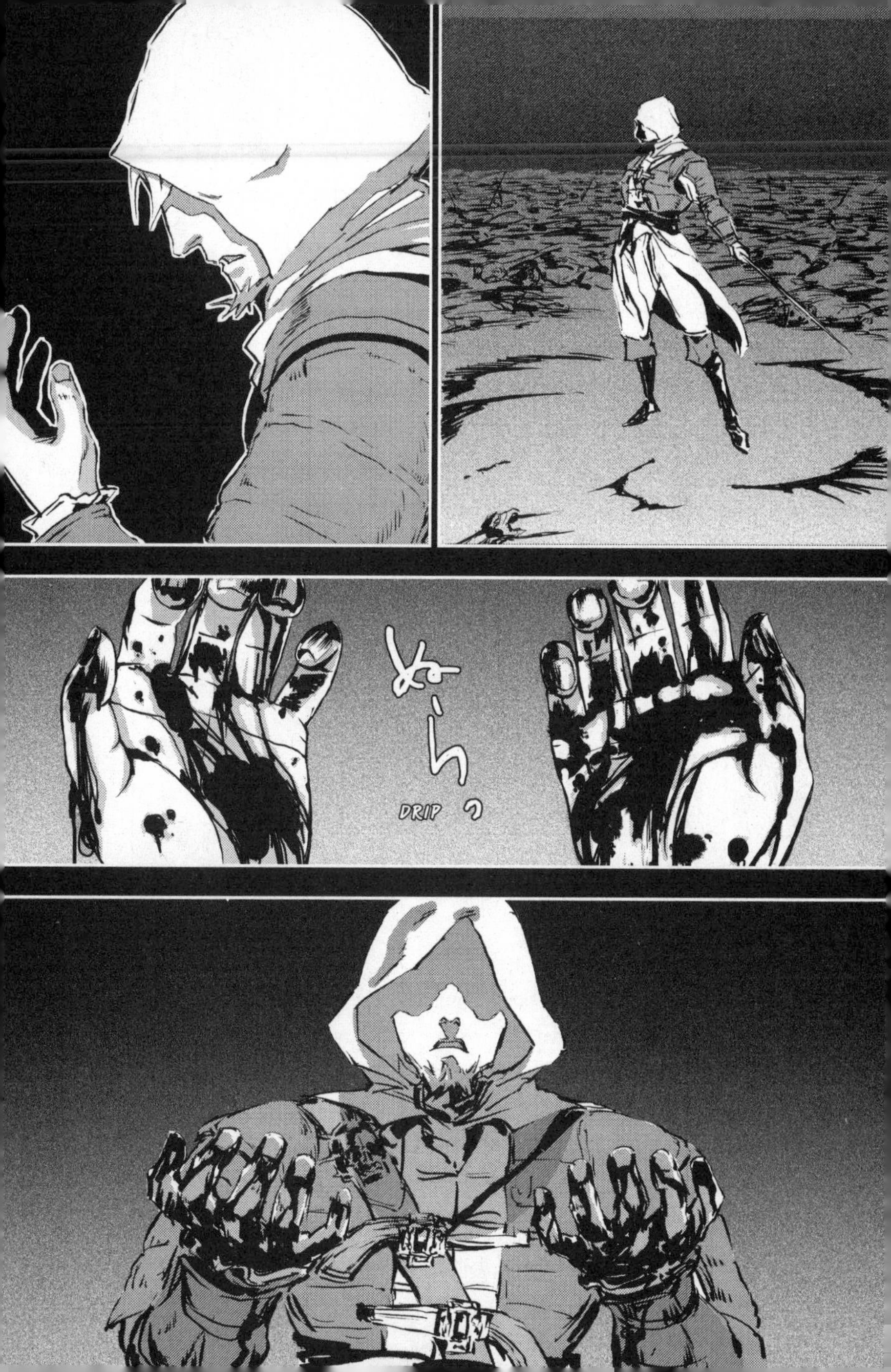
ぬらっ
DRIP

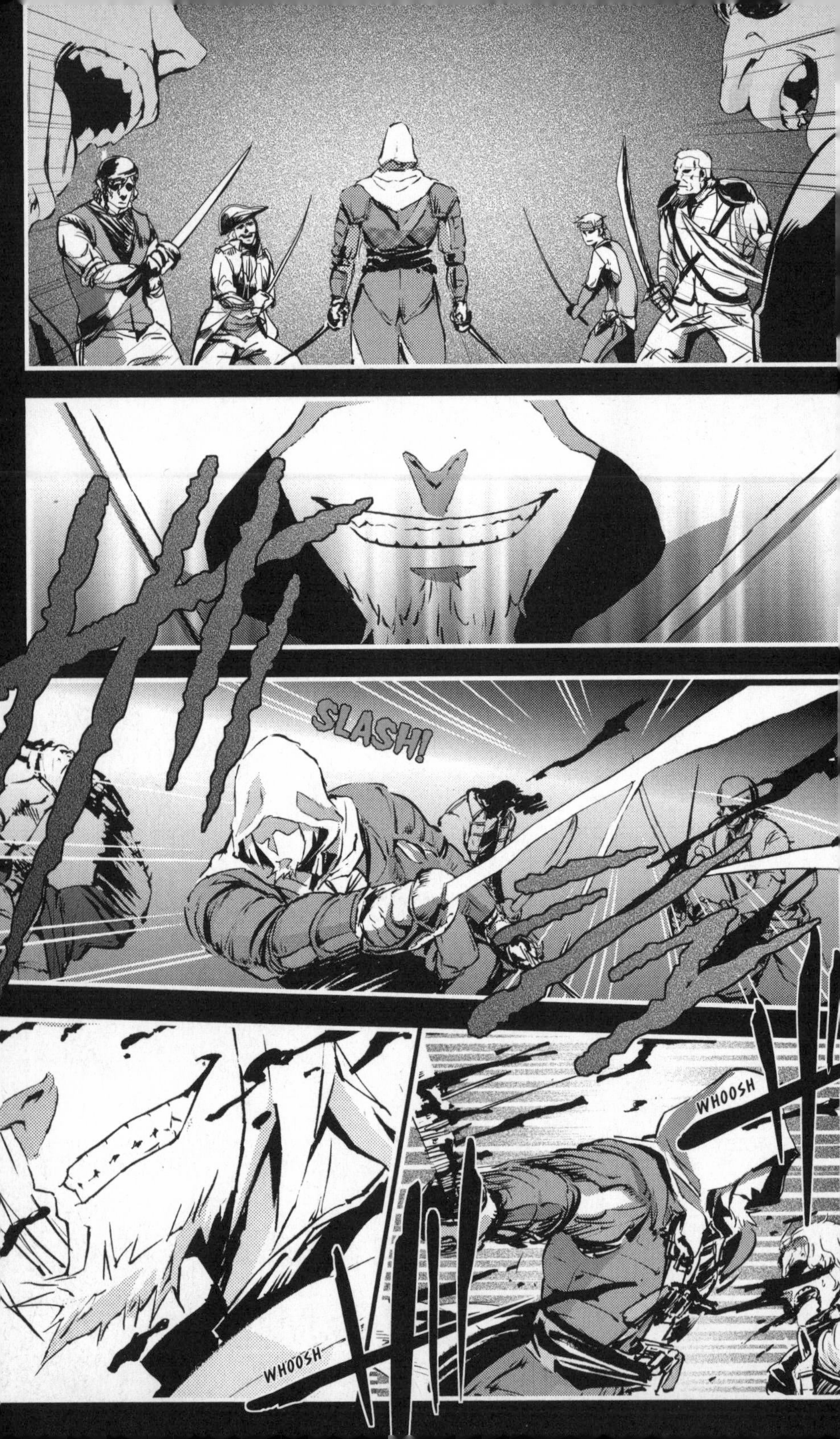
SLASH!
WHOOSH
WHOOSH

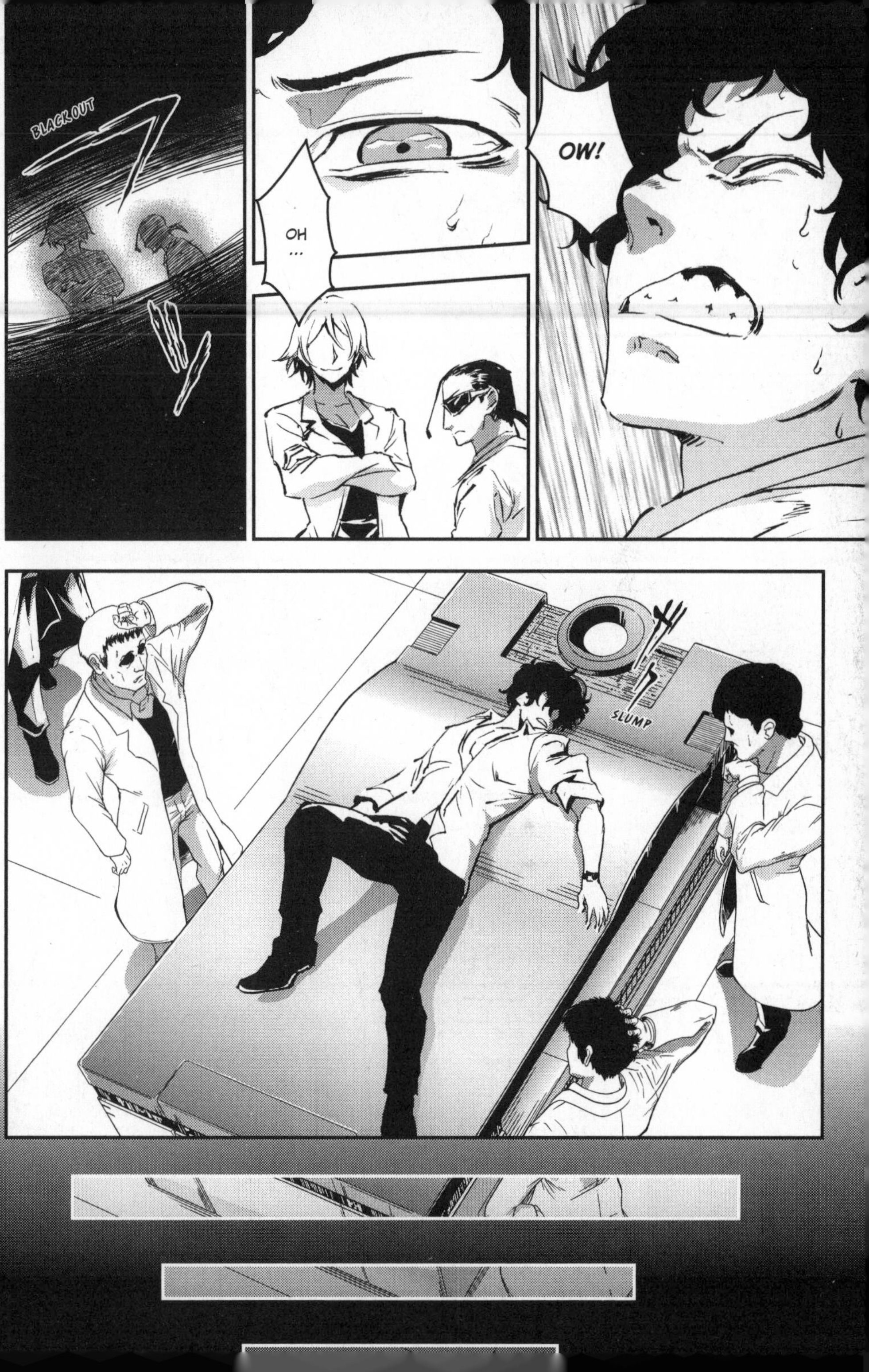
OW!
OH ...
BLACK OUT
SLUMP

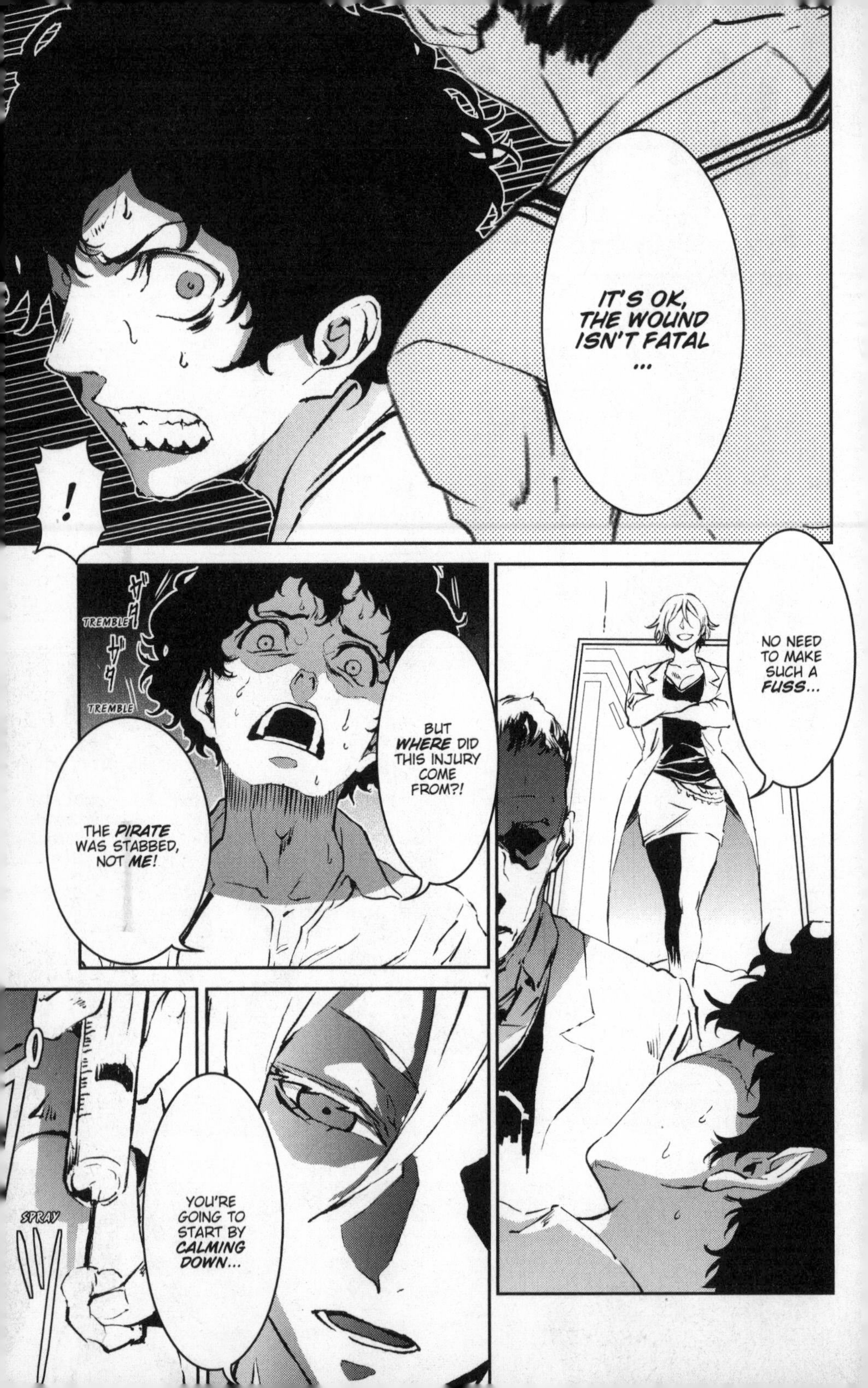
IT'S OK, THE WOUND ISN'T FATAL ...
!
NO NEED TO MAKE SUCH A FUSS...
TREMBLE
TREMBLE
BUT WHERE DID THIS INJURY COME FROM?!
THE PIRATE WAS STABBED, NOT ME!
YOU'RE GOING TO START BY CALMING DOWN...
SPRAY

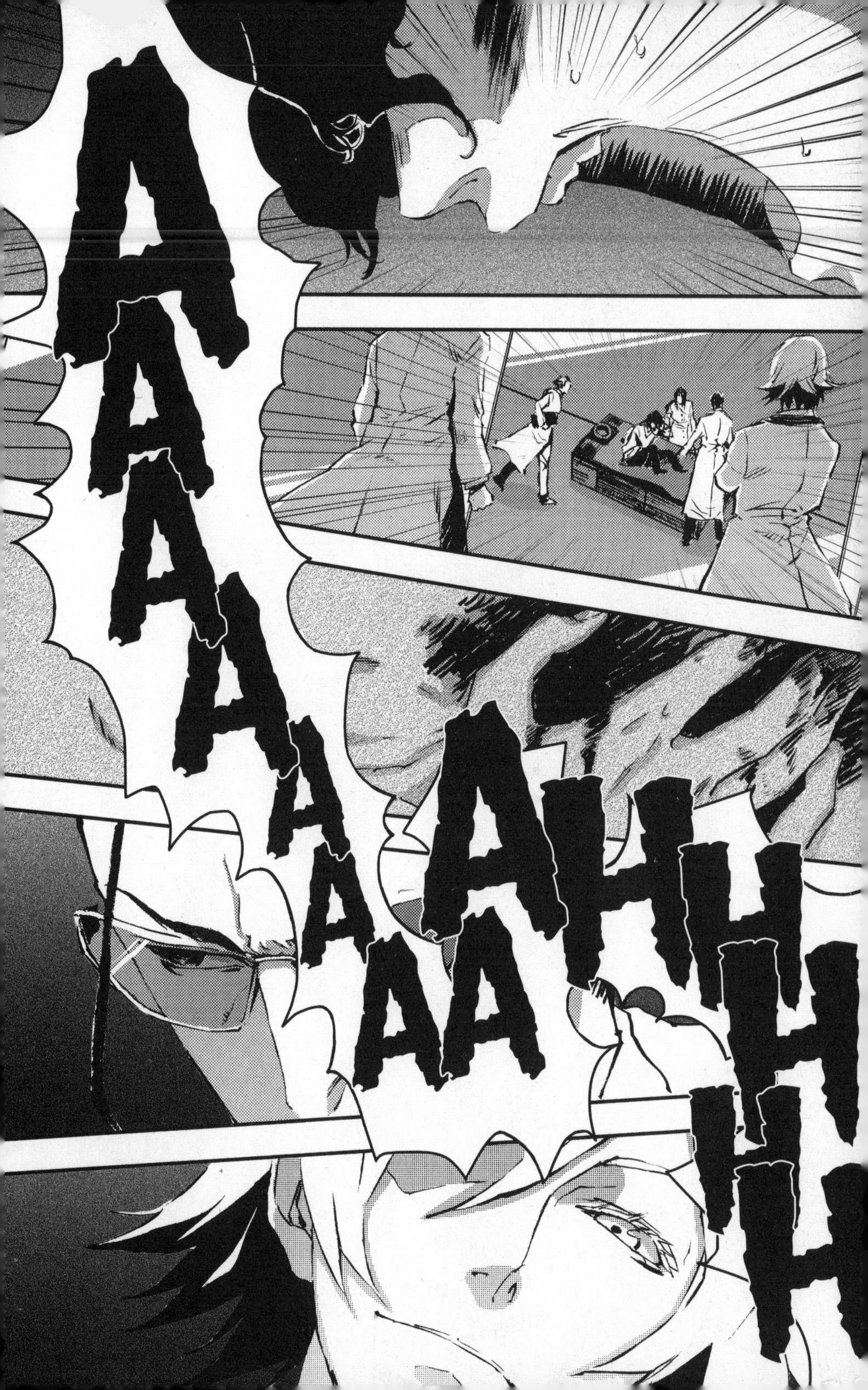
AAAAAAAAAAHHHHHH

Chapter VI

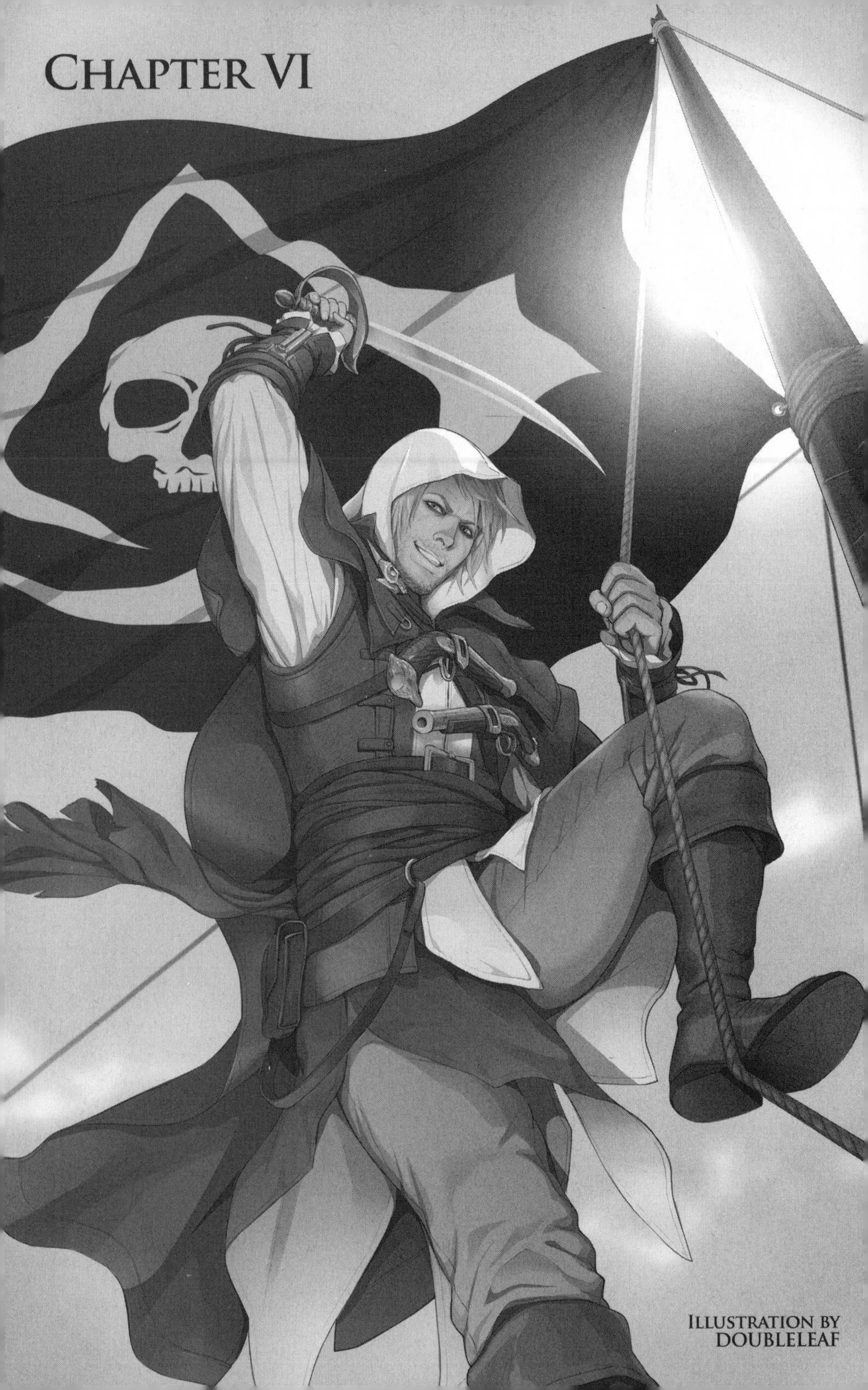

Illustration by
DOUBLELEAF

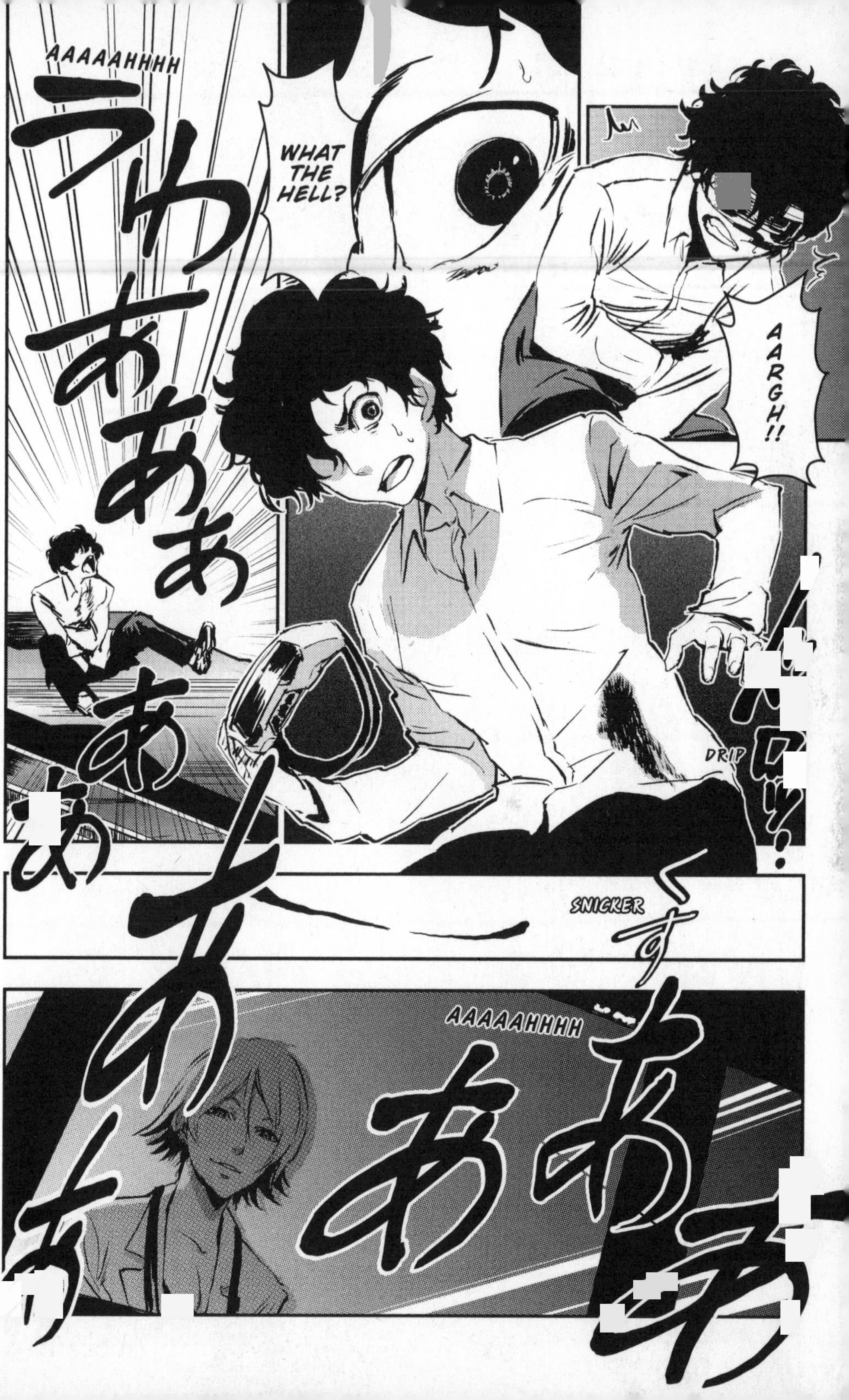
WHAT THE HELL?
AARGH!!
AAAAAHHHH
DRIP
SNICKER
AAAAAHHHH

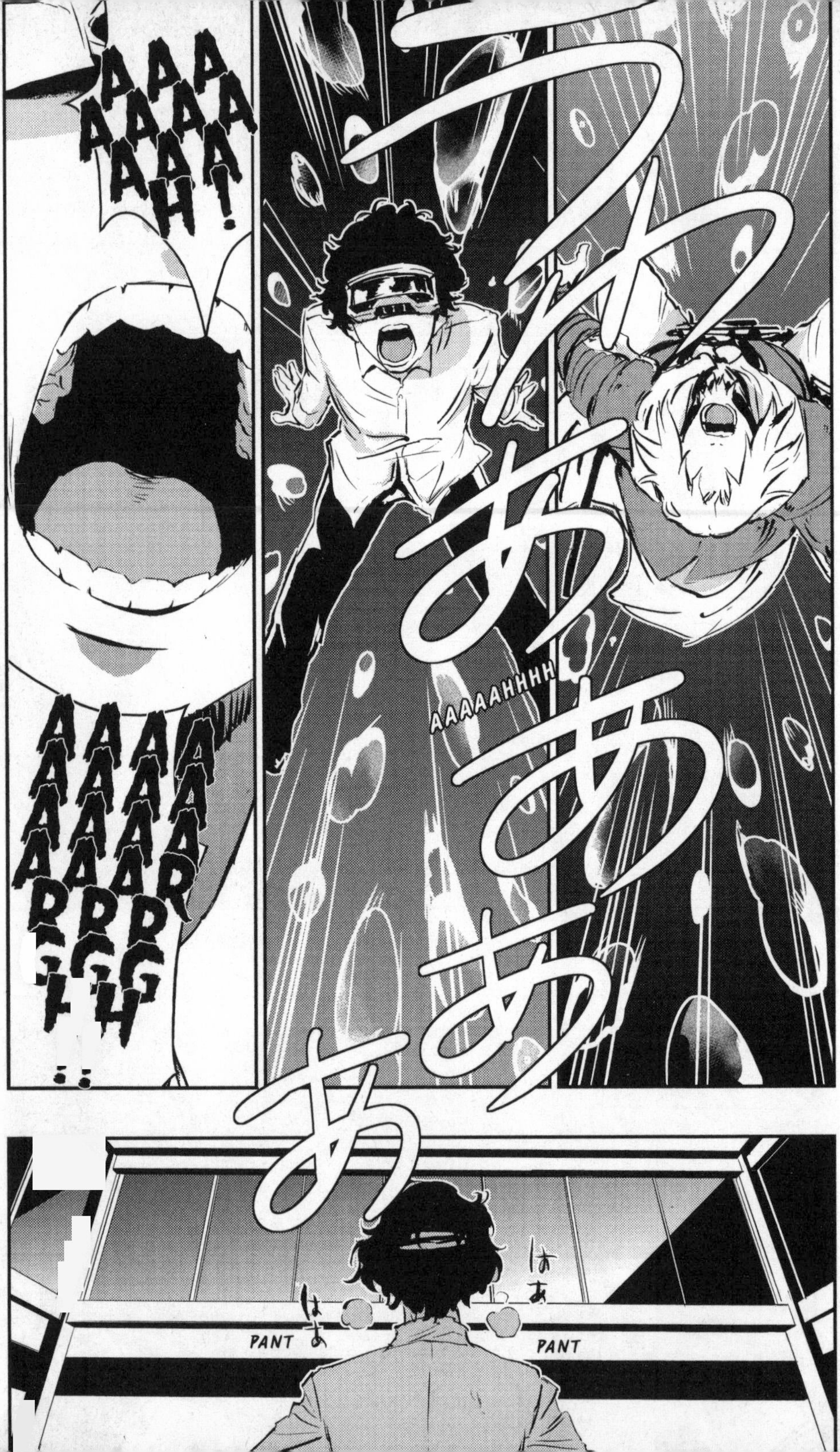
うわあああああ
AAAAAHHHH
AAAAAAAAAAAAH!
AAAAAAAAAAAAAAAARRRGGGHH!!
はあ
PANT
はあ
PANT

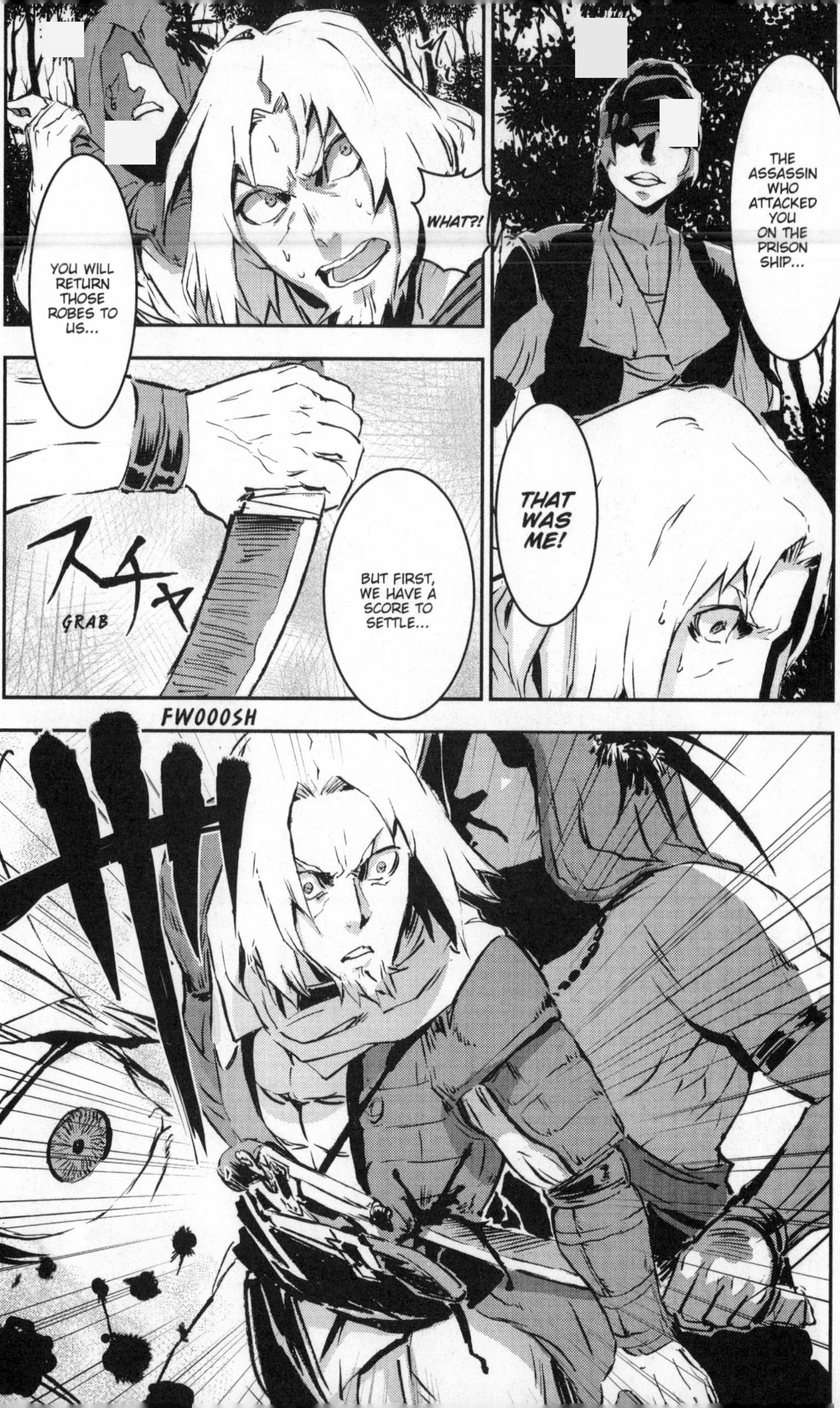
THE ASSASSIN WHO ATTACKED YOU ON THE PRISON SHIP...
THAT WAS ME!
YOU WILL RETURN THOSE ROBES TO US...
WHAT?!
BUT FIRST, WE HAVE A SCORE TO SETTLE...
スチャ
GRAB
FWOOOSH

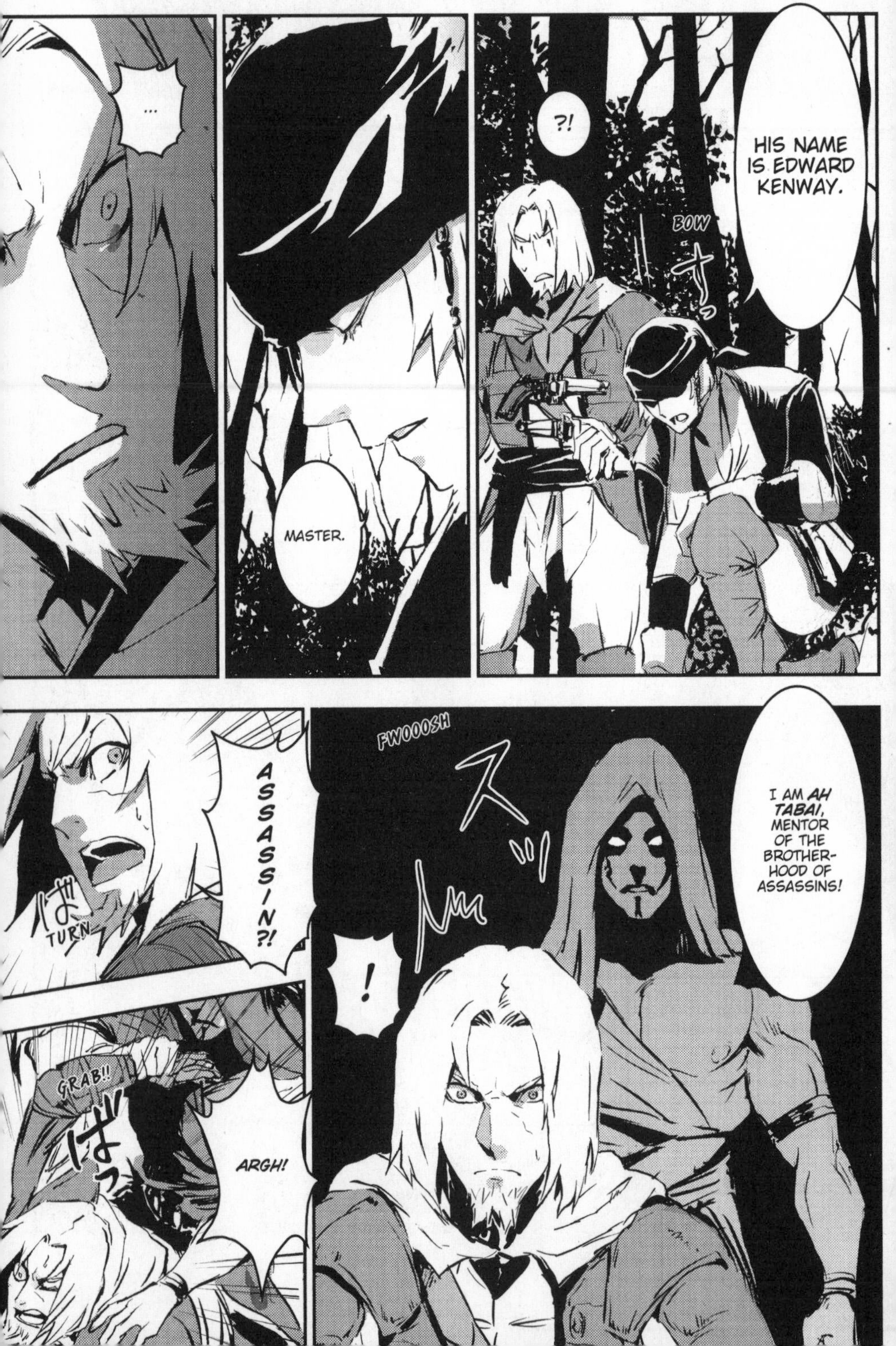
HIS NAME IS EDWARD KENWAY.
?!
BOW
MASTER.
...
FWOOOSH
I AM *AH TABAI*, MENTOR OF THE BROTHER-HOOD OF ASSASSINS!
!
ASSASSIN?!
TURN
GRAB!!
ARGH!

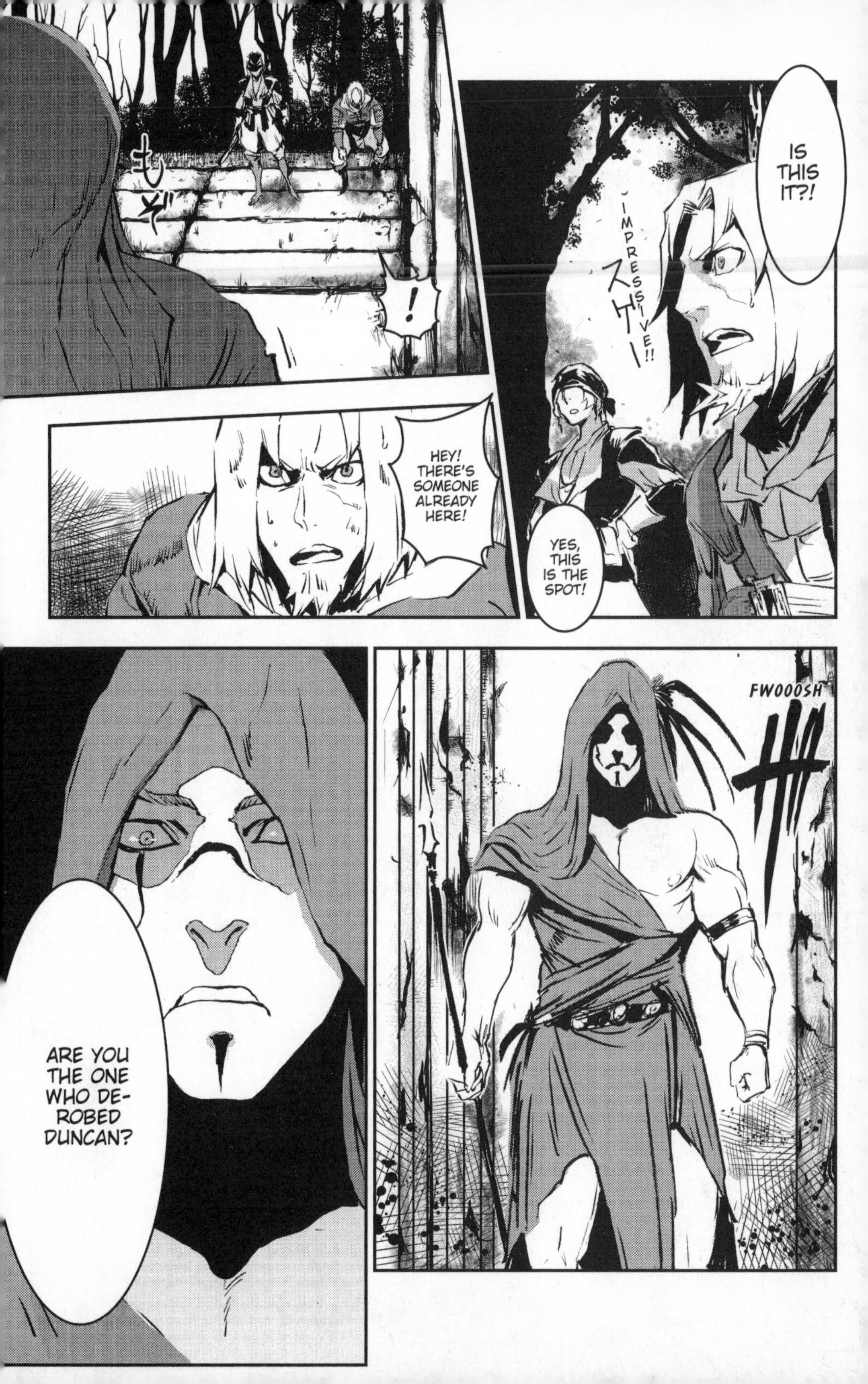
IS THIS IT?!
IMPRESSIVE!!
YES, THIS IS THE SPOT!
!
HEY! THERE'S SOMEONE ALREADY HERE!
FWOOOSH
ARE YOU THE ONE WHO DE-ROBED DUNCAN?

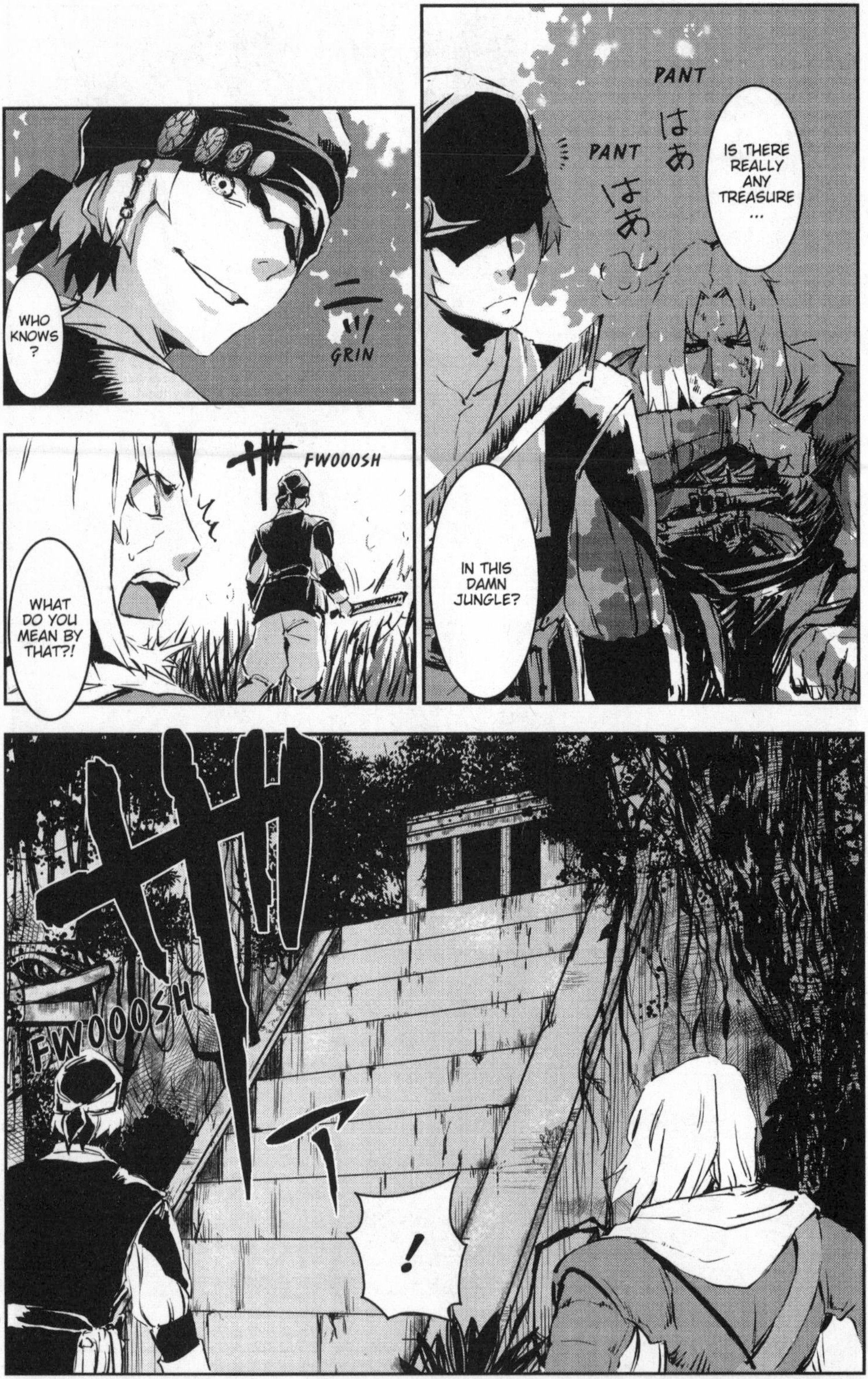
PANT
はあ
PANT
はあ
IS THERE REALLY ANY TREASURE ...
IN THIS DAMN JUNGLE?
WHO KNOWS?
GRIN
FWOOOSH
WHAT DO YOU MEAN BY THAT?!
FWOOOSH
!

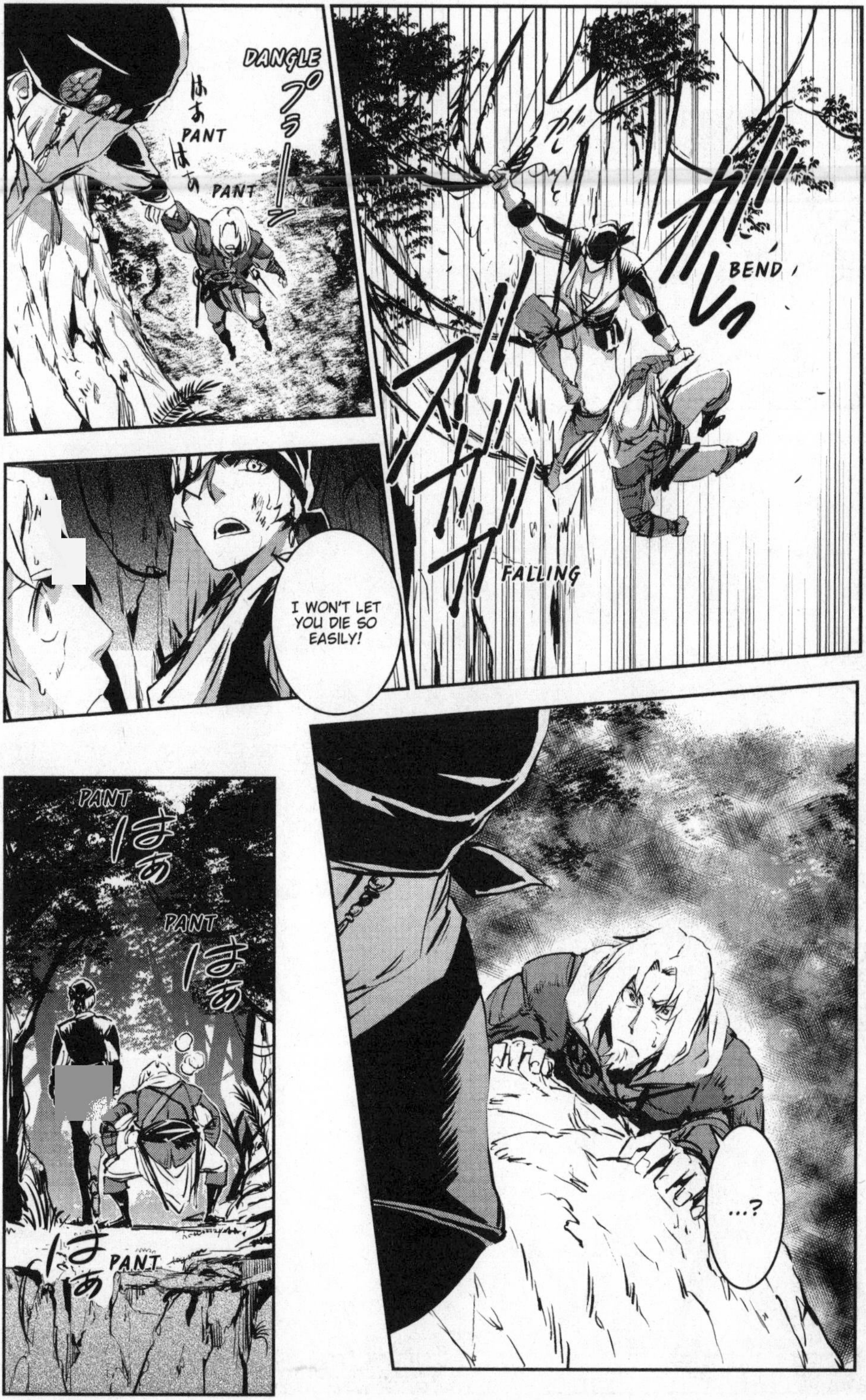
BEND
FALLING
DANGLE
プラーン
はあ
PANT
はあ
PANT
I WON'T LET YOU DIE SO EASILY!
...?
PANT
はぁ
PANT
はぁ
PANT

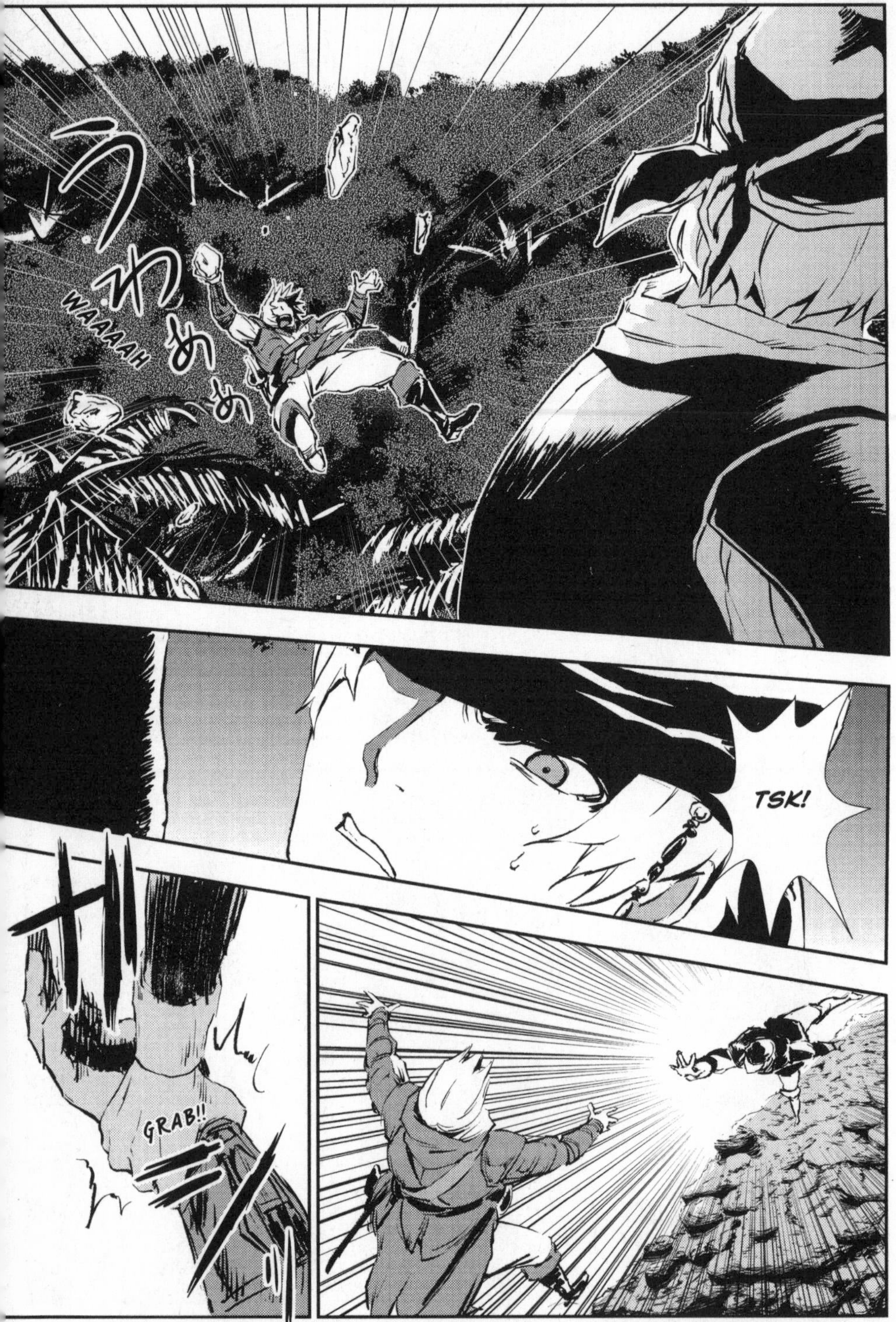
うわぁぁ
WAAAAH
TSK!
GRAB!!

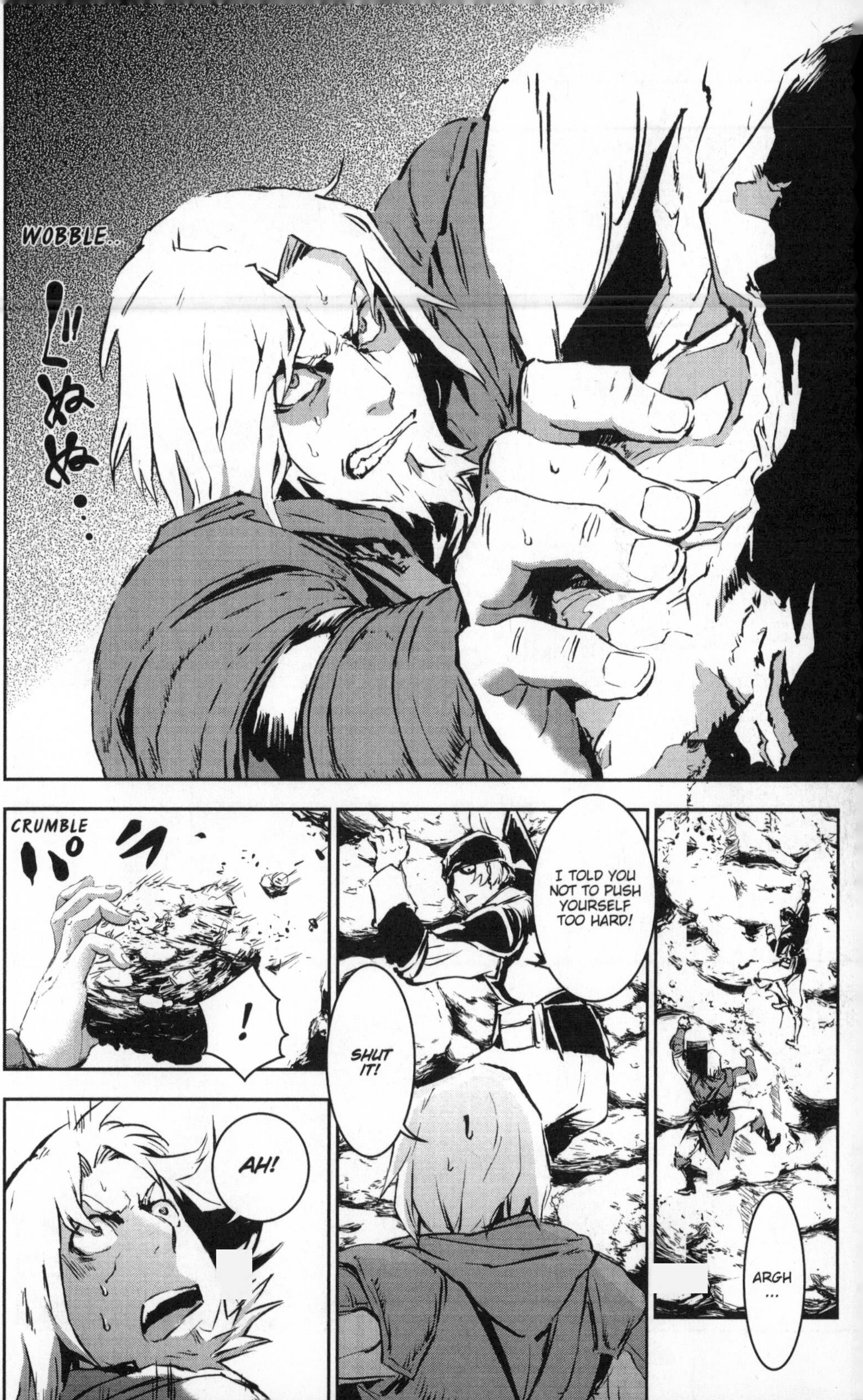
WOBBLE..
ぐぬぬ…
ARGH ...
I TOLD YOU NOT TO PUSH YOURSELF TOO HARD!
SHUT IT!
CRUMBLE
パッ
!
AH!

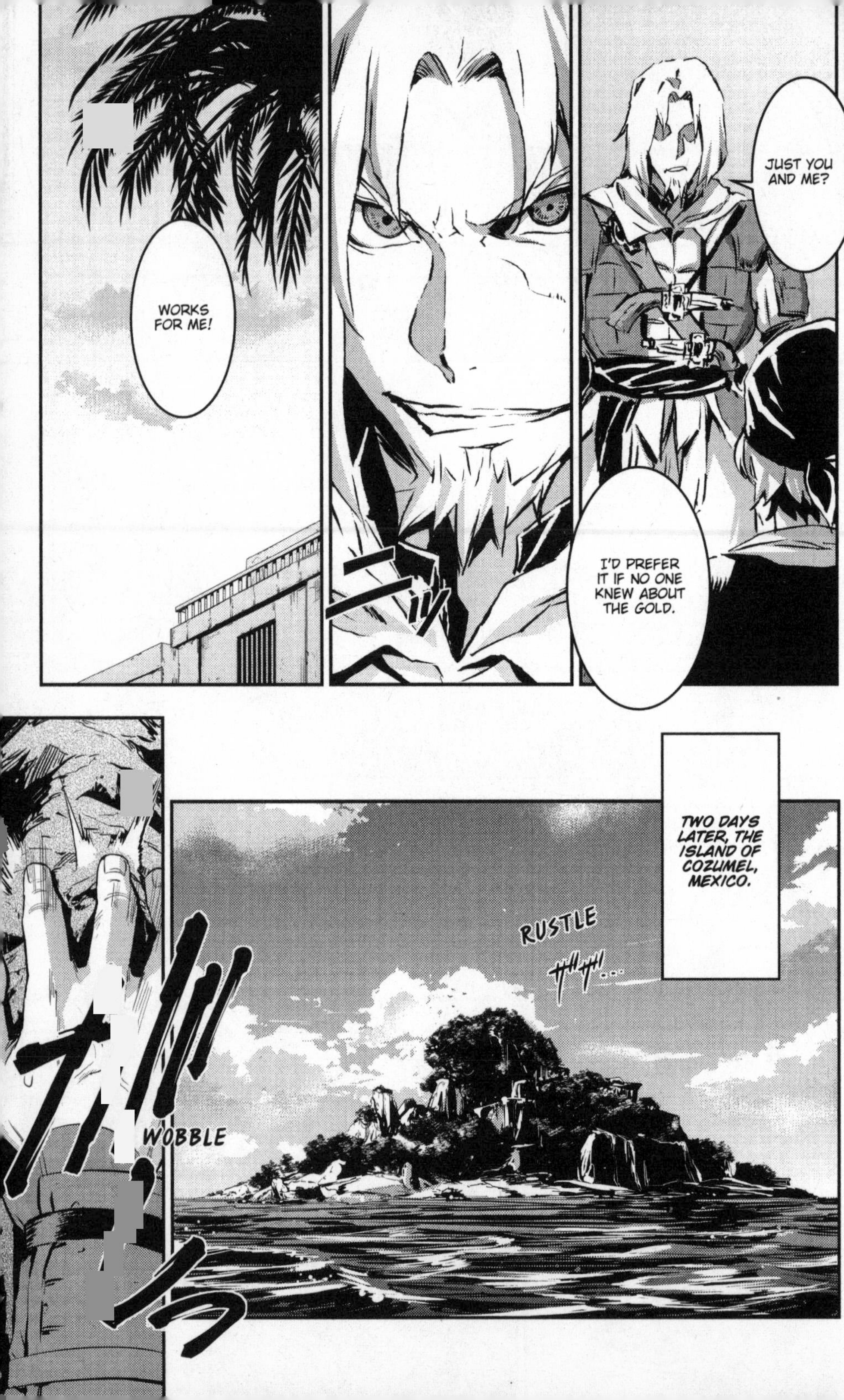
JUST YOU AND ME?
I'D PREFER IT IF NO ONE KNEW ABOUT THE GOLD.
WORKS FOR ME!
TWO DAYS LATER, THE ISLAND OF COZUMEL, MEXICO.
RUSTLE
WOBBLE

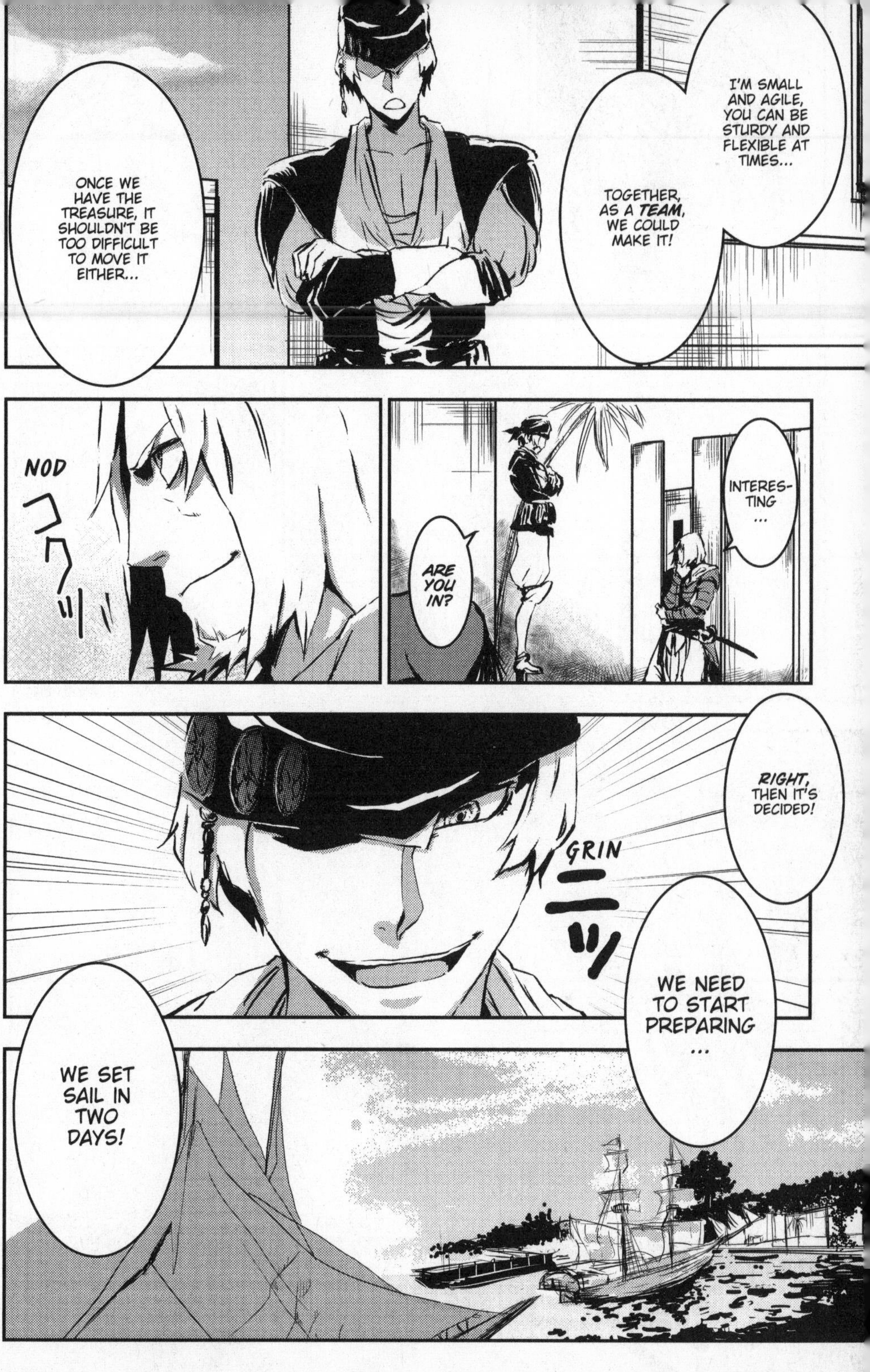
I'M SMALL AND AGILE, YOU CAN BE STURDY AND FLEXIBLE AT TIMES...
TOGETHER, AS A *TEAM*, WE COULD MAKE IT!
ONCE WE HAVE THE TREASURE, IT SHOULDN'T BE TOO DIFFICULT TO MOVE IT EITHER...
INTERES-TING ...
ARE YOU IN?
NOD
RIGHT, THEN IT'S DECIDED!
GRIN
WE NEED TO START PREPARING ...
WE SET SAIL IN TWO DAYS!

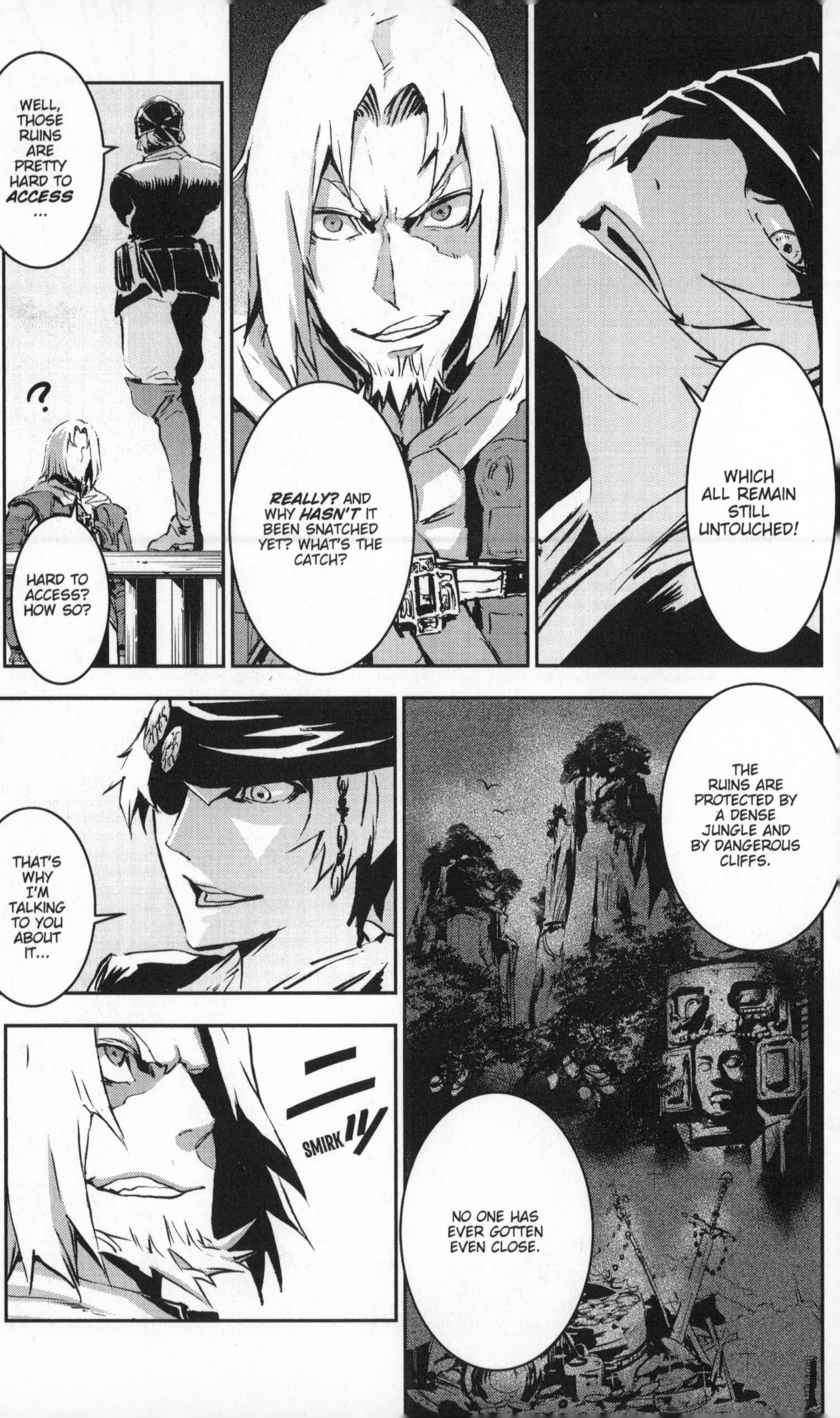
WHICH ALL REMAIN STILL UNTOUCHED!
REALLY? AND WHY HASN'T IT BEEN SNATCHED YET? WHAT'S THE CATCH?
WELL, THOSE RUINS ARE PRETTY HARD TO ACCESS ...
?
HARD TO ACCESS? HOW SO?
THE RUINS ARE PROTECTED BY A DENSE JUNGLE AND BY DANGEROUS CLIFFS.
NO ONE HAS EVER GOTTEN EVEN CLOSE.
THAT'S WHY I'M TALKING TO YOU ABOUT IT...
SMIRK

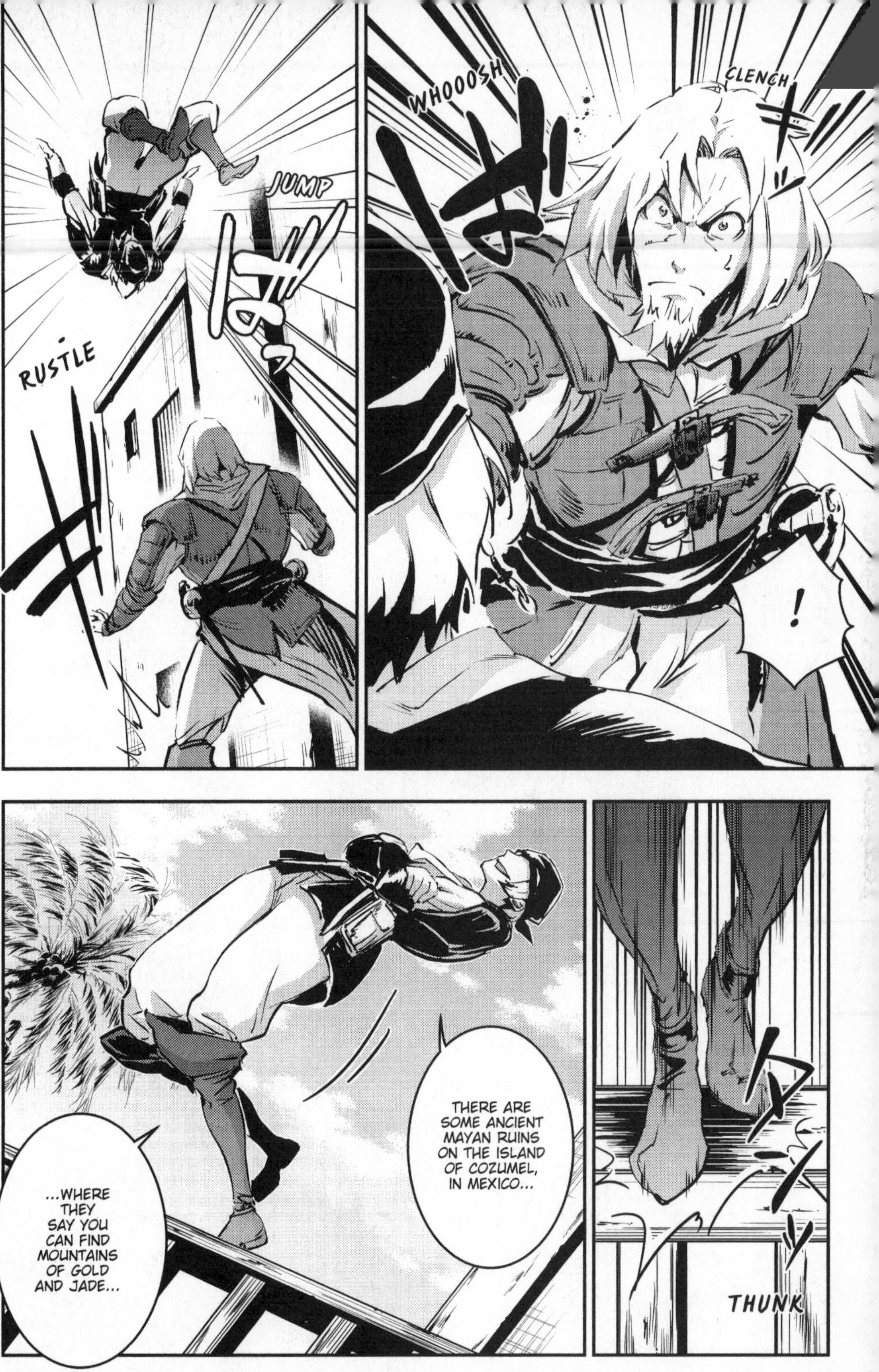
CLENCH
WHOOOSH
!
JUMP
RUSTLE
THUNK
THERE ARE SOME ANCIENT MAYAN RUINS ON THE ISLAND OF COZUMEL, IN MEXICO...
...WHERE THEY SAY YOU CAN FIND MOUNTAINS OF GOLD AND JADE...

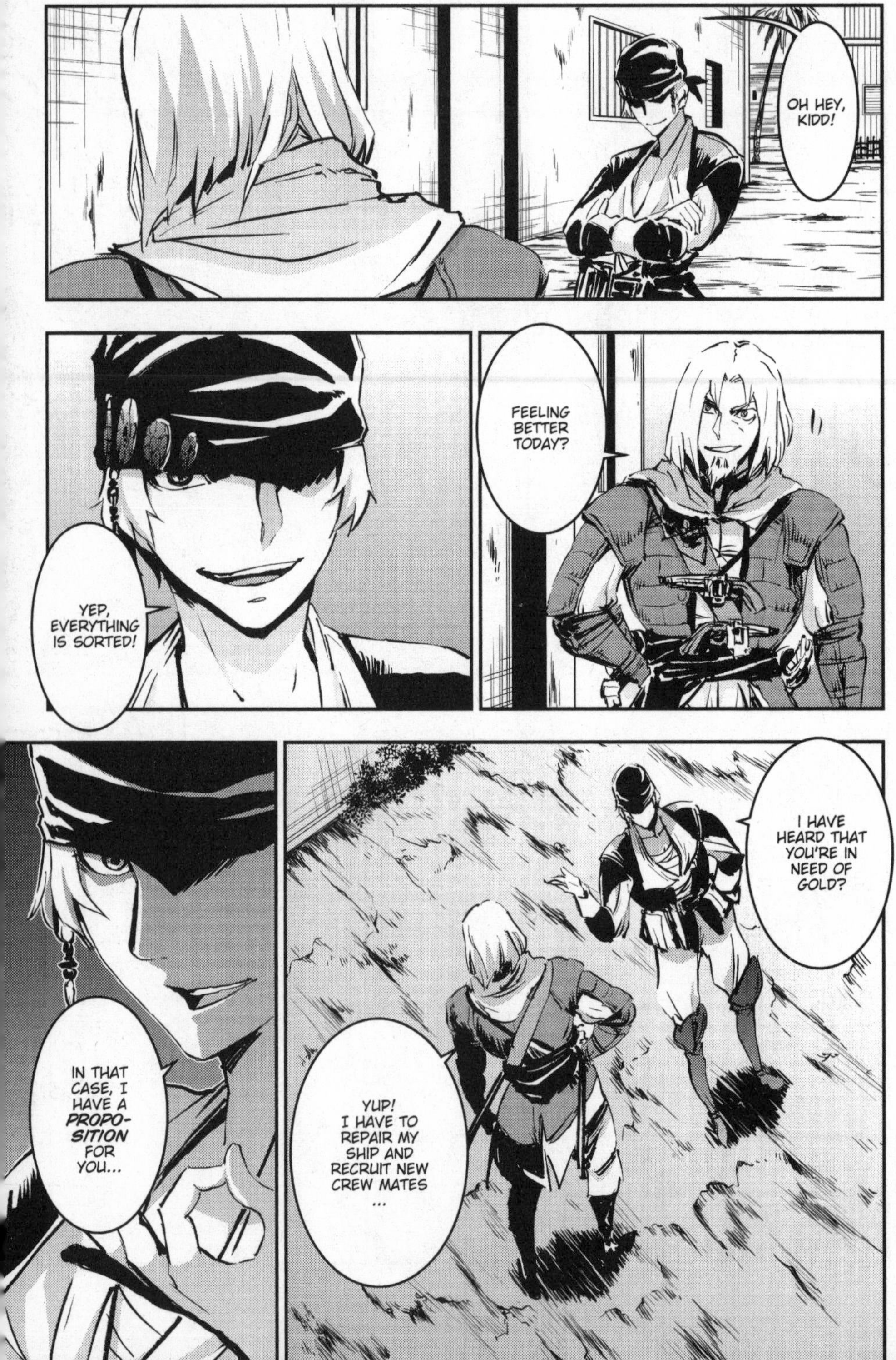
OH HEY, KIDD!
FEELING BETTER TODAY?
YEP, EVERYTHING IS SORTED!
I HAVE HEARD THAT YOU'RE IN NEED OF GOLD?
YUP! I HAVE TO REPAIR MY SHIP AND RECRUIT NEW CREW MATES ...
IN THAT CASE, I HAVE A ***PROPO-SITION*** FOR YOU...

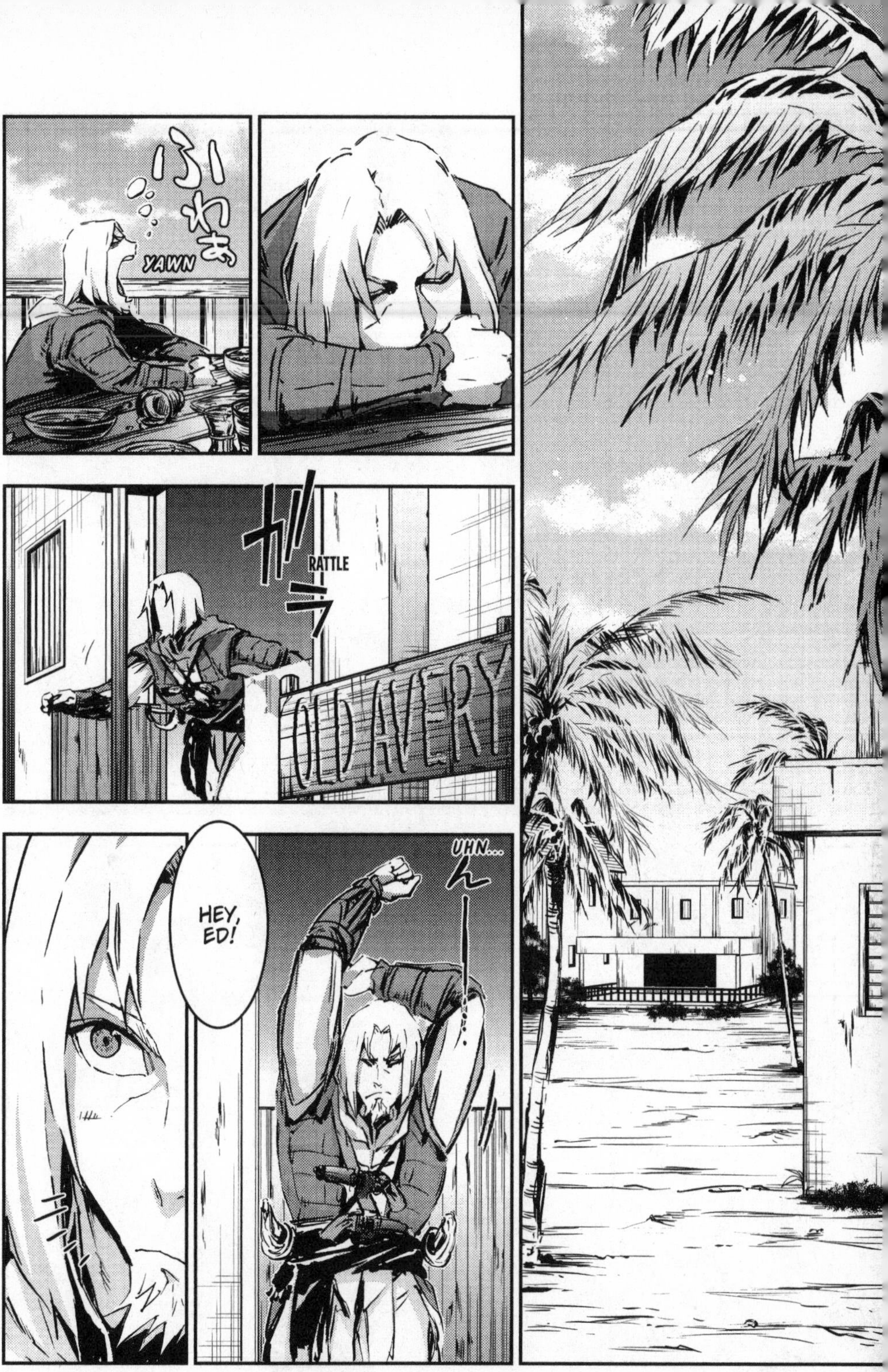
ふわぁ
YAWN
ガラ
RATTLE
OLD AVERY
UHN...
んー…
HEY, ED!

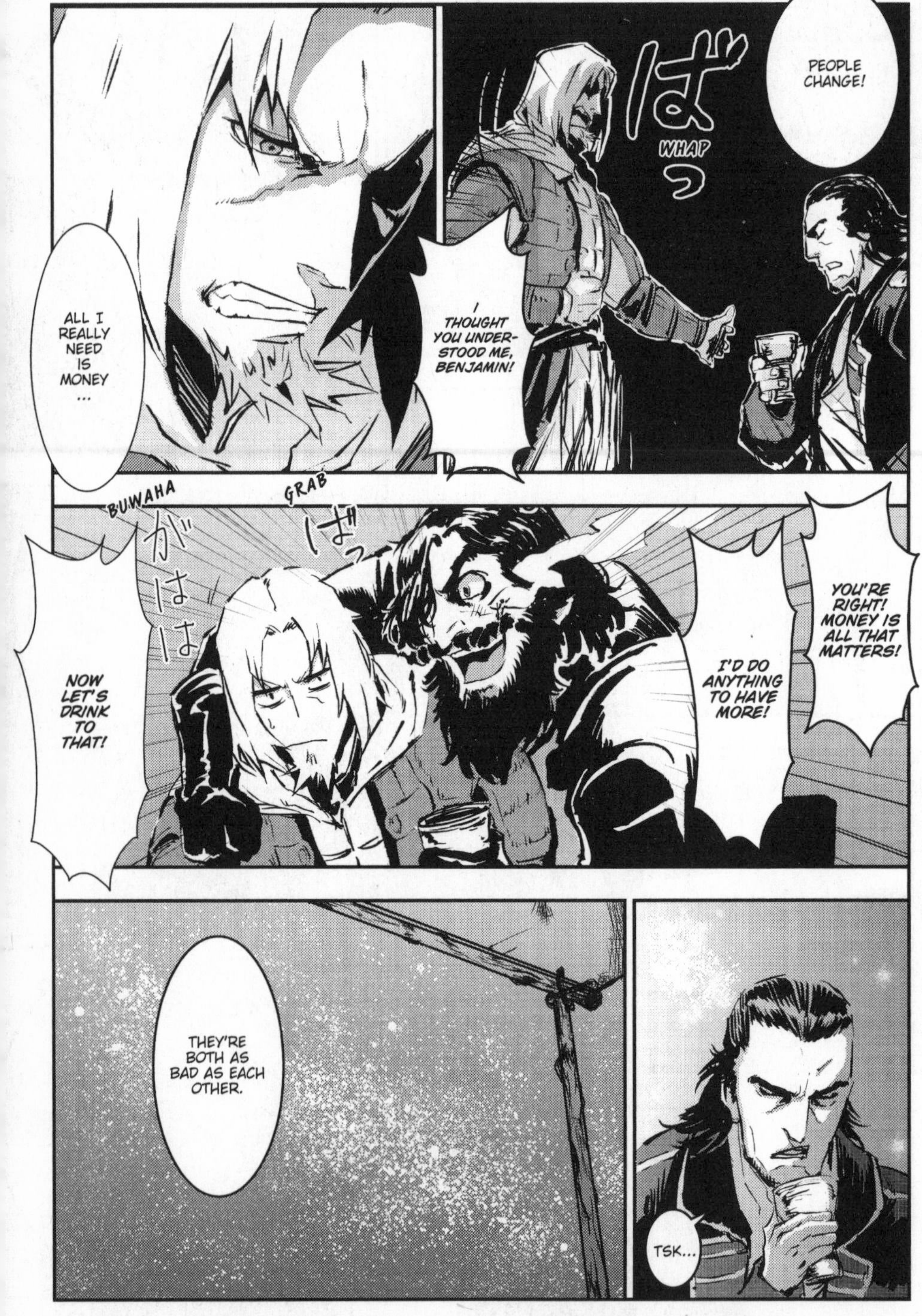
PEOPLE CHANGE!
ばっ
WHAP
I THOUGHT YOU UNDER-STOOD ME, BENJAMIN!
ALL I REALLY NEED IS MONEY ...
YOU'RE RIGHT! MONEY IS ALL THAT MATTERS!
I'D DO ANYTHING TO HAVE MORE!
ばっ
GRAB
がはは
BUWAHA
NOW LET'S DRINK TO THAT!
TSK...
THEY'RE BOTH AS BAD AS EACH OTHER.

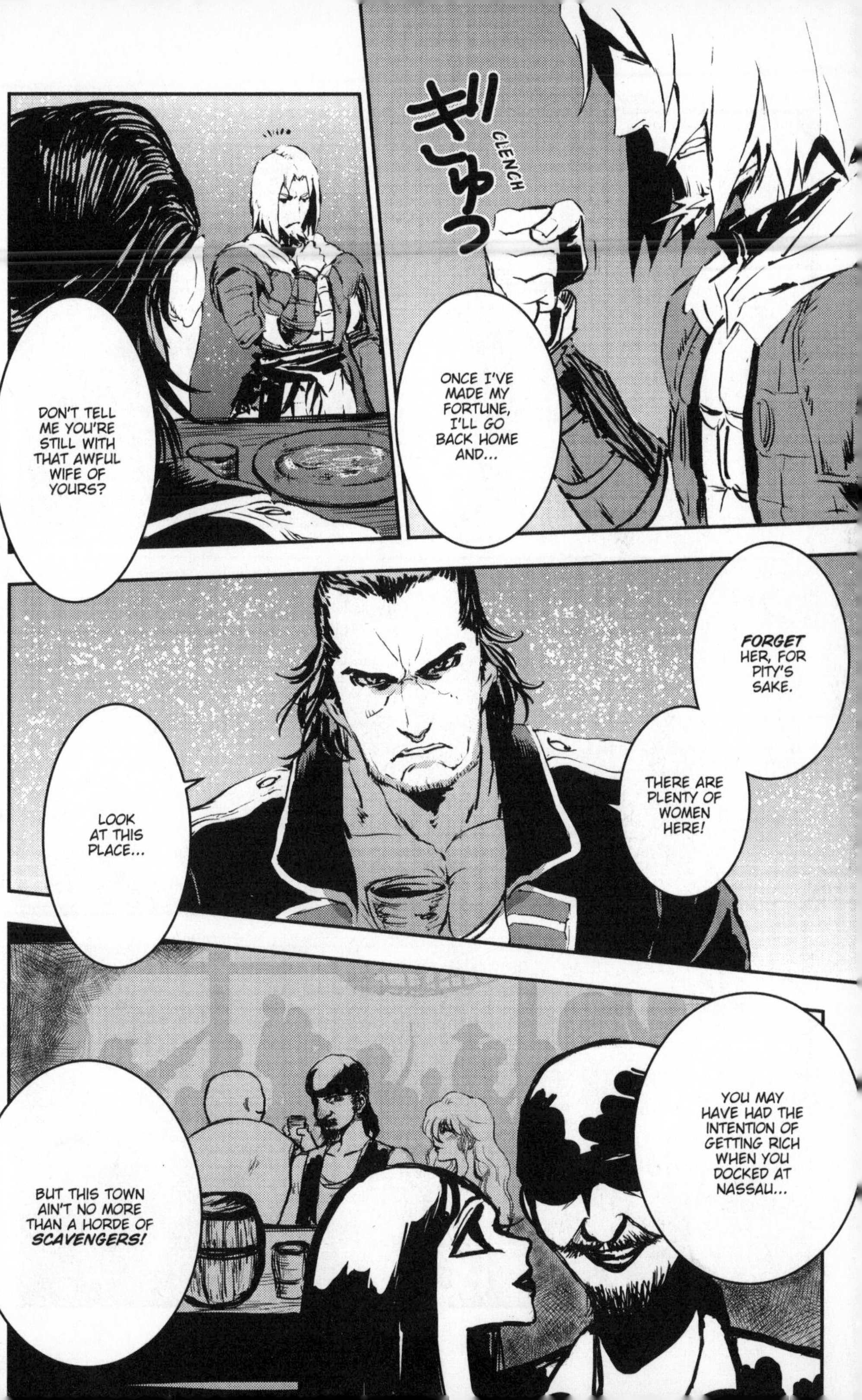

ぎゅっ
CLENCH
ONCE I'VE MADE MY FORTUNE, I'LL GO BACK HOME AND...
DON'T TELL ME YOU'RE STILL WITH THAT AWFUL WIFE OF YOURS?
FORGET HER, FOR PITY'S SAKE.
THERE ARE PLENTY OF WOMEN HERE!
LOOK AT THIS PLACE...
YOU MAY HAVE HAD THE INTENTION OF GETTING RICH WHEN YOU DOCKED AT NASSAU...
BUT THIS TOWN AIN'T NO MORE THAN A HORDE OF **SCAVENGERS!**

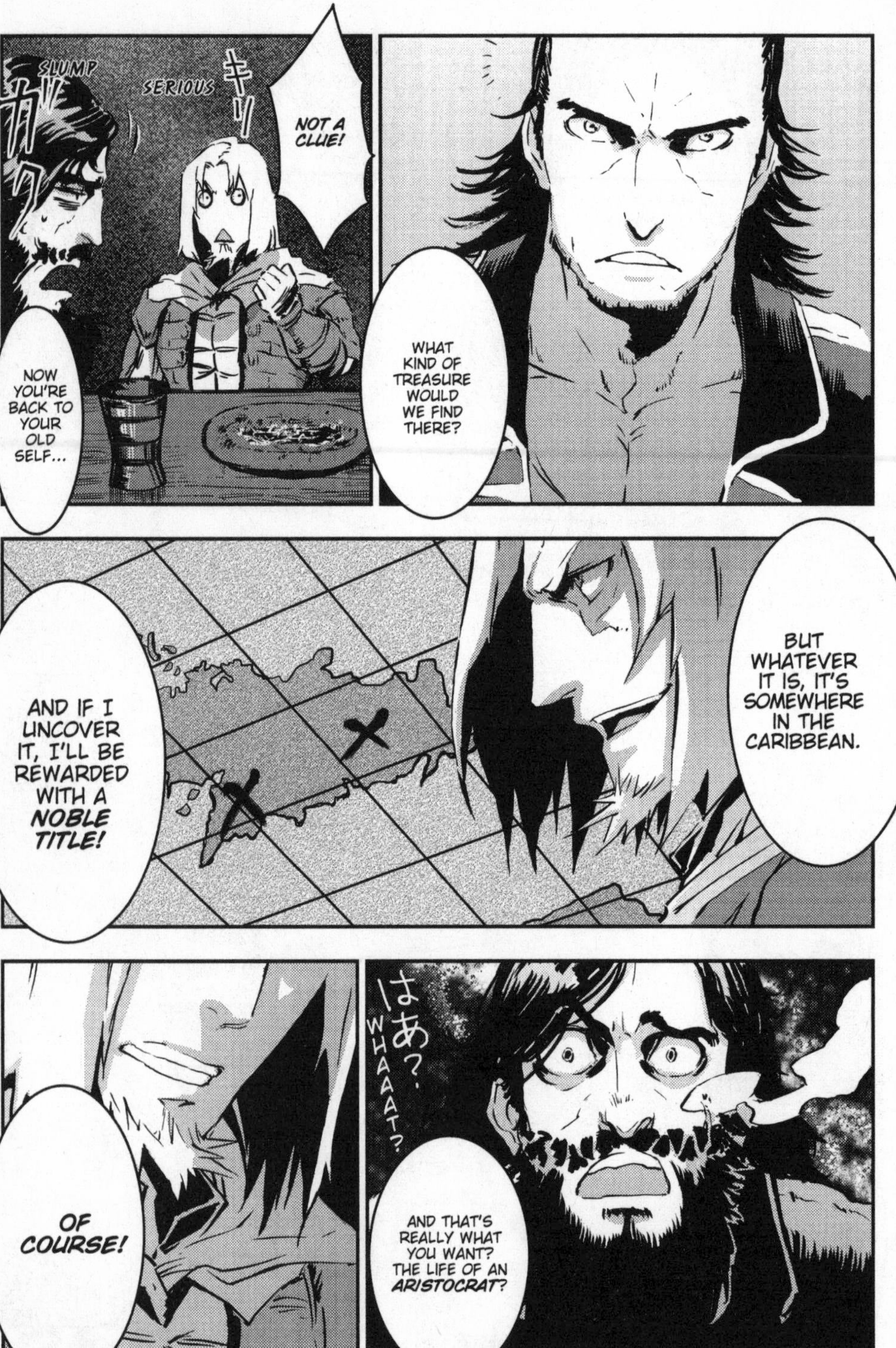

WHAT KIND OF TREASURE WOULD WE FIND THERE?
NOT A CLUE!
キリ
SERIOUS
ガク
SLUMP
NOW YOU'RE BACK TO YOUR OLD SELF...
BUT WHATEVER IT IS, IT'S SOMEWHERE IN THE CARIBBEAN.
AND IF I UNCOVER IT, I'LL BE REWARDED WITH A *NOBLE TITLE!*
はあ?
WHAAAT?
AND THAT'S REALLY WHAT YOU WANT? THE LIFE OF AN *ARISTOCRAT?*
OF COURSE!

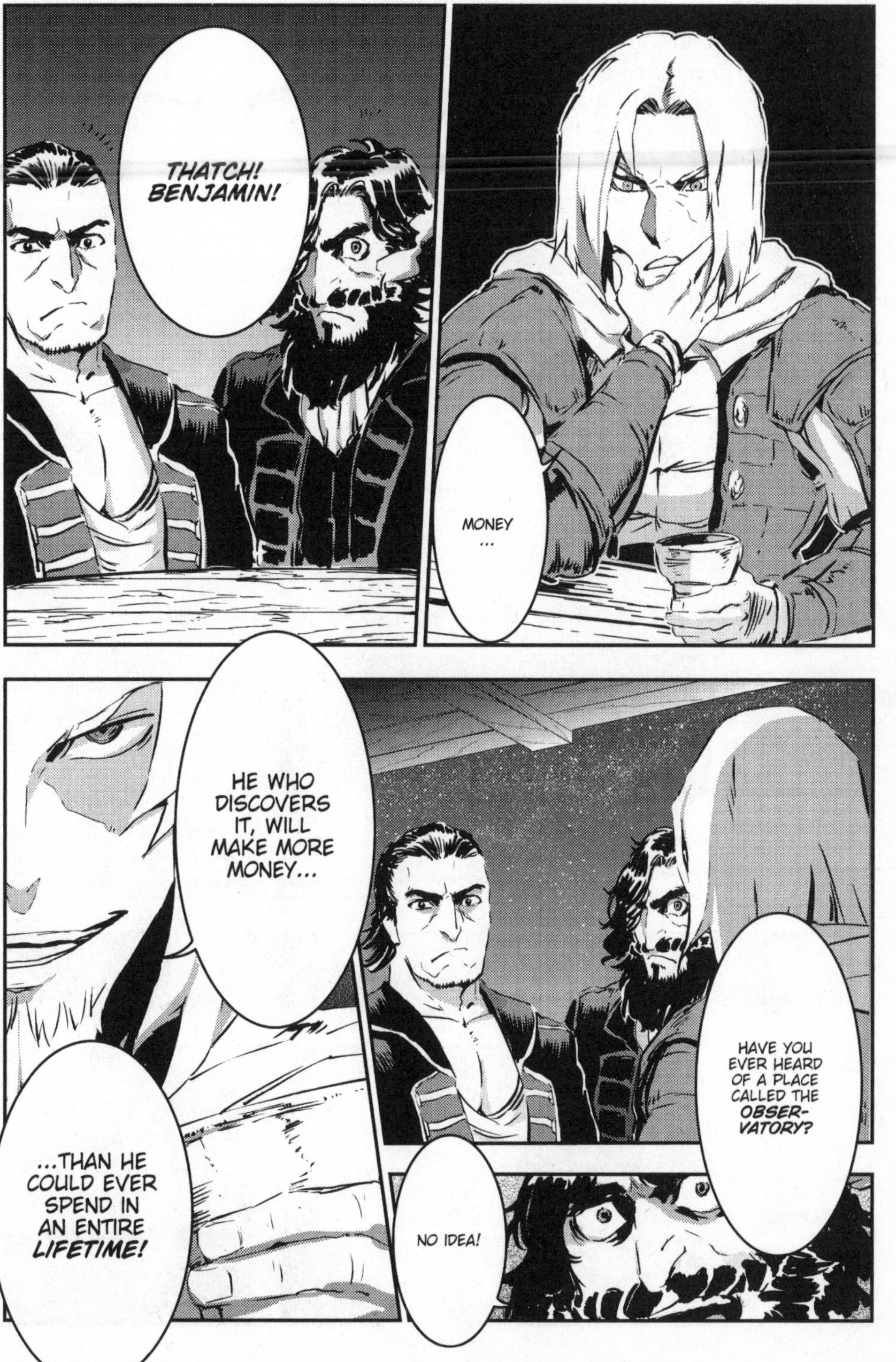
MONEY ...
THATCH! BENJAMIN!
HAVE YOU EVER HEARD OF A PLACE CALLED THE OBSER-VATORY?
NO IDEA!
HE WHO DISCOVERS IT, WILL MAKE MORE MONEY...
...THAN HE COULD EVER SPEND IN AN ENTIRE LIFETIME!

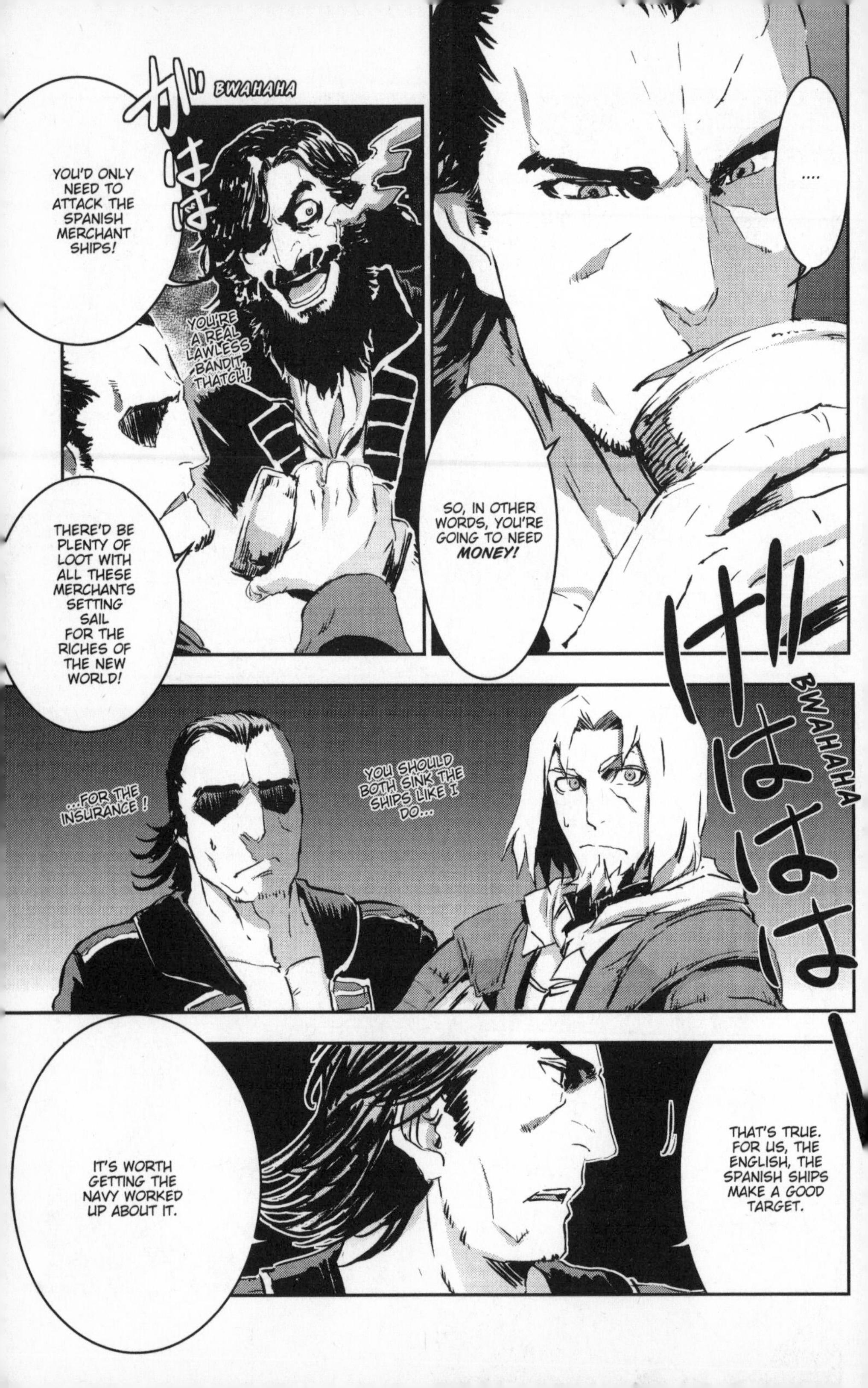
....
SO, IN OTHER WORDS, YOU'RE GOING TO NEED MONEY!
がはは BWAHAHA
YOU'D ONLY NEED TO ATTACK THE SPANISH MERCHANT SHIPS!
YOU'RE A REAL LAWLESS BANDIT, THATCH!
THERE'D BE PLENTY OF LOOT WITH ALL THESE MERCHANTS SETTING SAIL FOR THE RICHES OF THE NEW WORLD!
けははは BWAHAHA
YOU SHOULD BOTH SINK THE SHIPS LIKE I DO...
...FOR THE INSURANCE!
THAT'S TRUE. FOR US, THE ENGLISH, THE SPANISH SHIPS MAKE A GOOD TARGET.
IT'S WORTH GETTING THE NAVY WORKED UP ABOUT IT.

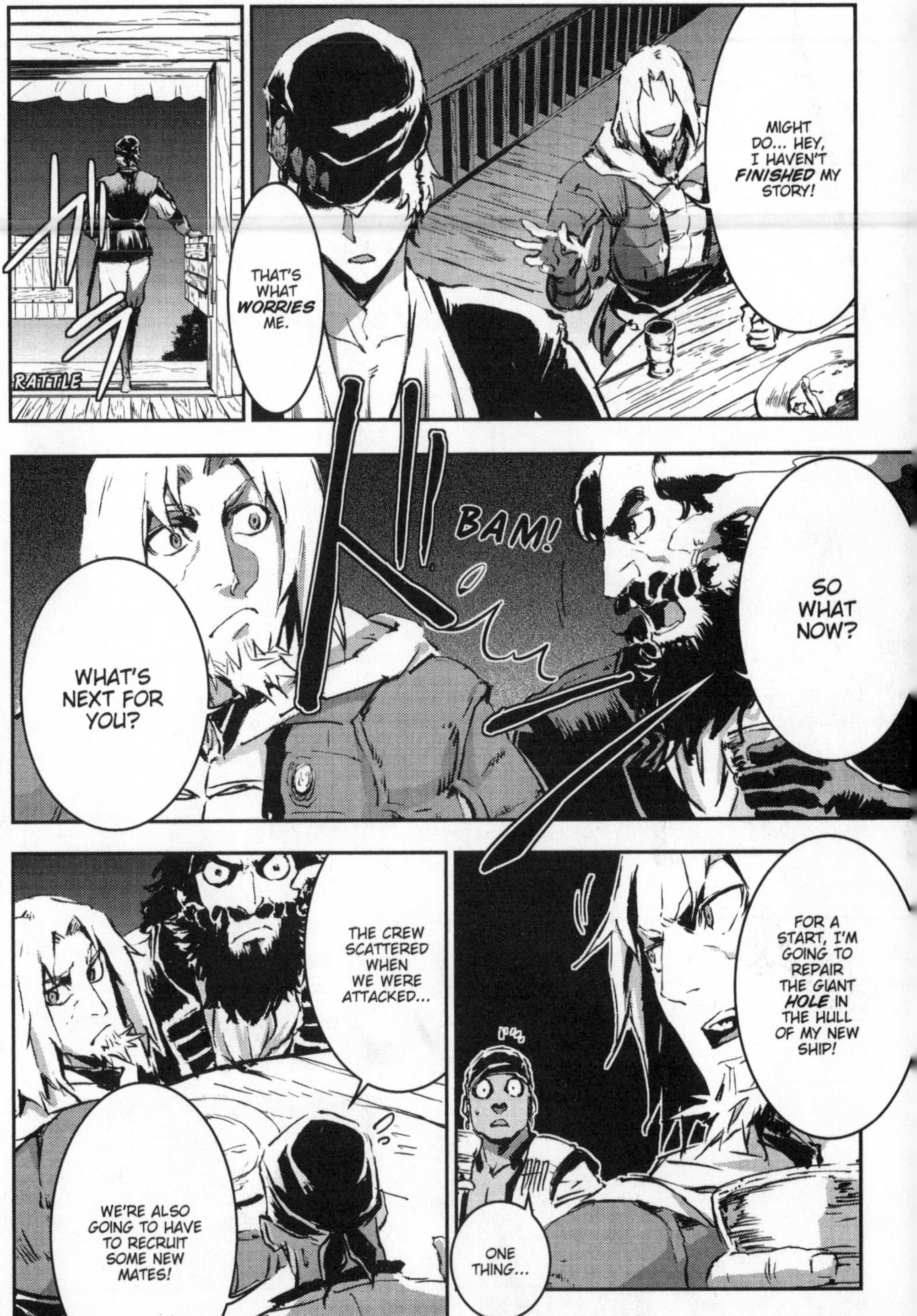
MIGHT DO... HEY, I HAVEN'T FINISHED MY STORY!
THAT'S WHAT WORRIES ME.
RATTLE
SO WHAT NOW?
BAM!
WHAT'S NEXT FOR YOU?
FOR A START, I'M GOING TO REPAIR THE GIANT HOLE IN THE HULL OF MY NEW SHIP!
ONE THING...
THE CREW SCATTERED WHEN WE WERE ATTACKED...
WE'RE ALSO GOING TO HAVE TO RECRUIT SOME NEW MATES!

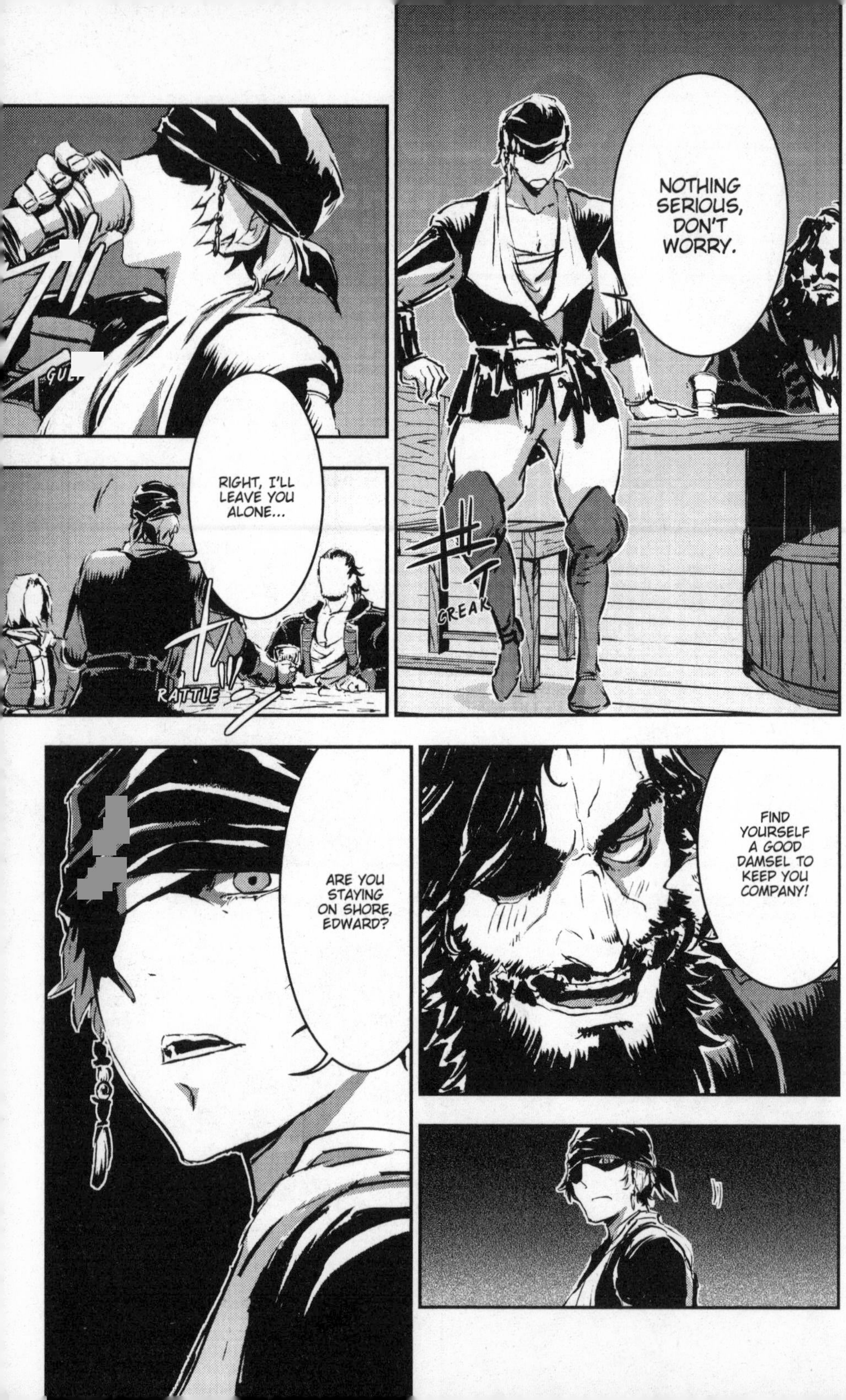
NOTHING SERIOUS, DON'T WORRY.
CREAK
RIGHT, I'LL LEAVE YOU ALONE...
RATTLE
FIND YOURSELF A GOOD DAMSEL TO KEEP YOU COMPANY!
ARE YOU STAYING ON SHORE, EDWARD?

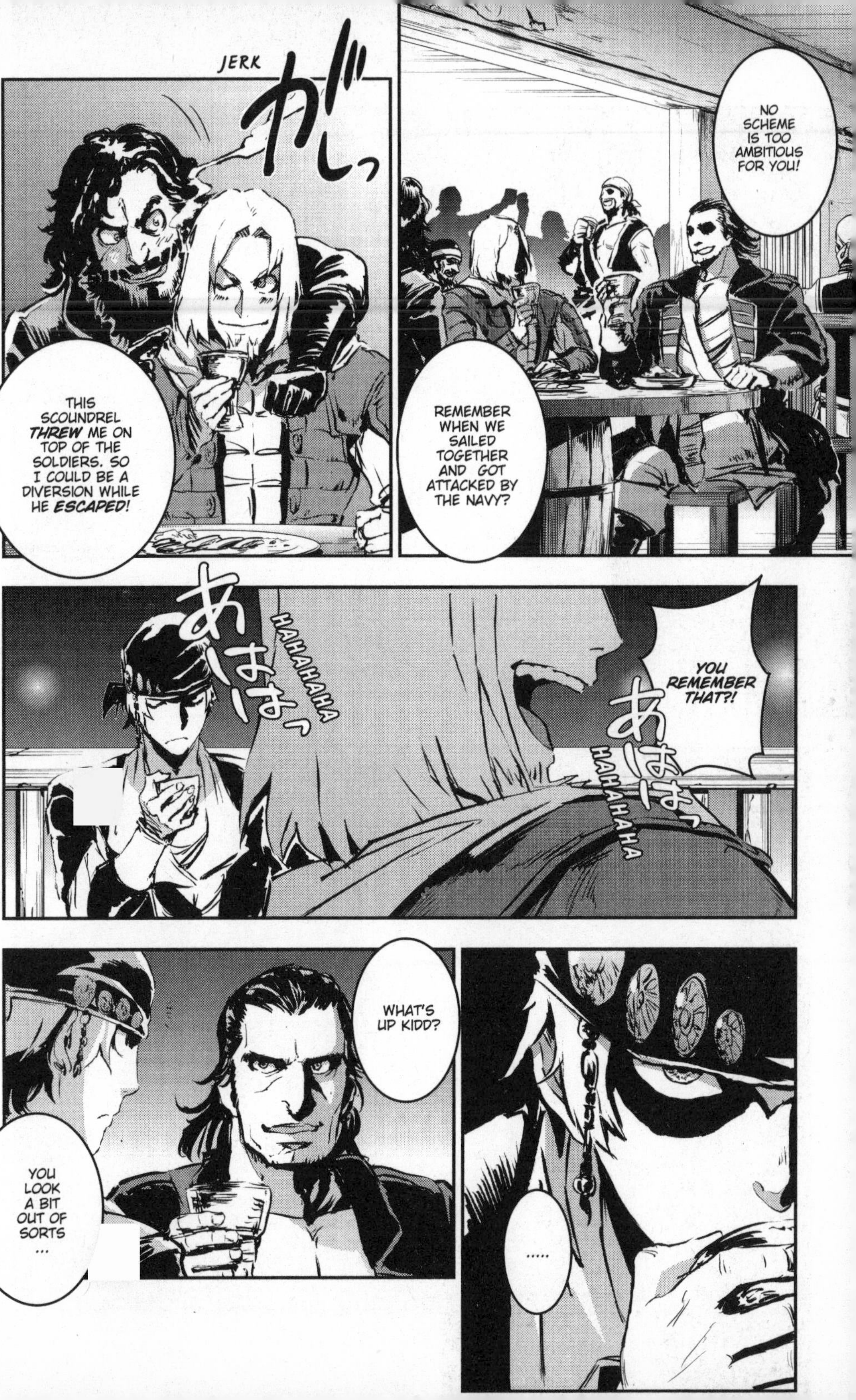
NO SCHEME IS TOO AMBITIOUS FOR YOU!
REMEMBER WHEN WE SAILED TOGETHER AND GOT ATTACKED BY THE NAVY?
JERK
がしっ
THIS SCOUNDREL *THREW* ME ON TOP OF THE SOLDIERS. SO I COULD BE A DIVERSION WHILE HE *ESCAPED*!
YOU REMEMBER THAT?!
あははっ
HAHAHAHA
あははっ
HAHAHAHA
.....
WHAT'S UP KIDD?
YOU LOOK A BIT OUT OF SORTS ...

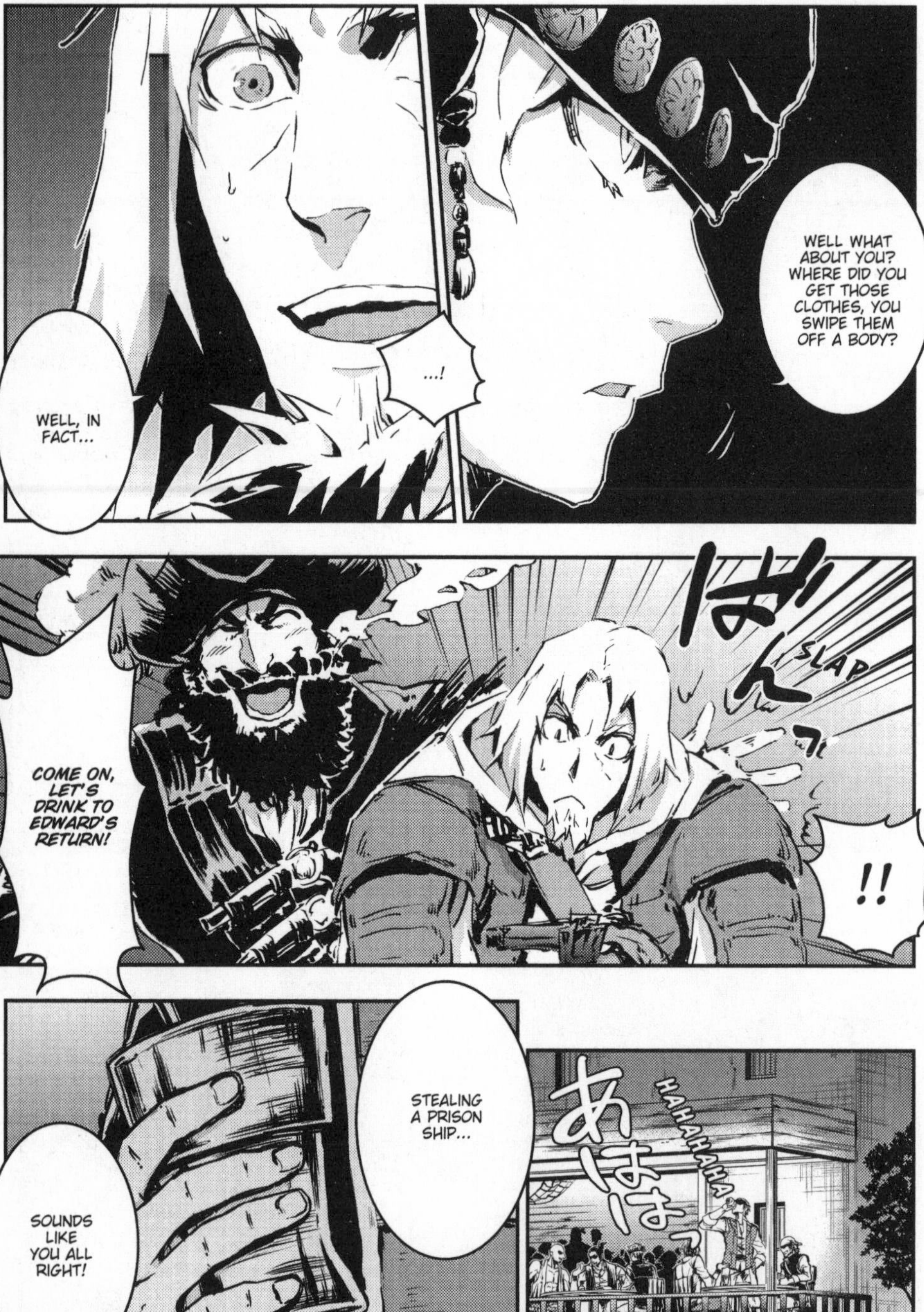
WELL WHAT ABOUT YOU? WHERE DID YOU GET THOSE CLOTHES, YOU SWIPE THEM OFF A BODY?
...!
WELL, IN FACT...
ばんっ
SLAP
!!
COME ON, LET'S DRINK TO EDWARD'S RETURN!
あははっ
HAHAHAHA
STEALING A PRISON SHIP...
SOUNDS LIKE YOU ALL RIGHT!

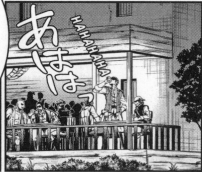

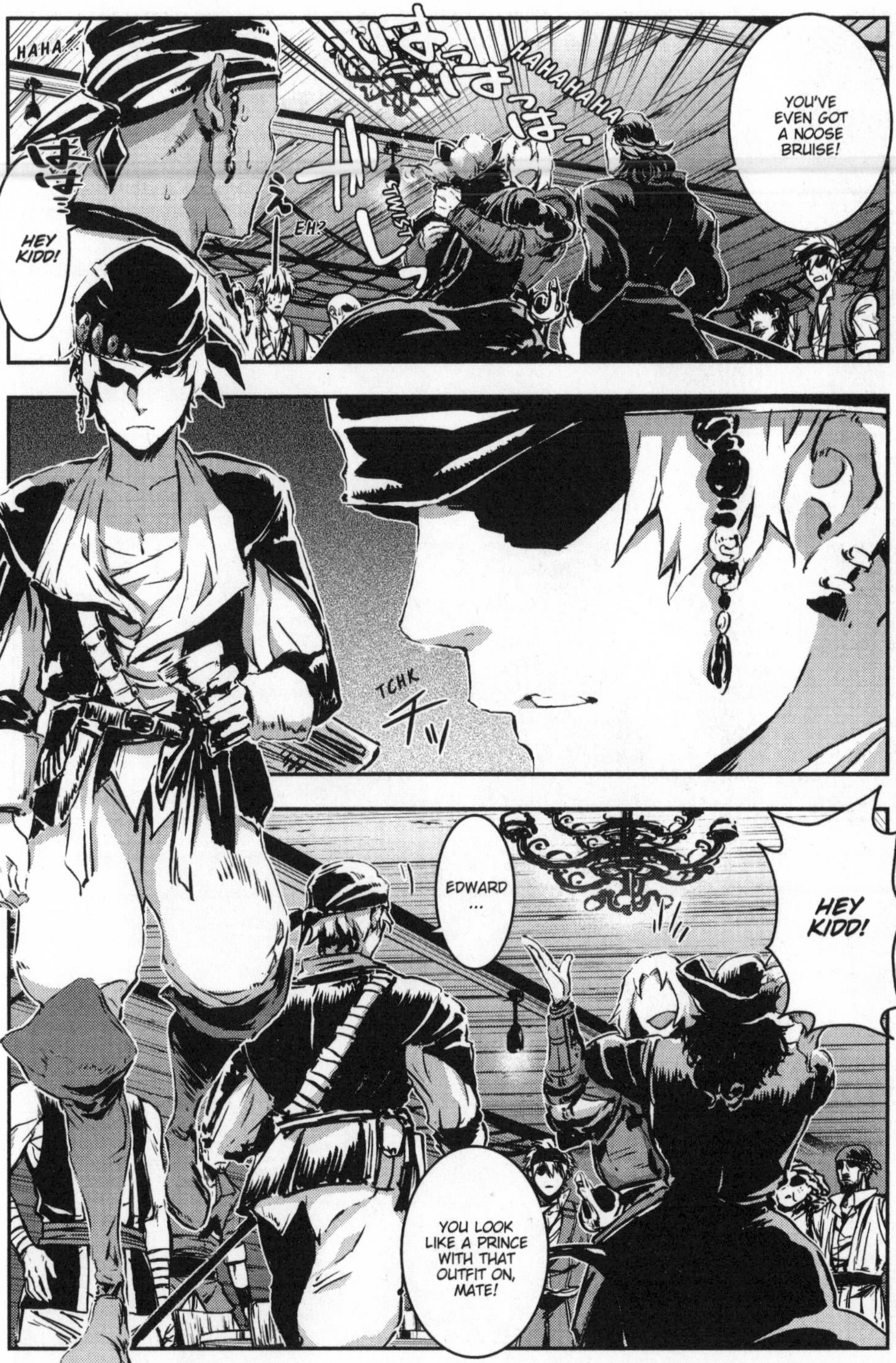
YOU'VE EVEN GOT A NOOSE BRUISE!
HAHAHAHA
TWIST
EH?
HAHA...
HEY KIDD!
TCHK
チッ
HEY KIDD!
EDWARD ...
YOU LOOK LIKE A PRINCE WITH THAT OUTFIT ON, MATE!

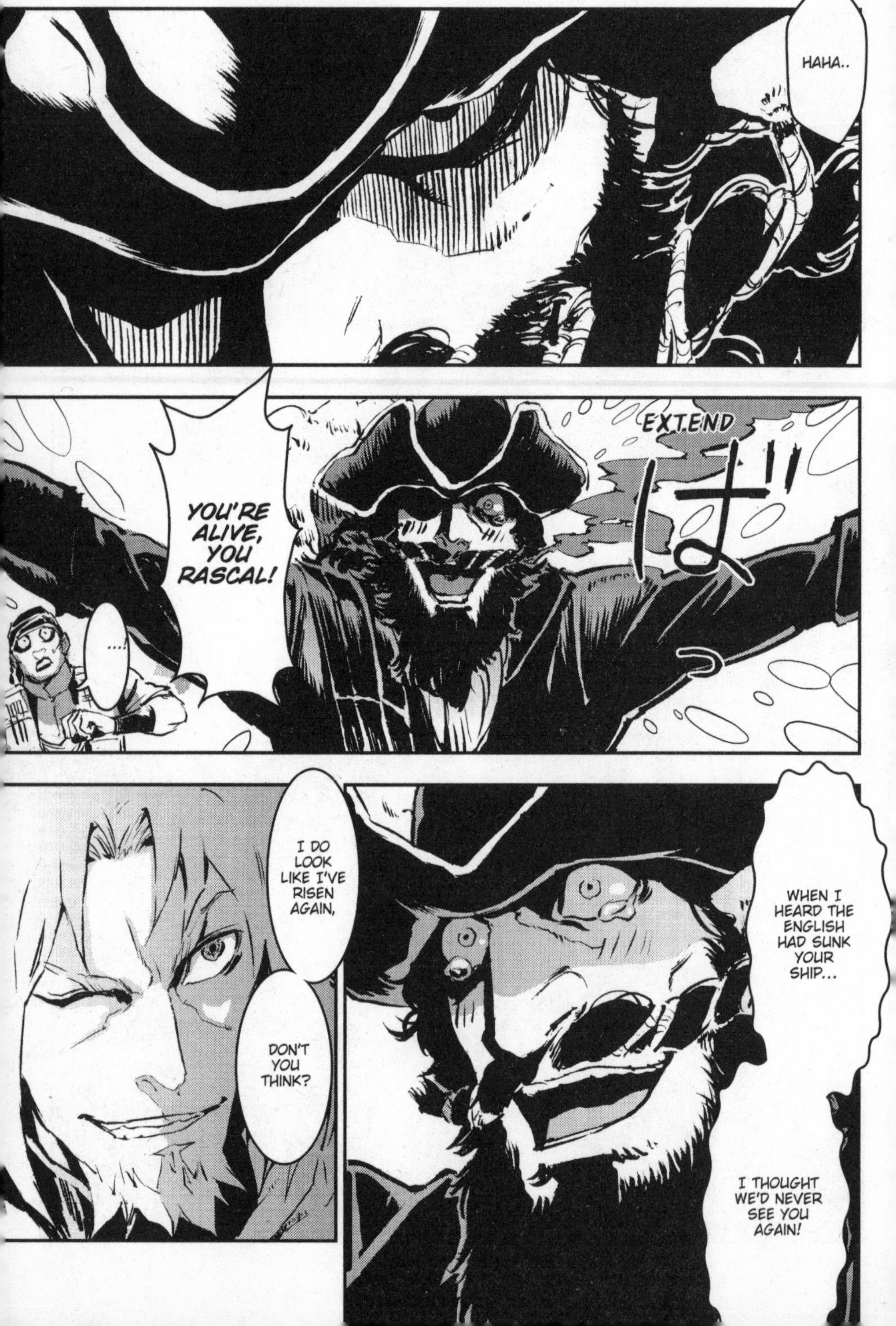
HAHA..
EXTEND
ば
YOU'RE ALIVE, YOU RASCAL!
....
WHEN I HEARD THE ENGLISH HAD SUNK YOUR SHIP...
I THOUGHT WE'D NEVER SEE YOU AGAIN!
I DO LOOK LIKE I'VE RISEN AGAIN,
DON'T YOU THINK?

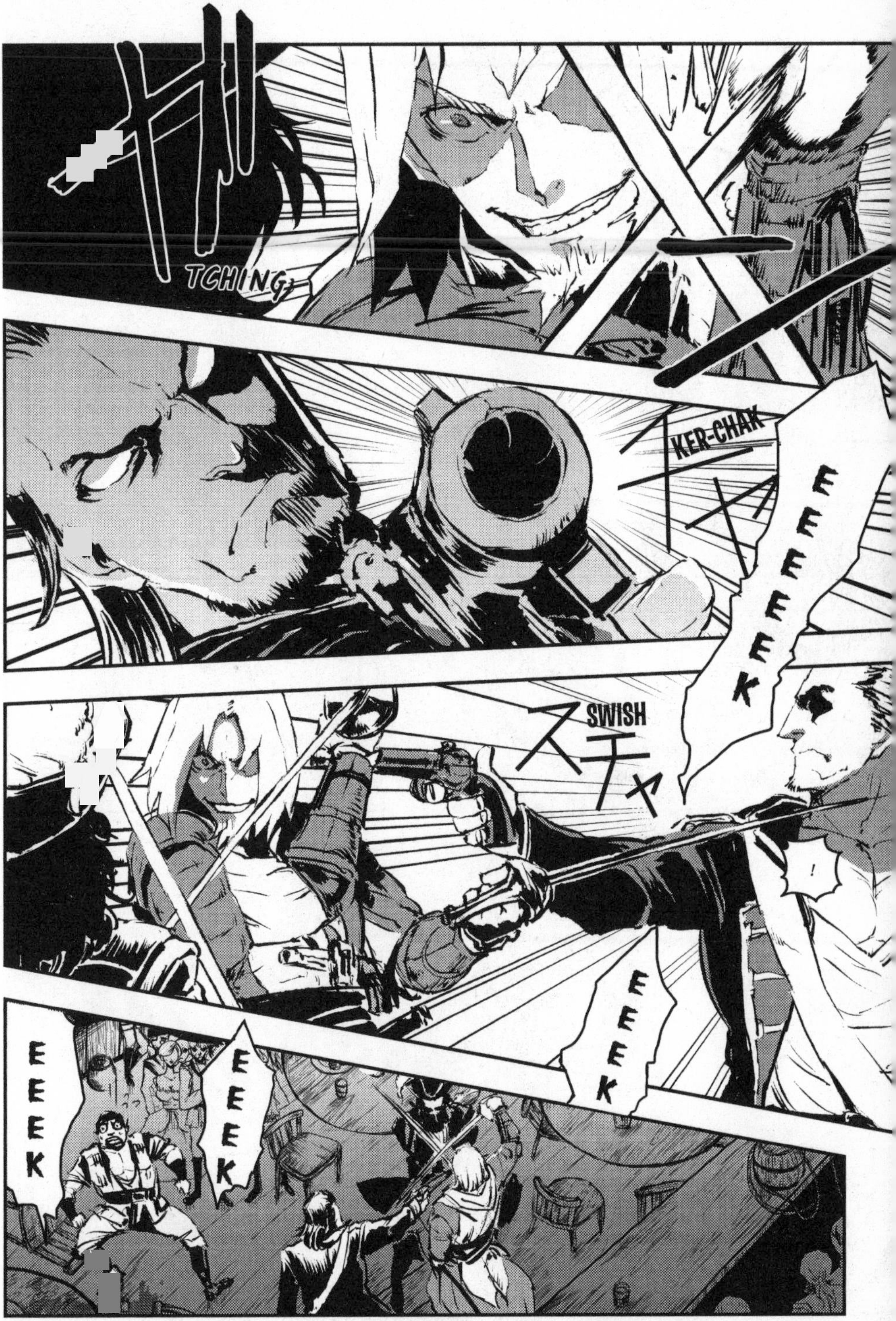
TCHING
KER-CHAK
EEEEEEK
SWISH
スチャ
!
EEEEK
EEEEK
EEEEK

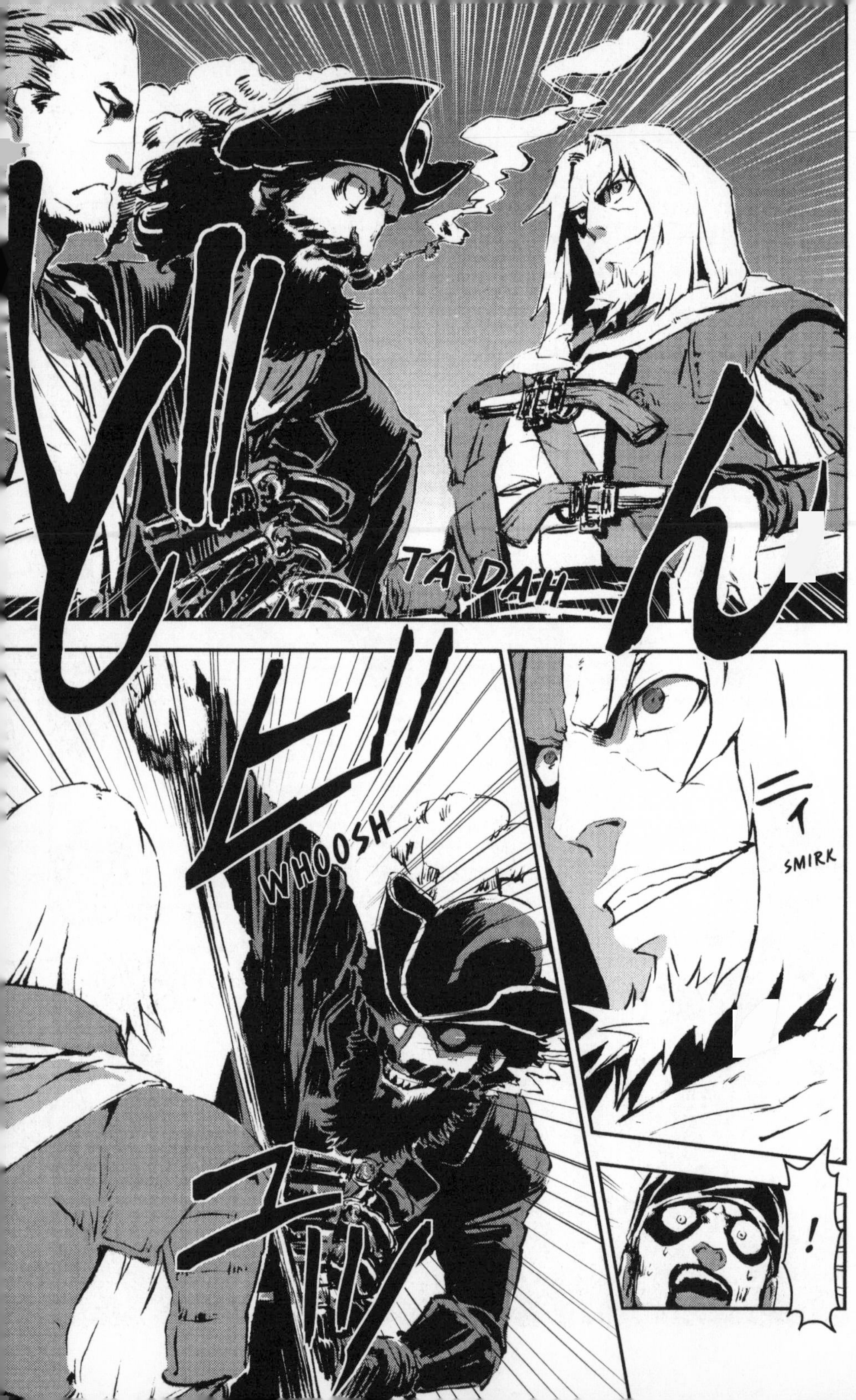
TA-DAH
SMIRK
!
WHOOSH

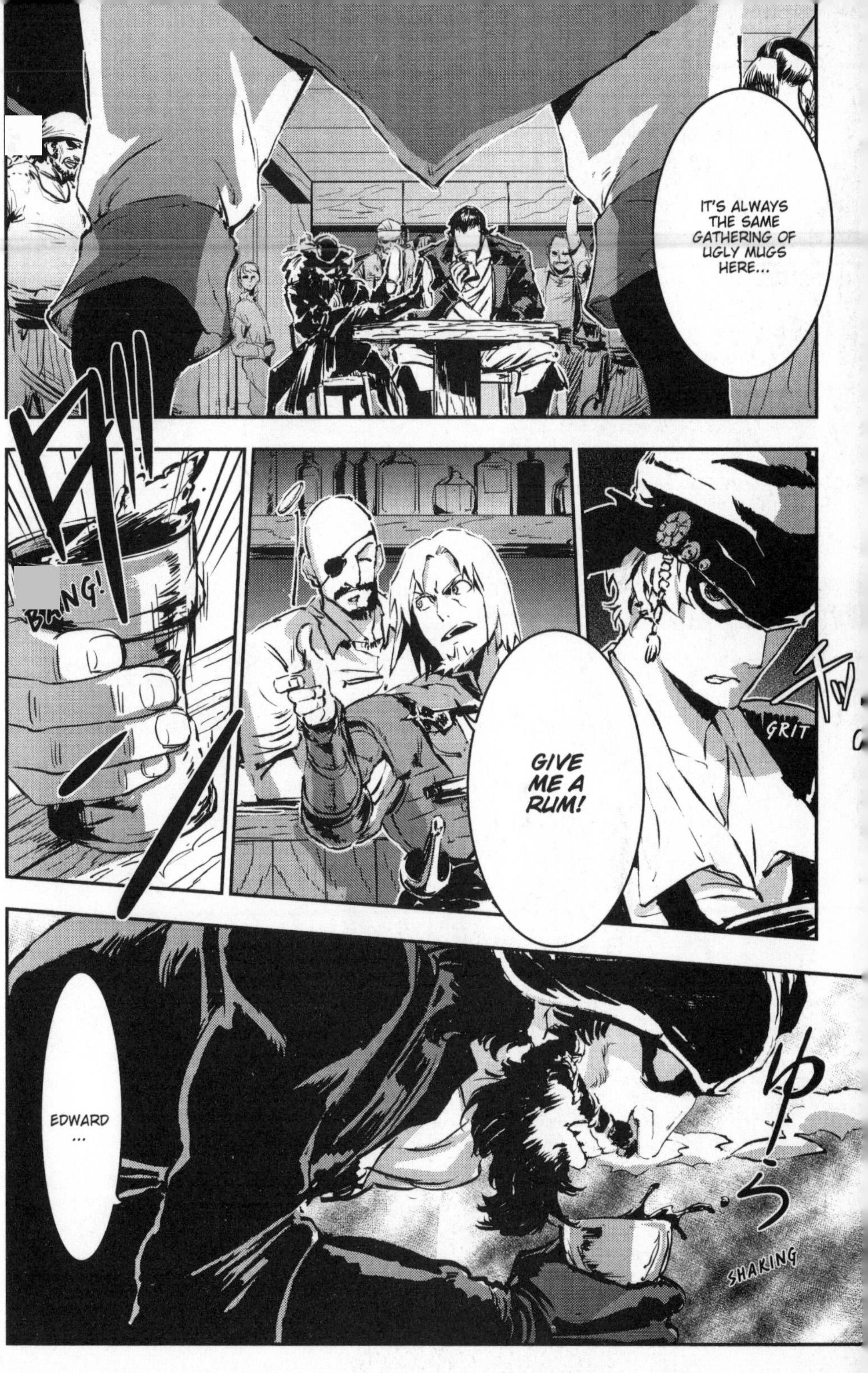
IT'S ALWAYS THE SAME GATHERING OF UGLY MUGS HERE...
GRIT
GIVE ME A RUM!
BANG!
EDWARD ...
SHAKING

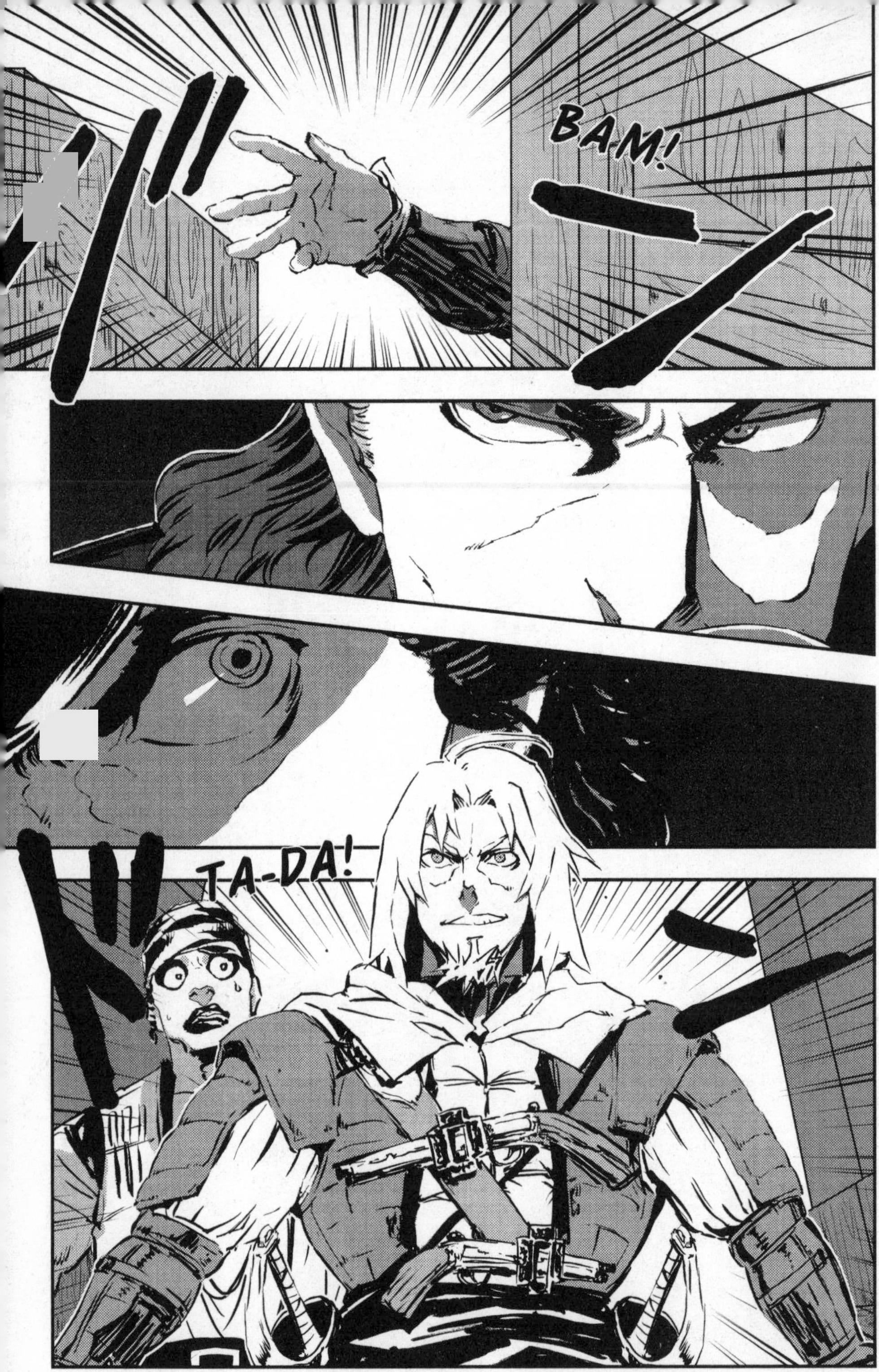
BAM!
TA-DA!

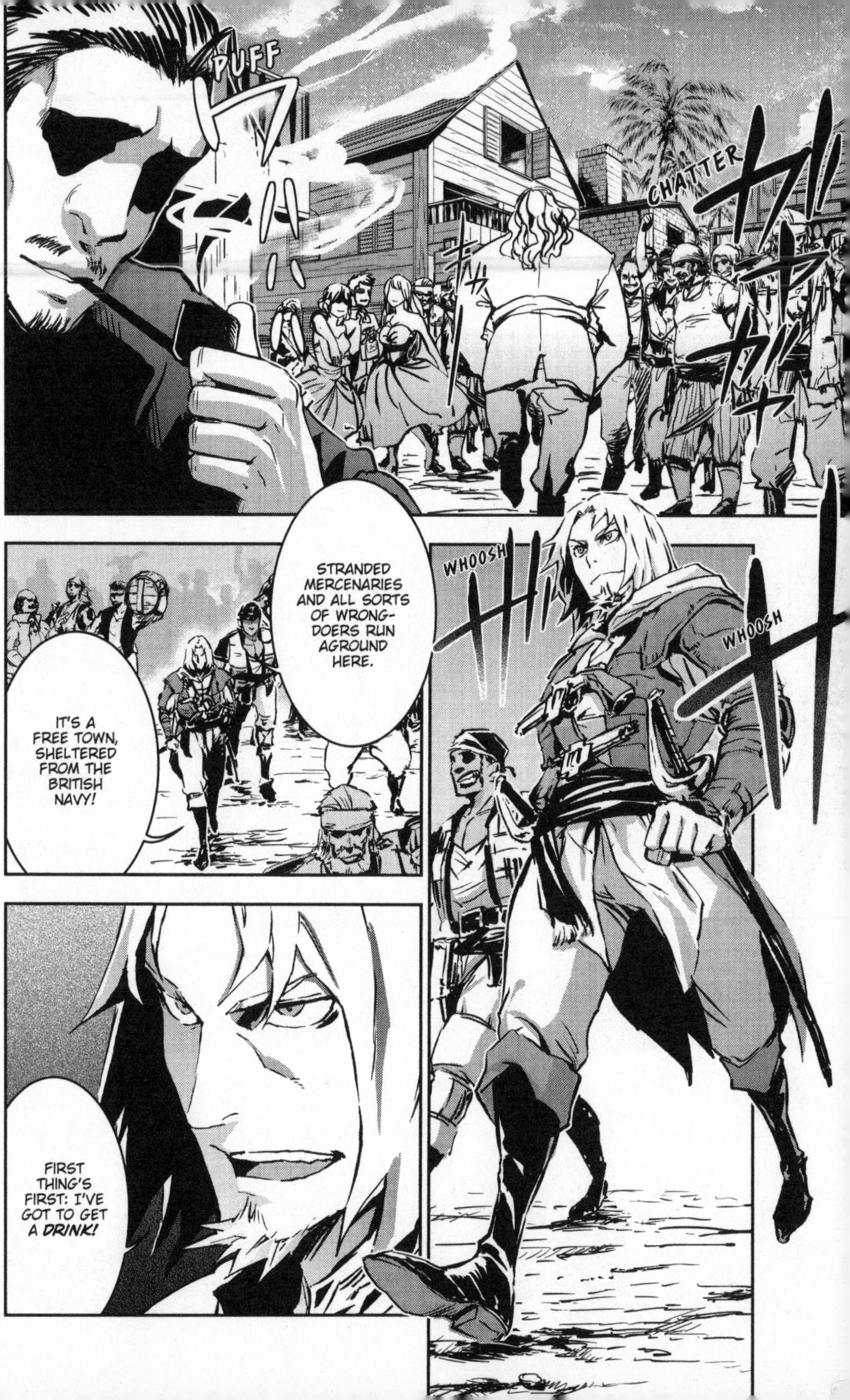
PUFF
CHATTER
WHOOSH
WHOOSH
STRANDED MERCENARIES AND ALL SORTS OF WRONG-DOERS RUN AGROUND HERE.
IT'S A FREE TOWN, SHELTERED FROM THE BRITISH NAVY!
FIRST THING'S FIRST: I'VE GOT TO GET A *DRINK!*

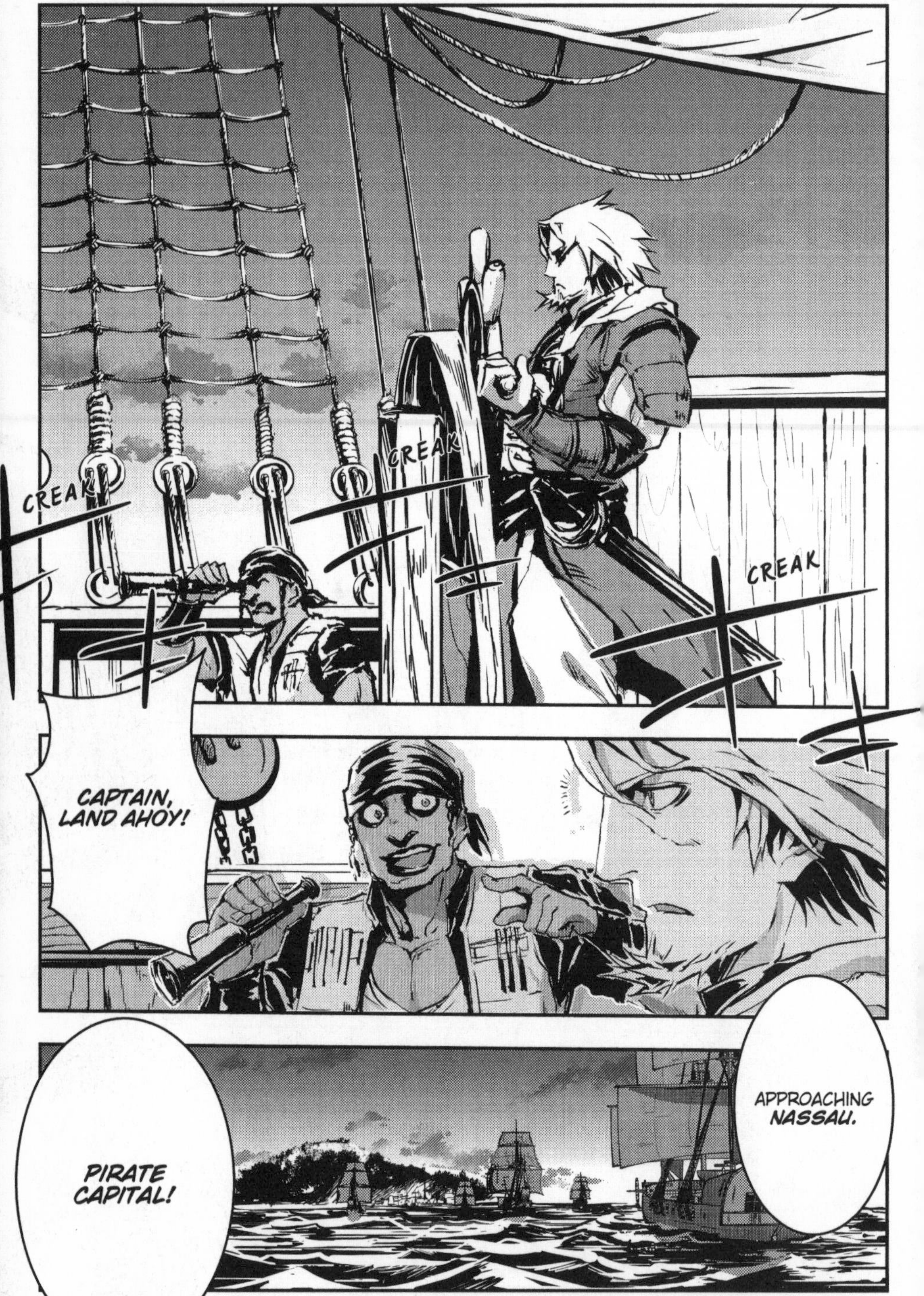
CREAK
CREAK
CREAK
CAPTAIN, LAND AHOY!
APPROACHING NASSAU.
PIRATE CAPITAL!

CHAPTER V

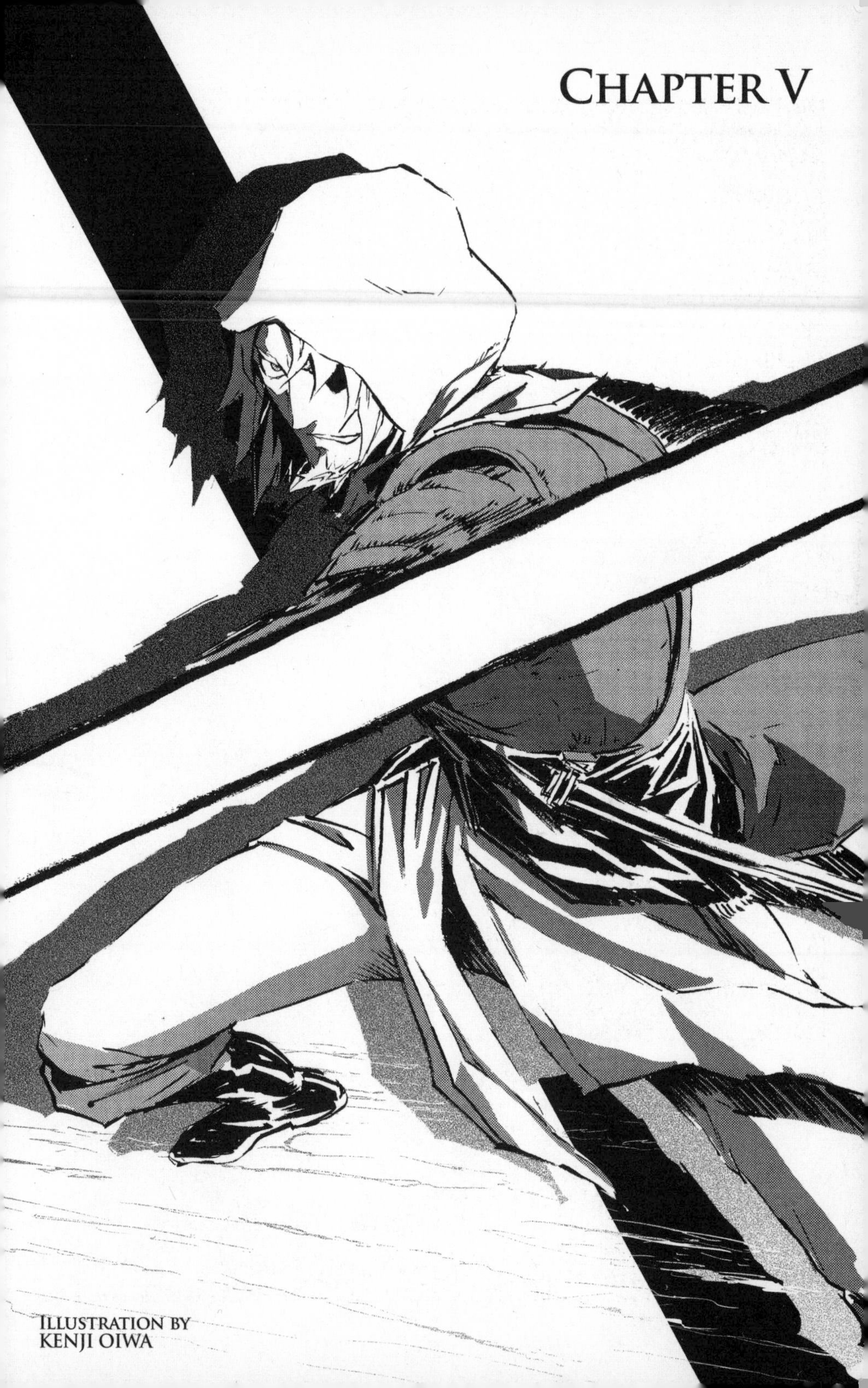

ILLUSTRATION BY
KENJI OIWA

CHAPTER V

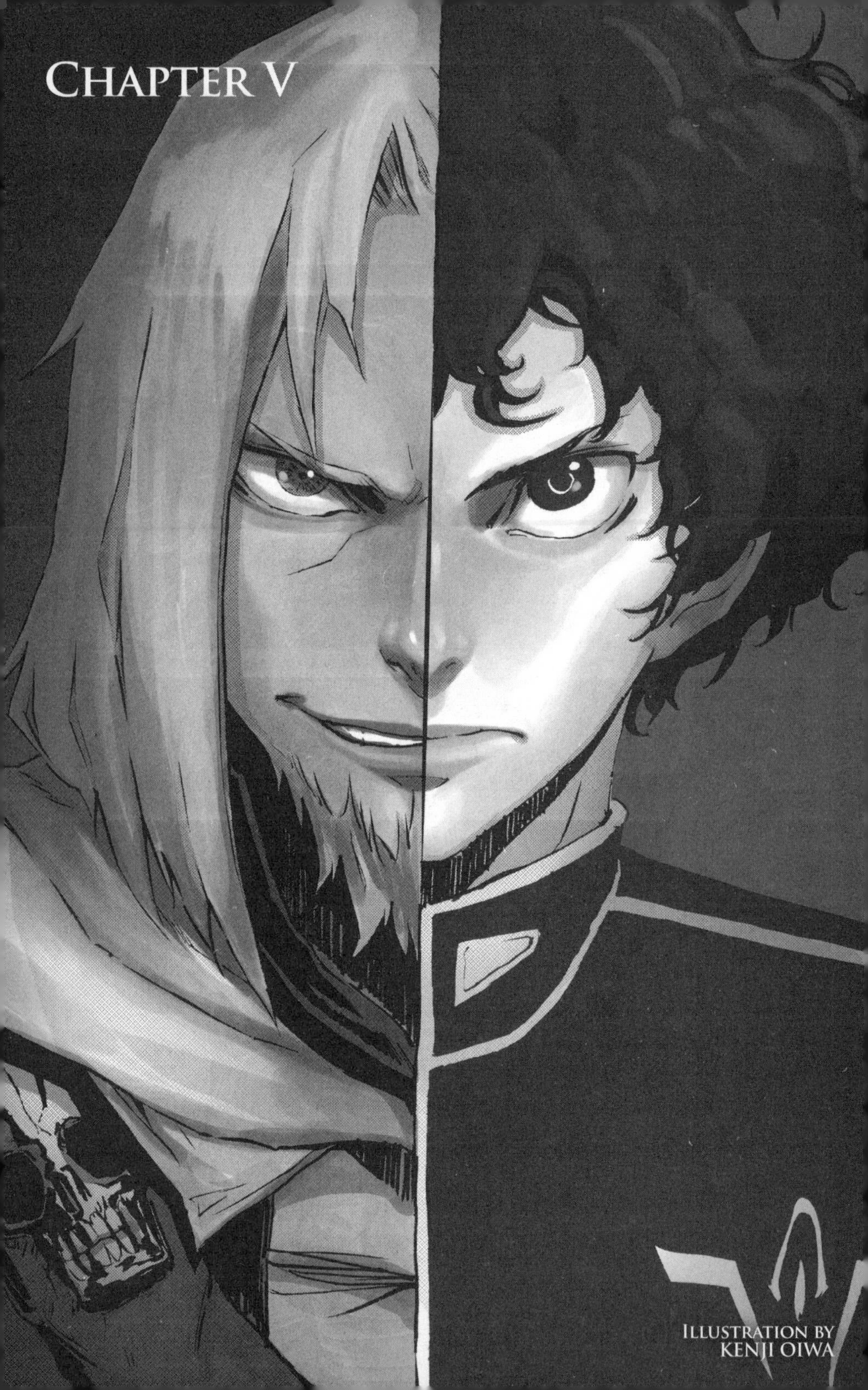

ILLUSTRATION BY
KENJI OIWA

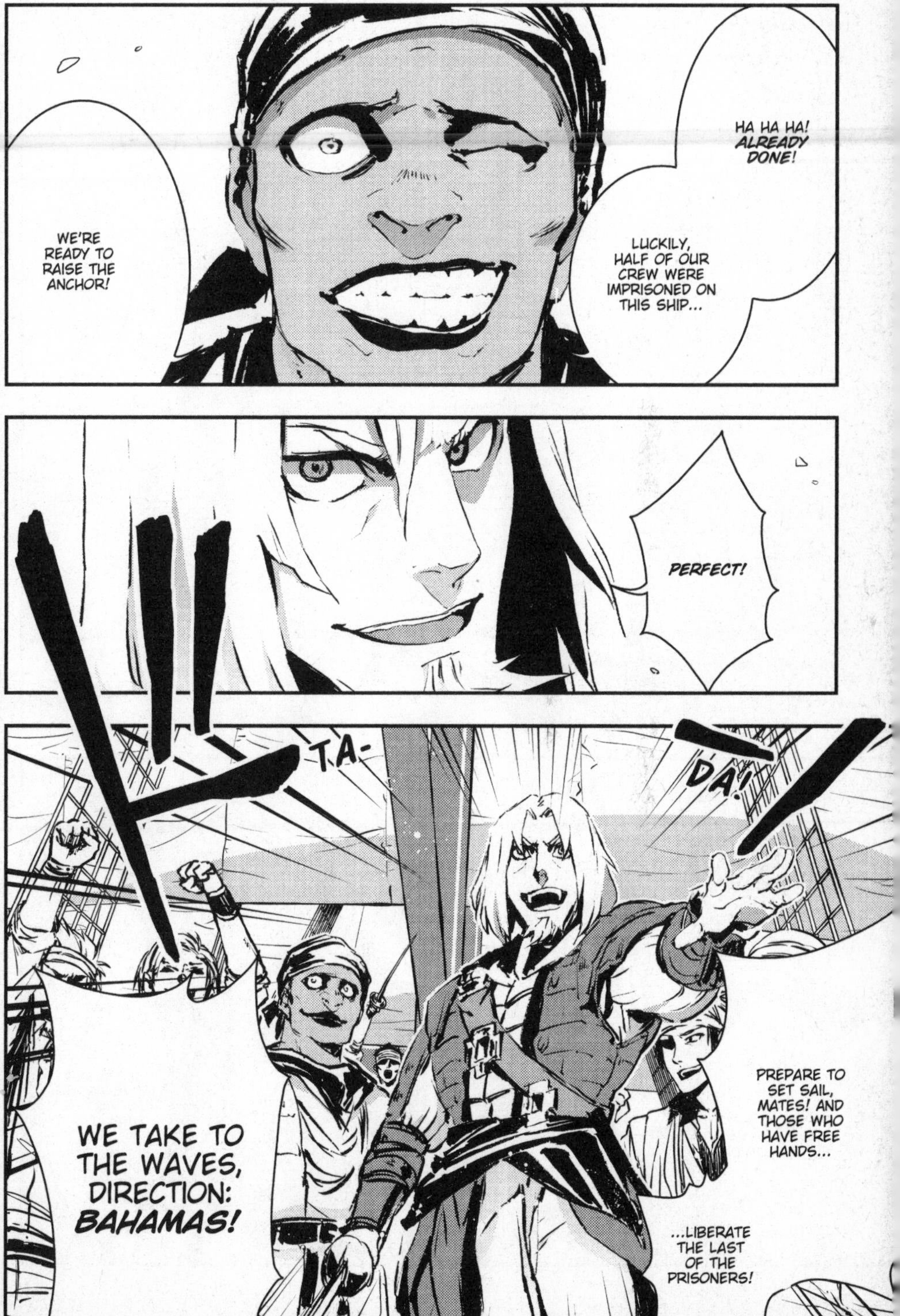
HA HA HA! ALREADY DONE!
LUCKILY, HALF OF OUR CREW WERE IMPRISONED ON THIS SHIP...
WE'RE READY TO RAISE THE ANCHOR!
PERFECT!
TA-
DA!
PREPARE TO SET SAIL, MATES! AND THOSE WHO HAVE FREE HANDS...
...LIBERATE THE LAST OF THE PRISONERS!
WE TAKE TO THE WAVES, DIRECTION: BAHAMAS!

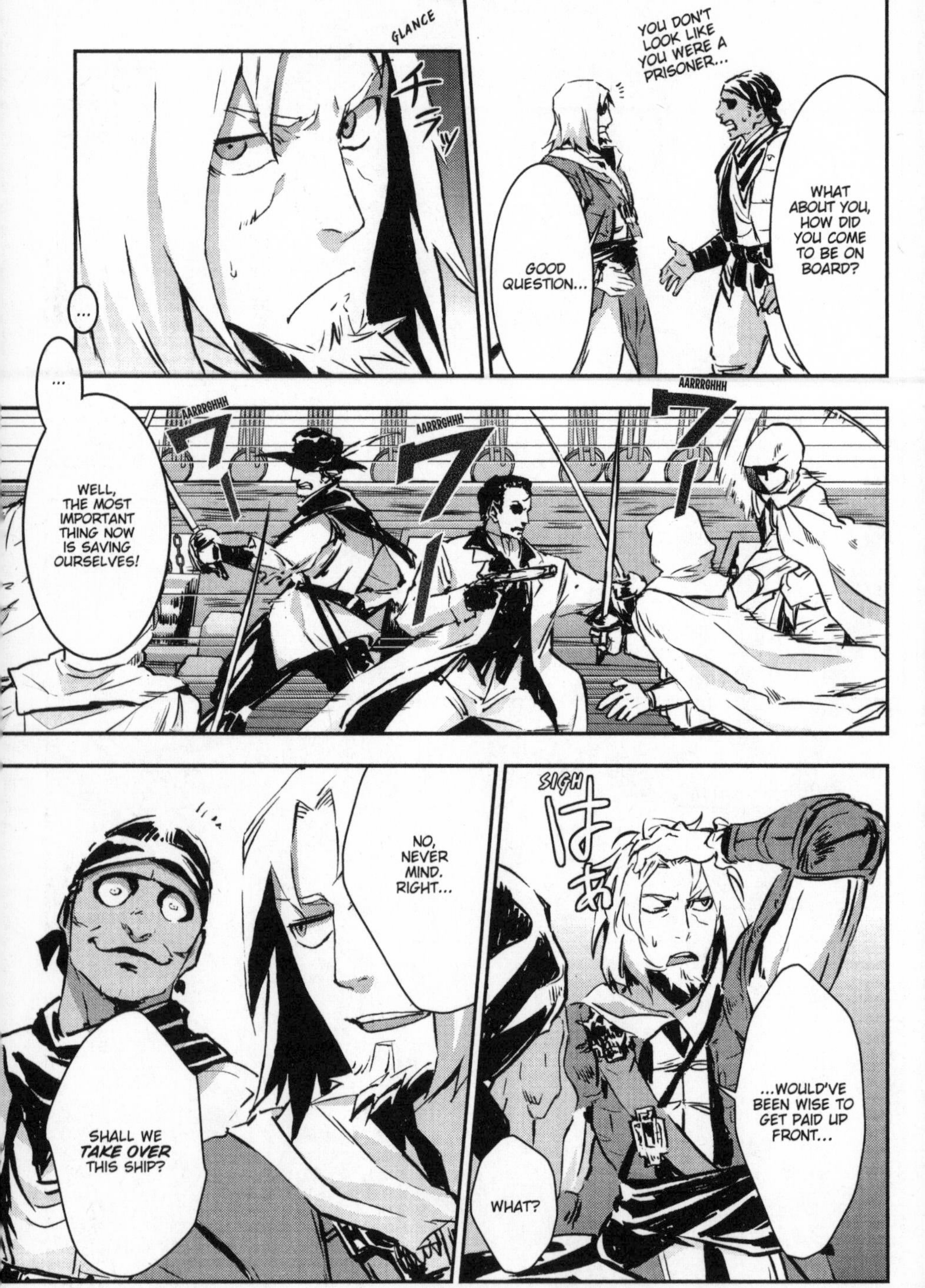
YOU DON'T LOOK LIKE YOU WERE A PRISONER...
WHAT ABOUT YOU, HOW DID YOU COME TO BE ON BOARD?
GOOD QUESTION...
GLANCE
チラッ
...
...
AARRRGHHH
AARRRGHHH
AARRRGHHH
WELL, THE MOST IMPORTANT THING NOW IS SAVING OURSELVES!
SIGH
はぁ
...WOULD'VE BEEN WISE TO GET PAID UP FRONT...
WHAT?
NO, NEVER MIND. RIGHT...
SHALL WE *TAKE OVER* THIS SHIP?

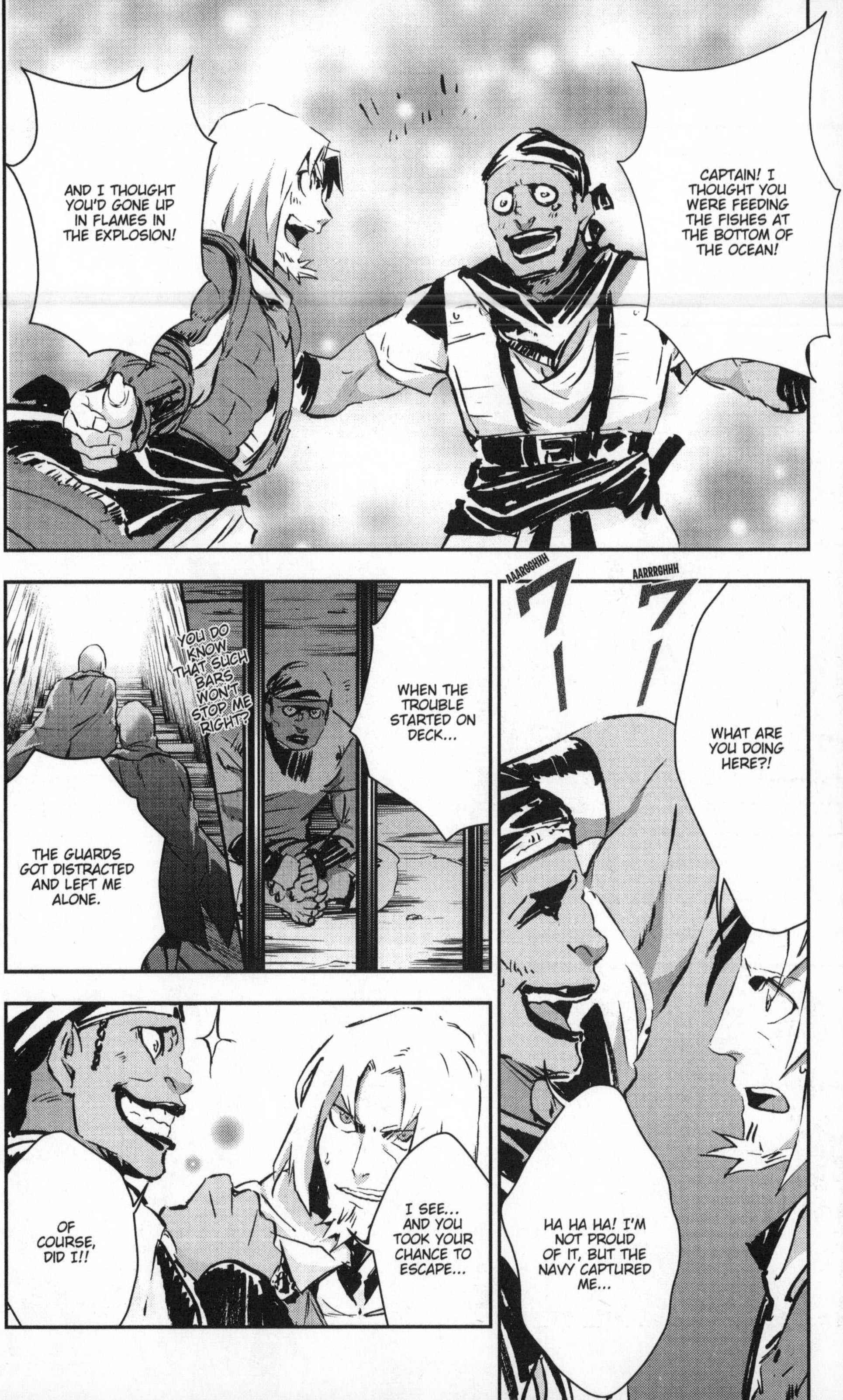
CAPTAIN! I THOUGHT YOU WERE FEEDING THE FISHES AT THE BOTTOM OF THE OCEAN!
AND I THOUGHT YOU'D GONE UP IN FLAMES IN THE EXPLOSION!
AARRRGHHH
AAARGGHHH
WHAT ARE YOU DOING HERE?!
HA HA HA! I'M NOT PROUD OF IT, BUT THE NAVY CAPTURED ME...
WHEN THE TROUBLE STARTED ON DECK...
YOU DO KNOW THAT SUCH BARS WON'T STOP ME RIGHT?
THE GUARDS GOT DISTRACTED AND LEFT ME ALONE.
I SEE... AND YOU TOOK YOUR CHANCE TO ESCAPE...
OF COURSE, DID I!!

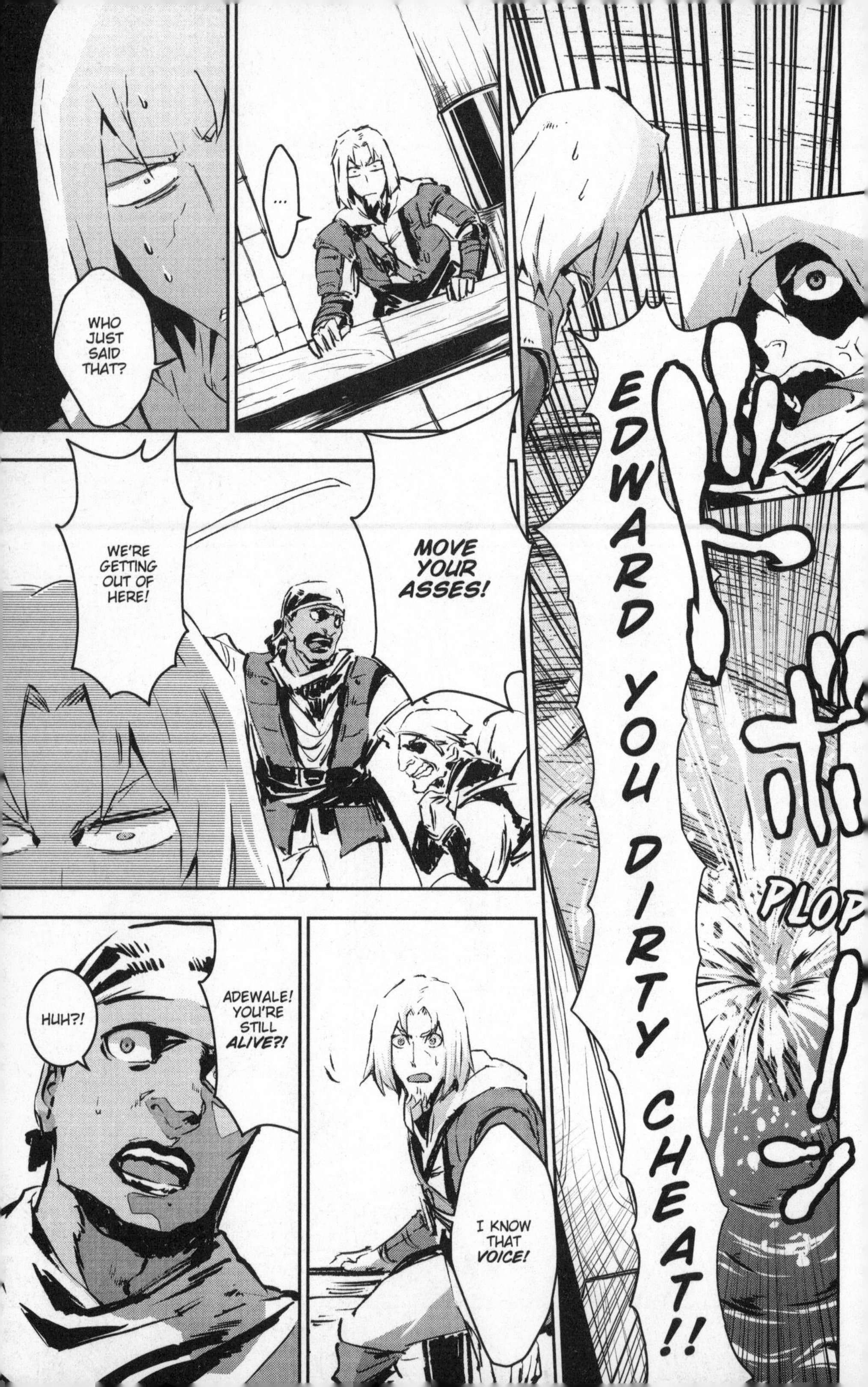
PLOP
EDWARD YOU DIRTY CHEAT!!
...
WHO JUST SAID THAT?
MOVE YOUR ASSES!
WE'RE GETTING OUT OF HERE!
I KNOW THAT VOICE!
ADEWALE! YOU'RE STILL ALIVE?!
HUH?!

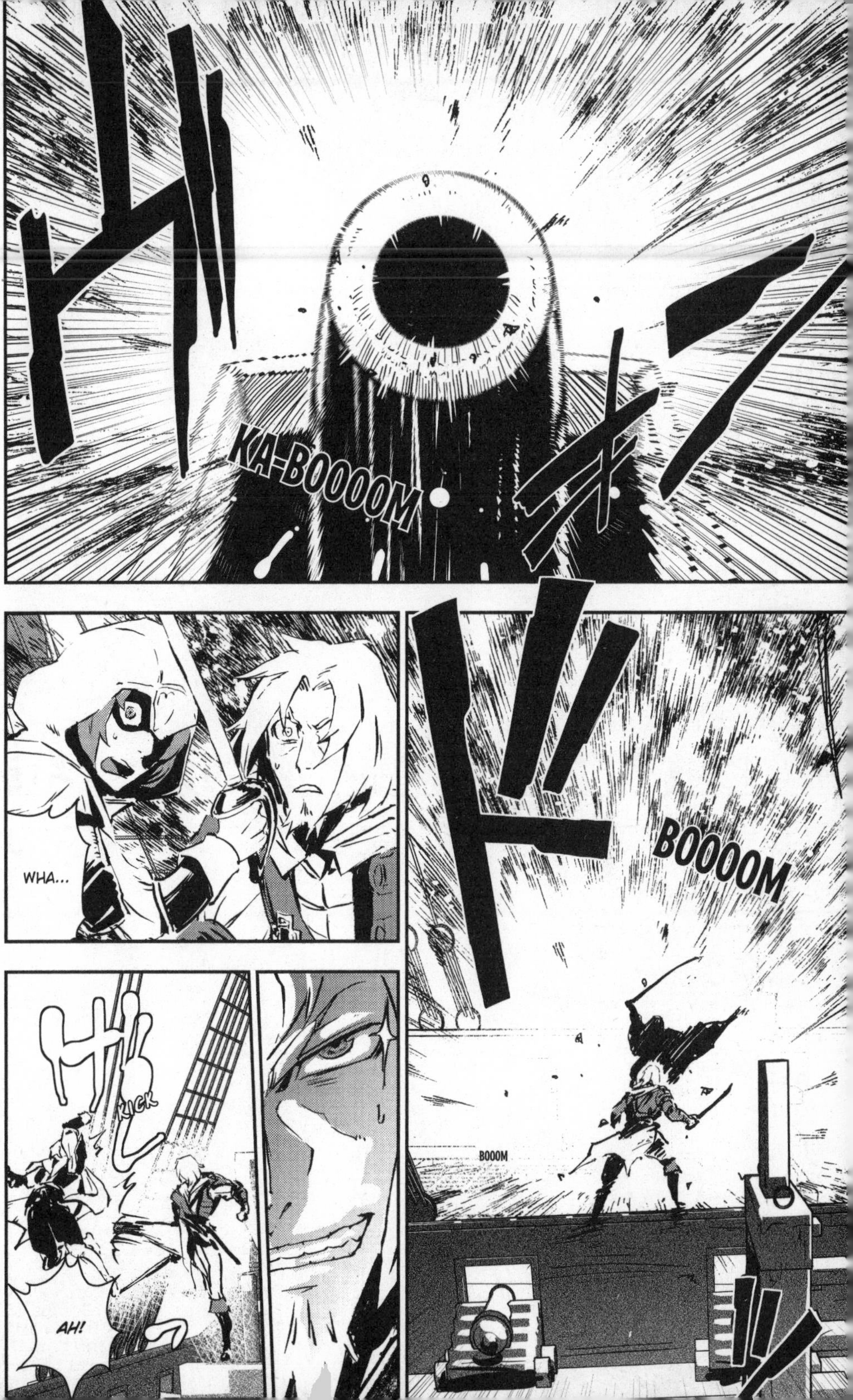
KA-BOOOOM
BOOOOM
WHA...
BOOOM
KICK
AH!

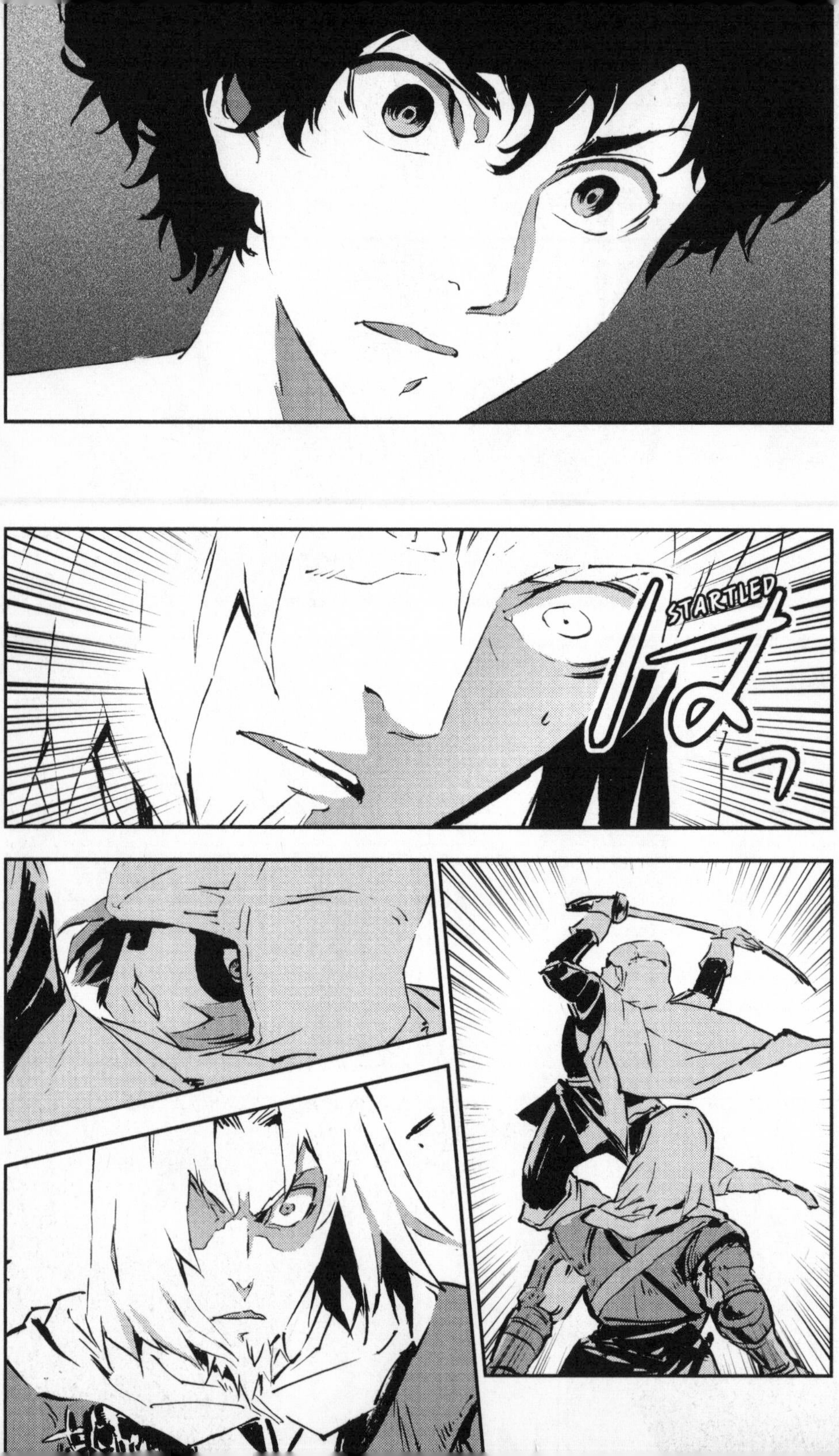
STARTLED
はっ

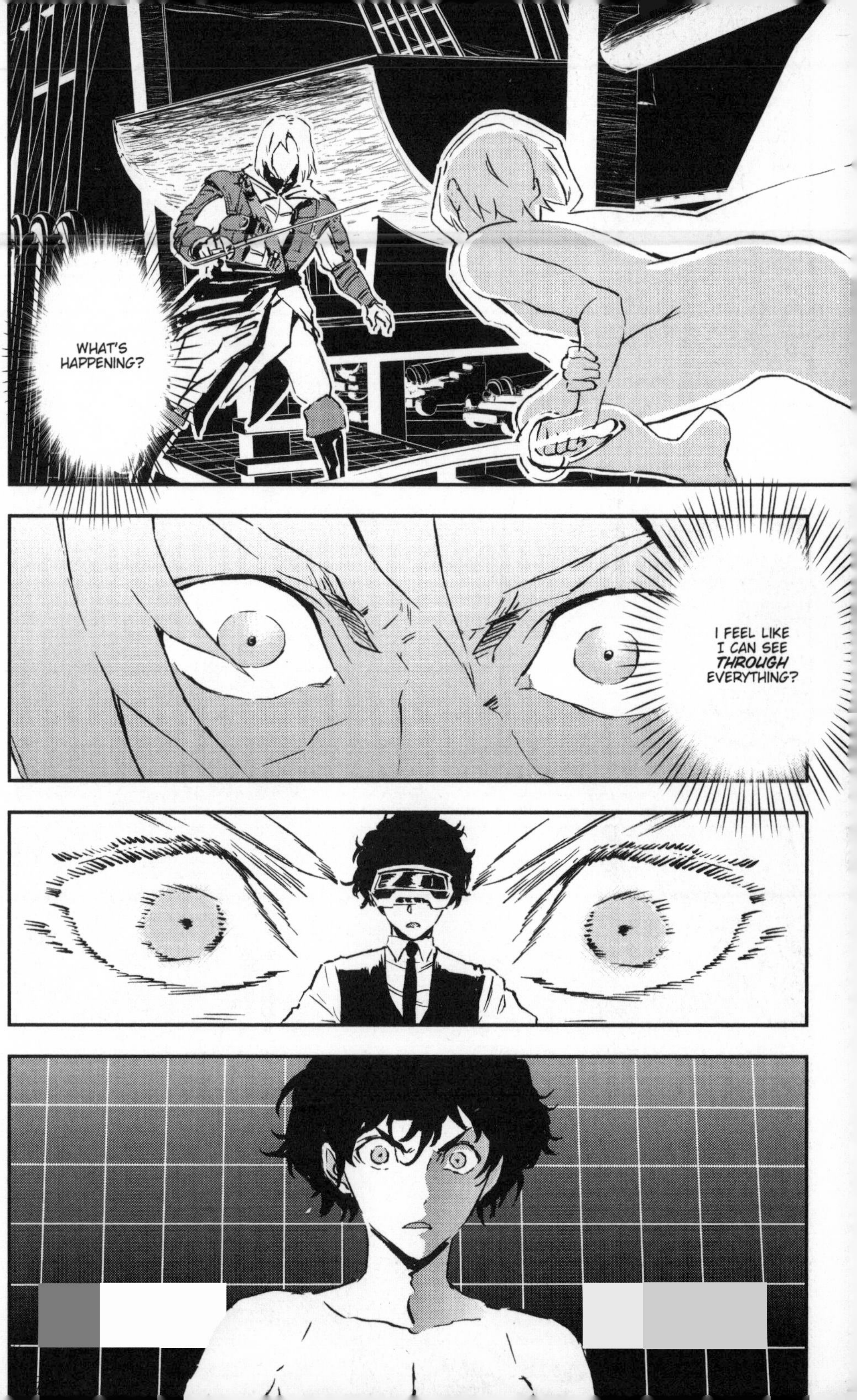
WHAT'S HAPPENING?
I FEEL LIKE I CAN SEE *THROUGH* EVERYTHING?

BA-DUMP
BA-DUMP

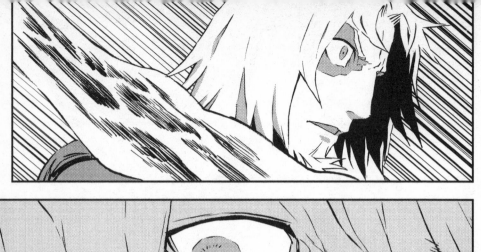

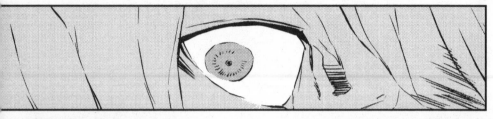

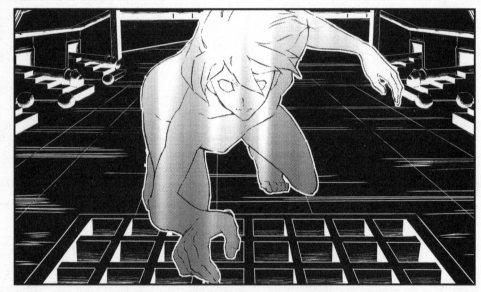

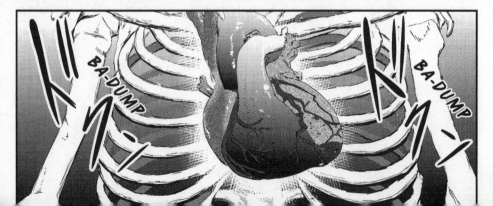

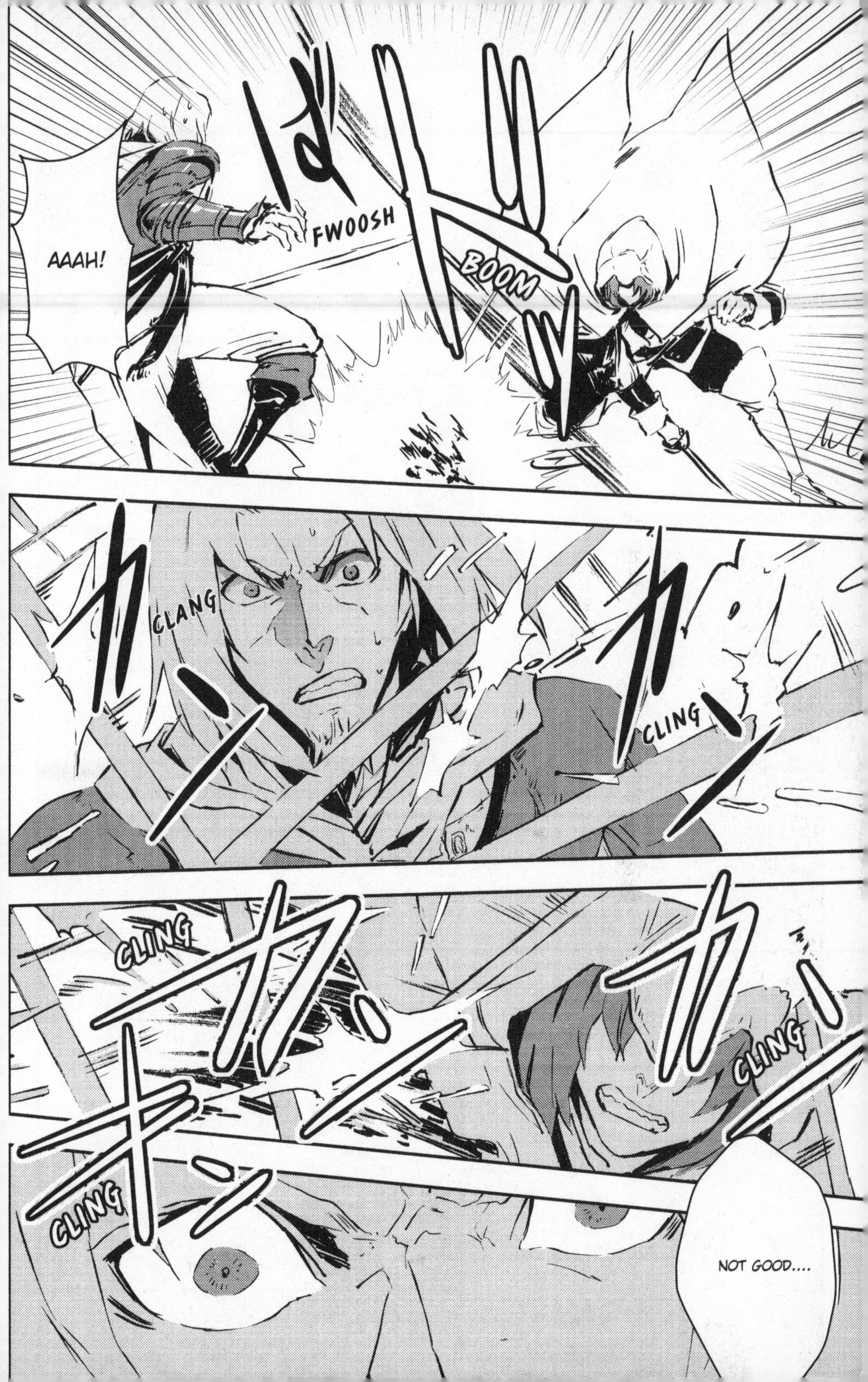
BOOM
FWOOSH
AAAH!
CLING
CLANG
CLING
CLING
NOT GOOD....
CLING

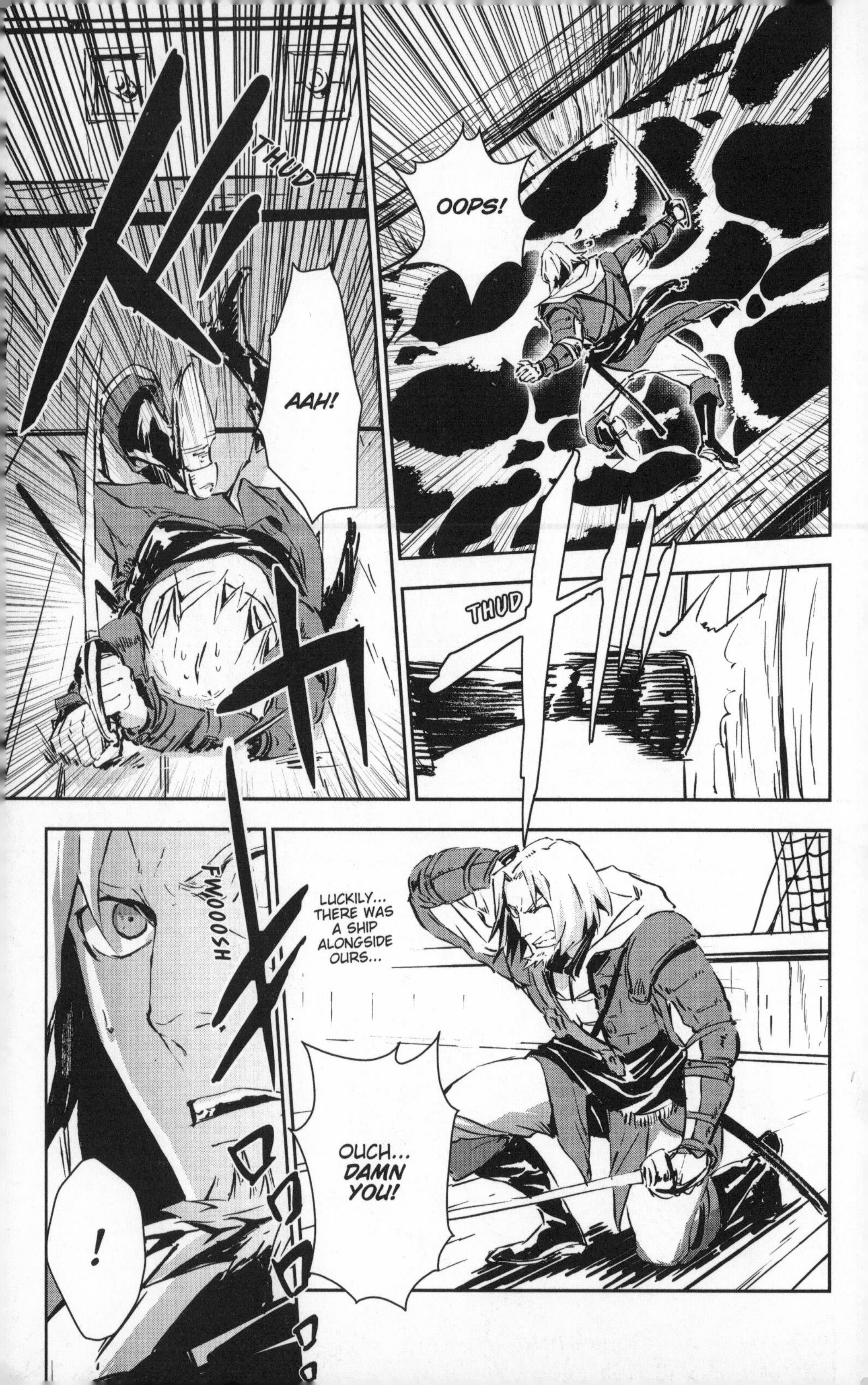
OOPS!
THUD
THUD
AAH!
LUCKILY... THERE WAS A SHIP ALONGSIDE OURS...
OUCH... DAMN YOU!
FWOOOSH
!

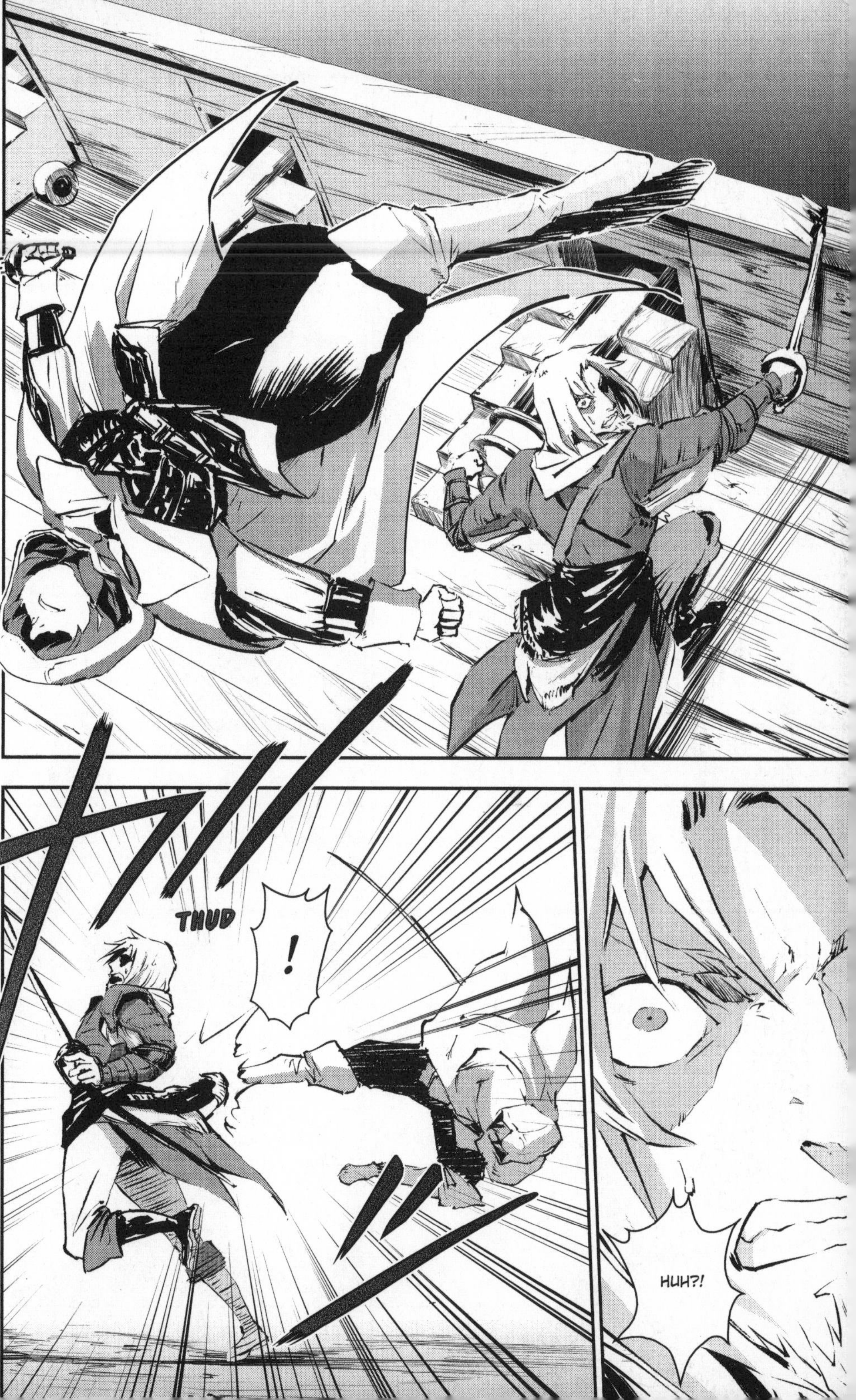
HUH?!
THUD
!

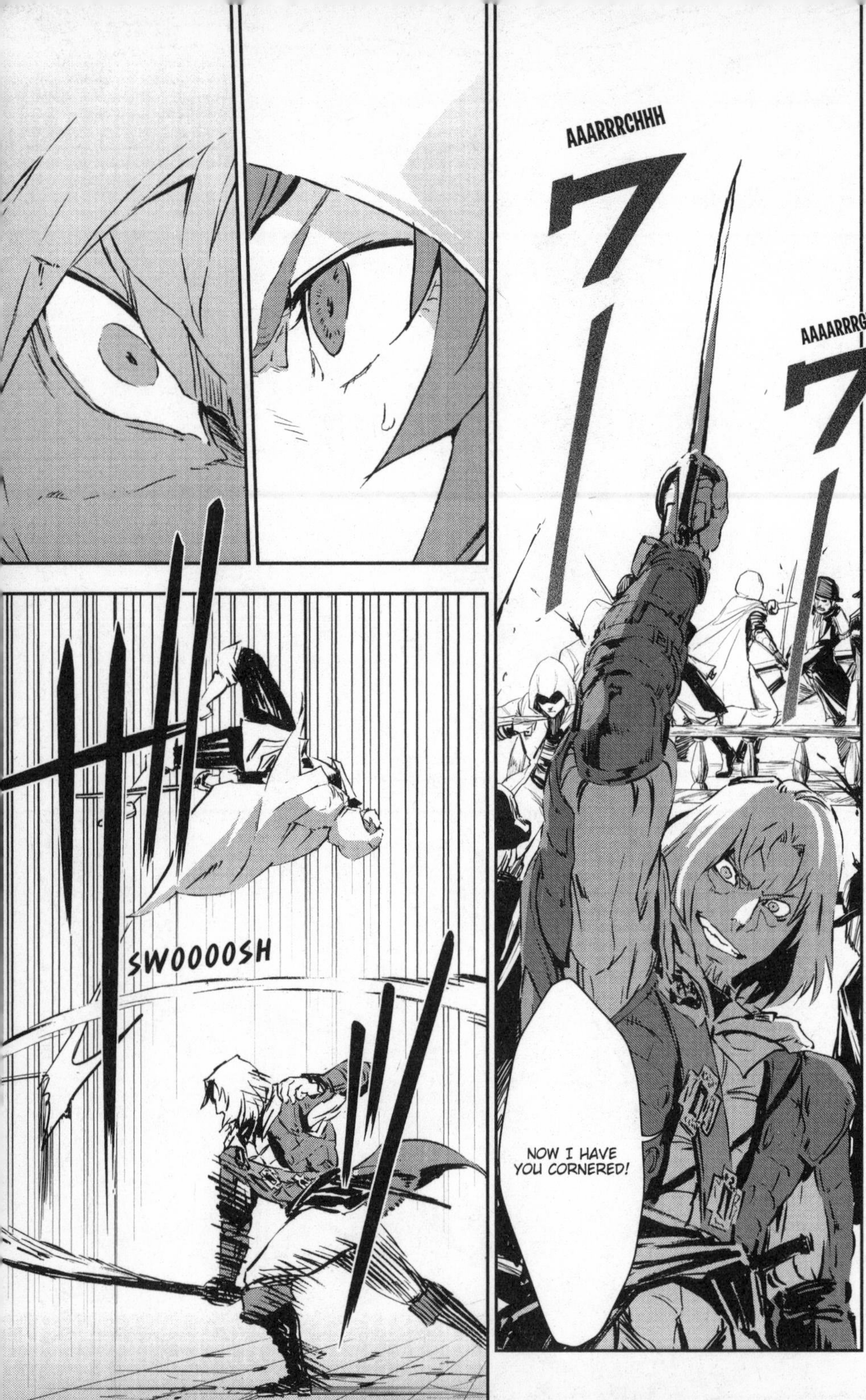
AAARRRCHHH
AAAARRRGHH
NOW I HAVE YOU CORNERED!
SWOOOOSH

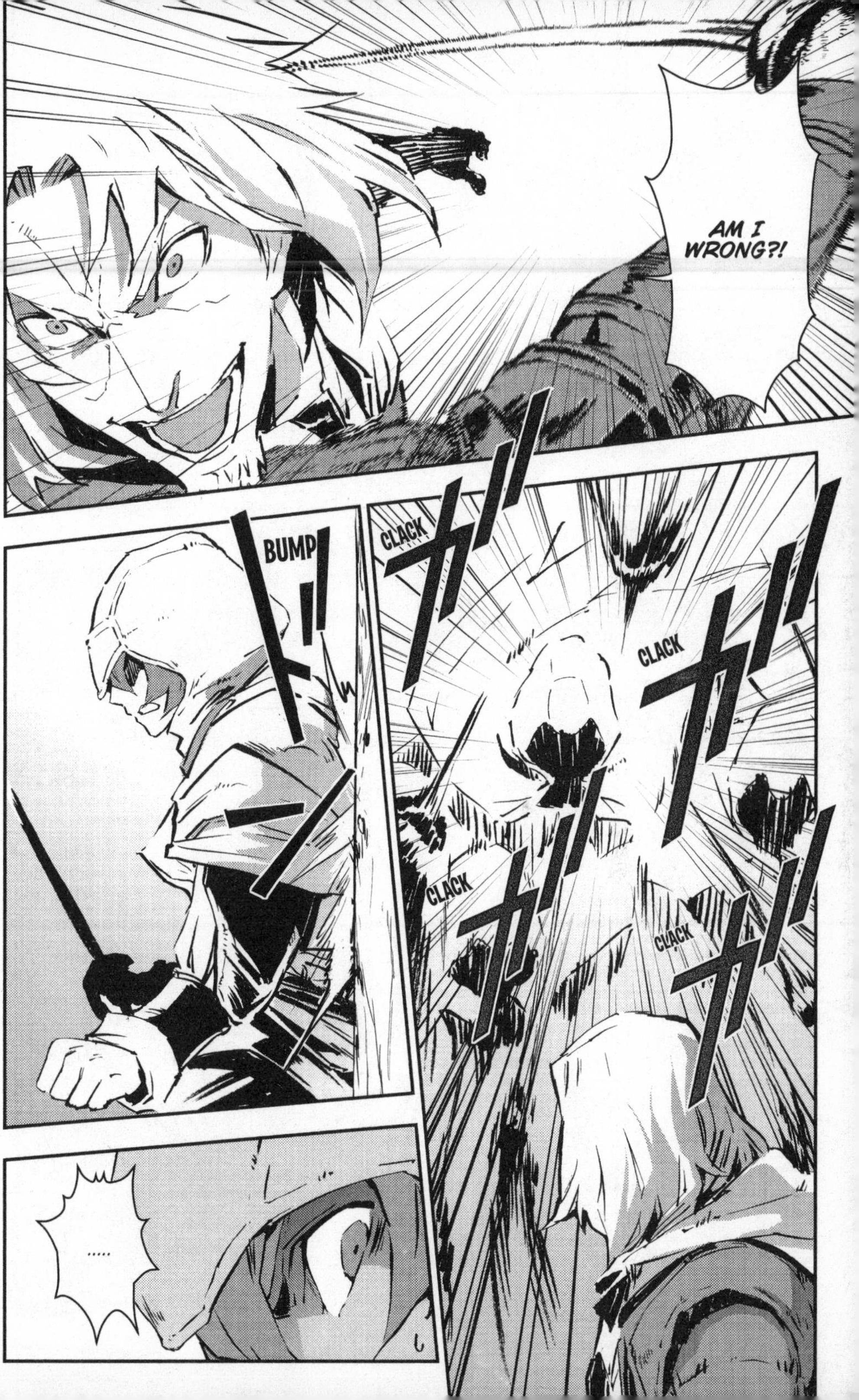
AM I WRONG?!
CLACK
CLACK
CLACK
CLACK
BUMP
.....

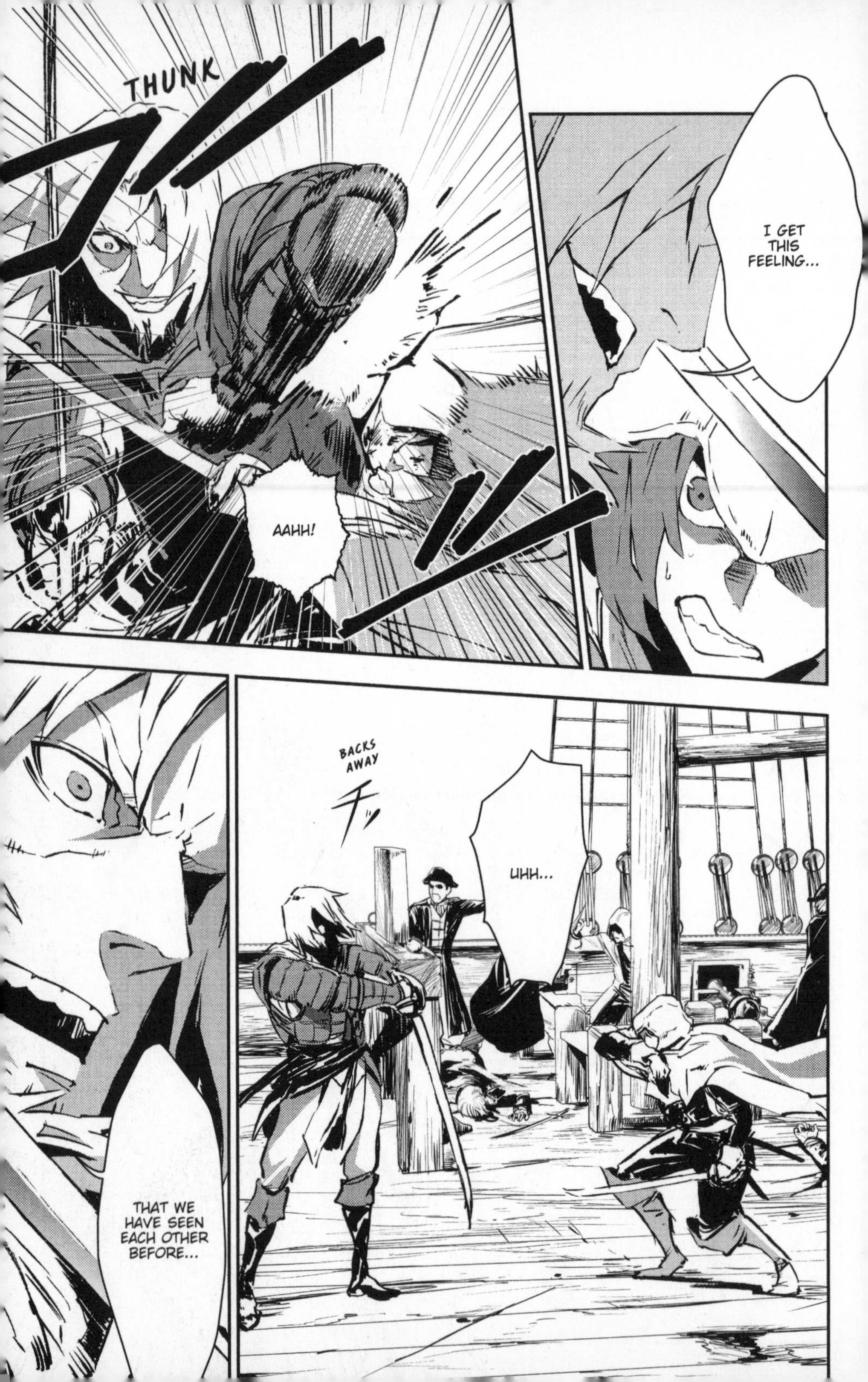
I GET THIS FEELING...
THUNK
AAHH!
BACKS AWAY
UHH...
THAT WE HAVE SEEN EACH OTHER BEFORE...

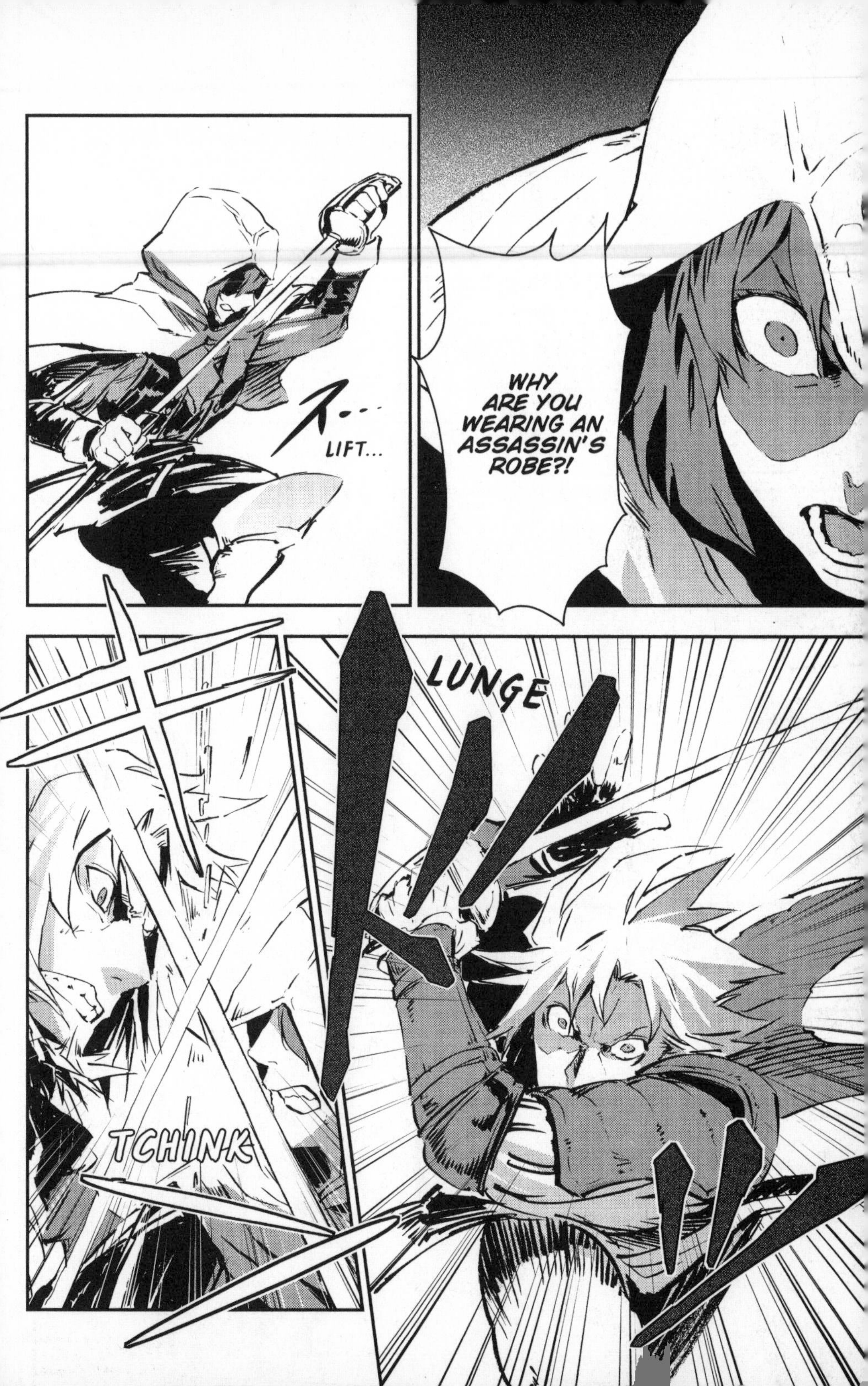
WHY ARE YOU WEARING AN ASSASSIN'S ROBE?!
ス・・・
LIFT...
LUNGE
TCHINK

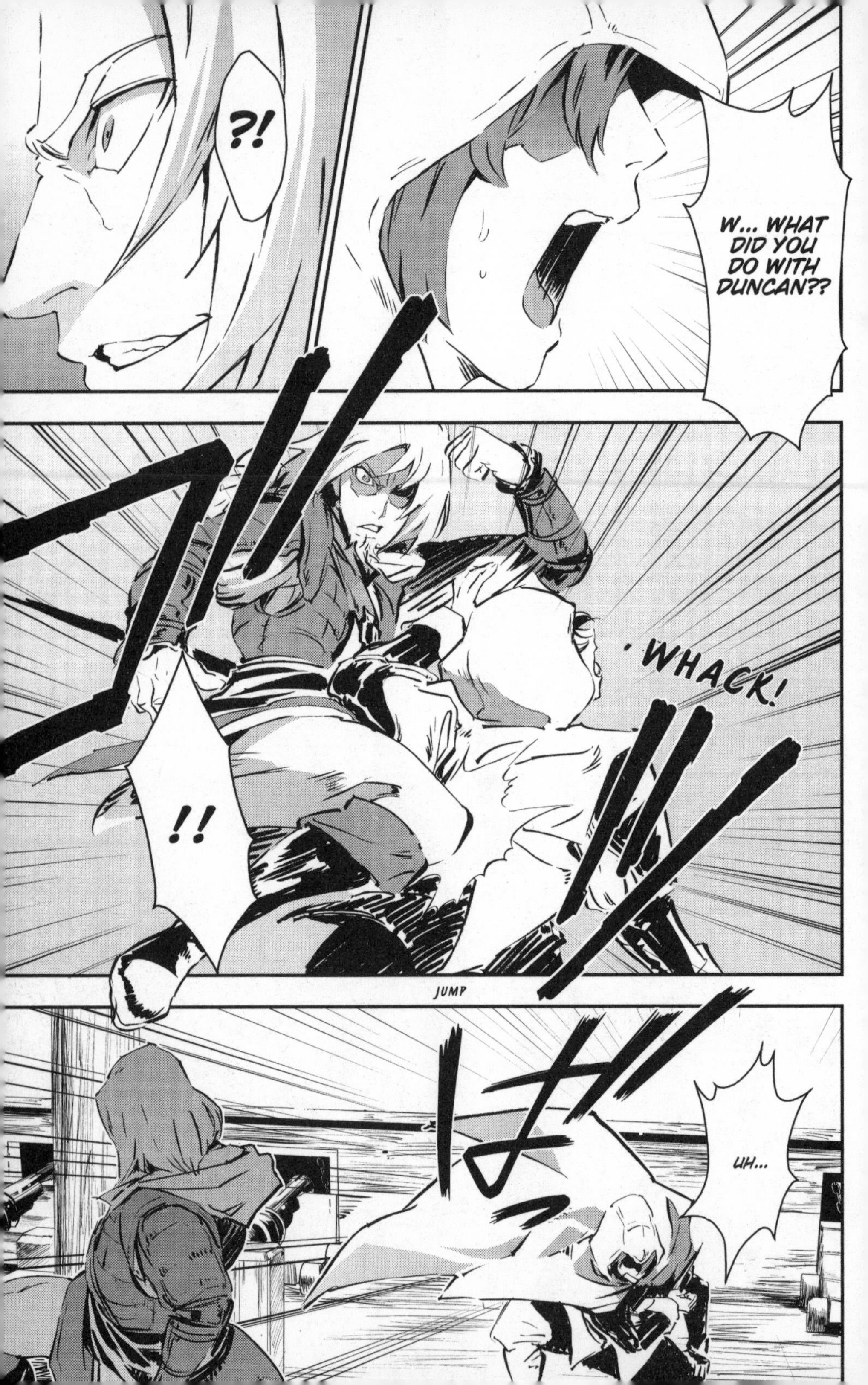
W... WHAT DID YOU DO WITH DUNCAN??
?!
WHACK!
!!
JUMP
UH...

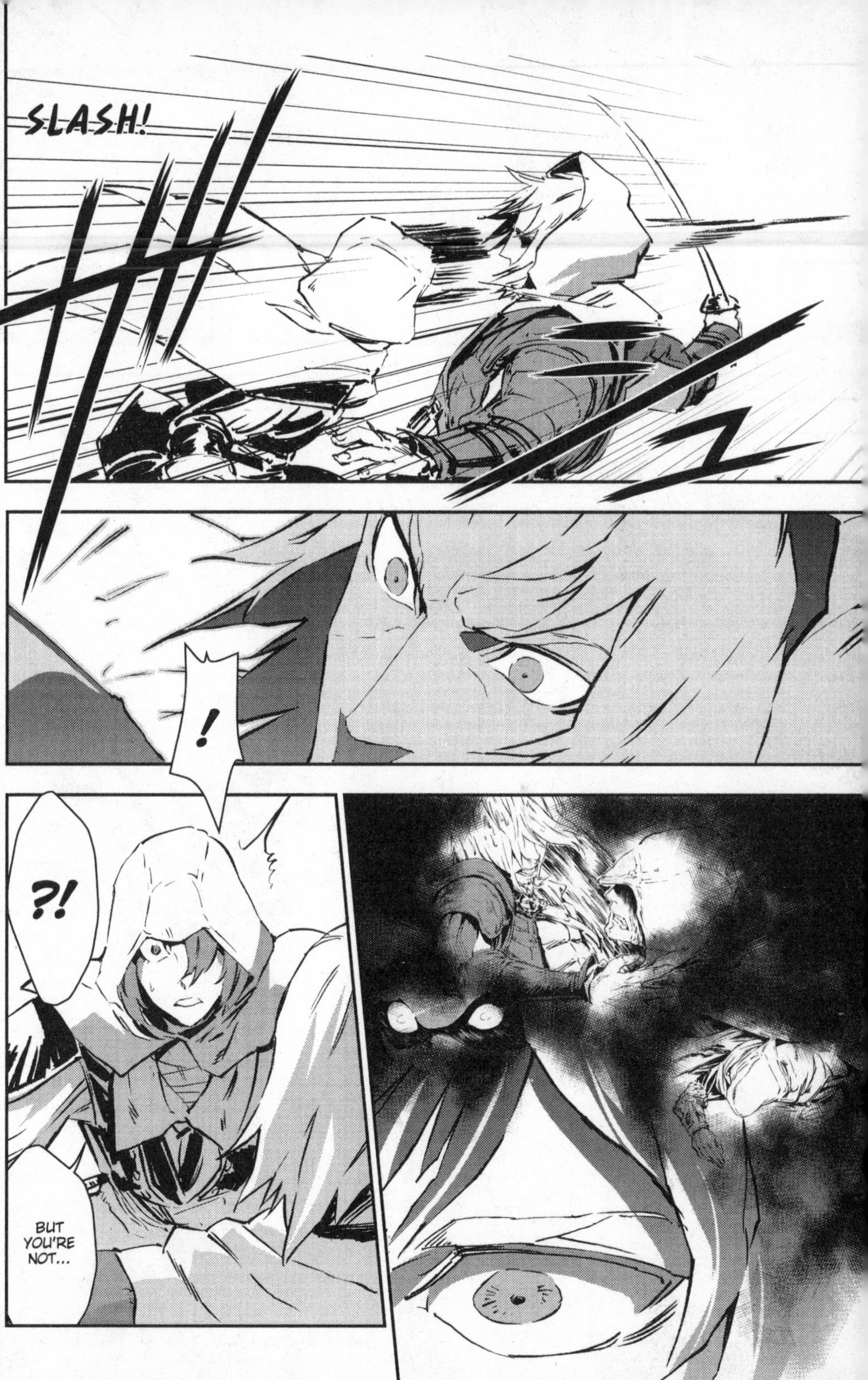
SLASH!
!
?!
BUT YOU'RE NOT...

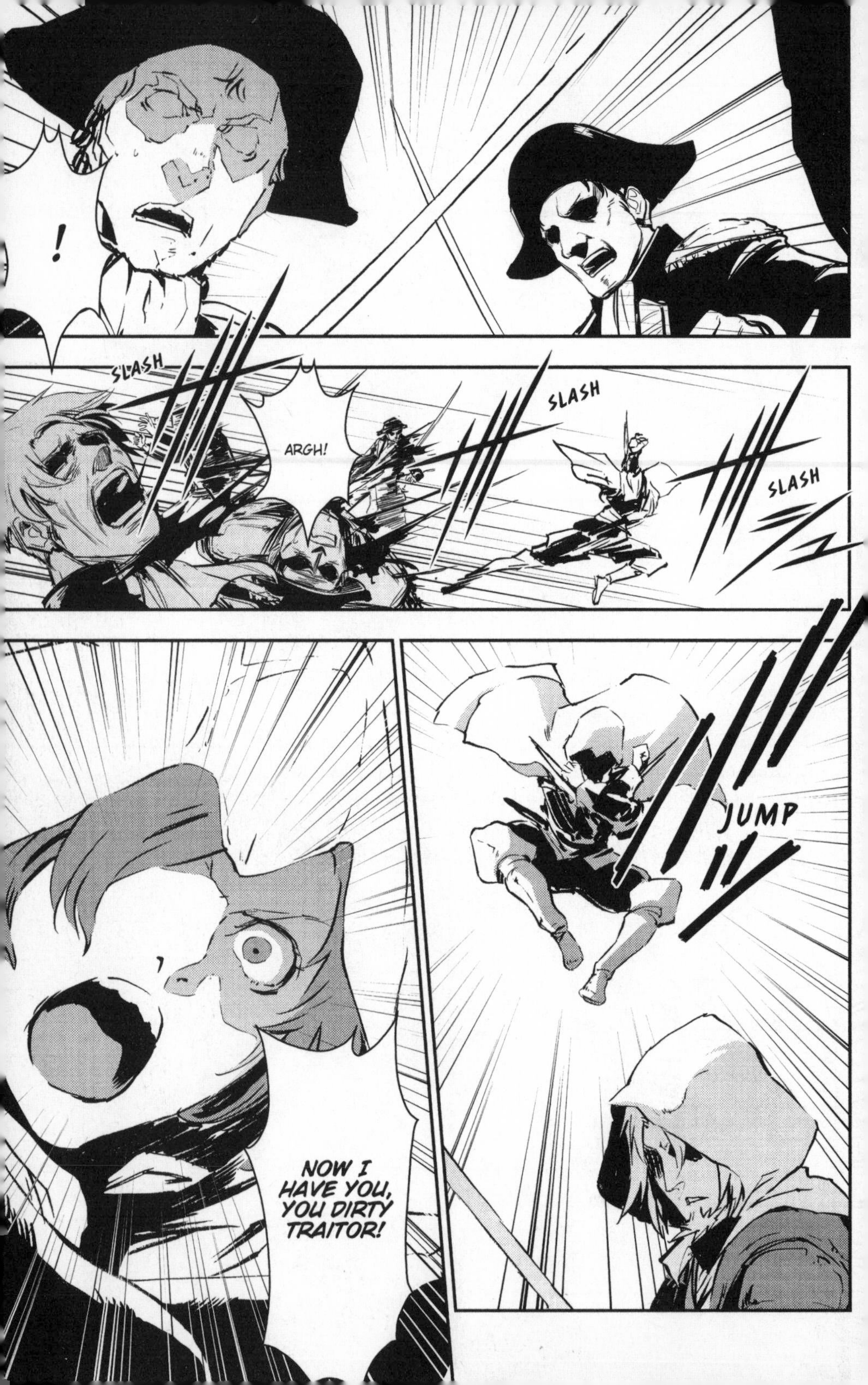
!
SLASH
SLASH
ARGH!
SLASH
JUMP
NOW I HAVE YOU, YOU DIRTY TRAITOR!

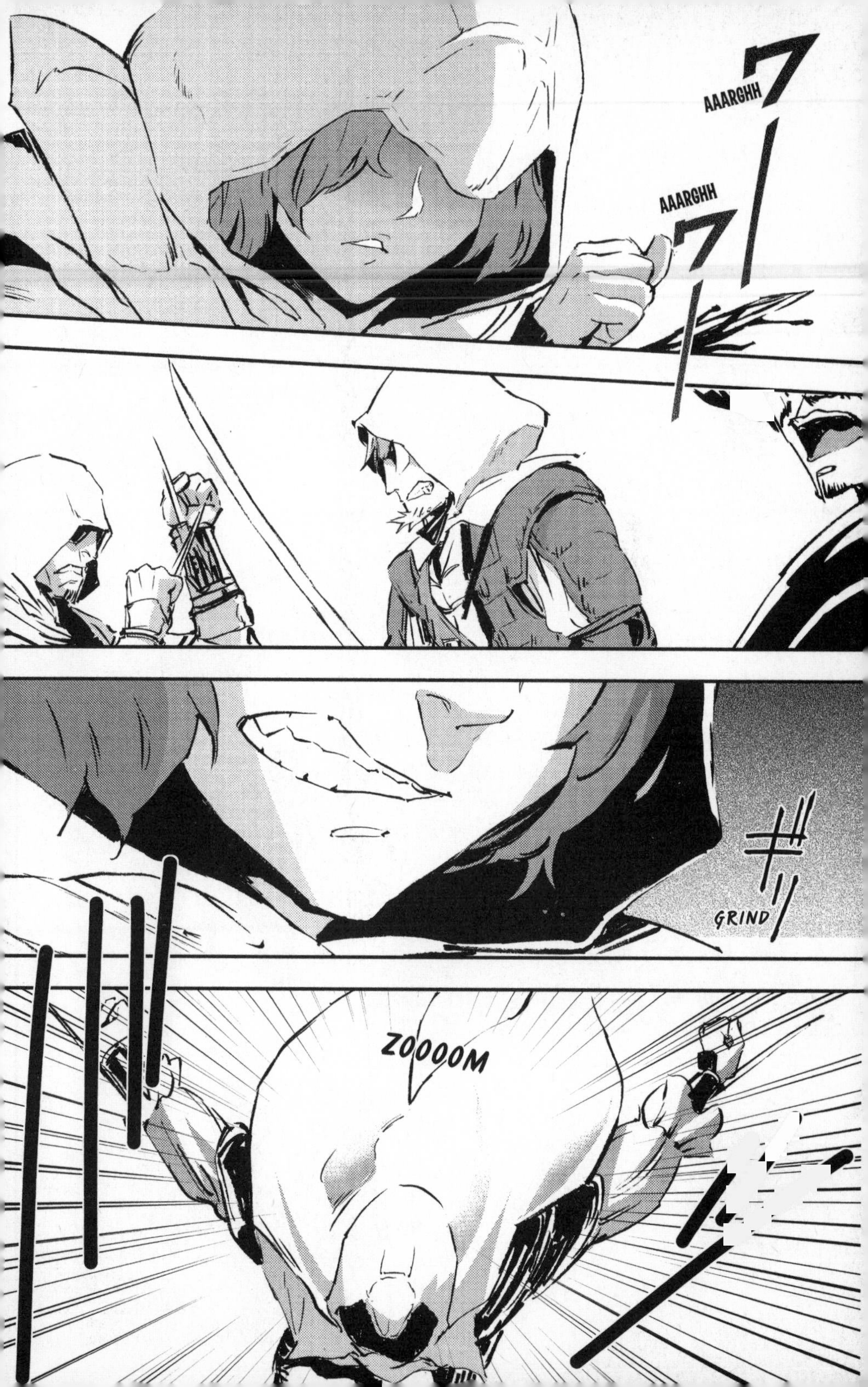
AAARGHH
AAARGHH
GRIND
ZOOOOM

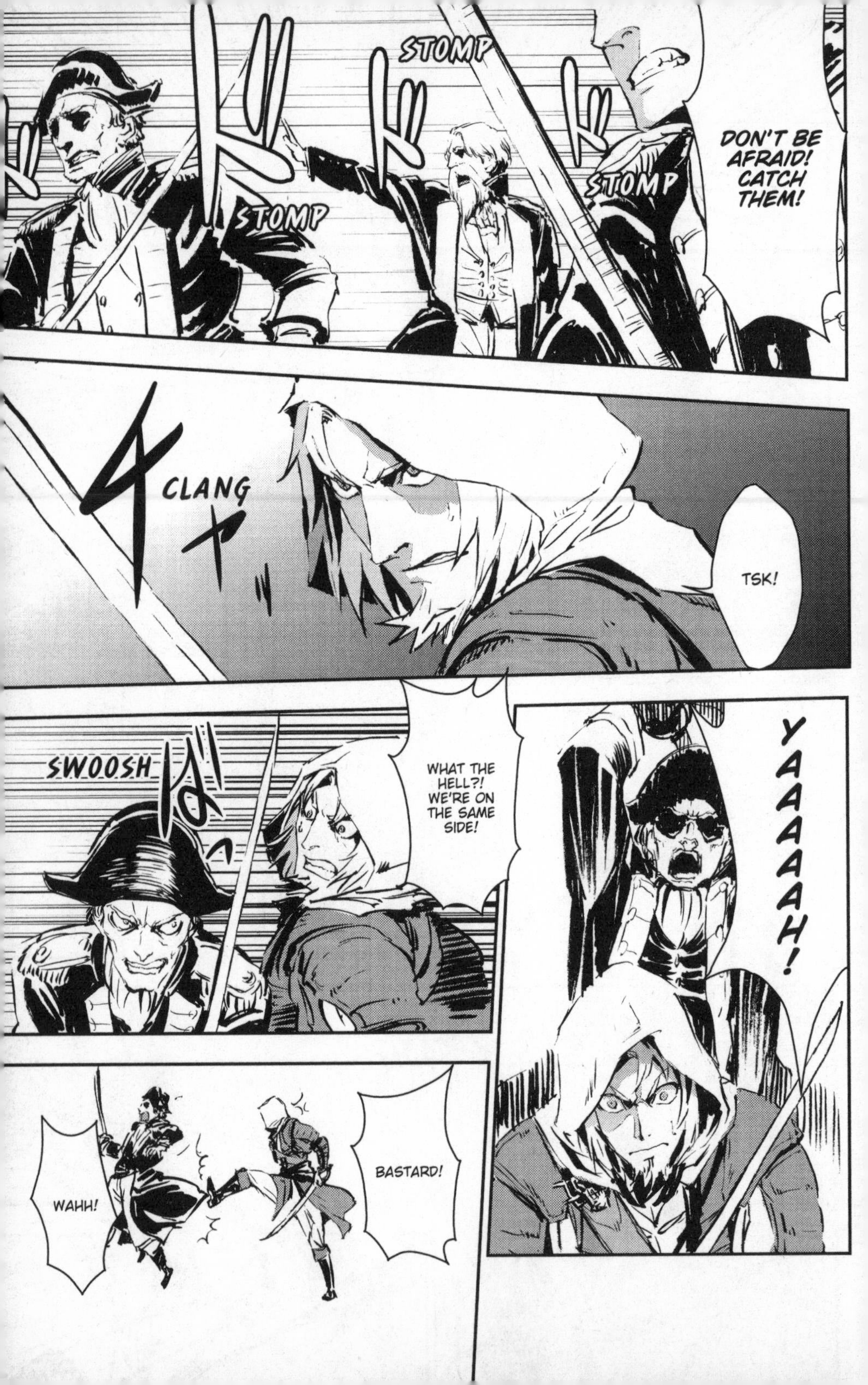
STOMP
DON'T BE AFRAID! CATCH THEM!
STOMP
STOMP
TSK!
CLANG
YAAAAAAH!
WHAT THE HELL?! WE'RE ON THE SAME SIDE!
SWOOSH
BASTARD!
WAHH!

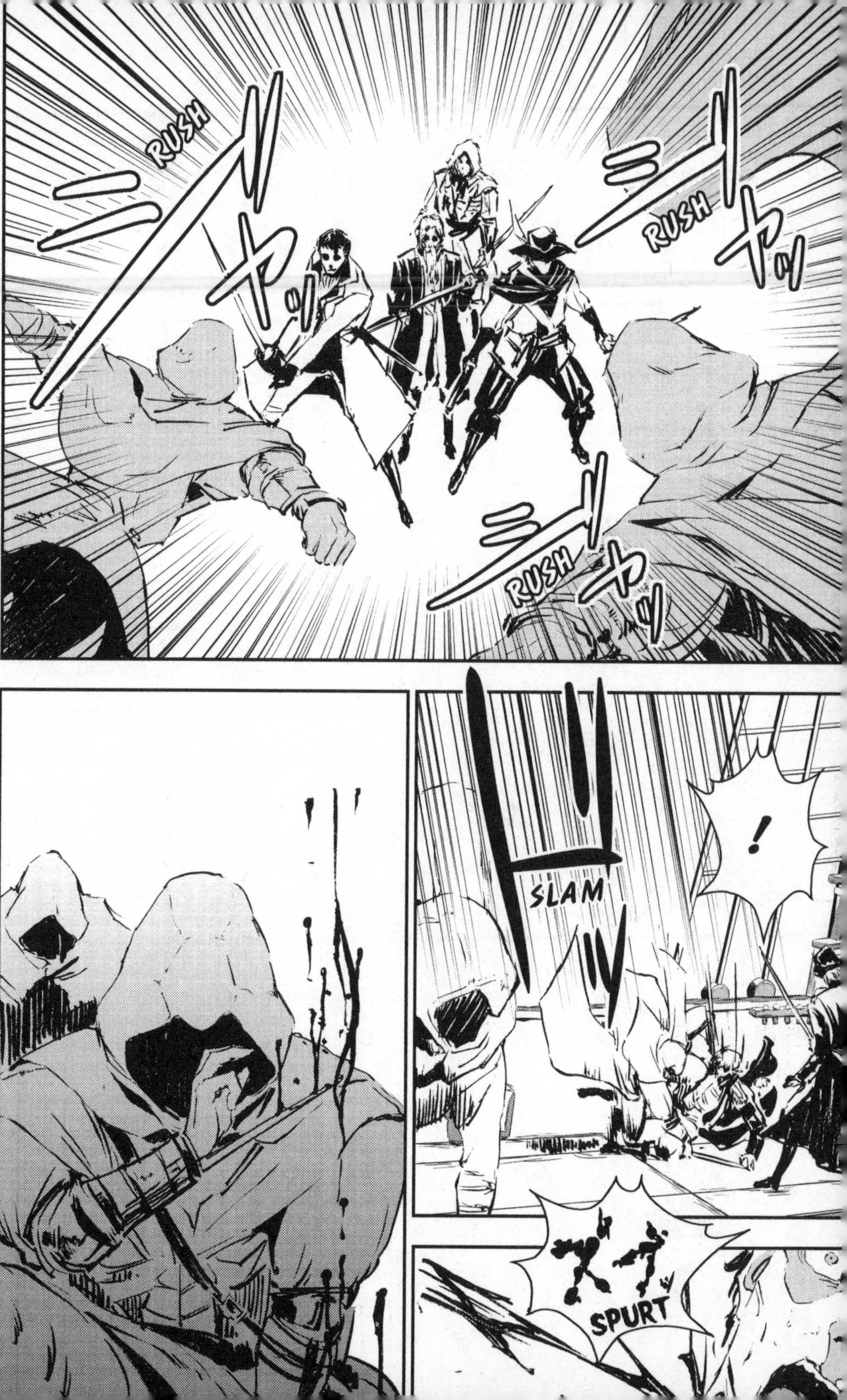
RUSH
RUSH
RUSH
!
SLAM
SPURT

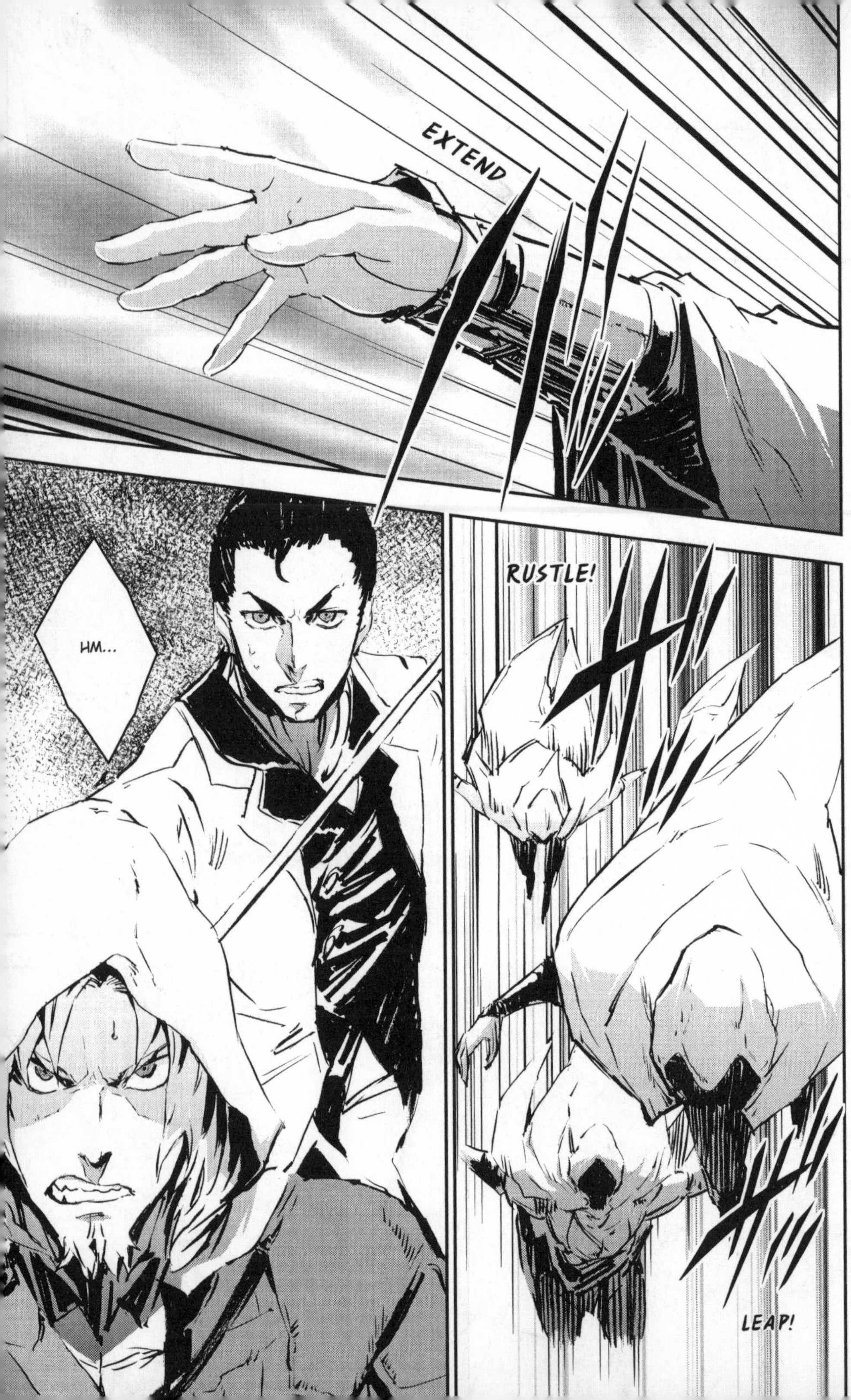
EXTEND
RUSTLE!
LEAP!
HM...

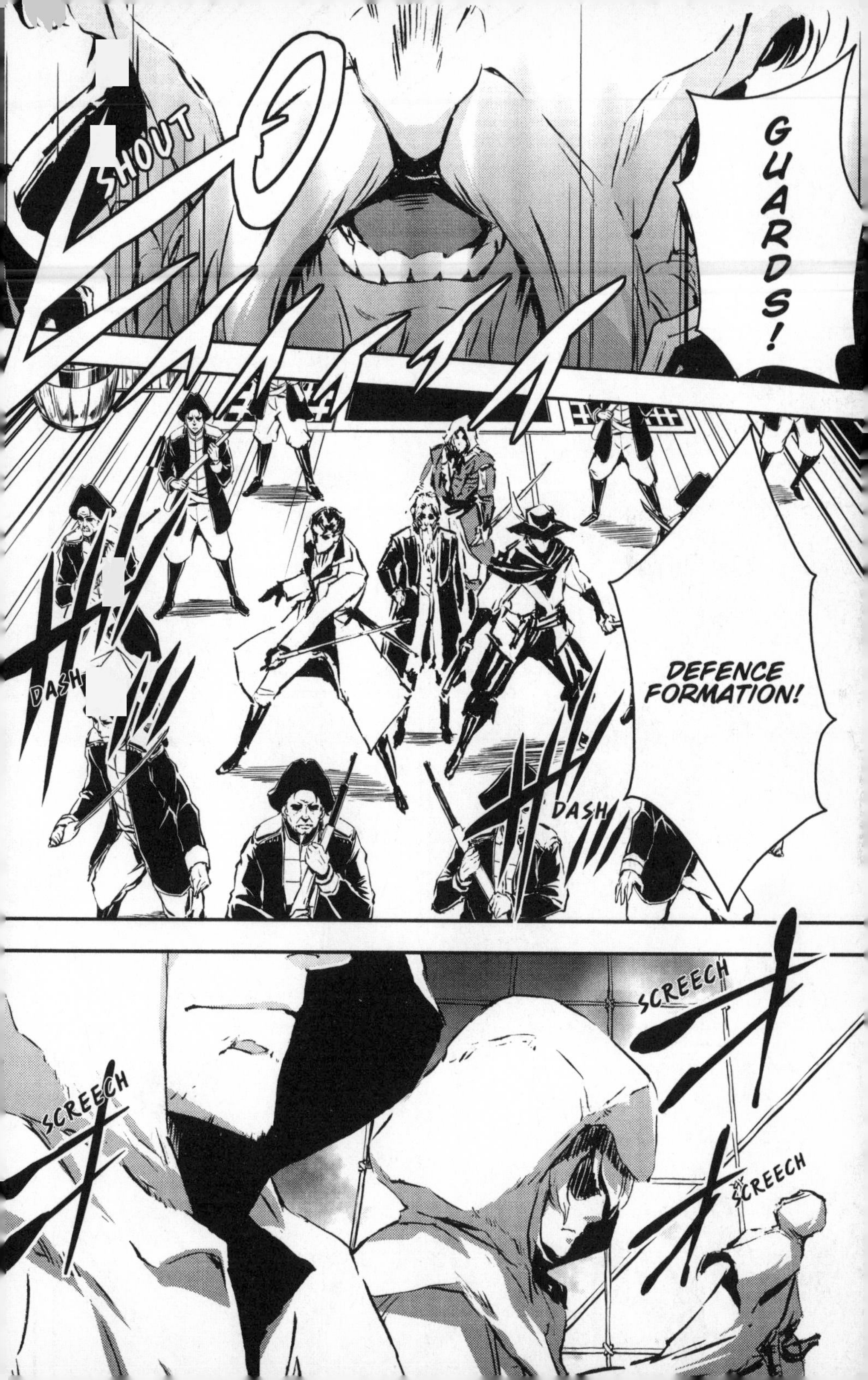
GUARDS!
SHOUT
DEFENCE FORMATION!
DASH
DASH
SCREECH
SCREECH
SCREECH

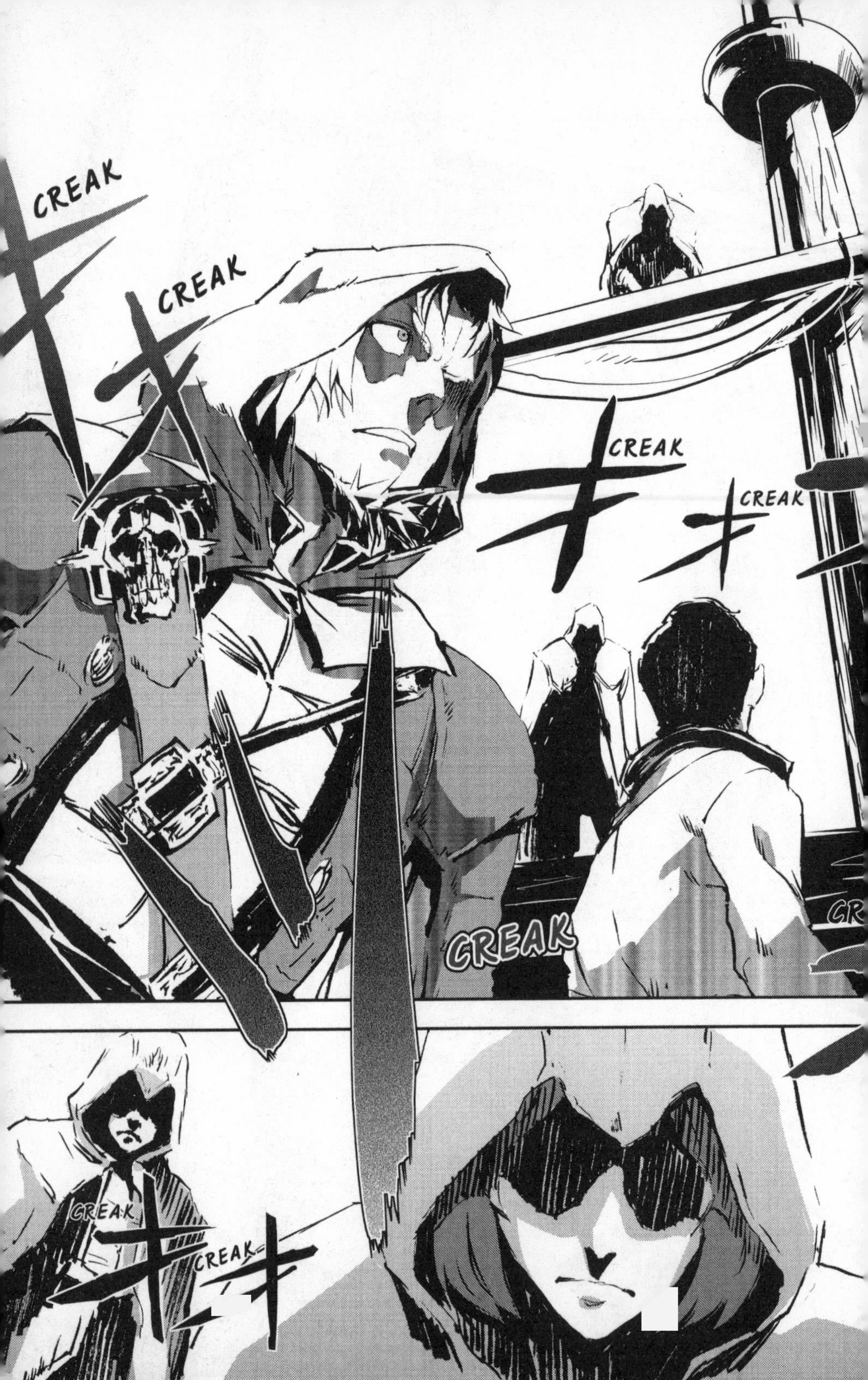
CREAK
CREAK
CREAK
CREAK
CREAK
CREAK
CREAK

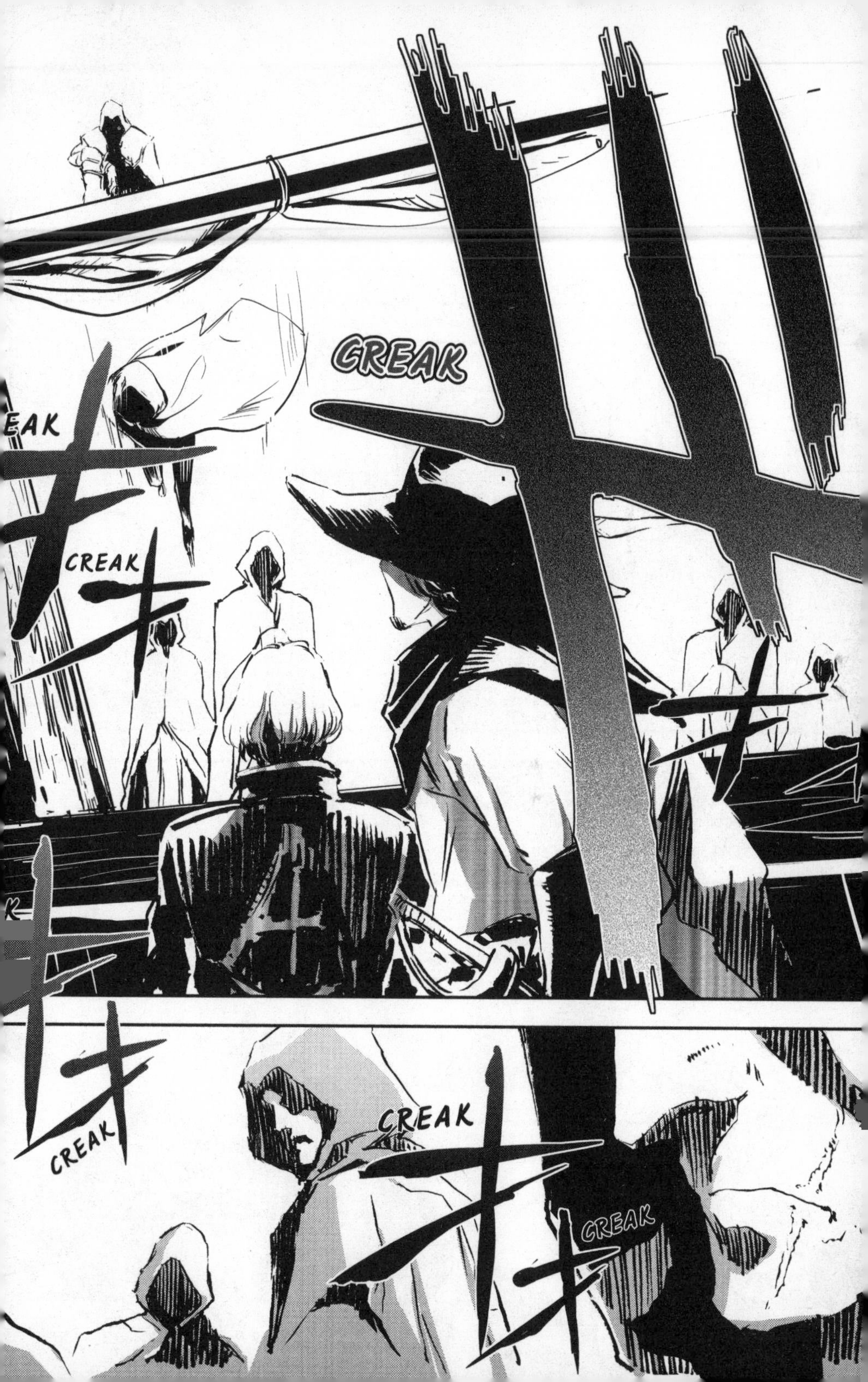
CREAK
EAK
CREAK
CREAK
CREAK
CREAK

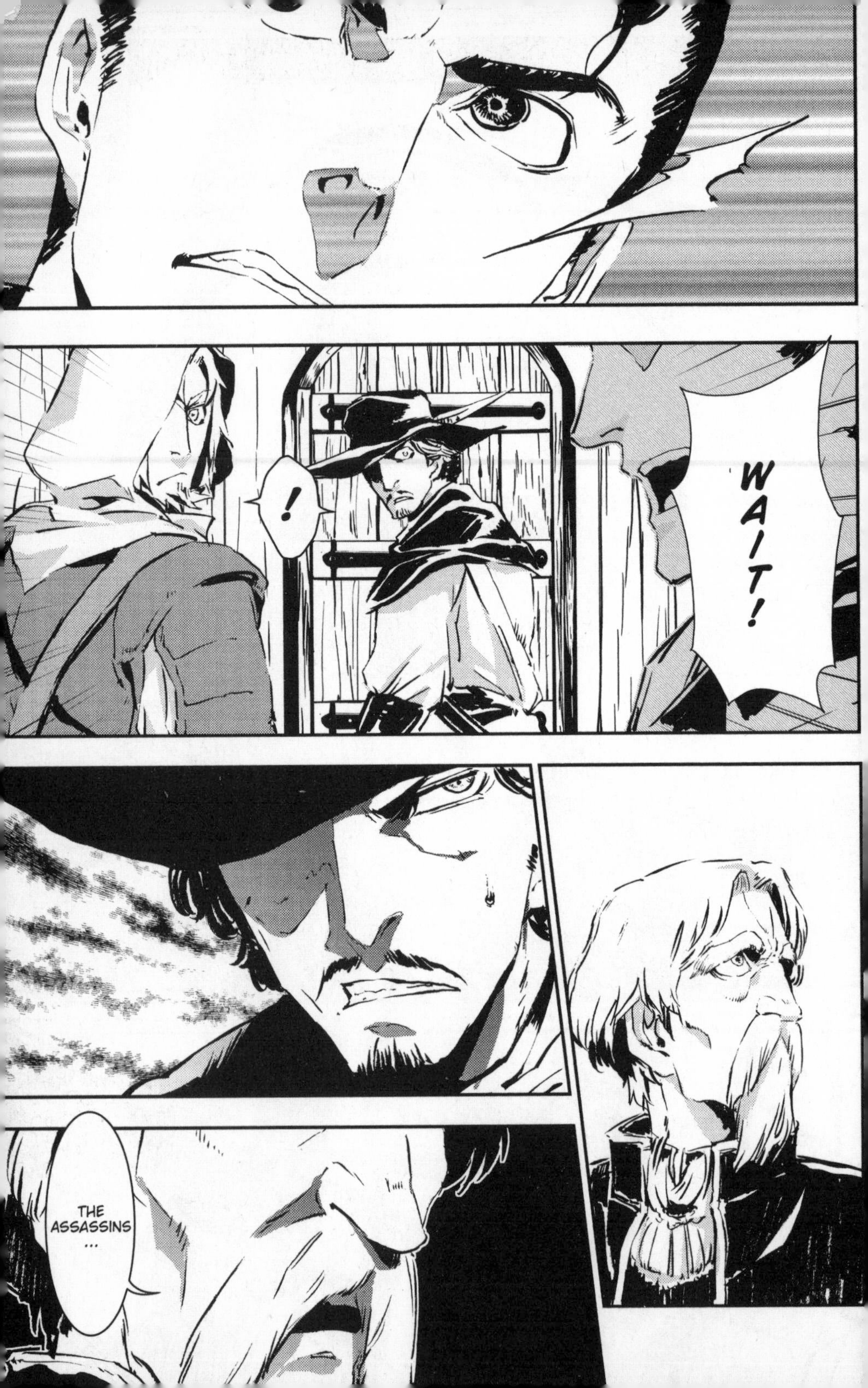
WAIT!
!
THE ASSASSINS ...

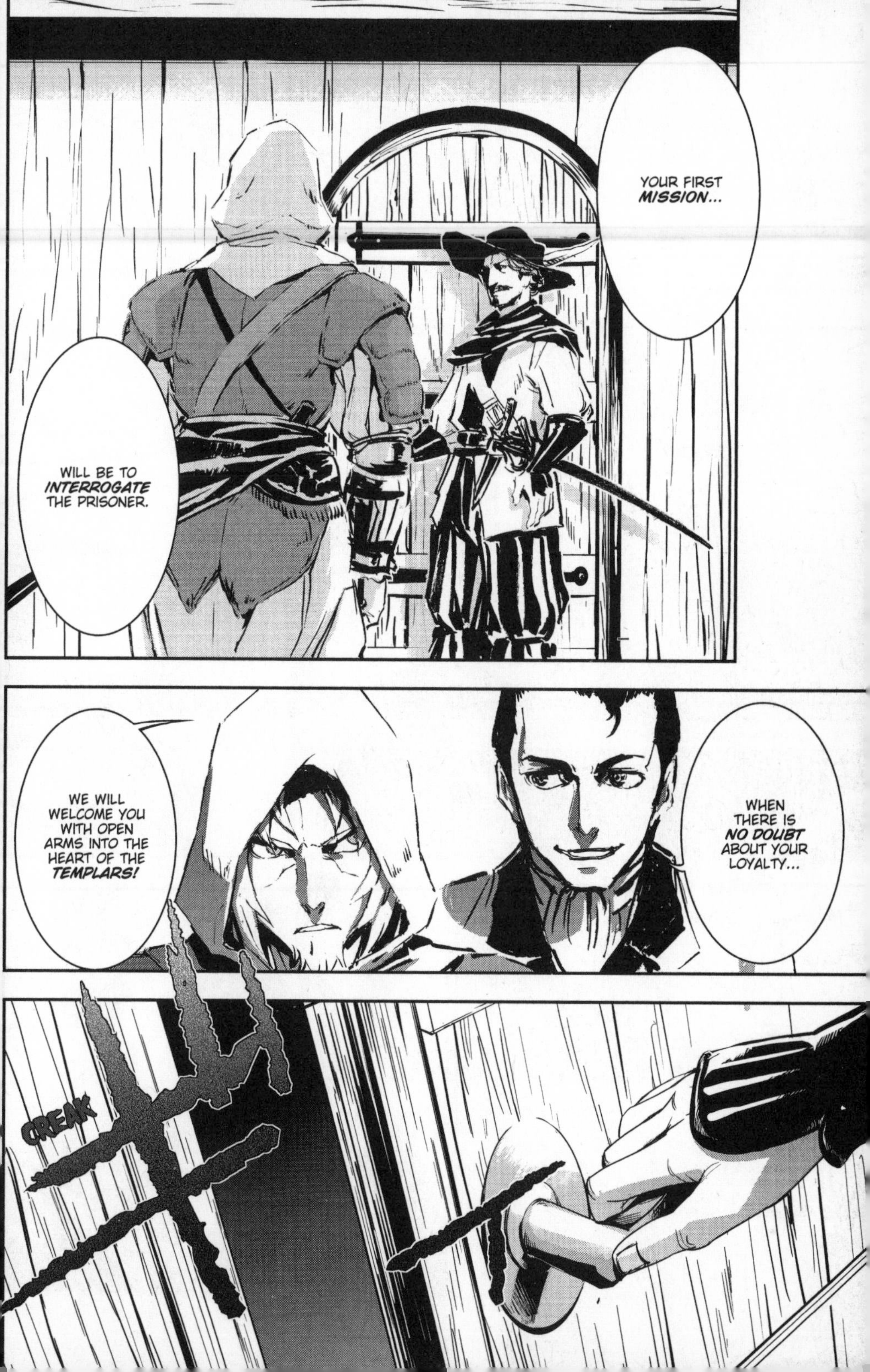
YOUR FIRST MISSION...
WILL BE TO INTERROGATE THE PRISONER.
WHEN THERE IS NO DOUBT ABOUT YOUR LOYALTY...
WE WILL WELCOME YOU WITH OPEN ARMS INTO THE HEART OF THE TEMPLARS!
CREAK

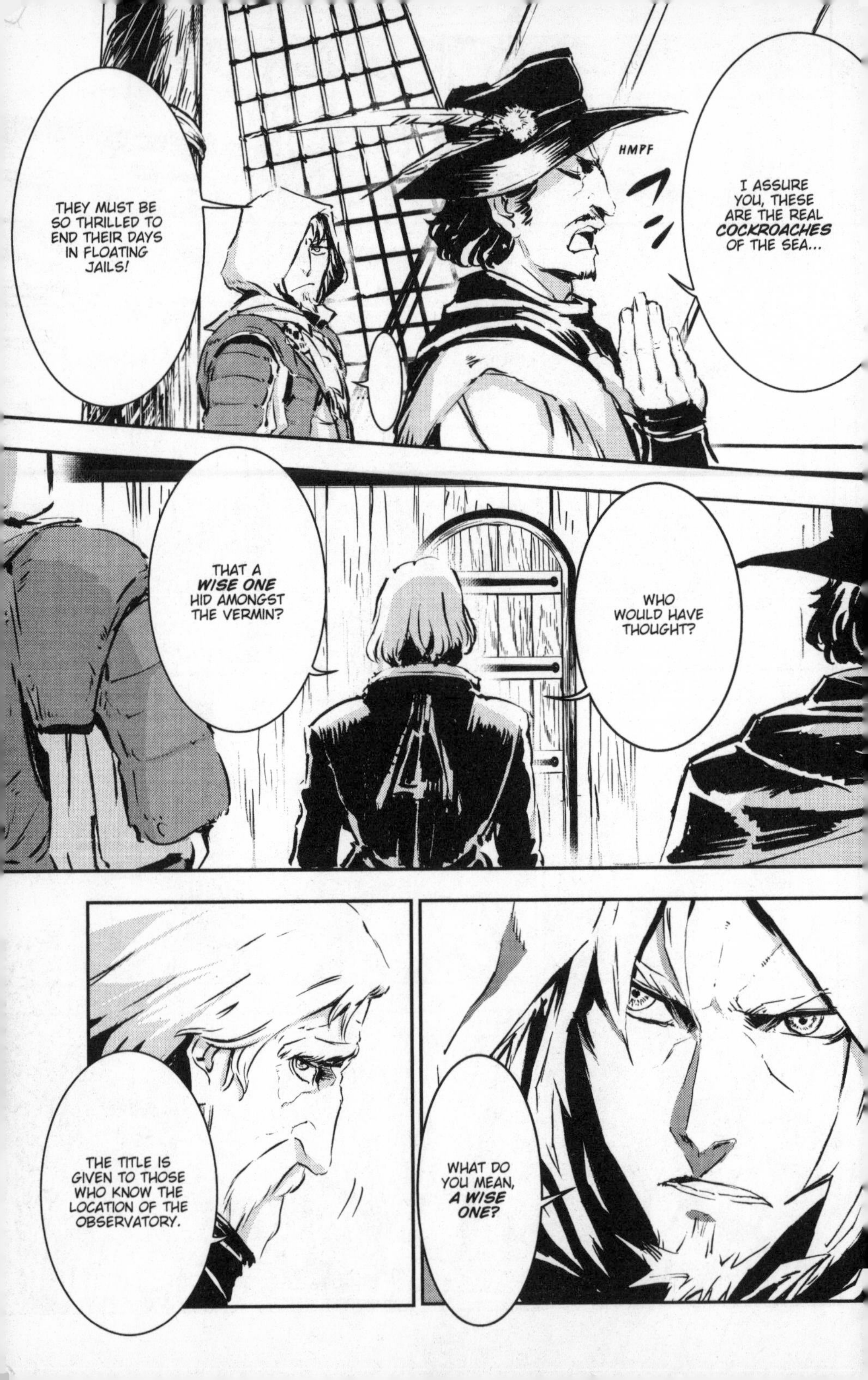
I ASSURE YOU, THESE ARE THE REAL **COCKROACHES** OF THE SEA...
HMPF
THEY MUST BE SO THRILLED TO END THEIR DAYS IN FLOATING JAILS!
WHO WOULD HAVE THOUGHT?
THAT A **WISE ONE** HID AMONGST THE VERMIN?
WHAT DO YOU MEAN, **A WISE ONE?**
THE TITLE IS GIVEN TO THOSE WHO KNOW THE LOCATION OF THE OBSERVATORY.

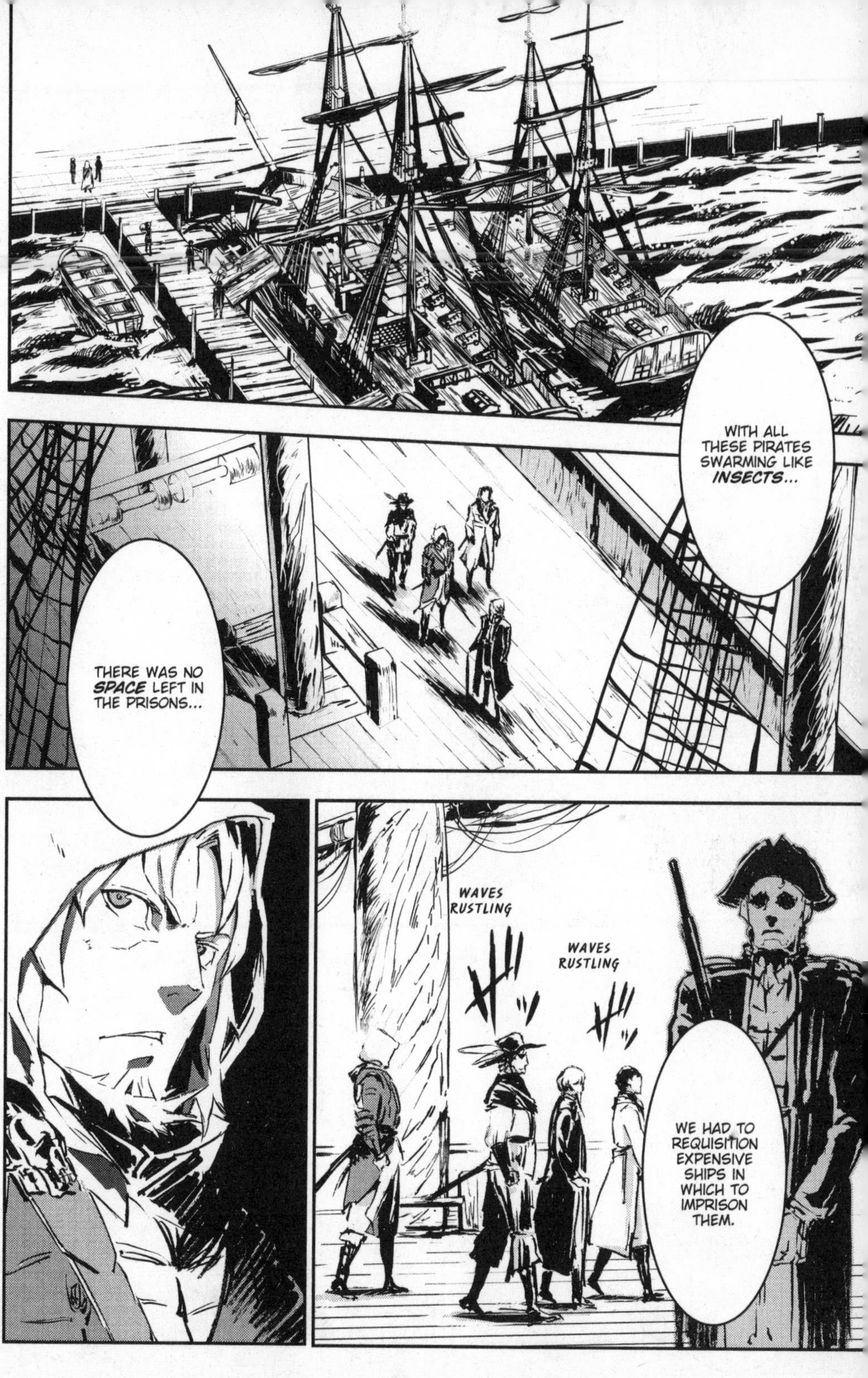
WITH ALL THESE PIRATES SWARMING LIKE INSECTS...
THERE WAS NO SPACE LEFT IN THE PRISONS...
WAVES RUSTLING
WAVES RUSTLING
WE HAD TO REQUISITION EXPENSIVE SHIPS IN WHICH TO IMPRISON THEM.

CHAPTER IV

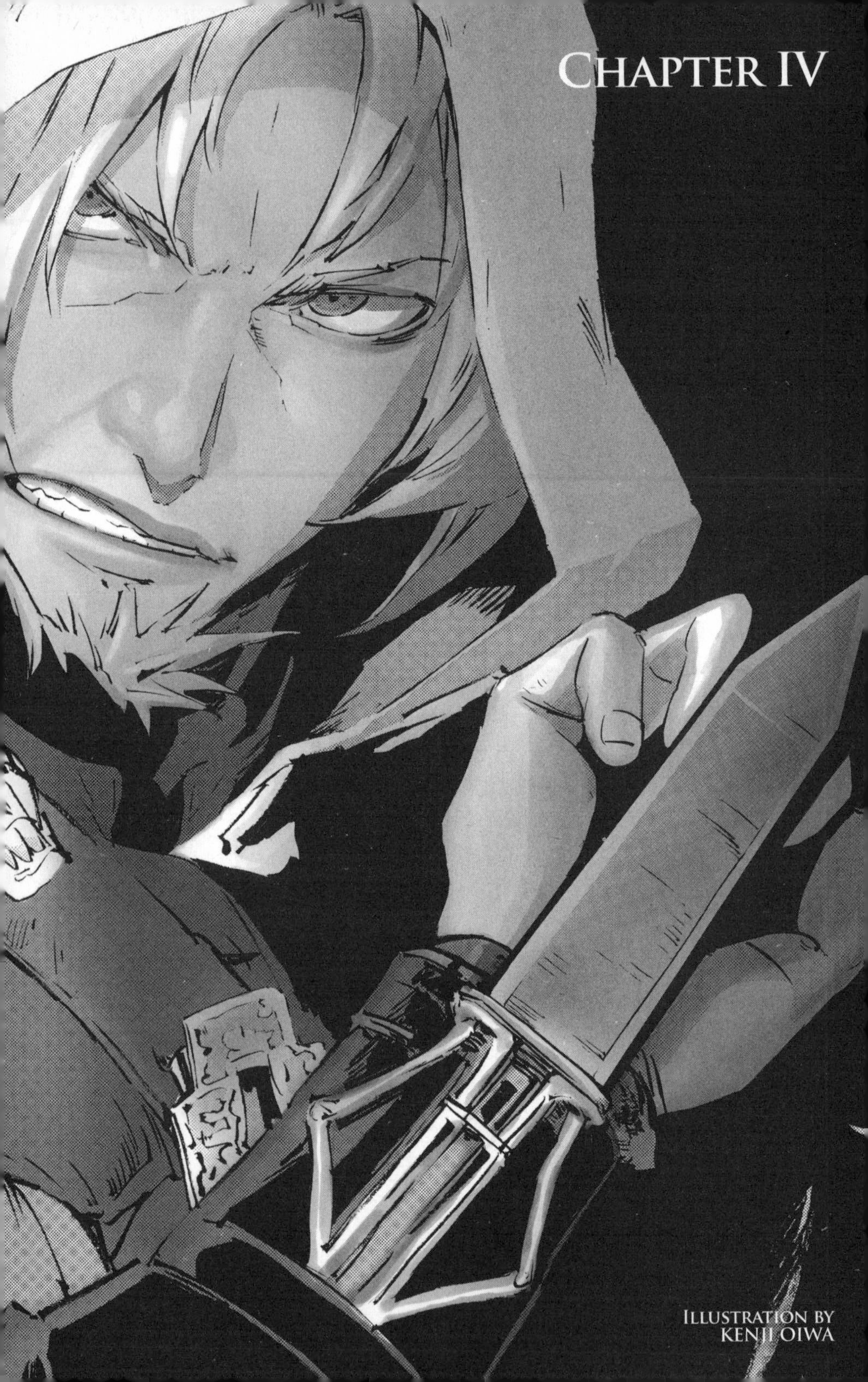

ILLUSTRATION BY
KENJI OIWA

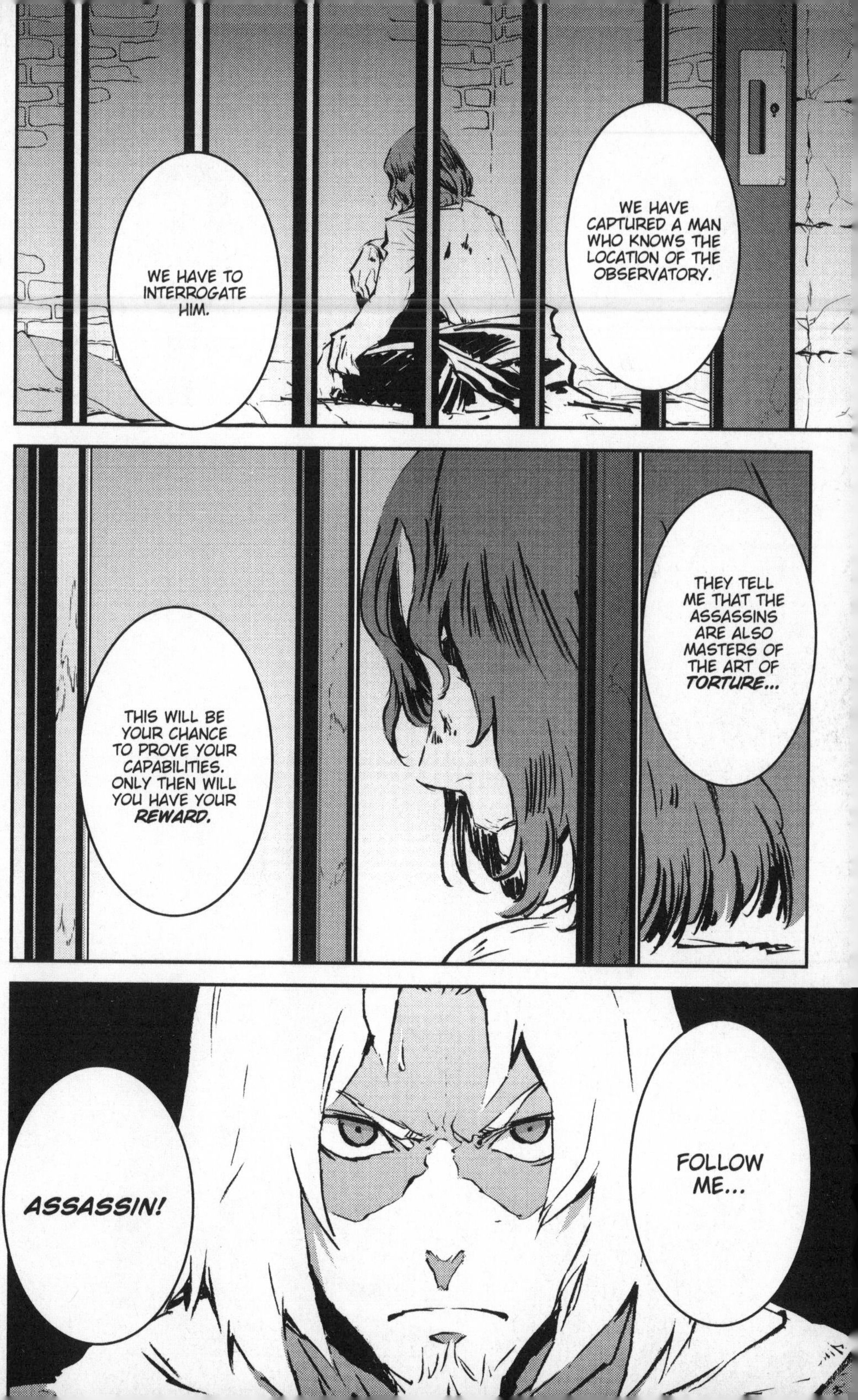
WE HAVE CAPTURED A MAN WHO KNOWS THE LOCATION OF THE OBSERVATORY.
WE HAVE TO INTERROGATE HIM.
THEY TELL ME THAT THE ASSASSINS ARE ALSO MASTERS OF THE ART OF *TORTURE...*
THIS WILL BE YOUR CHANCE TO PROVE YOUR CAPABILITIES. ONLY THEN WILL YOU HAVE YOUR *REWARD.*
FOLLOW ME...
ASSASSIN!

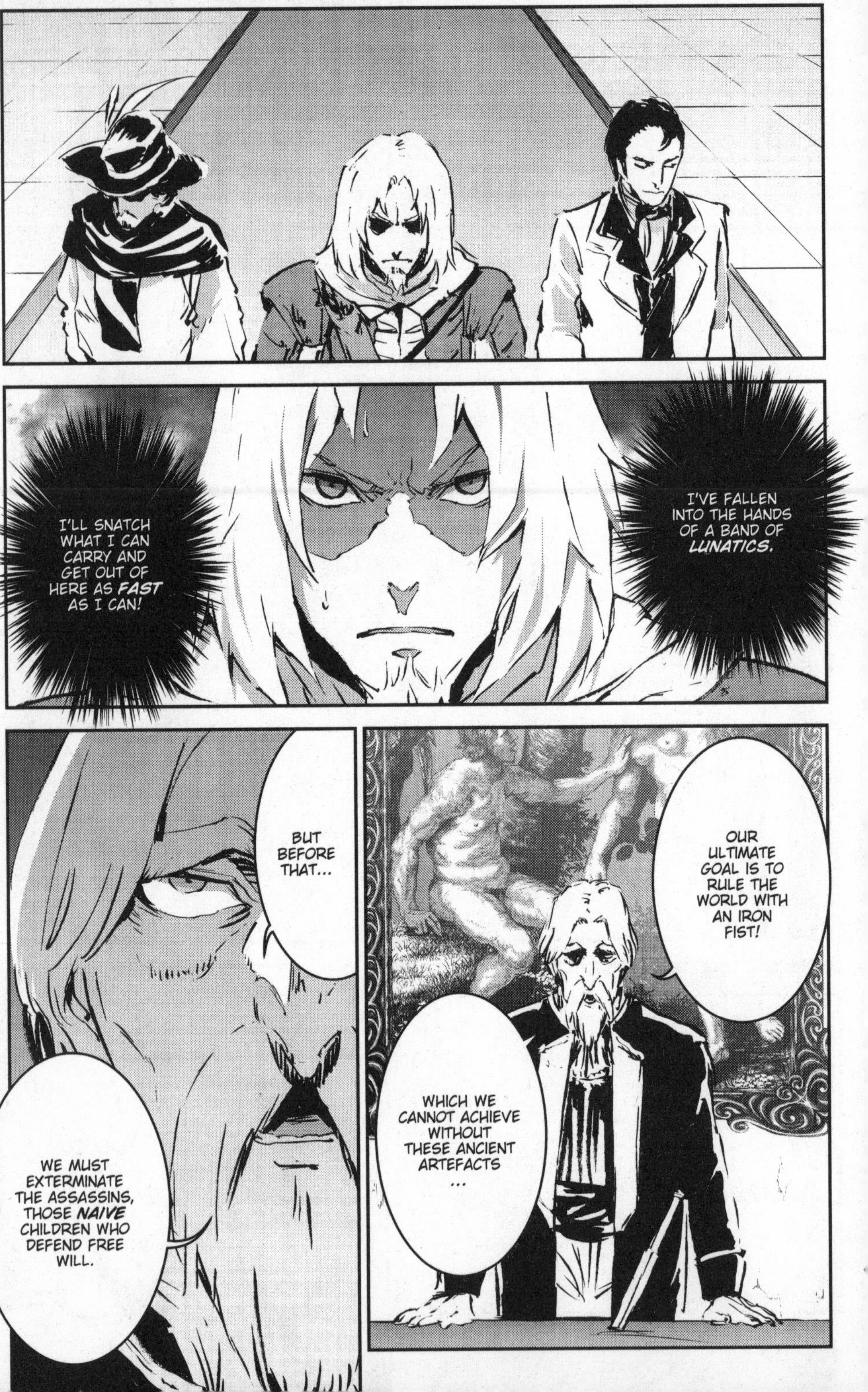
I'VE FALLEN INTO THE HANDS OF A BAND OF *LUNATICS.*
I'LL SNATCH WHAT I CAN CARRY AND GET OUT OF HERE AS *FAST* AS I CAN!
OUR ULTIMATE GOAL IS TO RULE THE WORLD WITH AN IRON FIST!
WHICH WE CANNOT ACHIEVE WITHOUT THESE ANCIENT ARTEFACTS ...
BUT BEFORE THAT...
WE MUST EXTERMINATE THE ASSASSINS, THOSE *NAIVE* CHILDREN WHO DEFEND FREE WILL.

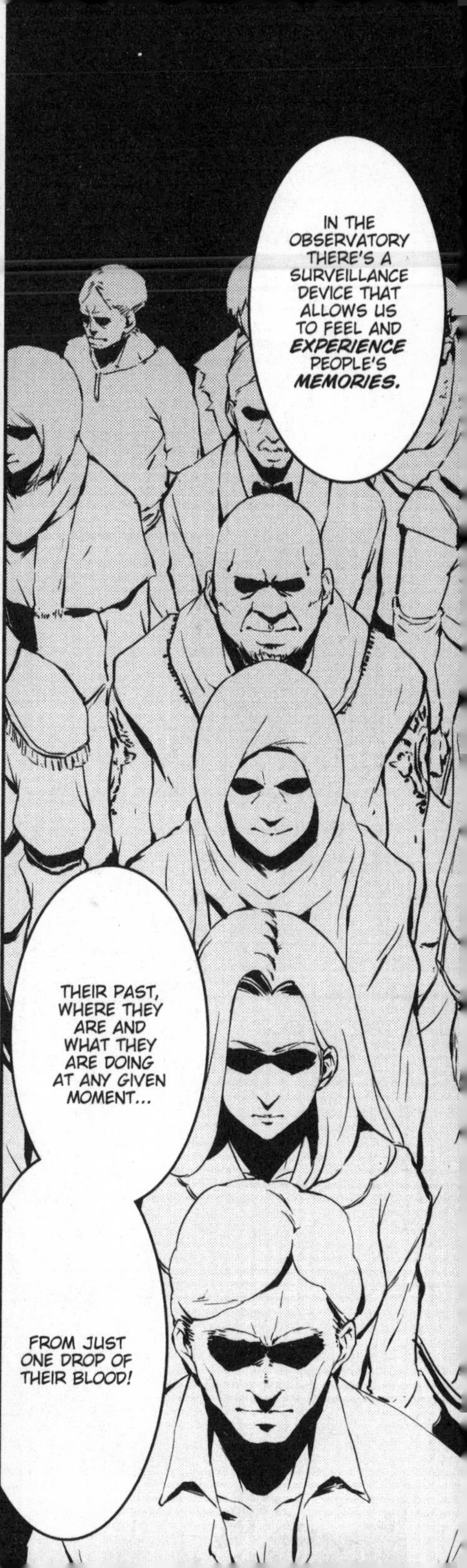
IN THE OBSERVATORY THERE'S A SURVEILLANCE DEVICE THAT ALLOWS US TO FEEL AND *EXPERIENCE* PEOPLE'S *MEMORIES.*
THEIR PAST, WHERE THEY ARE AND WHAT THEY ARE DOING AT ANY GIVEN MOMENT...
FROM JUST ONE DROP OF THEIR BLOOD!

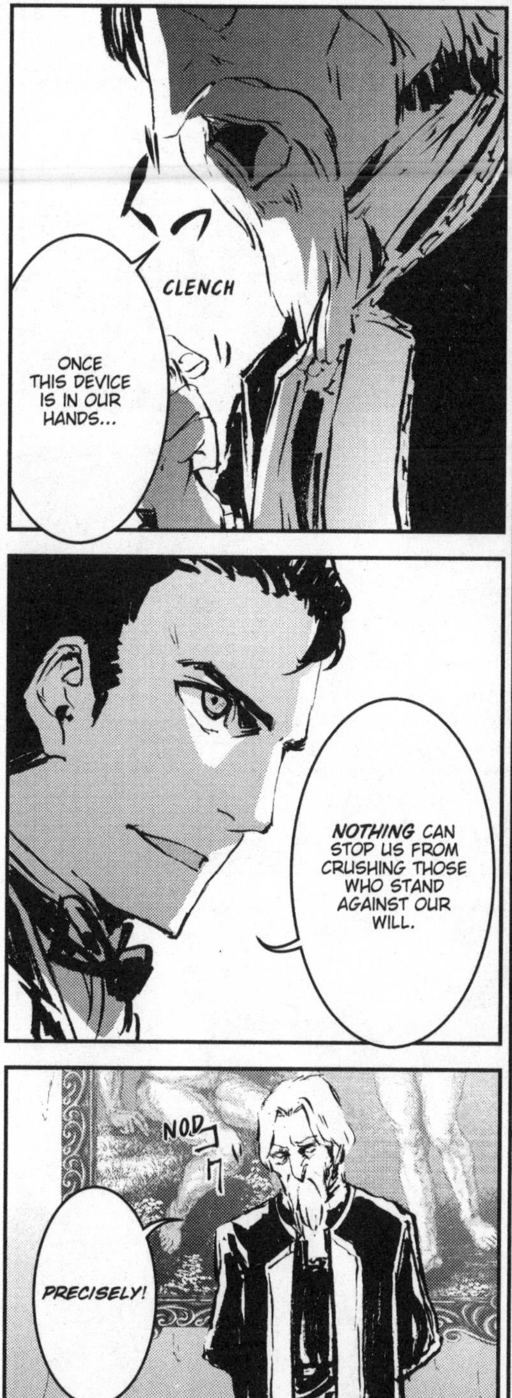
CLENCH
ONCE THIS DEVICE IS IN OUR HANDS...
NOTHING CAN STOP US FROM CRUSHING THOSE WHO STAND AGAINST OUR WILL.
NOD
PRECISELY!

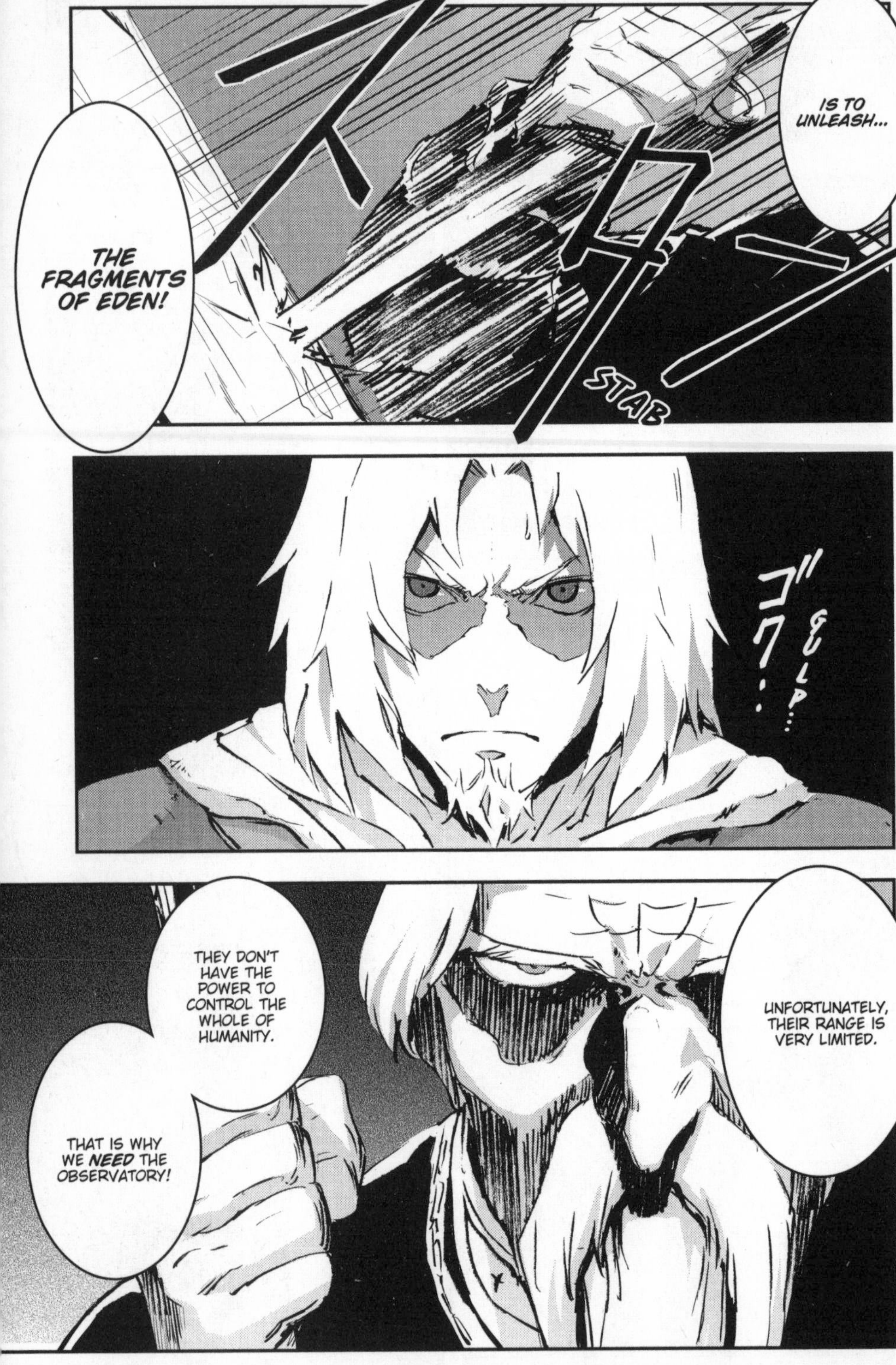
IS TO UNLEASH...
THE FRAGMENTS OF EDEN!
STAB
GULP...
UNFORTUNATELY, THEIR RANGE IS VERY LIMITED.
THEY DON'T HAVE THE POWER TO CONTROL THE WHOLE OF HUMANITY.
THAT IS WHY WE *NEED* THE OBSERVATORY!

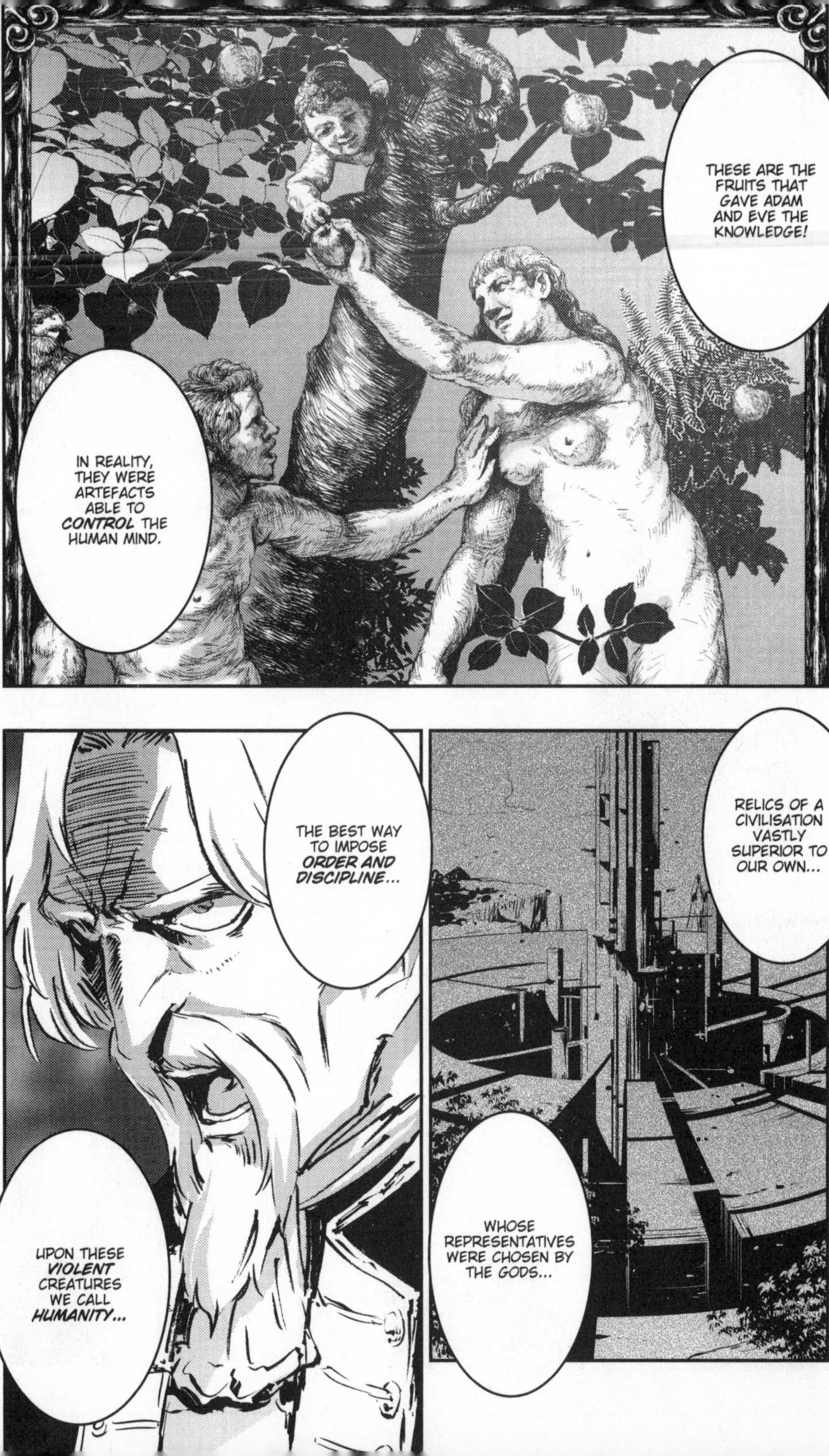
THESE ARE THE FRUITS THAT GAVE ADAM AND EVE THE KNOWLEDGE!
IN REALITY, THEY WERE ARTEFACTS ABLE TO CONTROL THE HUMAN MIND.
RELICS OF A CIVILISATION VASTLY SUPERIOR TO OUR OWN...
WHOSE REPRESENTATIVES WERE CHOSEN BY THE GODS...
THE BEST WAY TO IMPOSE ORDER AND DISCIPLINE...
UPON THESE VIOLENT CREATURES WE CALL HUMANITY...

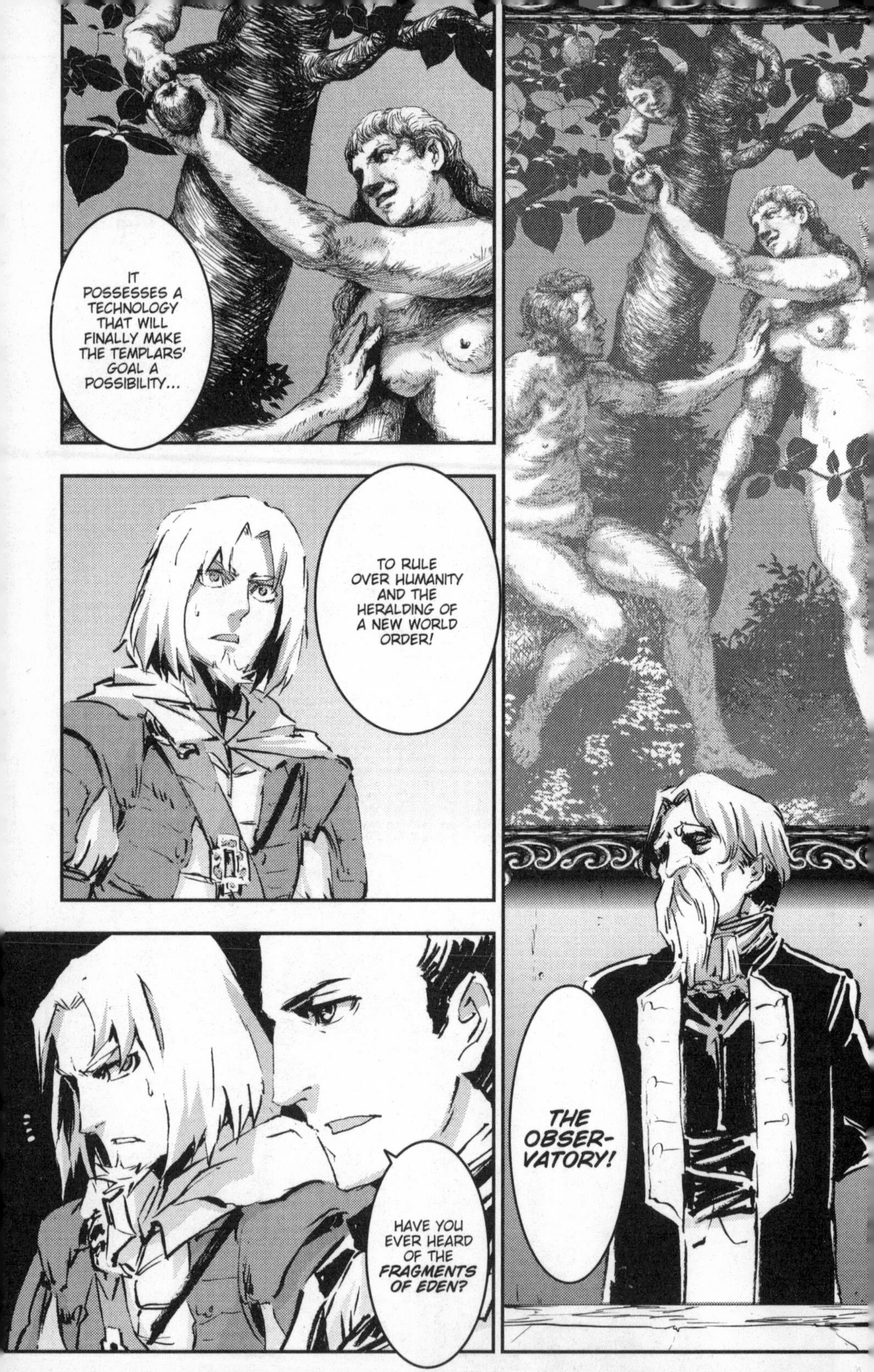
IT POSSESSES A TECHNOLOGY THAT WILL FINALLY MAKE THE TEMPLARS' GOAL A POSSIBILITY...
TO RULE OVER HUMANITY AND THE HERALDING OF A NEW WORLD ORDER!
THE OBSER-VATORY!
HAVE YOU EVER HEARD OF THE *FRAGMENTS OF EDEN*?
...

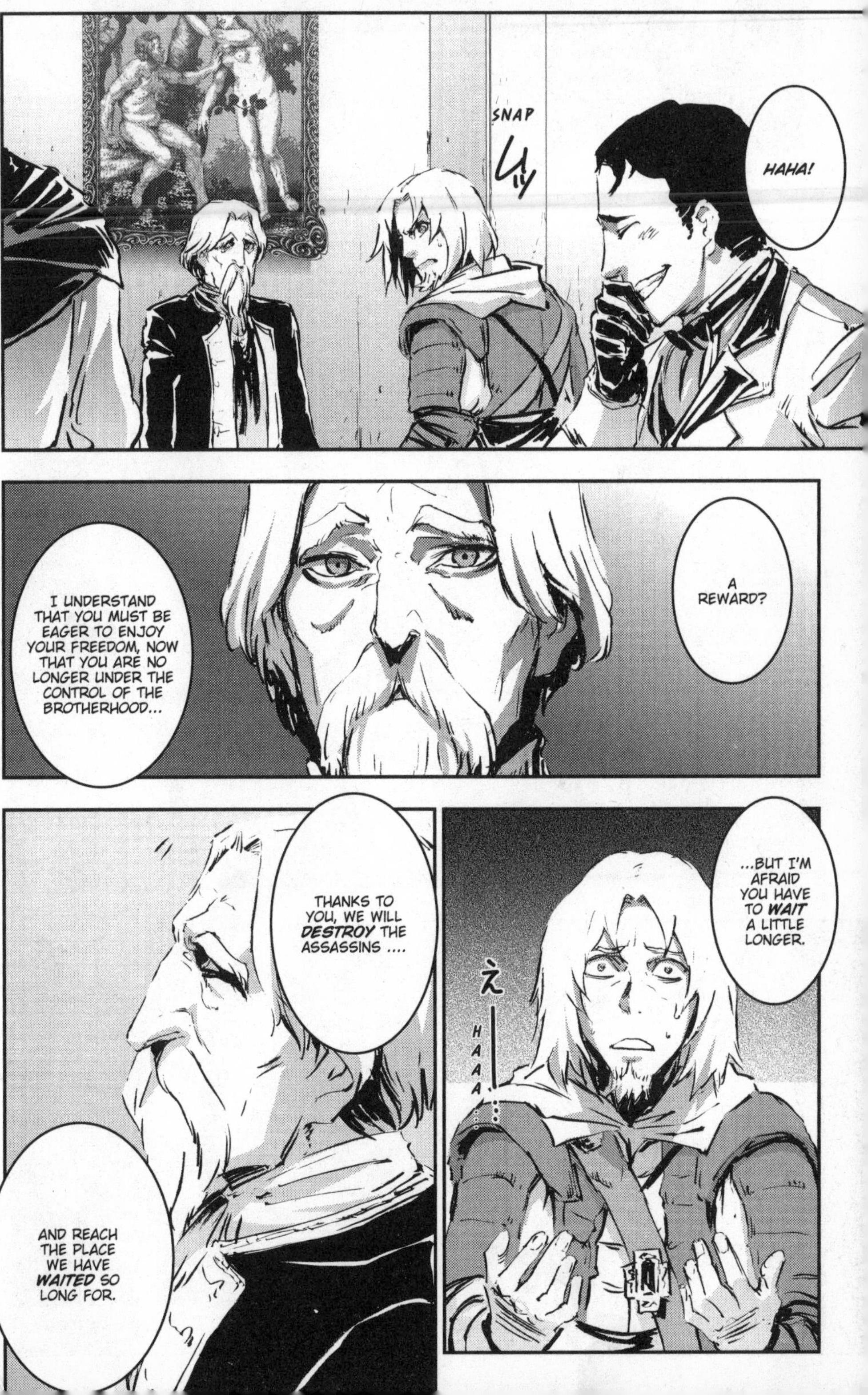
HAHA!
SNAP
A REWARD?
I UNDERSTAND THAT YOU MUST BE EAGER TO ENJOY YOUR FREEDOM, NOW THAT YOU ARE NO LONGER UNDER THE CONTROL OF THE BROTHERHOOD...
...BUT I'M AFRAID YOU HAVE TO **WAIT** A LITTLE LONGER.
え
HAAA...
THANKS TO YOU, WE WILL **DESTROY** THE ASSASSINS ....
AND REACH THE PLACE WE HAVE **WAITED** SO LONG FOR.

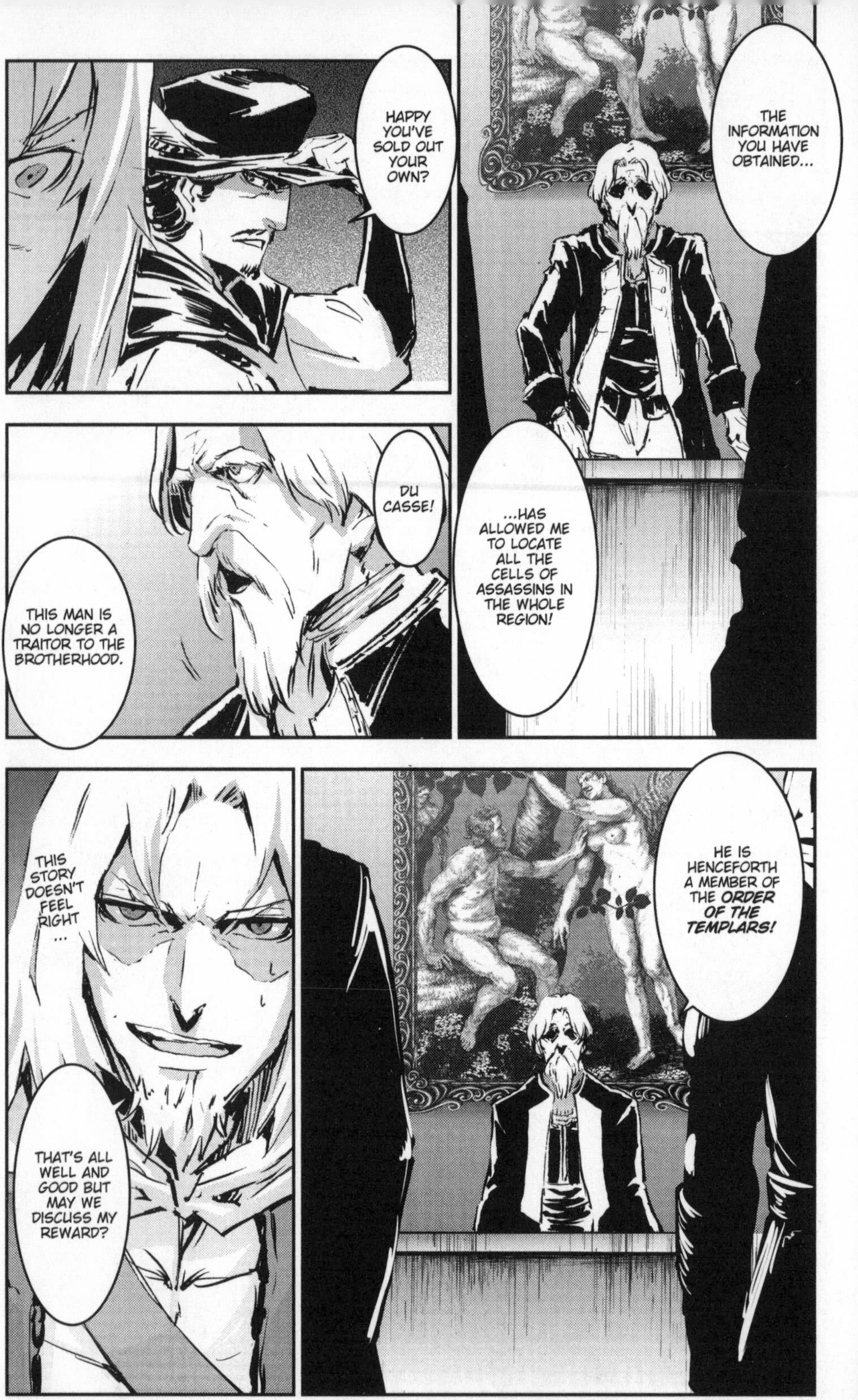
THE INFORMATION YOU HAVE OBTAINED...
...HAS ALLOWED ME TO LOCATE ALL THE CELLS OF ASSASSINS IN THE WHOLE REGION!
HAPPY YOU'VE SOLD OUT YOUR OWN?
DU CASSE!
THIS MAN IS NO LONGER A TRAITOR TO THE BROTHERHOOD.
HE IS HENCEFORTH A MEMBER OF THE *ORDER OF THE TEMPLARS!*
THIS STORY DOESN'T FEEL RIGHT ...
THAT'S ALL WELL AND GOOD BUT MAY WE DISCUSS MY REWARD?

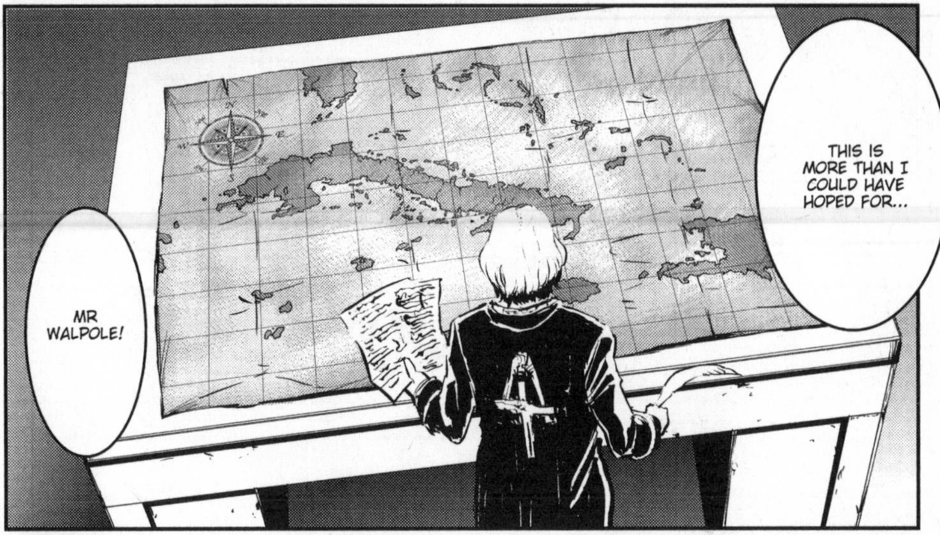
THIS IS MORE THAN I COULD HAVE HOPED FOR...
MR WALPOLE!

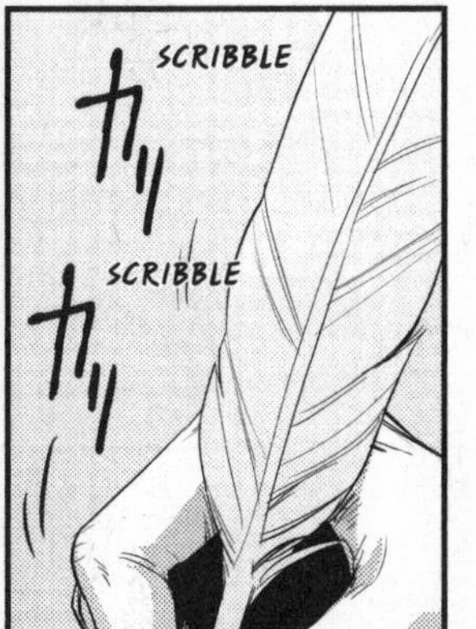
SCRIBBLE
カリ
SCRIBBLE
カリ

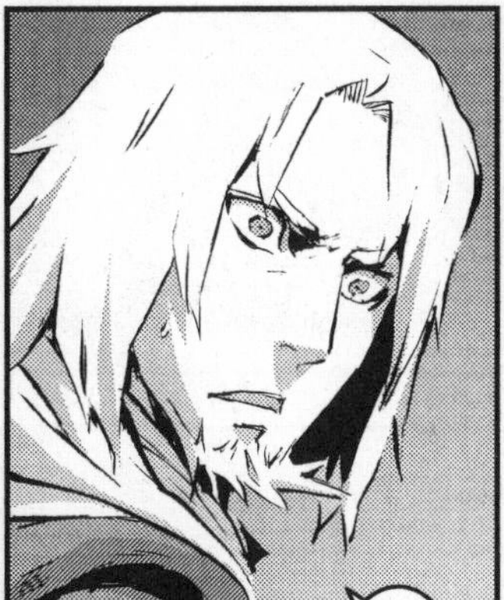
?

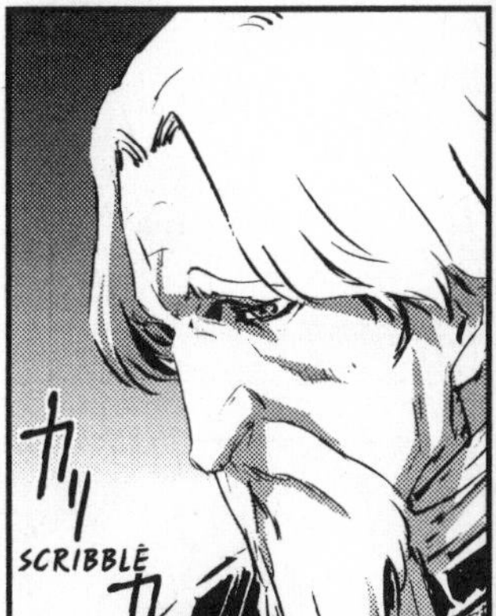
カリ
SCRIBBLE
カリ
SCRIBBLE

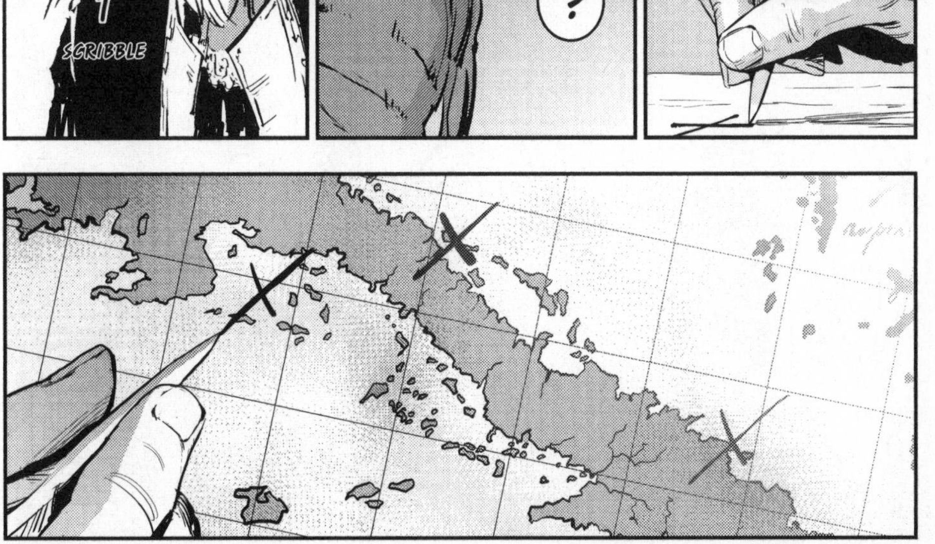

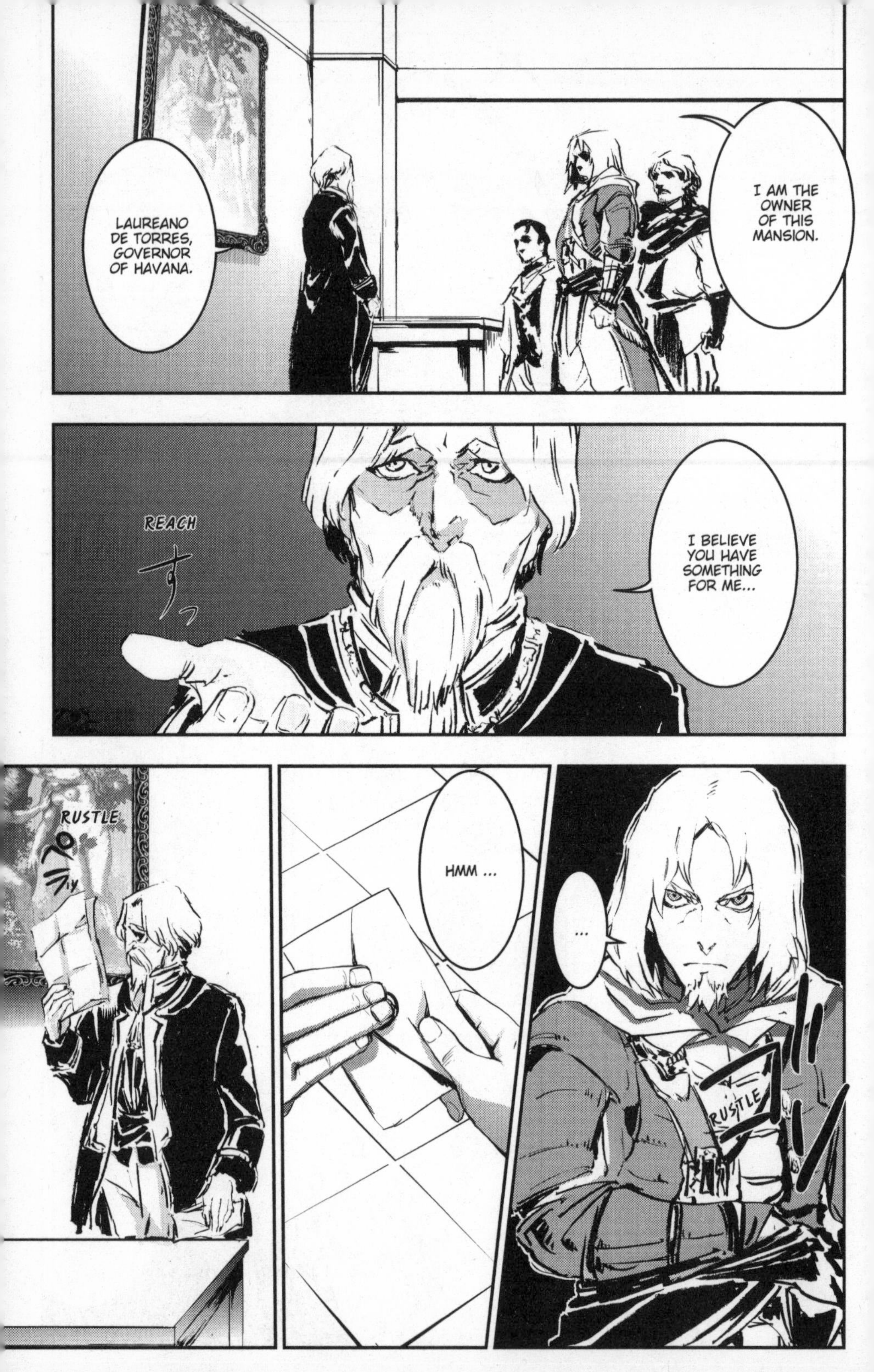
I AM THE OWNER OF THIS MANSION.
LAUREANO DE TORRES, GOVERNOR OF HAVANA.
I BELIEVE YOU HAVE SOMETHING FOR ME...
REACH
...
RUSTLE
HMM ...
RUSTLE

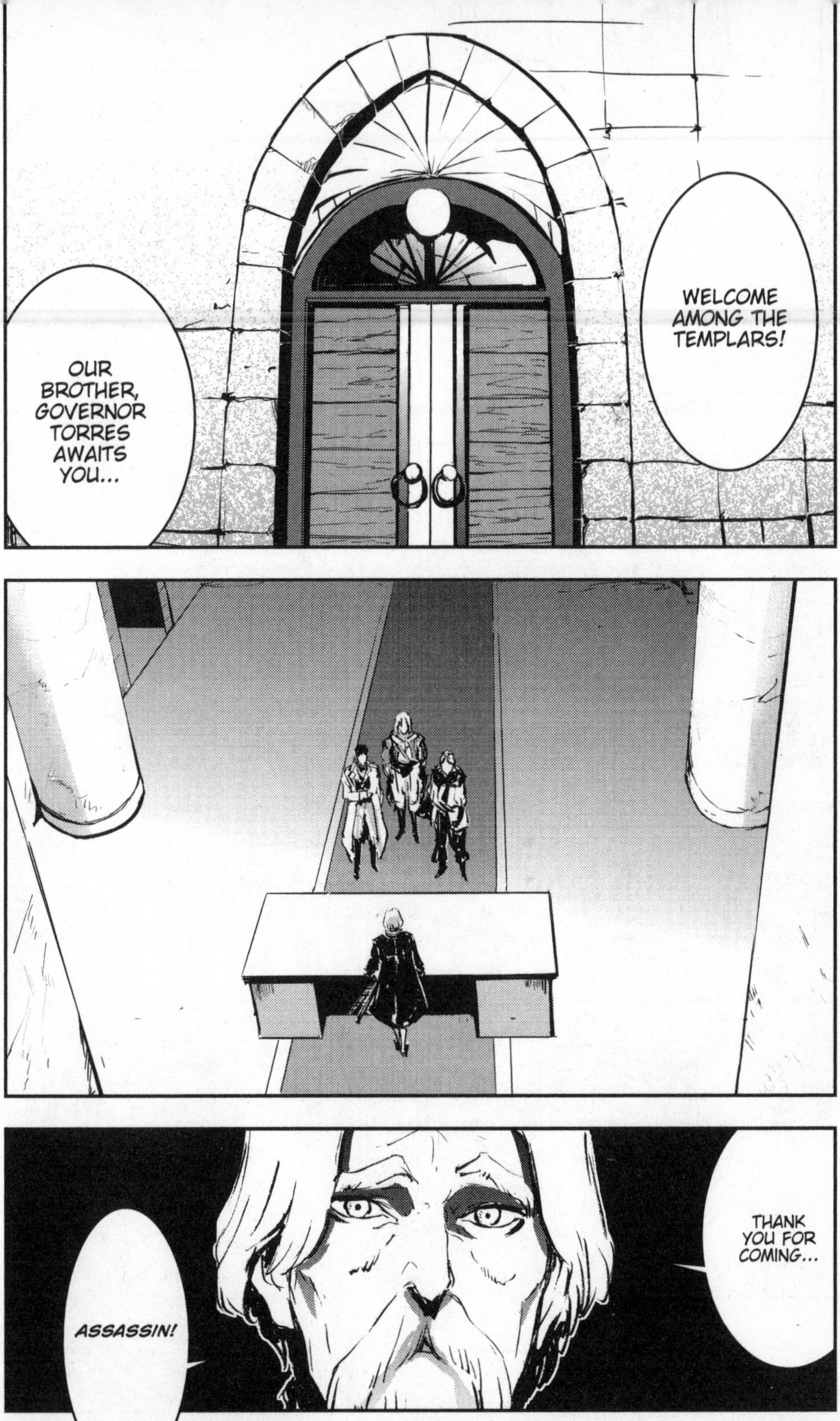
WELCOME AMONG THE TEMPLARS!
OUR BROTHER, GOVERNOR TORRES AWAITS YOU...
THANK YOU FOR COMING...
ASSASSIN!

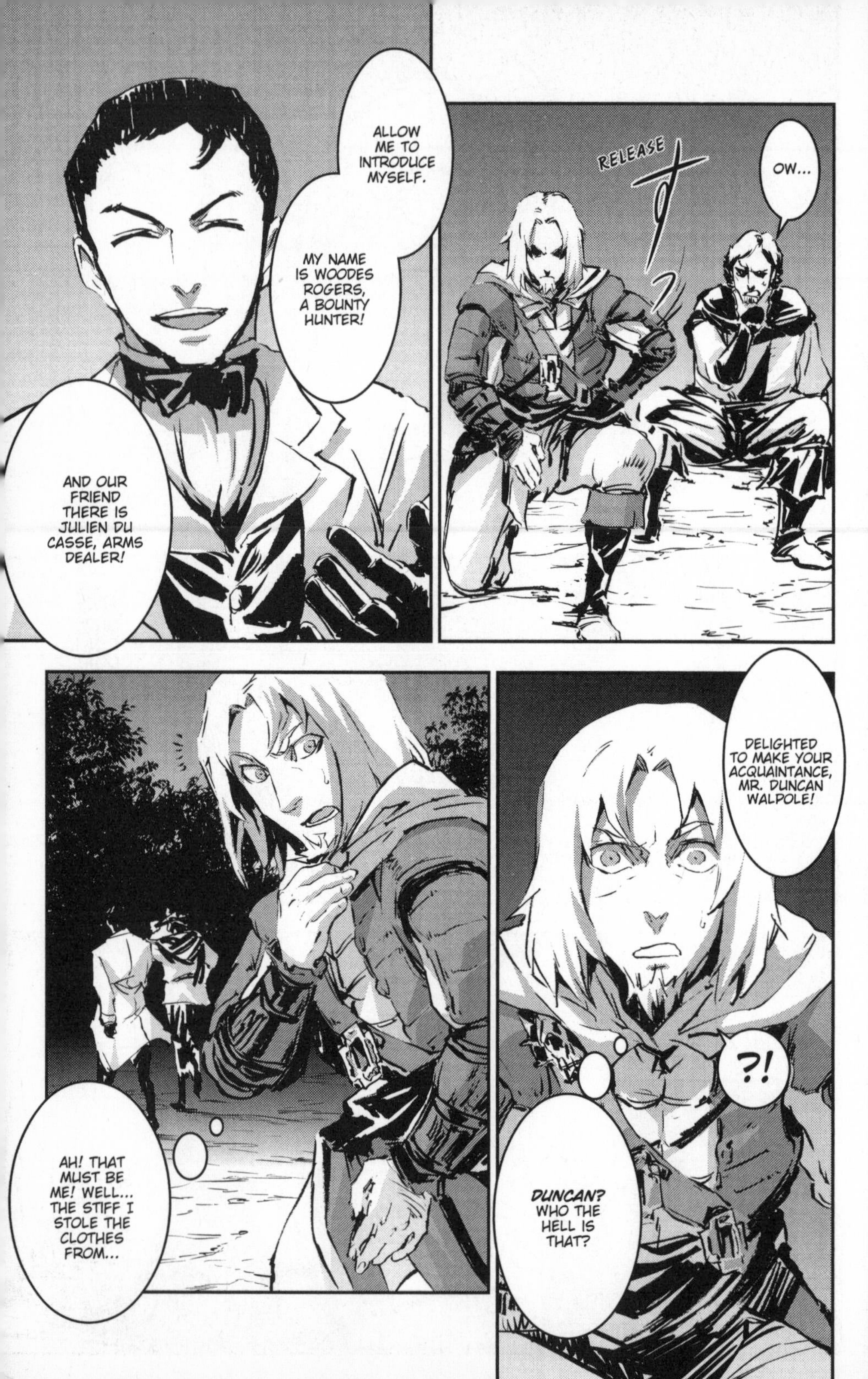
OW...
RELEASE
ALLOW ME TO INTRODUCE MYSELF.
MY NAME IS WOODES ROGERS, A BOUNTY HUNTER!
AND OUR FRIEND THERE IS JULIEN DU CASSE, ARMS DEALER!
DELIGHTED TO MAKE YOUR ACQUAINTANCE, MR. DUNCAN WALPOLE!
?!
DUNCAN? WHO THE HELL IS THAT?
AH! THAT MUST BE ME! WELL... THE STIFF I STOLE THE CLOTHES FROM...

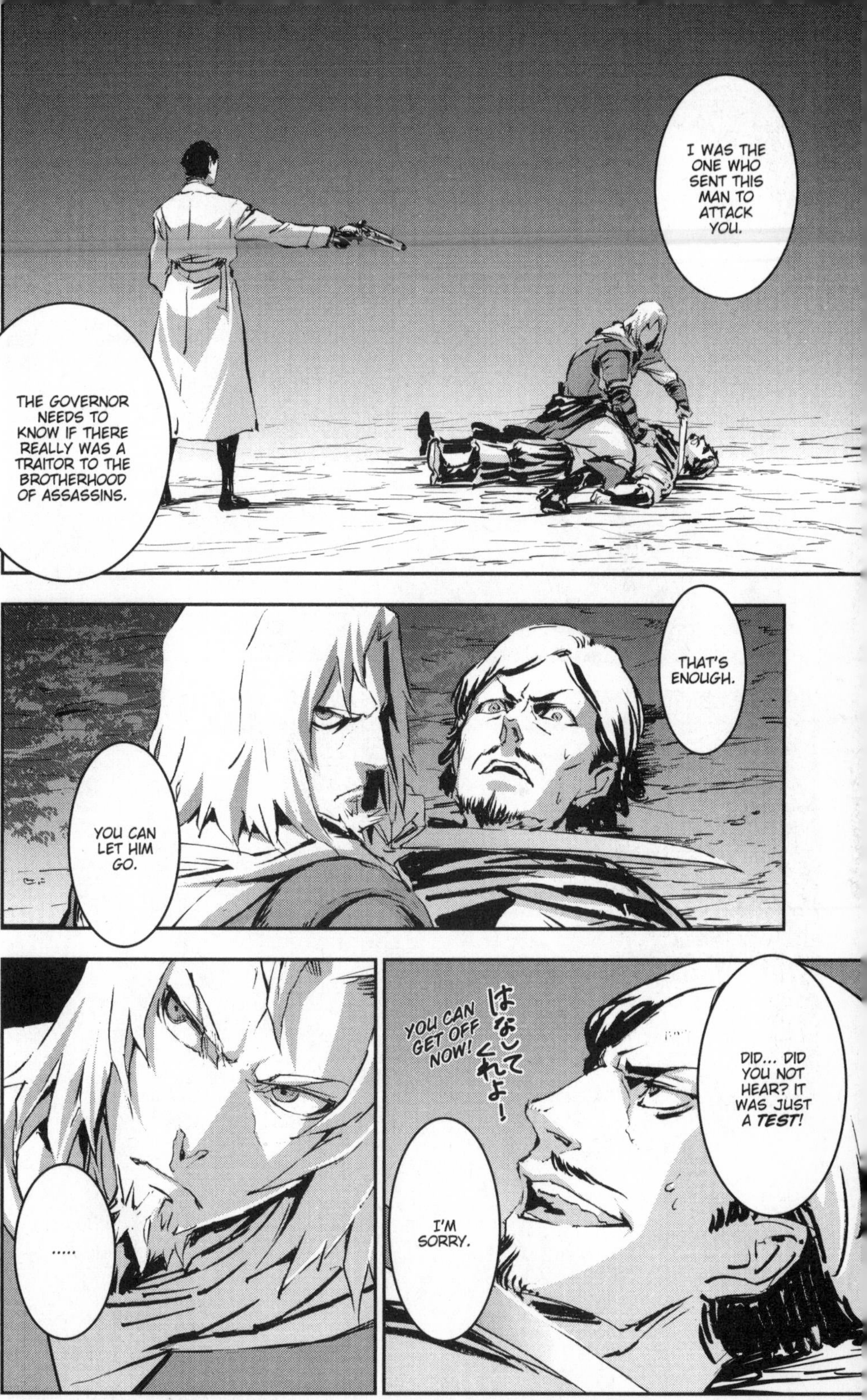
I WAS THE ONE WHO SENT THIS MAN TO ATTACK YOU.
THE GOVERNOR NEEDS TO KNOW IF THERE REALLY WAS A TRAITOR TO THE BROTHERHOOD OF ASSASSINS.
THAT'S ENOUGH.
YOU CAN LET HIM GO.
DID... DID YOU NOT HEAR? IT WAS JUST A *TEST*!
はなしてくれよ!
YOU CAN GET OFF NOW!
I'M SORRY.
.....

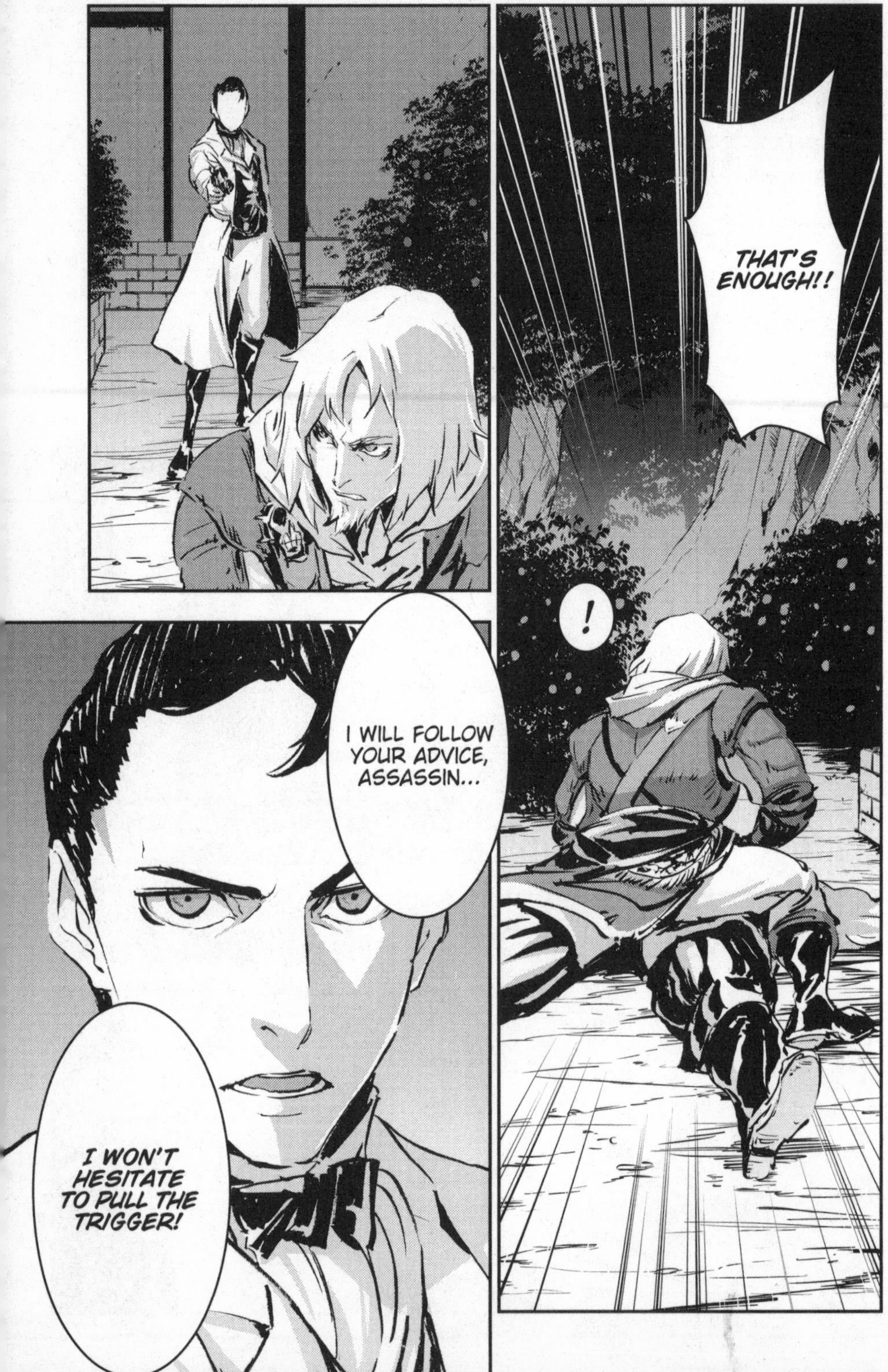
THAT'S ENOUGH!!
!
I WILL FOLLOW YOUR ADVICE, ASSASSIN...
I WON'T HESITATE TO PULL THE TRIGGER!

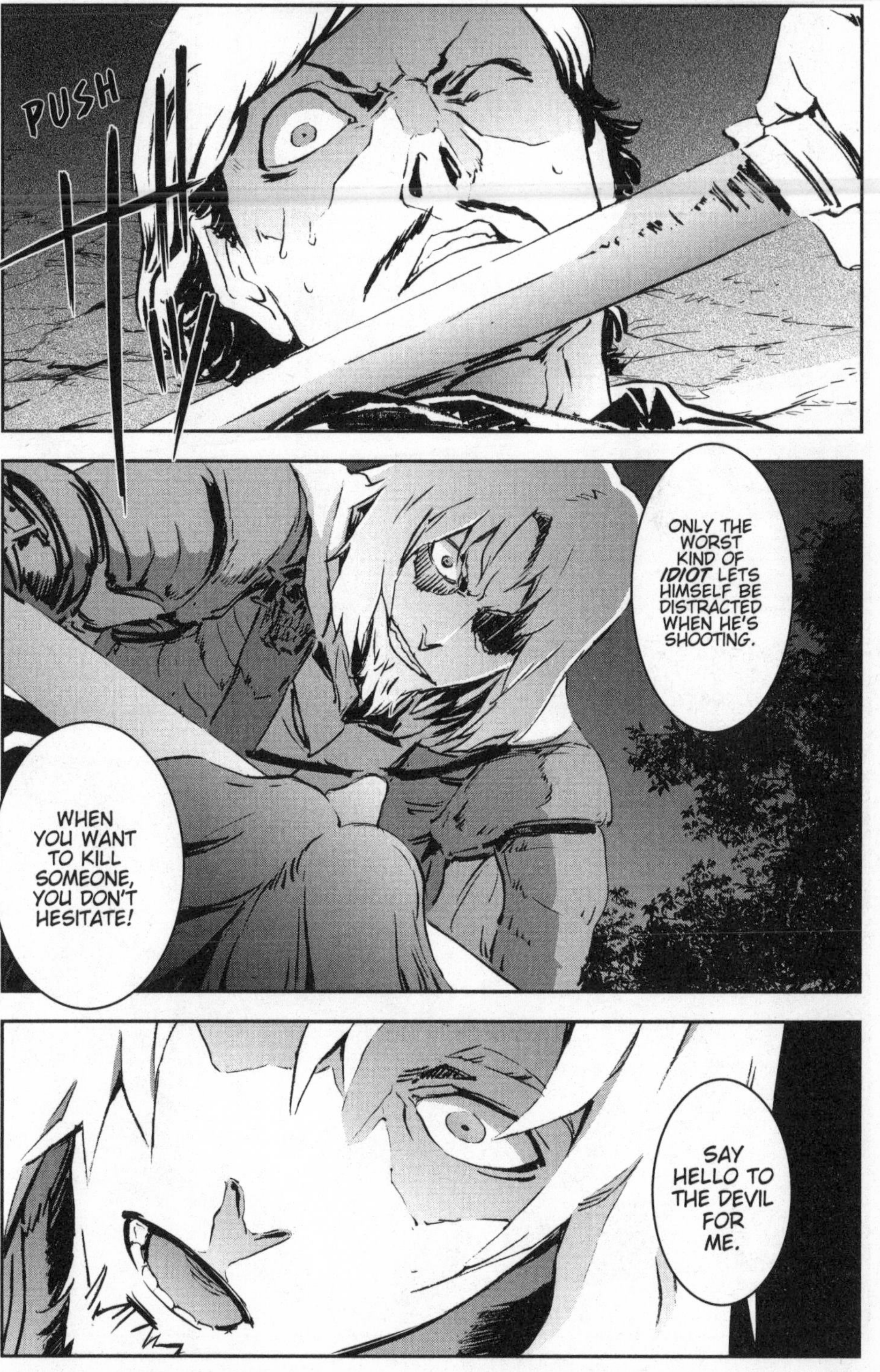
PUSH
ONLY THE WORST KIND OF IDIOT LETS HIMSELF BE DISTRACTED WHEN HE'S SHOOTING.
WHEN YOU WANT TO KILL SOMEONE, YOU DON'T HESITATE!
SAY HELLO TO THE DEVIL FOR ME.

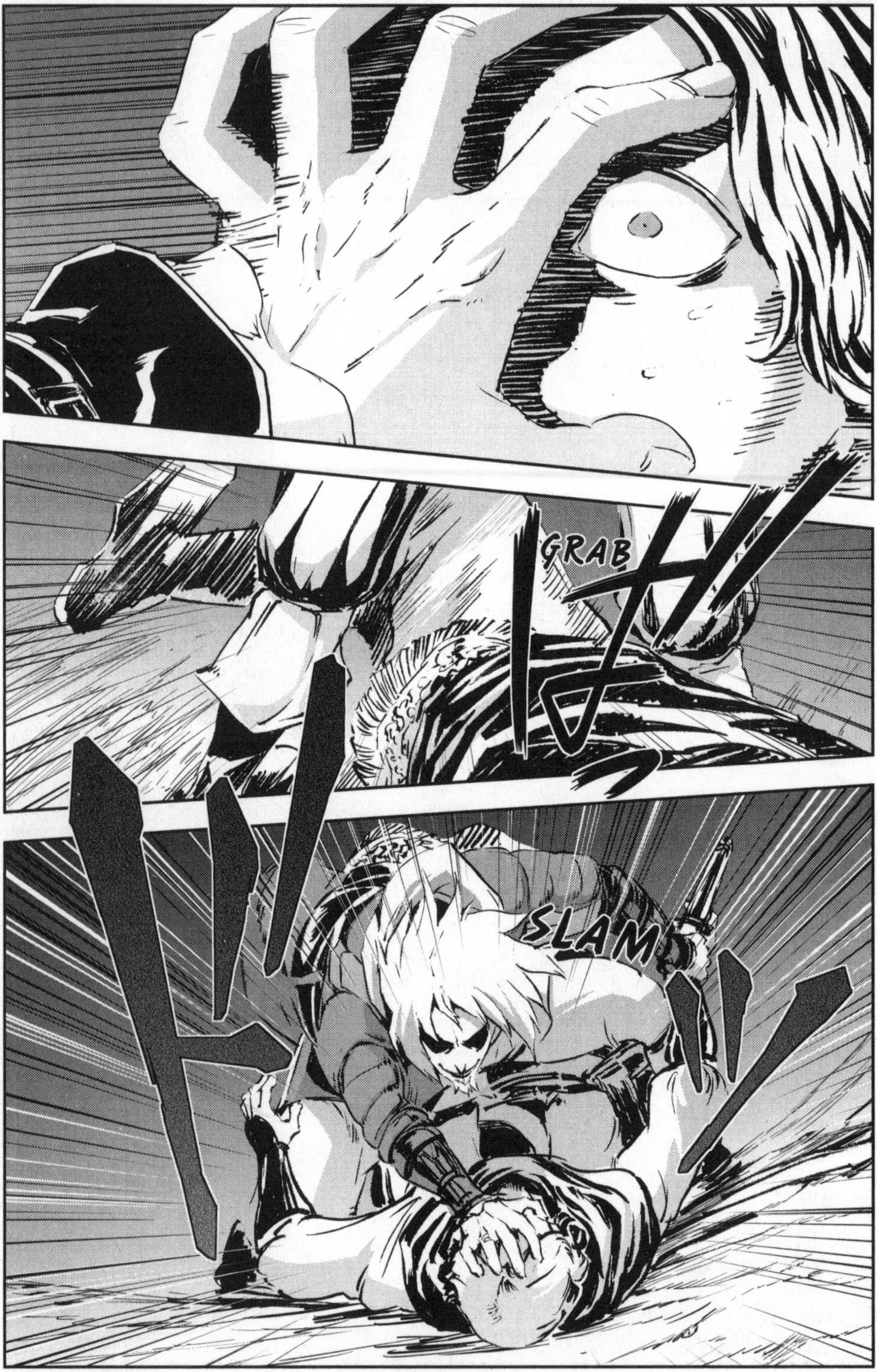
GRAB
SLAM

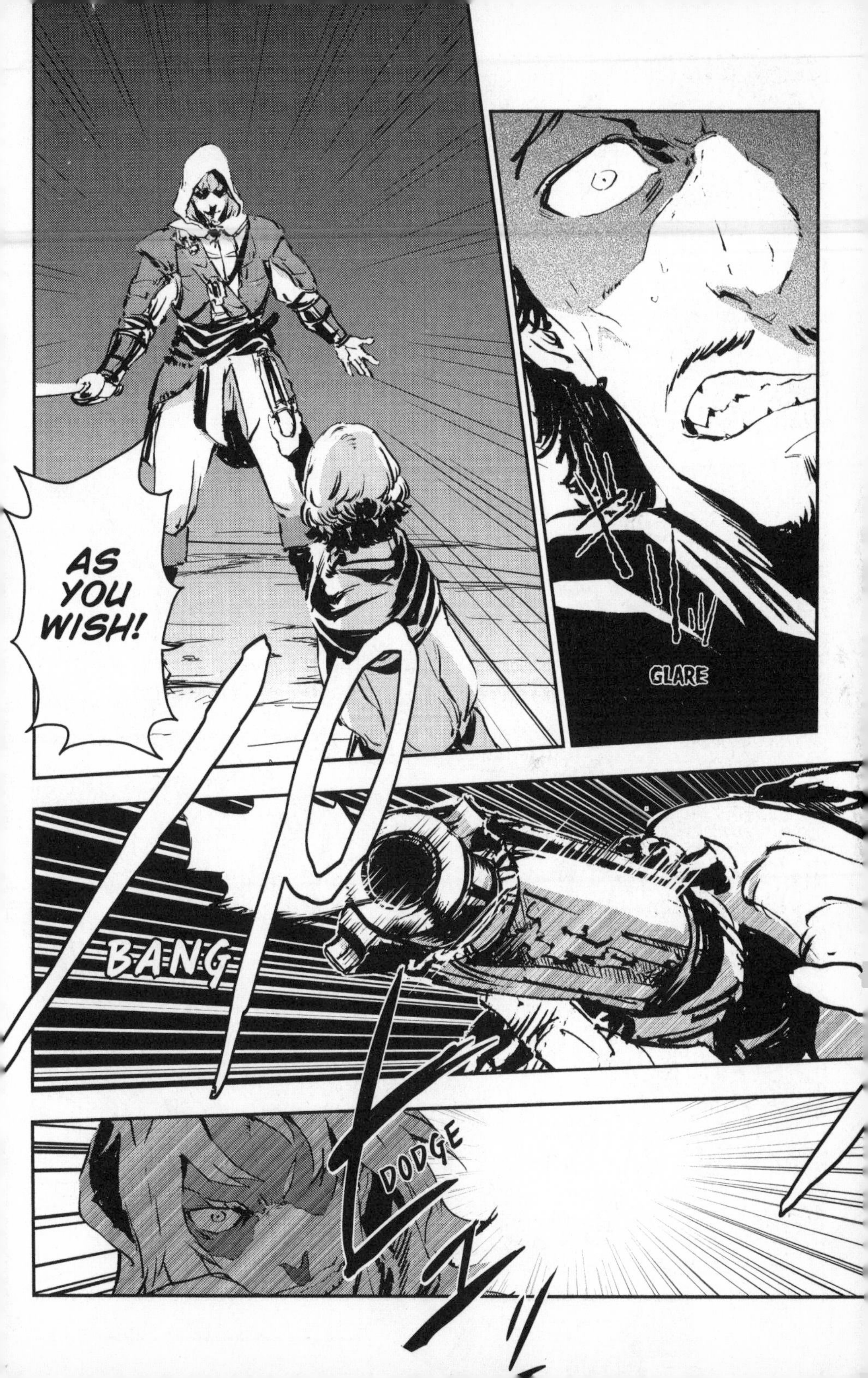
GLARE
AS YOU WISH!
BANG
DODGE

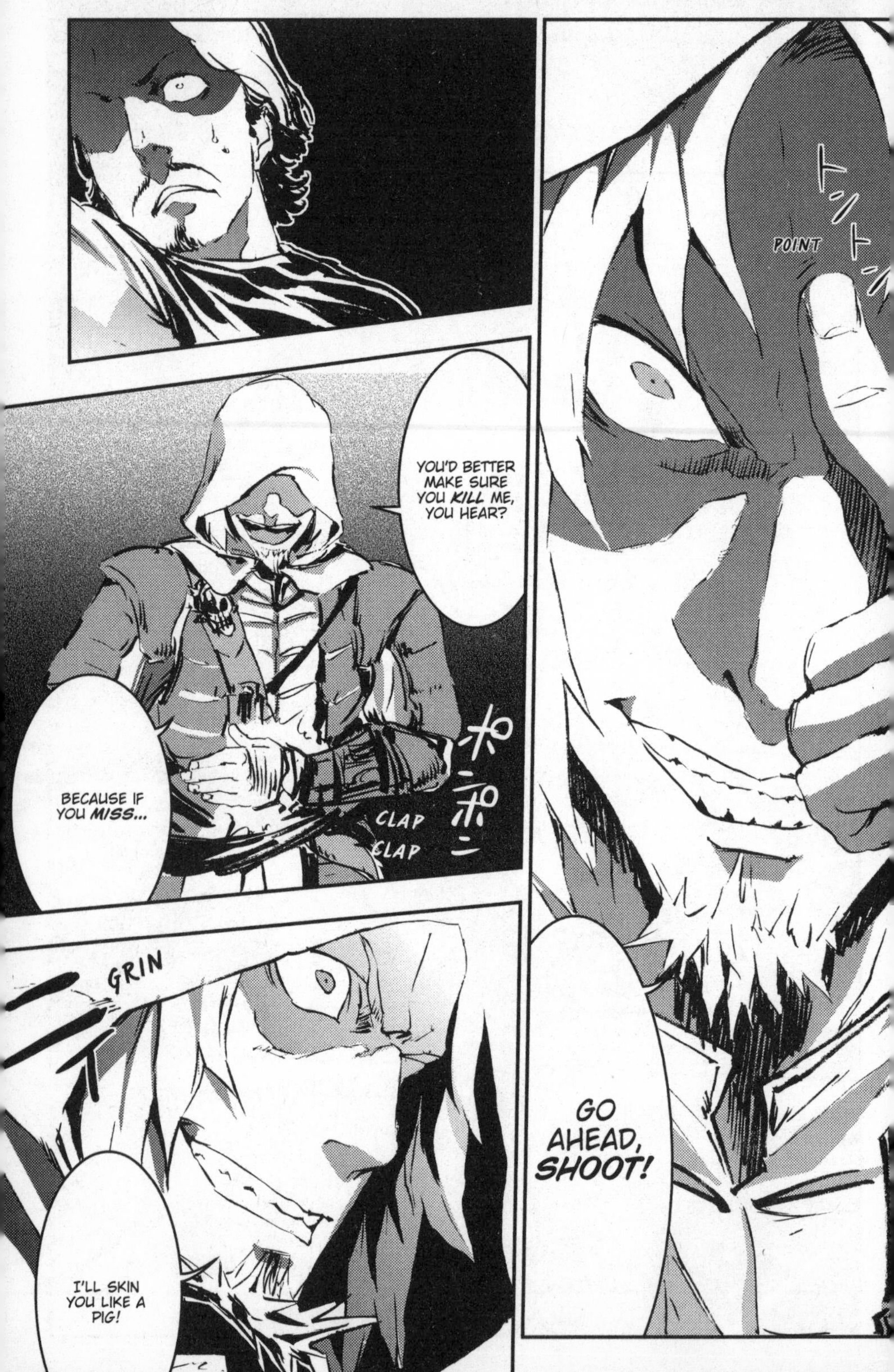
POINT
GO AHEAD, SHOOT!
YOU'D BETTER MAKE SURE YOU KILL ME, YOU HEAR?
BECAUSE IF YOU MISS...
CLAP CLAP
GRIN
I'LL SKIN YOU LIKE A PIG!

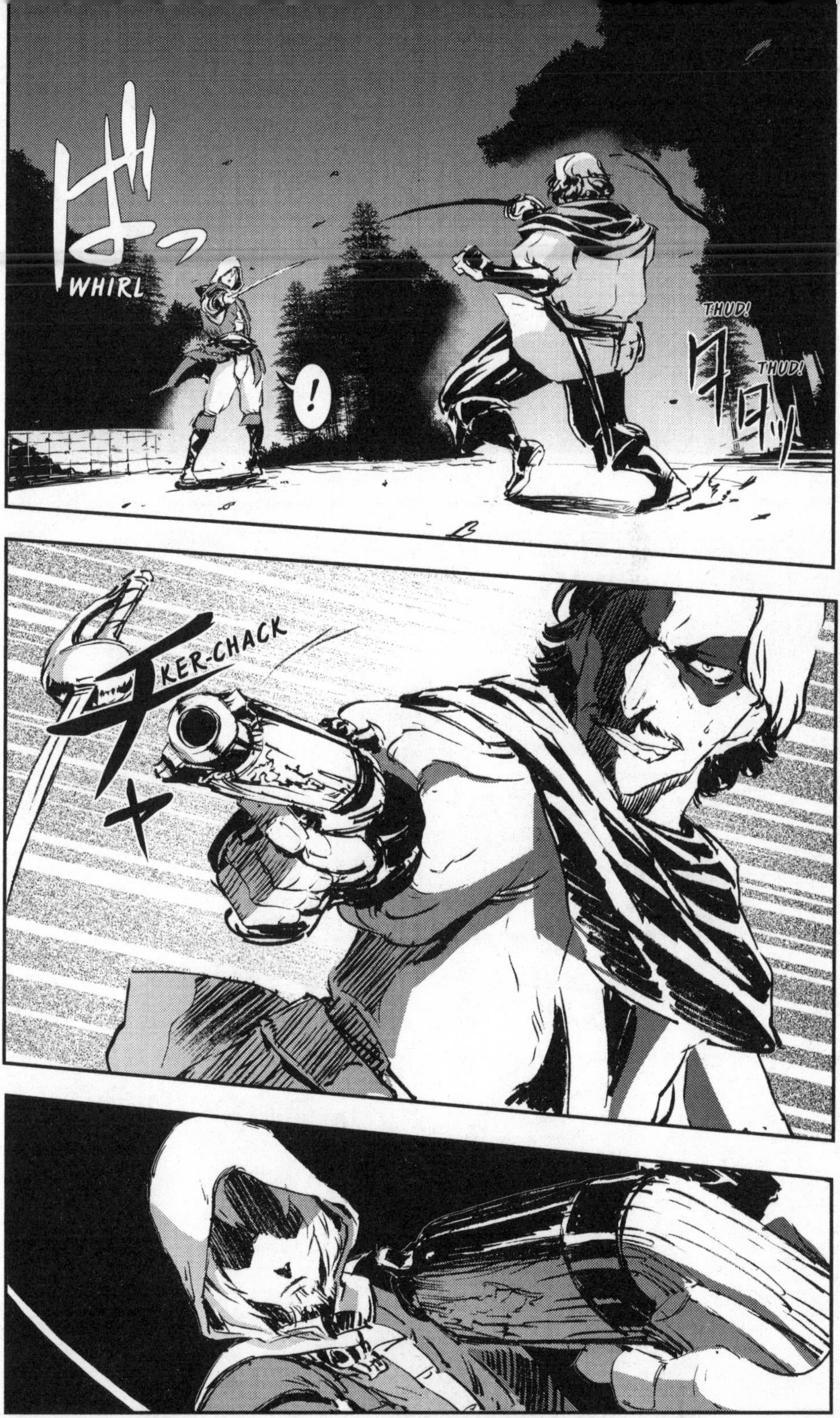
THUD!
THUD!
タタッ
!
ぱっ
WHIRL
KER-CHACK
チャ

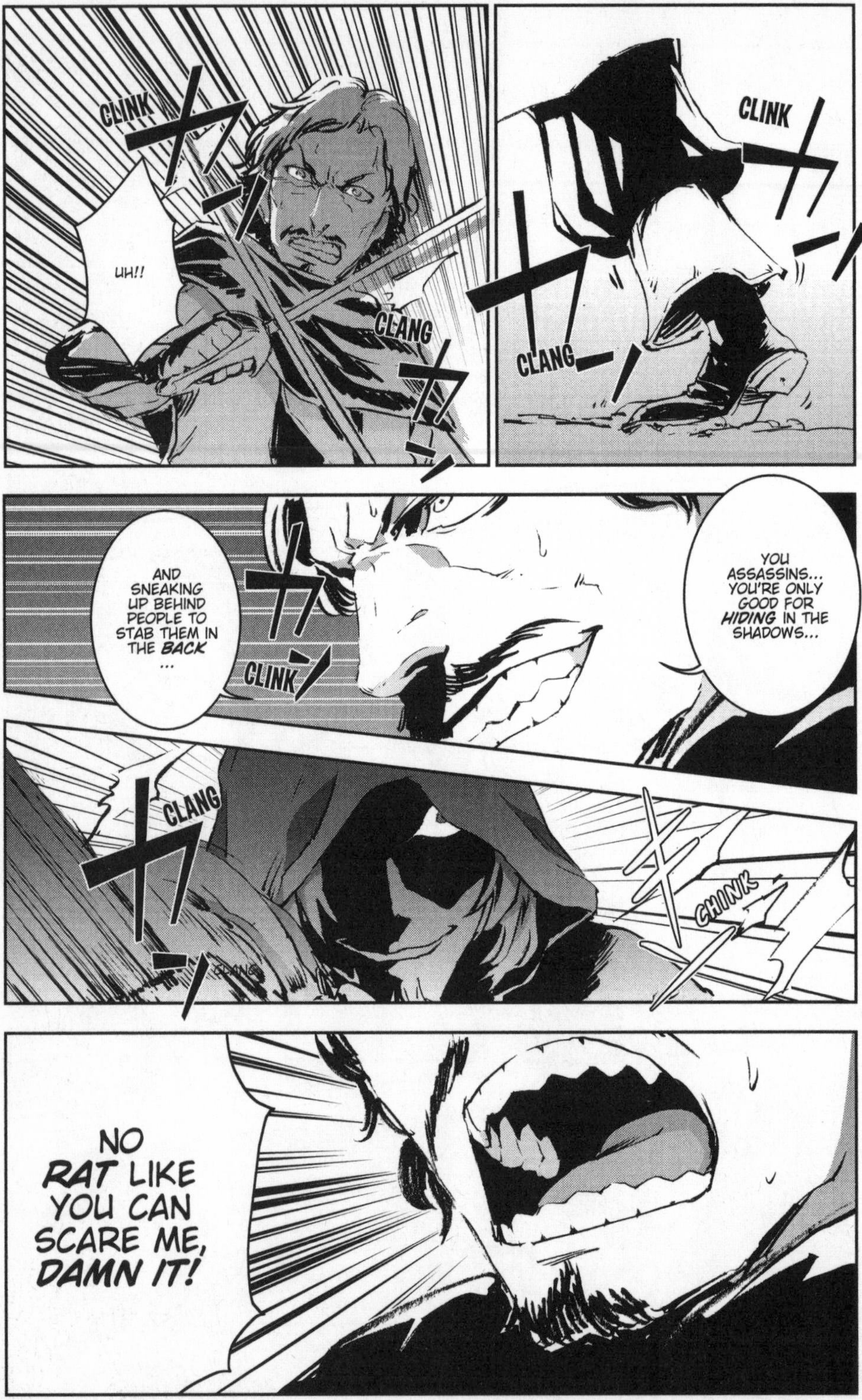
CLINK
CLANG
CLINK
UH!!
CLANG
YOU ASSASSINS... YOU'RE ONLY GOOD FOR *HIDING* IN THE SHADOWS...
AND SNEAKING UP BEHIND PEOPLE TO STAB THEM IN THE *BACK* ...
CLINK
CHINK
CLANG
CLANG
NO *RAT* LIKE YOU CAN SCARE ME, *DAMN IT!*

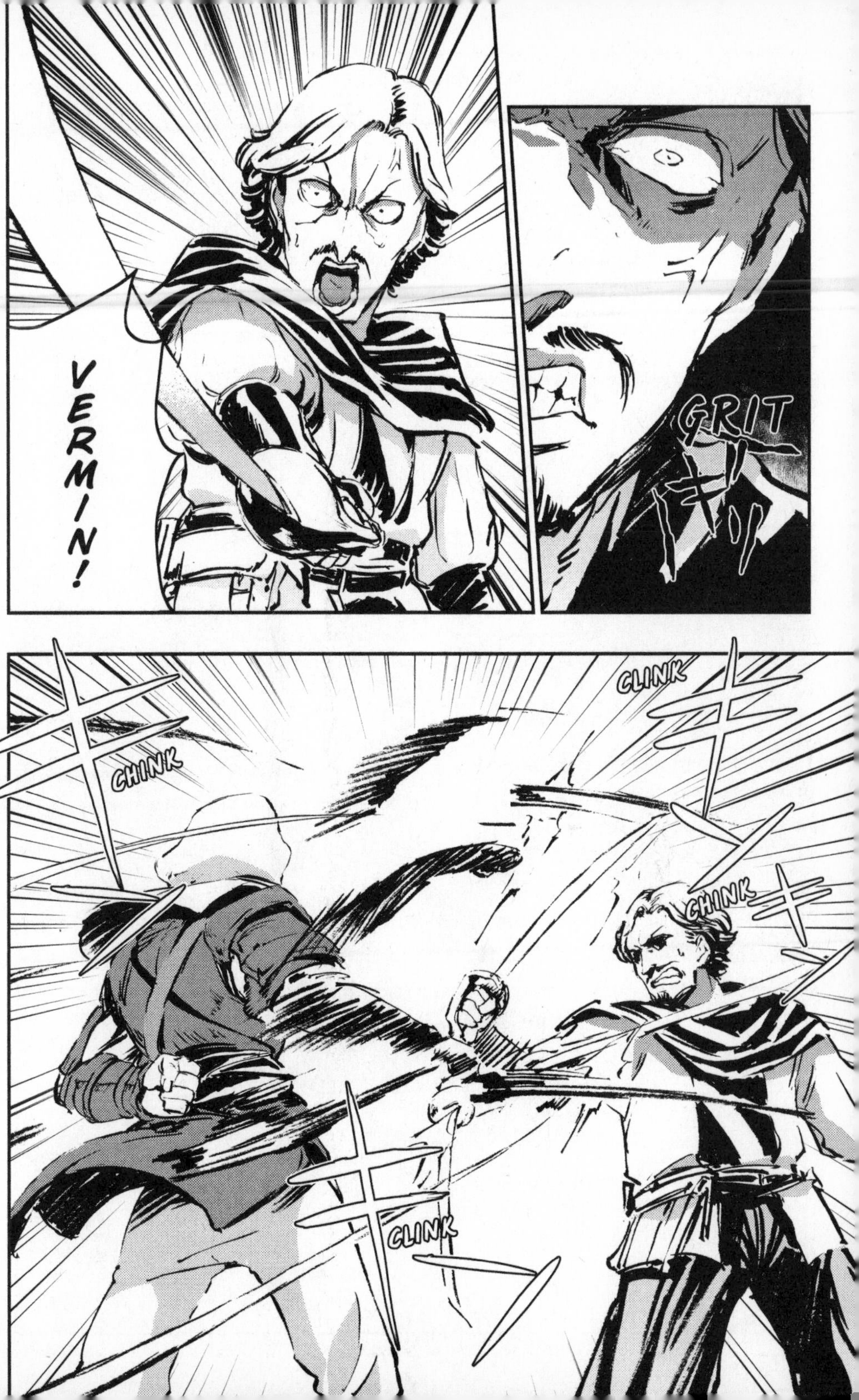
GRIT
VERMIN!
CLINK
CHINK
CHINK
CLINK

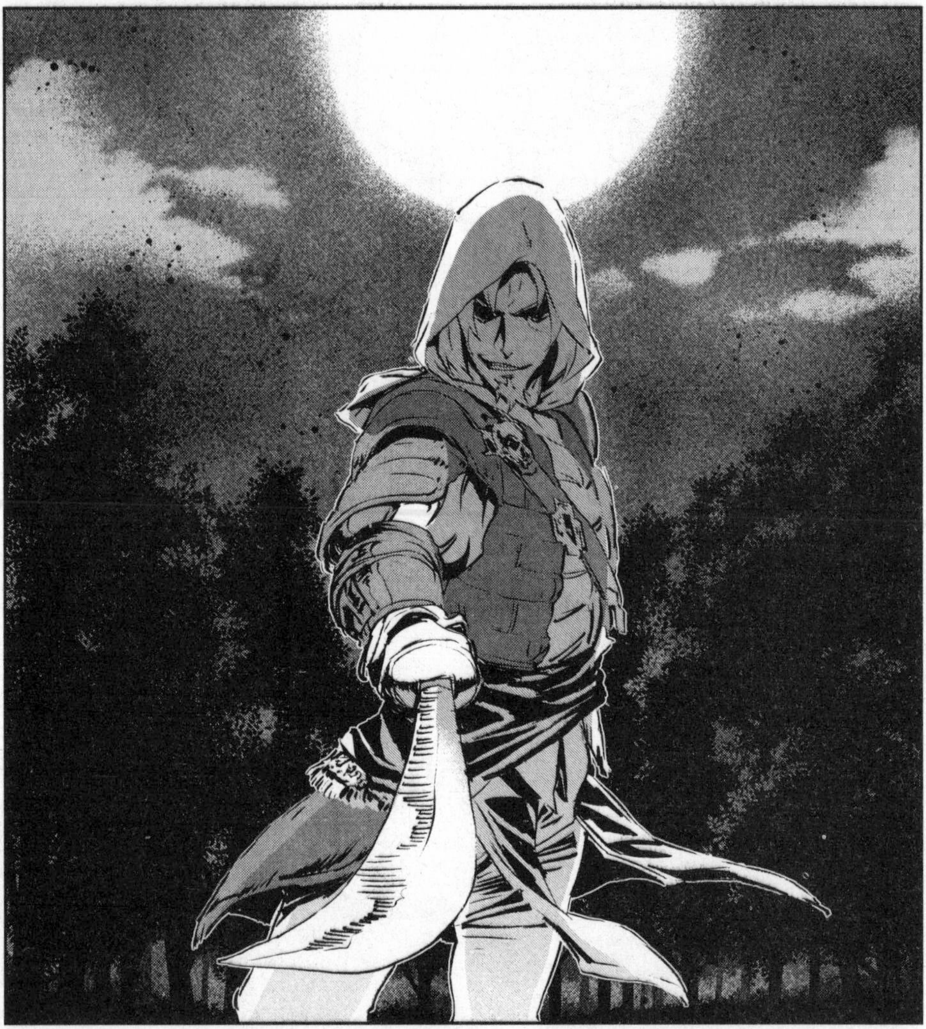
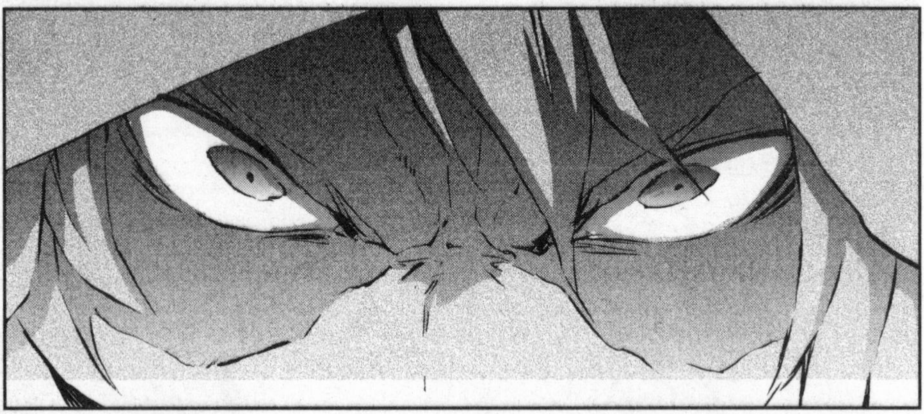

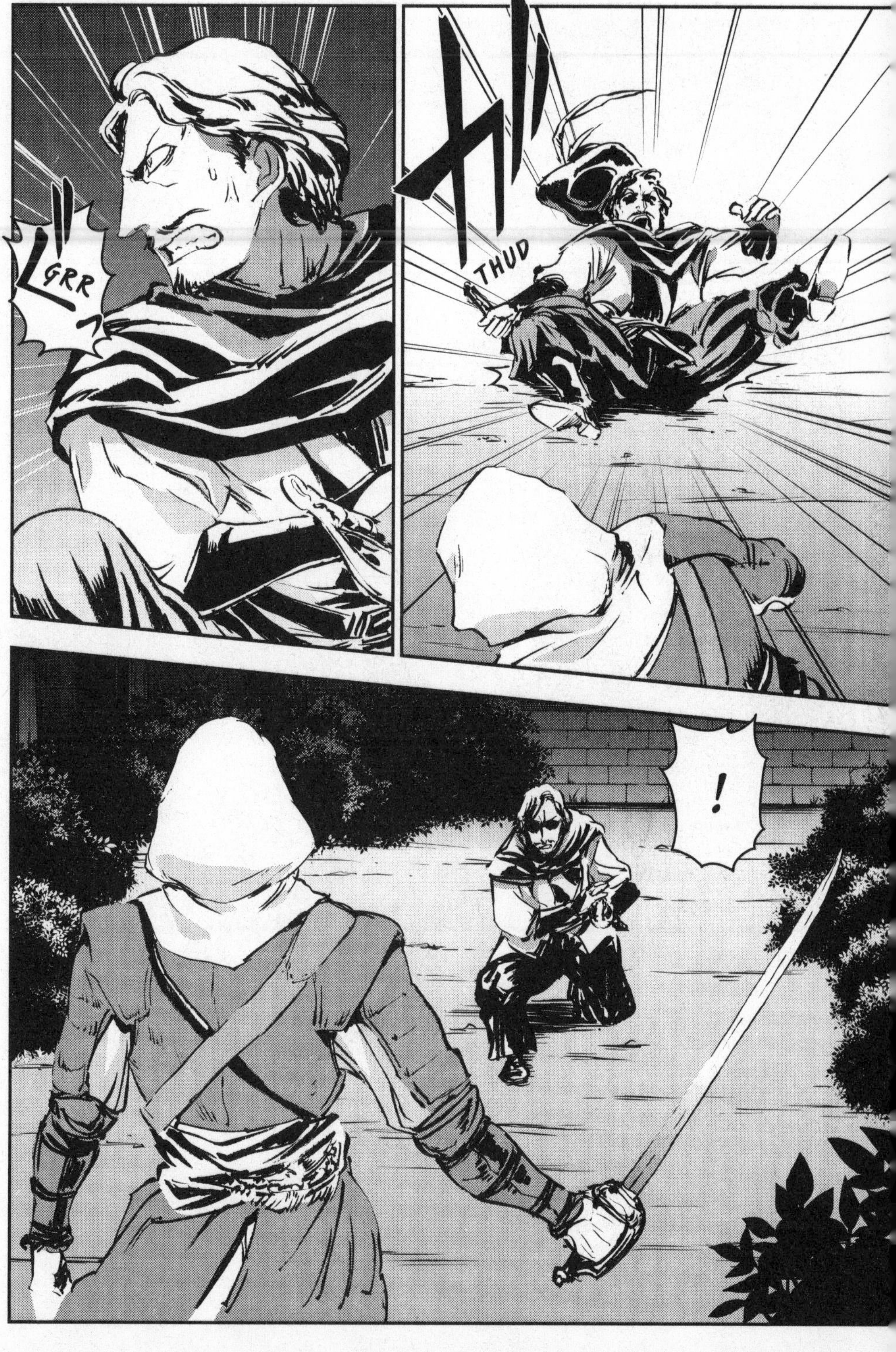
THUD
GRR
!

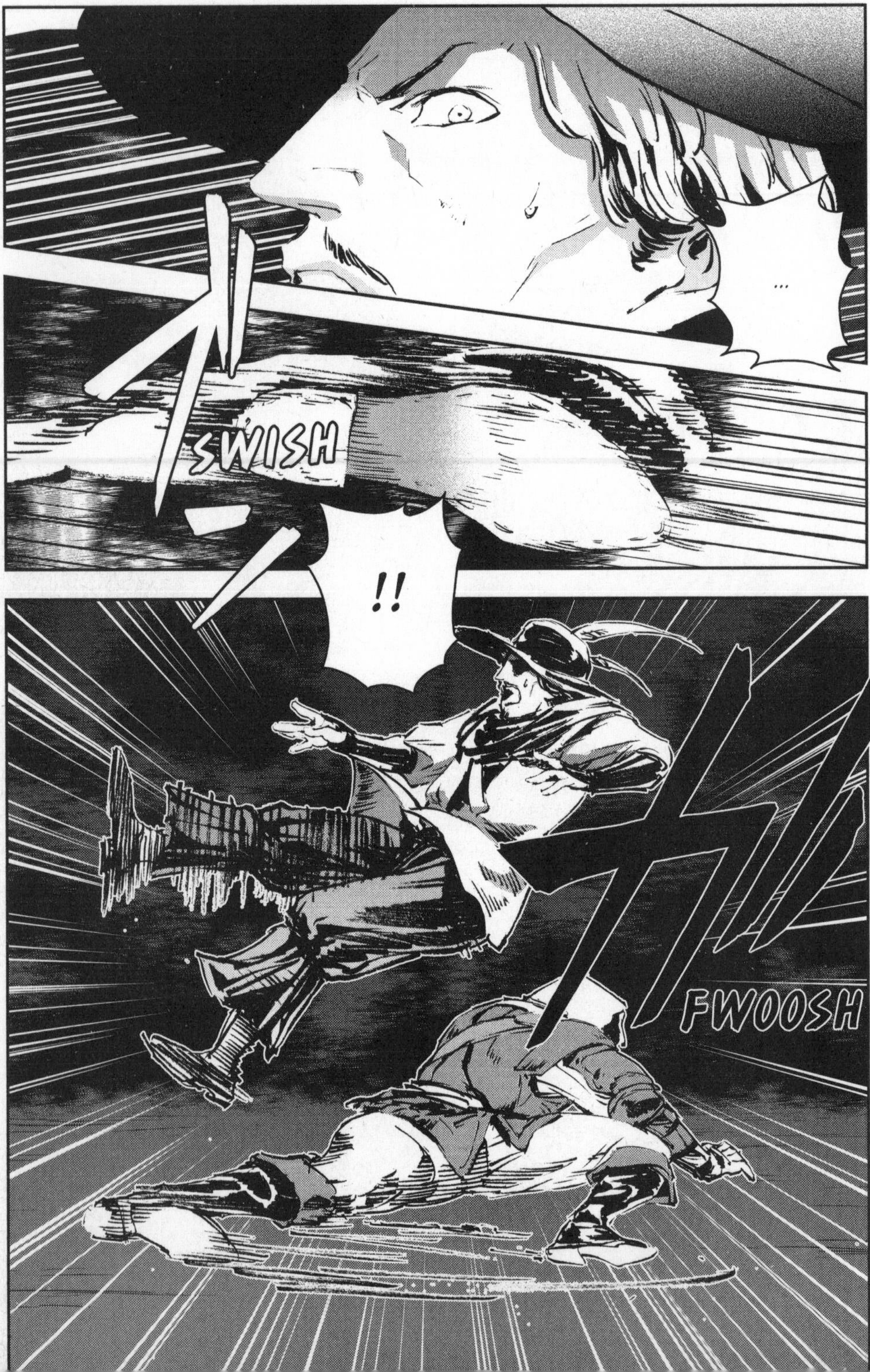
...
SWISH
!!
FWOOSH

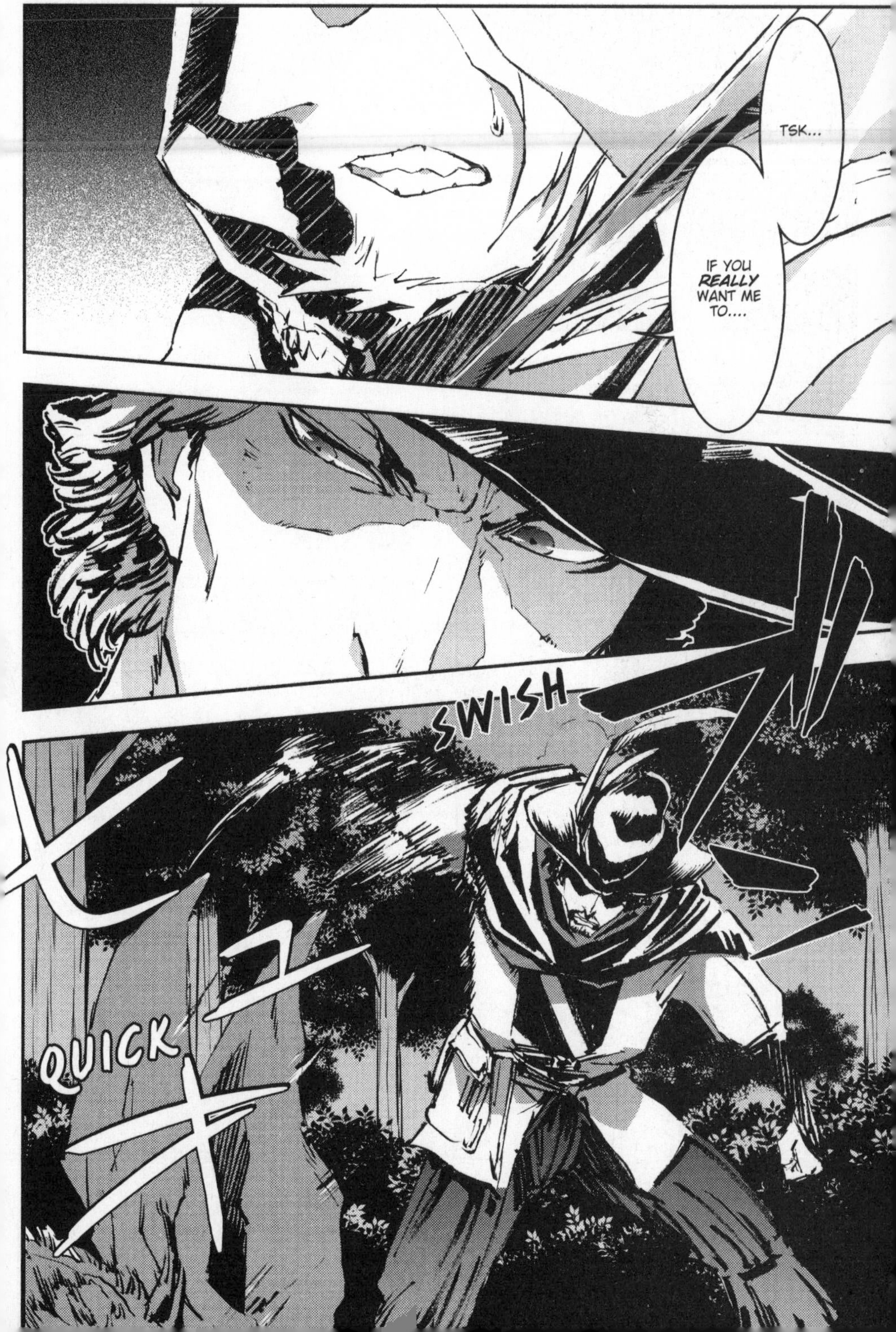
TSK...
IF YOU *REALLY* WANT ME TO....
SWISH
QUICK

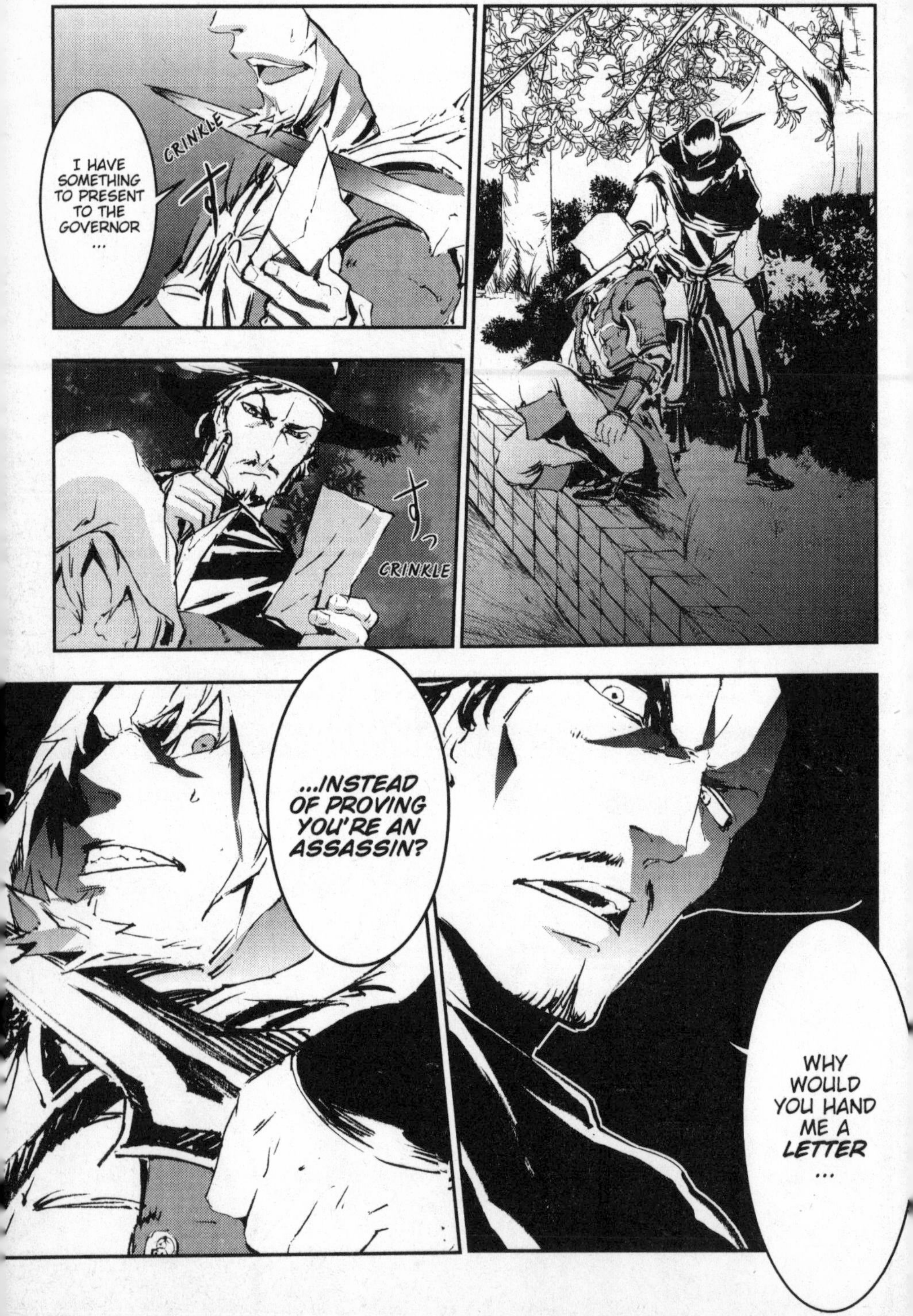
I HAVE SOMETHING TO PRESENT TO THE GOVERNOR ...
CRINKLE
す
すっ
CRINKLE
WHY WOULD YOU HAND ME A LETTER ...
...INSTEAD OF PROVING YOU'RE AN ASSASSIN?

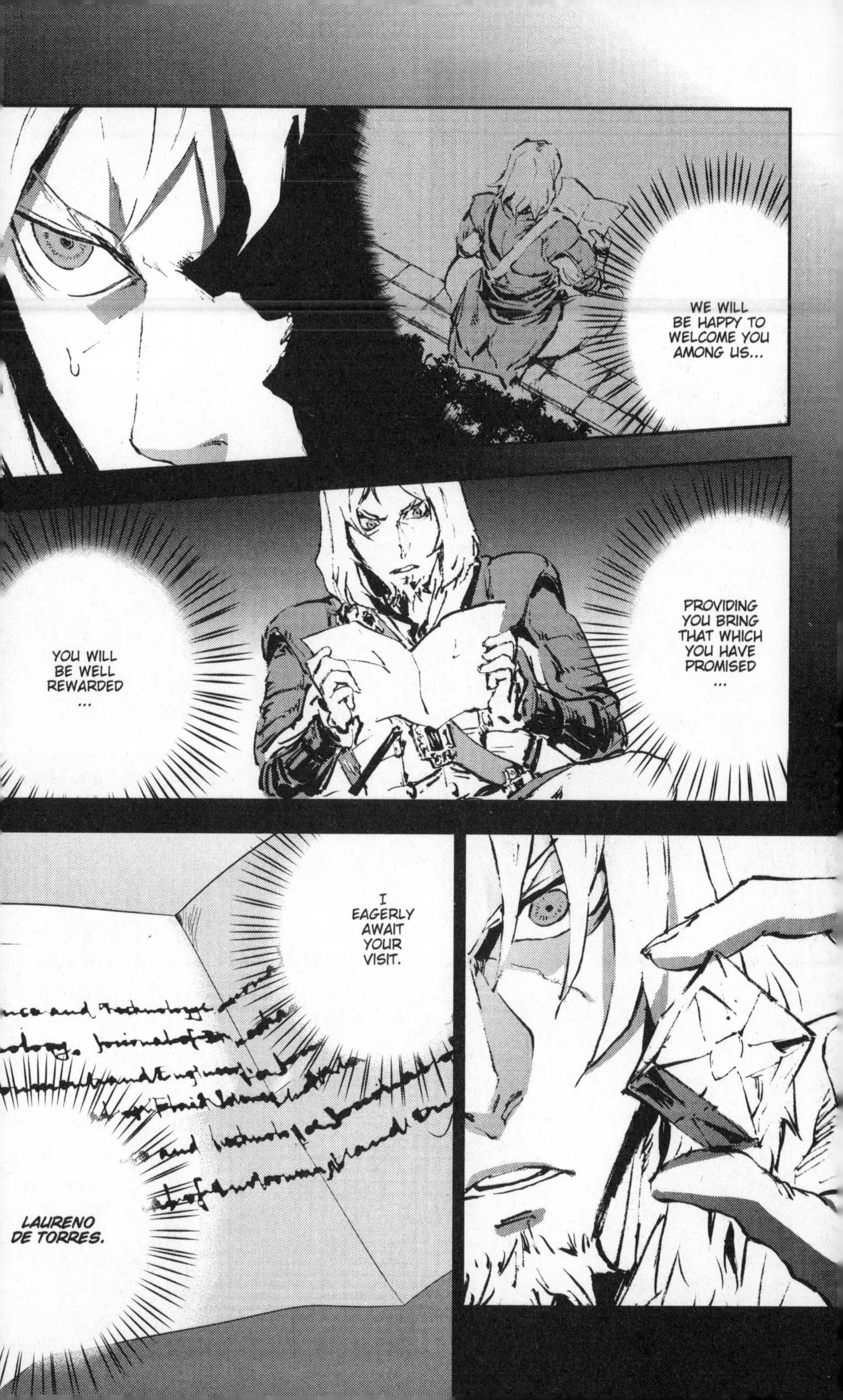
WE WILL BE HAPPY TO WELCOME YOU AMONG US...
PROVIDING YOU BRING THAT WHICH YOU HAVE PROMISED ...
YOU WILL BE WELL REWARDED ...
I EAGERLY AWAIT YOUR VISIT.
LAURENO DE TORRES.

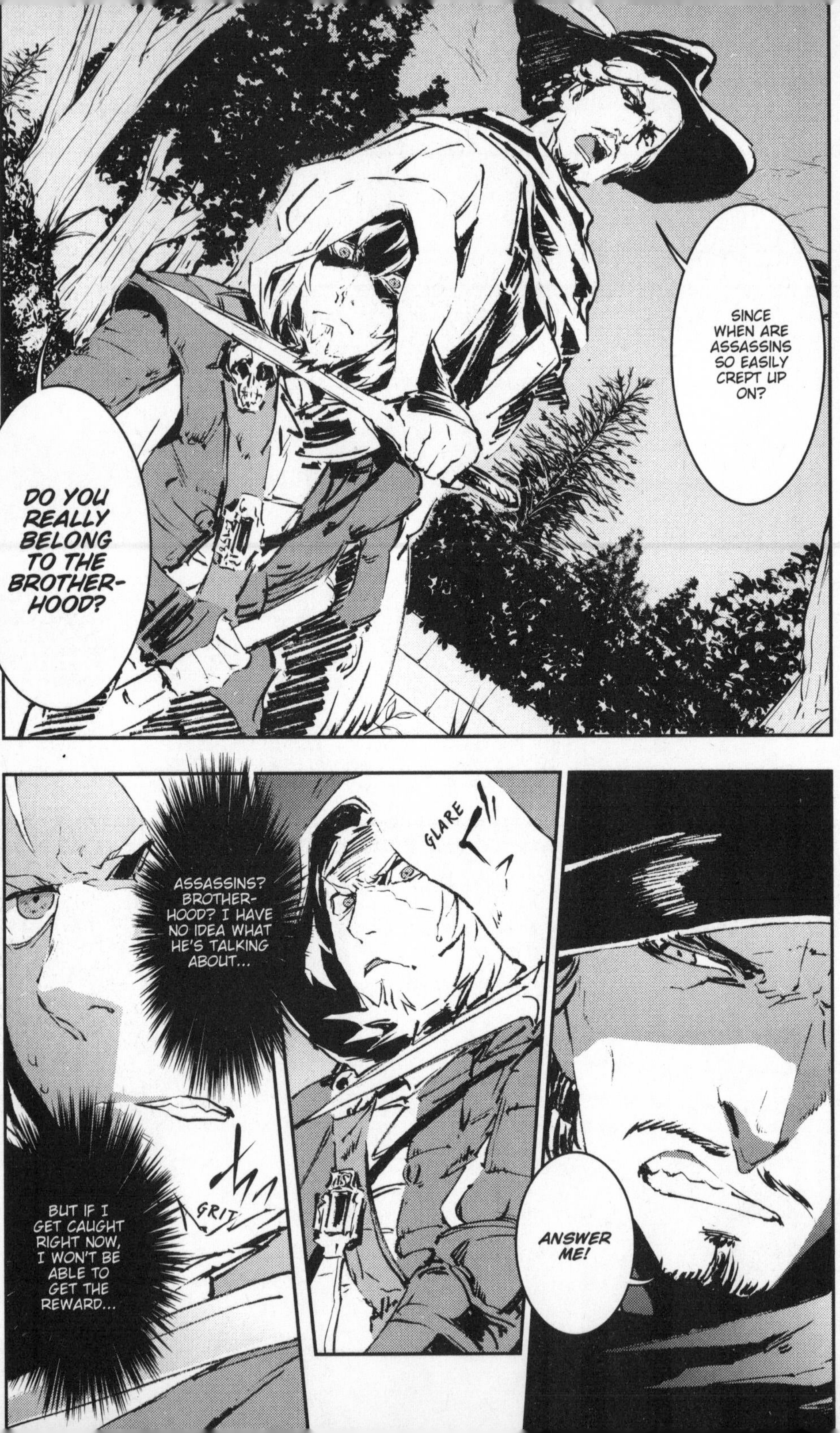
SINCE WHEN ARE ASSASSINS SO EASILY CREPT UP ON?
DO YOU REALLY BELONG TO THE BROTHER-HOOD?
ANSWER ME!
GLARE
ASSASSINS? BROTHER-HOOD? I HAVE NO IDEA WHAT HE'S TALKING ABOUT...
GRIT
BUT IF I GET CAUGHT RIGHT NOW, I WON'T BE ABLE TO GET THE REWARD...

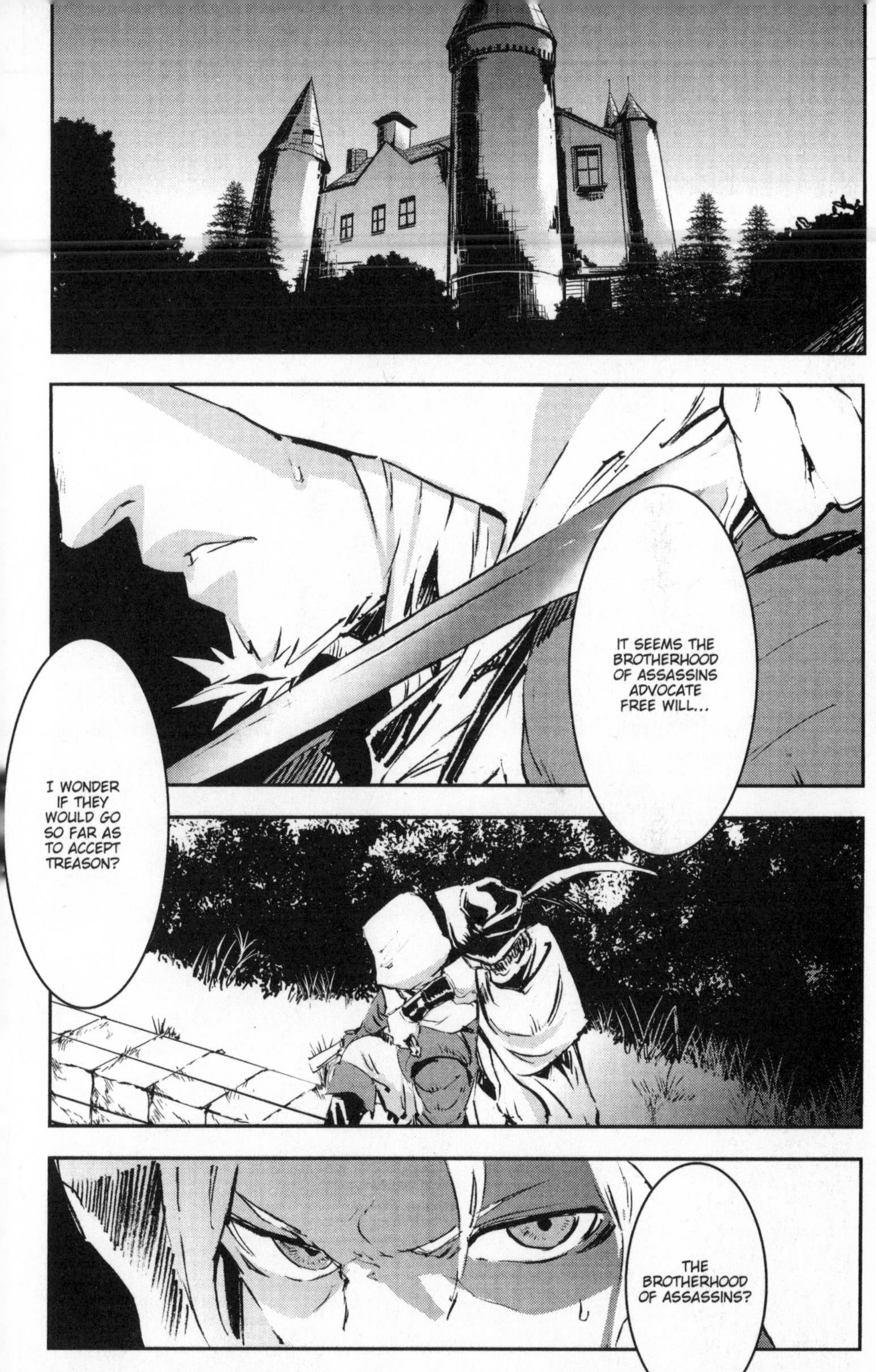
IT SEEMS THE BROTHERHOOD OF ASSASSINS ADVOCATE FREE WILL...
I WONDER IF THEY WOULD GO SO FAR AS TO ACCEPT TREASON?
THE BROTHERHOOD OF ASSASSINS?

CHAPTER III

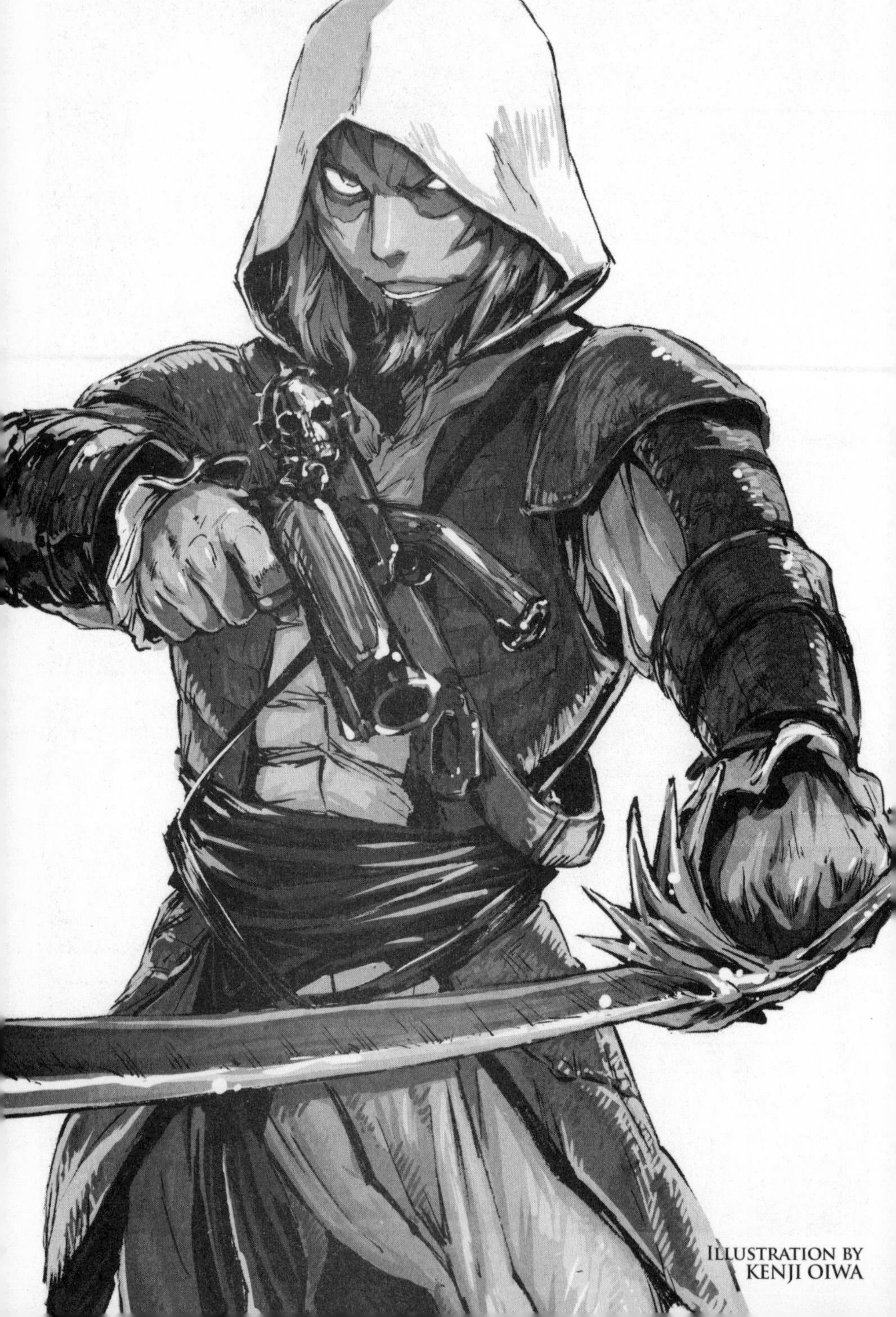

ILLUSTRATION BY
KENJI OIWA

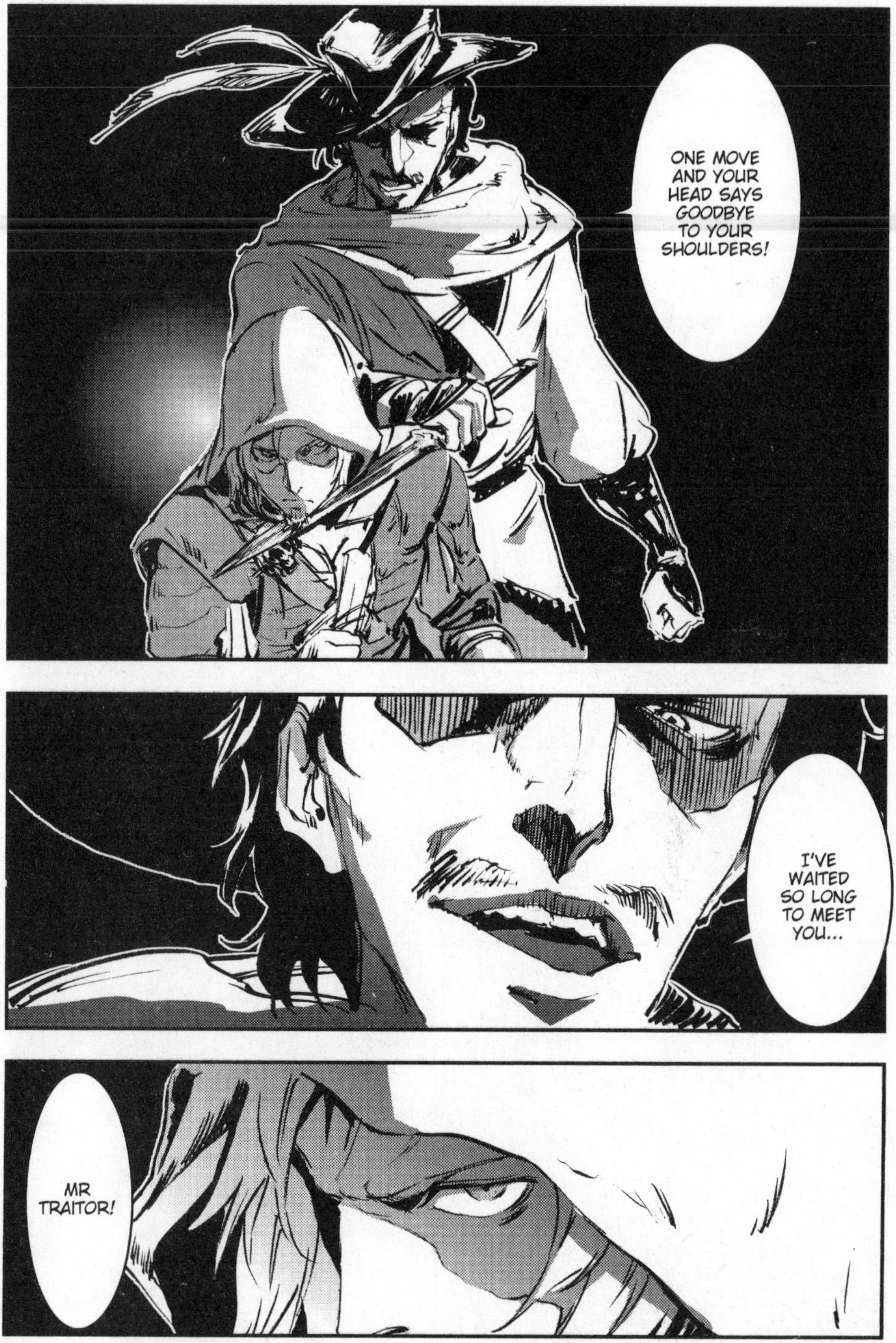
ONE MOVE AND YOUR HEAD SAYS GOODBYE TO YOUR SHOULDERS!
I'VE WAITED SO LONG TO MEET YOU...
MR TRAITOR!

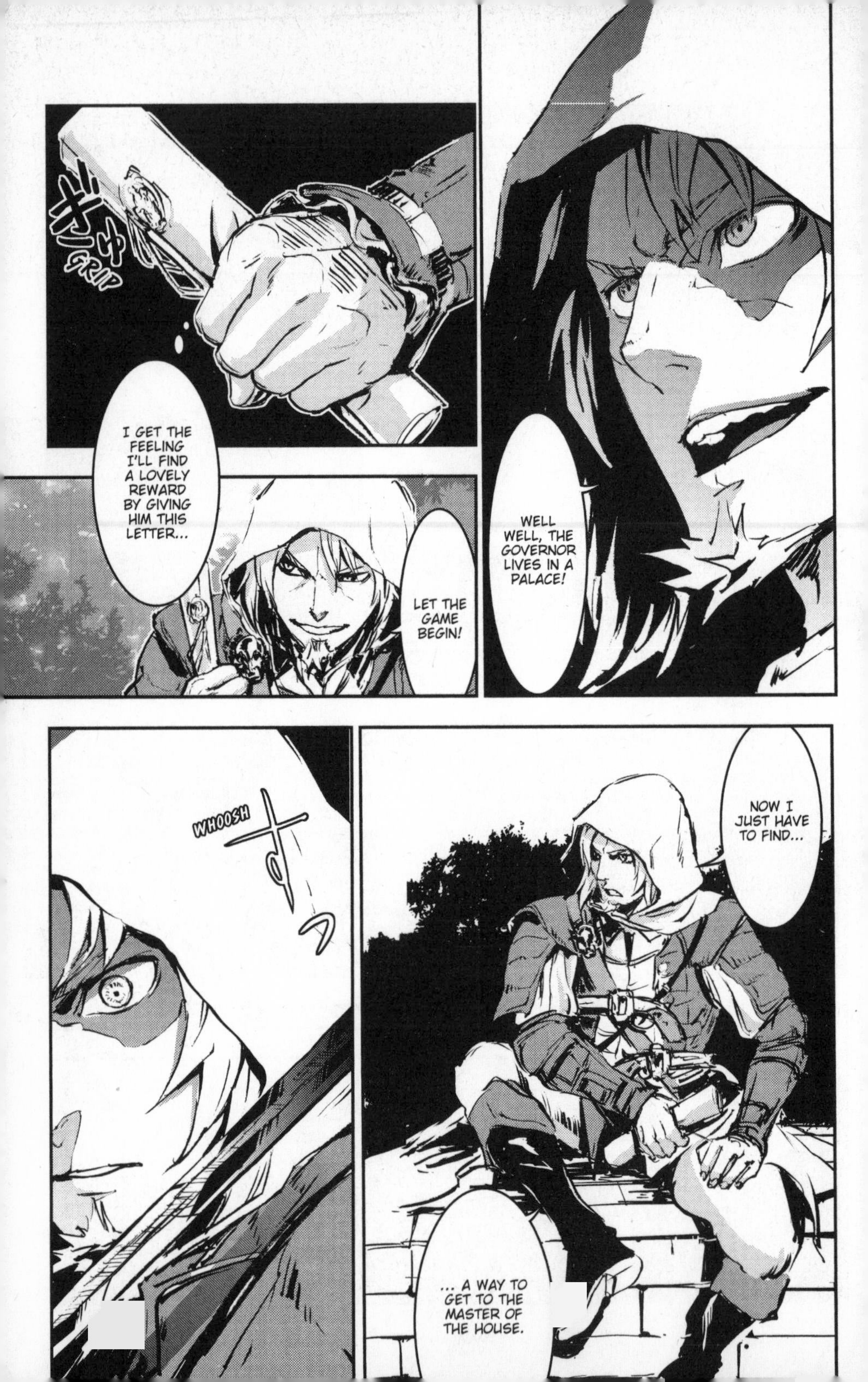
WELL WELL, THE GOVERNOR LIVES IN A PALACE!
GRIP
I GET THE FEELING I'LL FIND A LOVELY REWARD BY GIVING HIM THIS LETTER...
LET THE GAME BEGIN!
NOW I JUST HAVE TO FIND...
... A WAY TO GET TO THE MASTER OF THE HOUSE.
WHOOSH

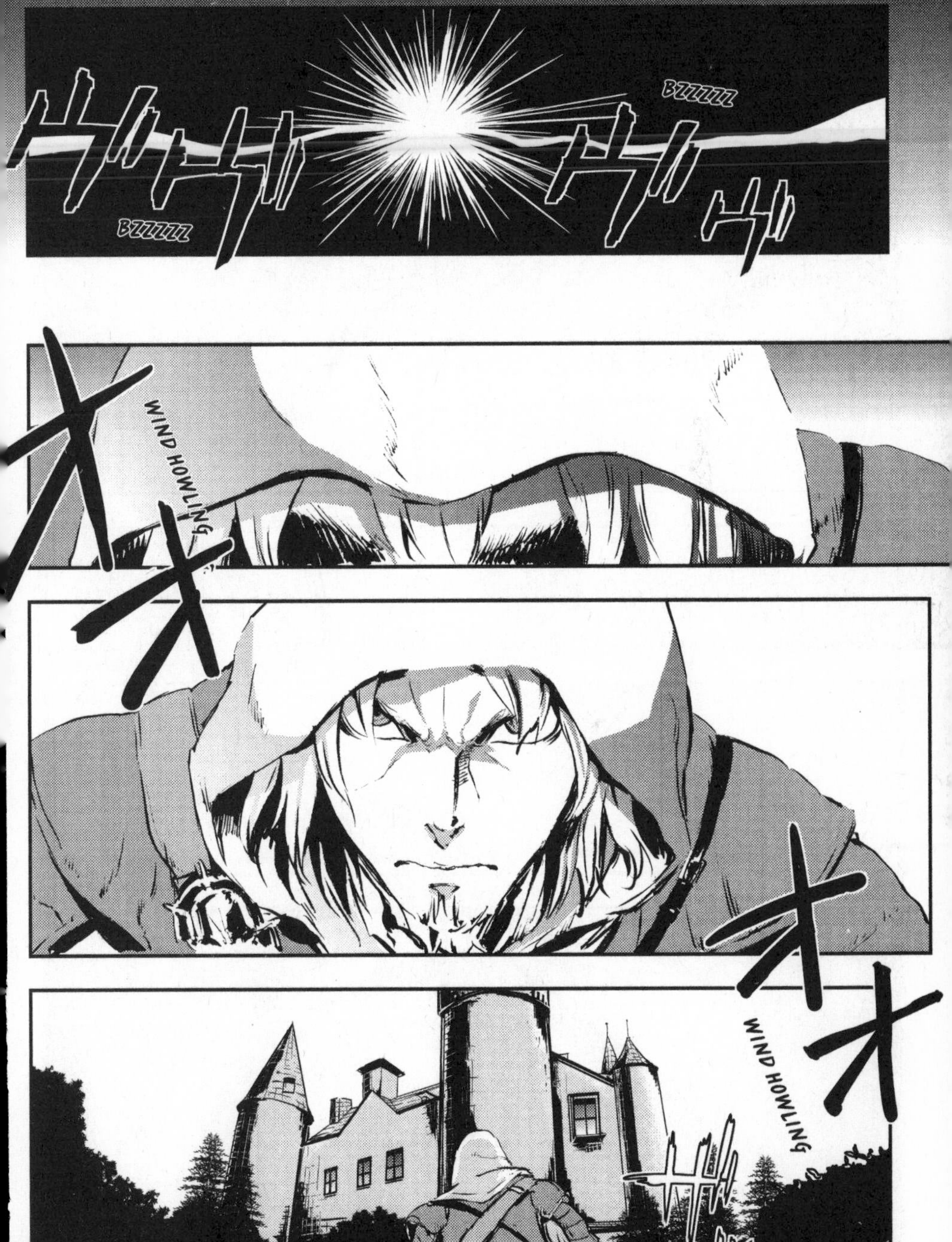
BZZZZZZ
BZZZZZZ
WIND HOWLING
WIND HOWLING
RUSTLING

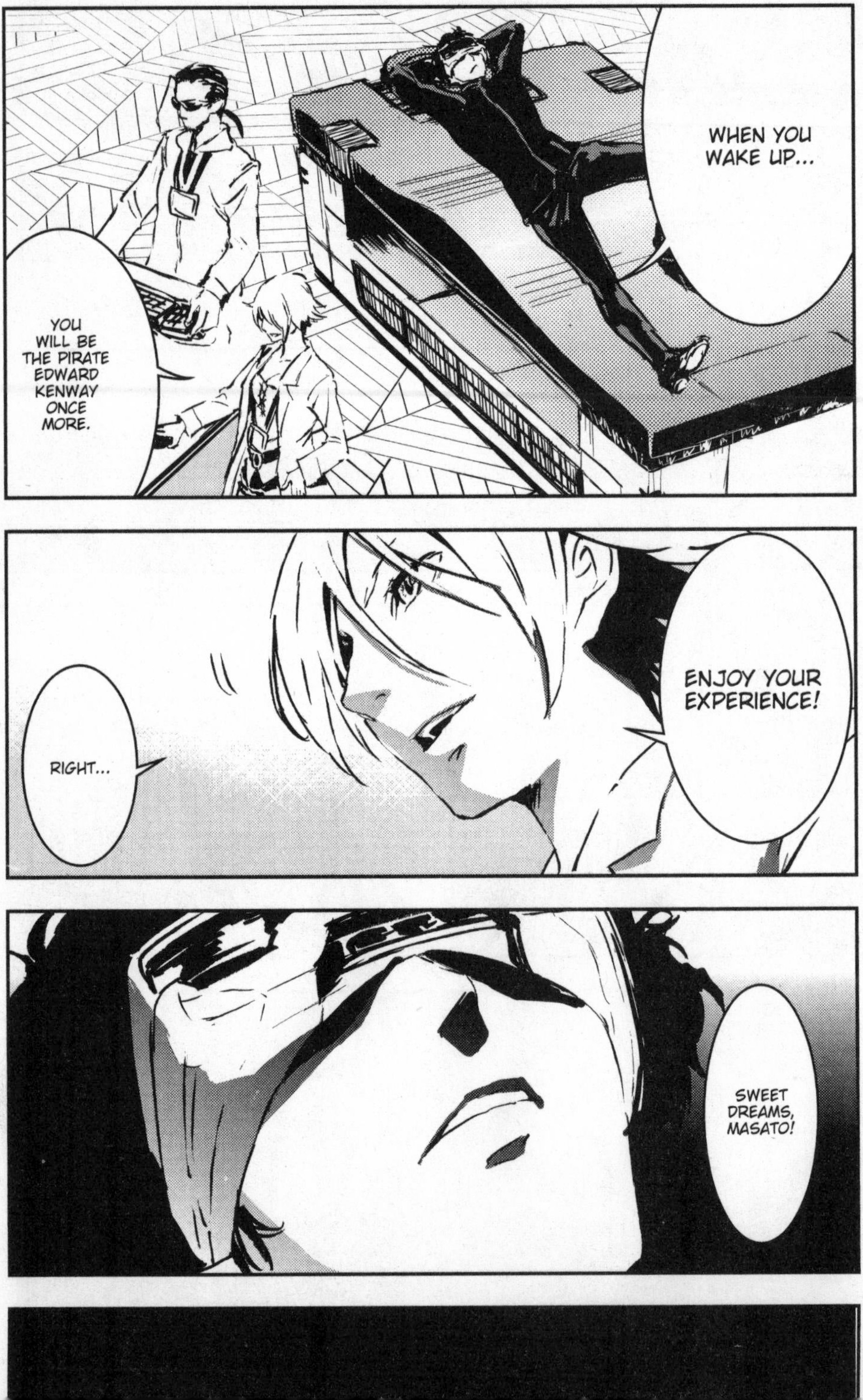
WHEN YOU WAKE UP...
YOU WILL BE THE PIRATE EDWARD KENWAY ONCE MORE.
ENJOY YOUR EXPERIENCE!
RIGHT...
SWEET DREAMS, MASATO!

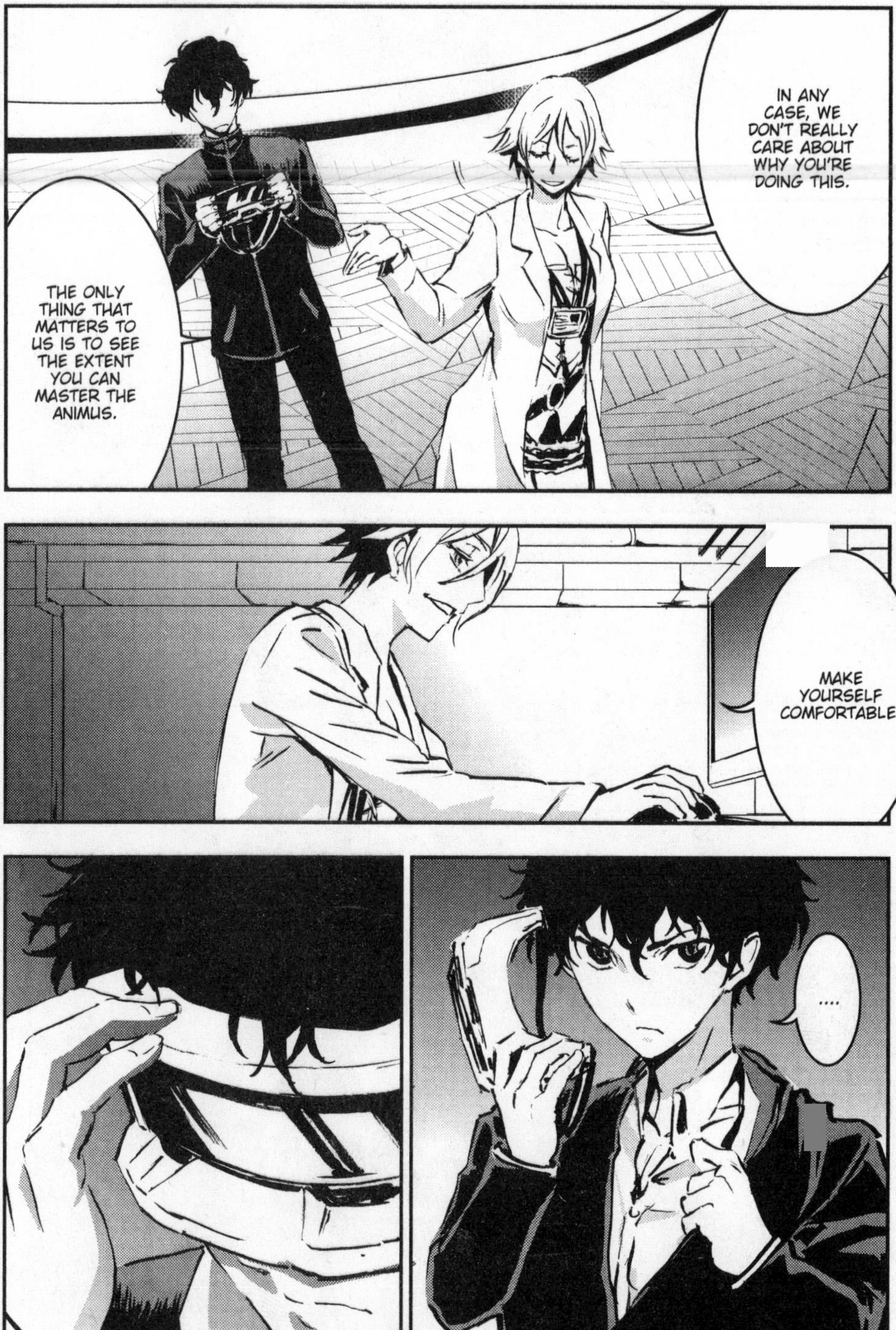
IN ANY CASE, WE DON'T REALLY CARE ABOUT WHY YOU'RE DOING THIS.
THE ONLY THING THAT MATTERS TO US IS TO SEE THE EXTENT YOU CAN MASTER THE ANIMUS.
MAKE YOURSELF COMFORTABLE.
....

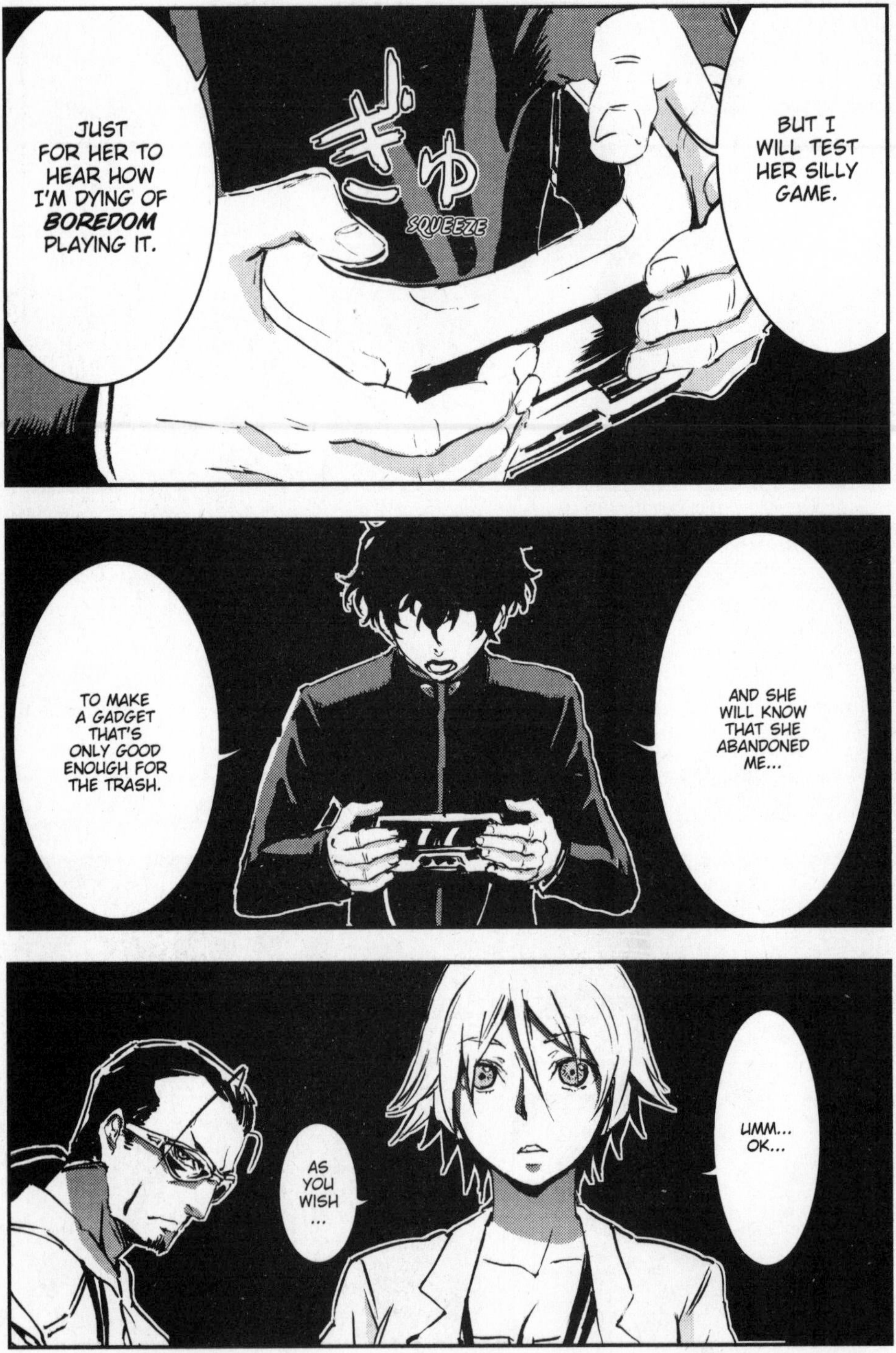
BUT I WILL TEST HER SILLY GAME.
ぎゅ
SQUEEZE
JUST FOR HER TO HEAR HOW I'M DYING OF **BOREDOM** PLAYING IT.
AND SHE WILL KNOW THAT SHE ABANDONED ME...
TO MAKE A GADGET THAT'S ONLY GOOD ENOUGH FOR THE TRASH.
UMM... OK...
AS YOU WISH ...

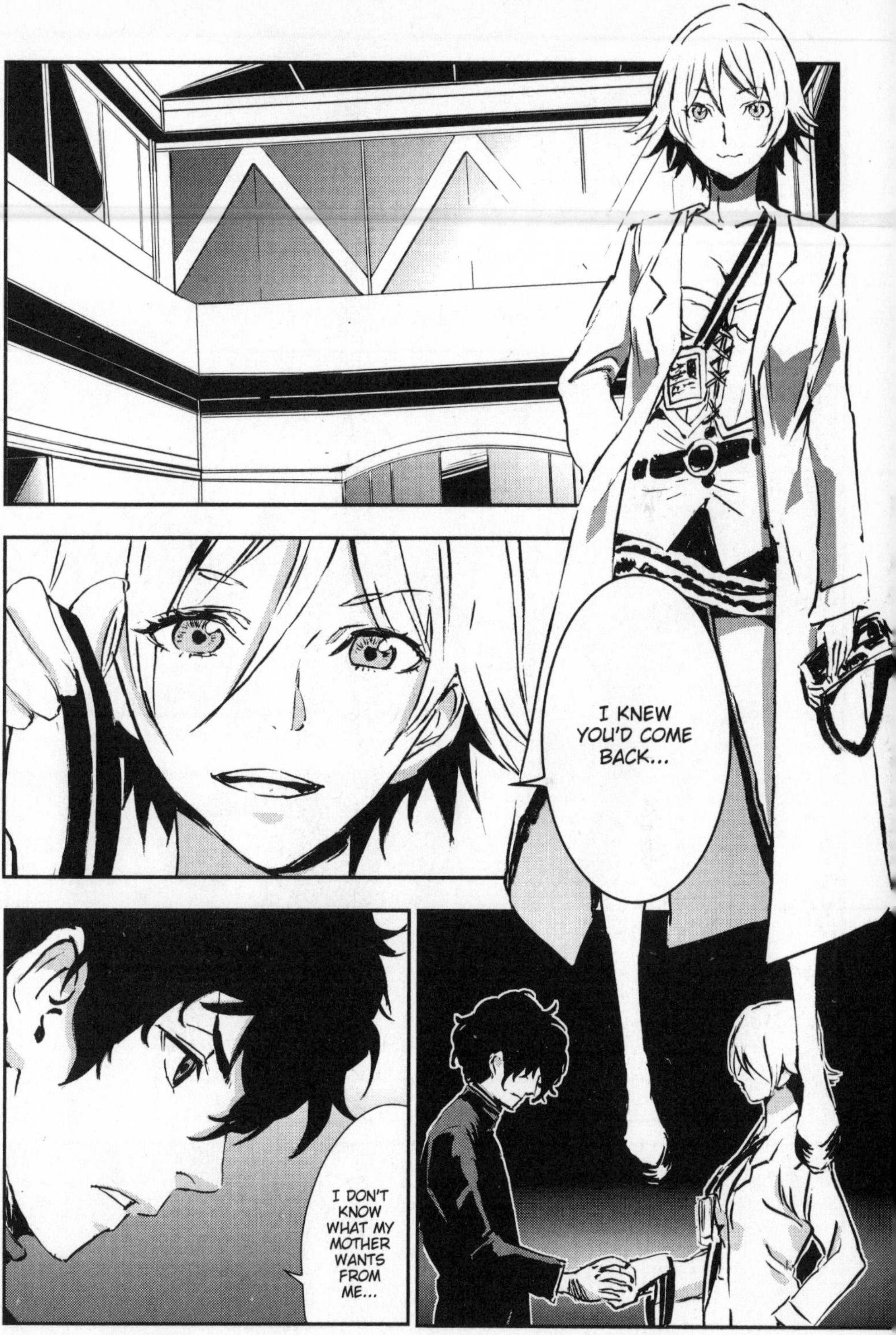
I KNEW YOU'D COME BACK...
I DON'T KNOW WHAT MY MOTHER WANTS FROM ME...

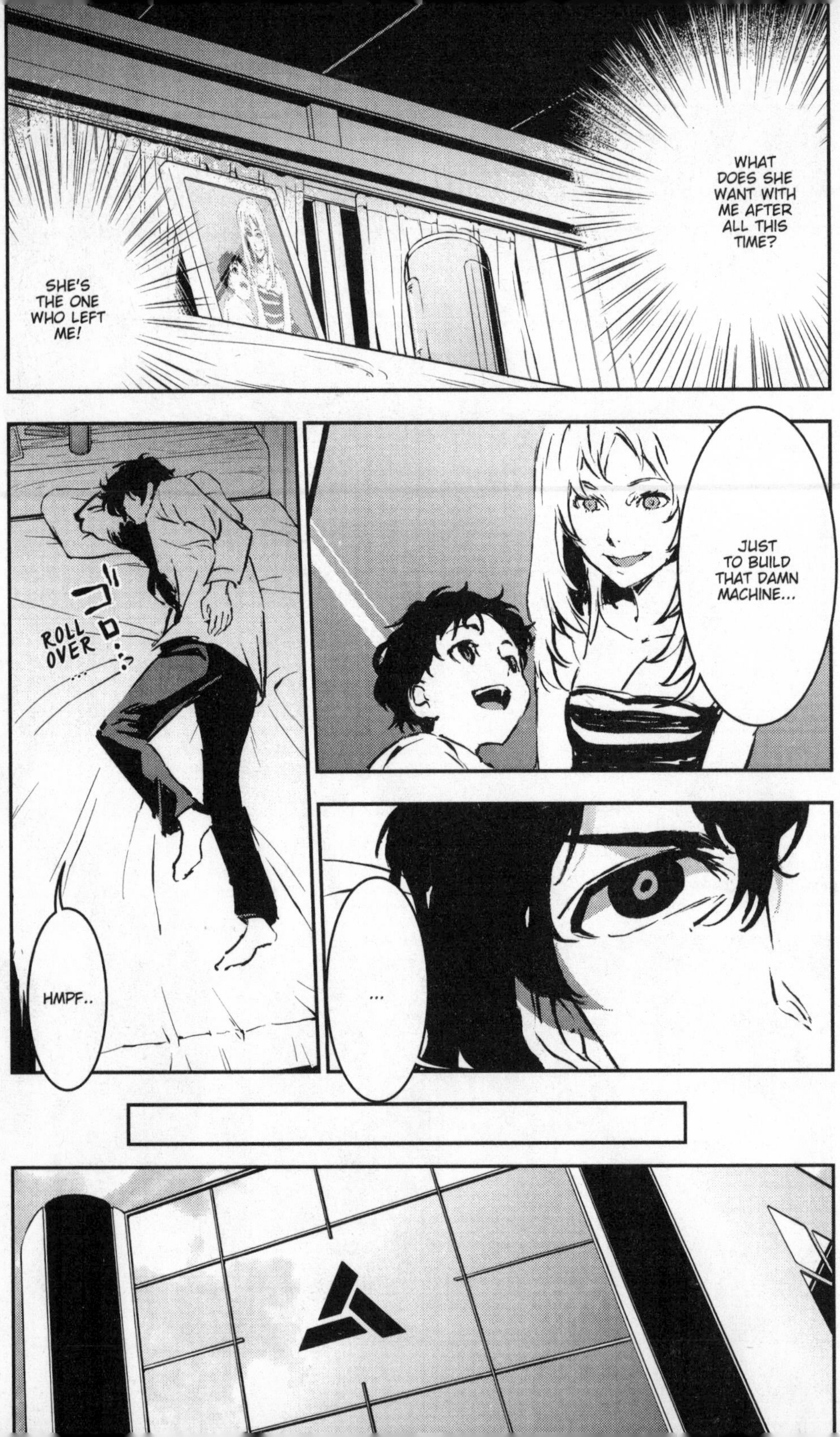
WHAT DOES SHE WANT WITH ME AFTER ALL THIS TIME?
SHE'S THE ONE WHO LEFT ME!
JUST TO BUILD THAT DAMN MACHINE...
...
ゴロ...
ROLL OVER
HMPF..

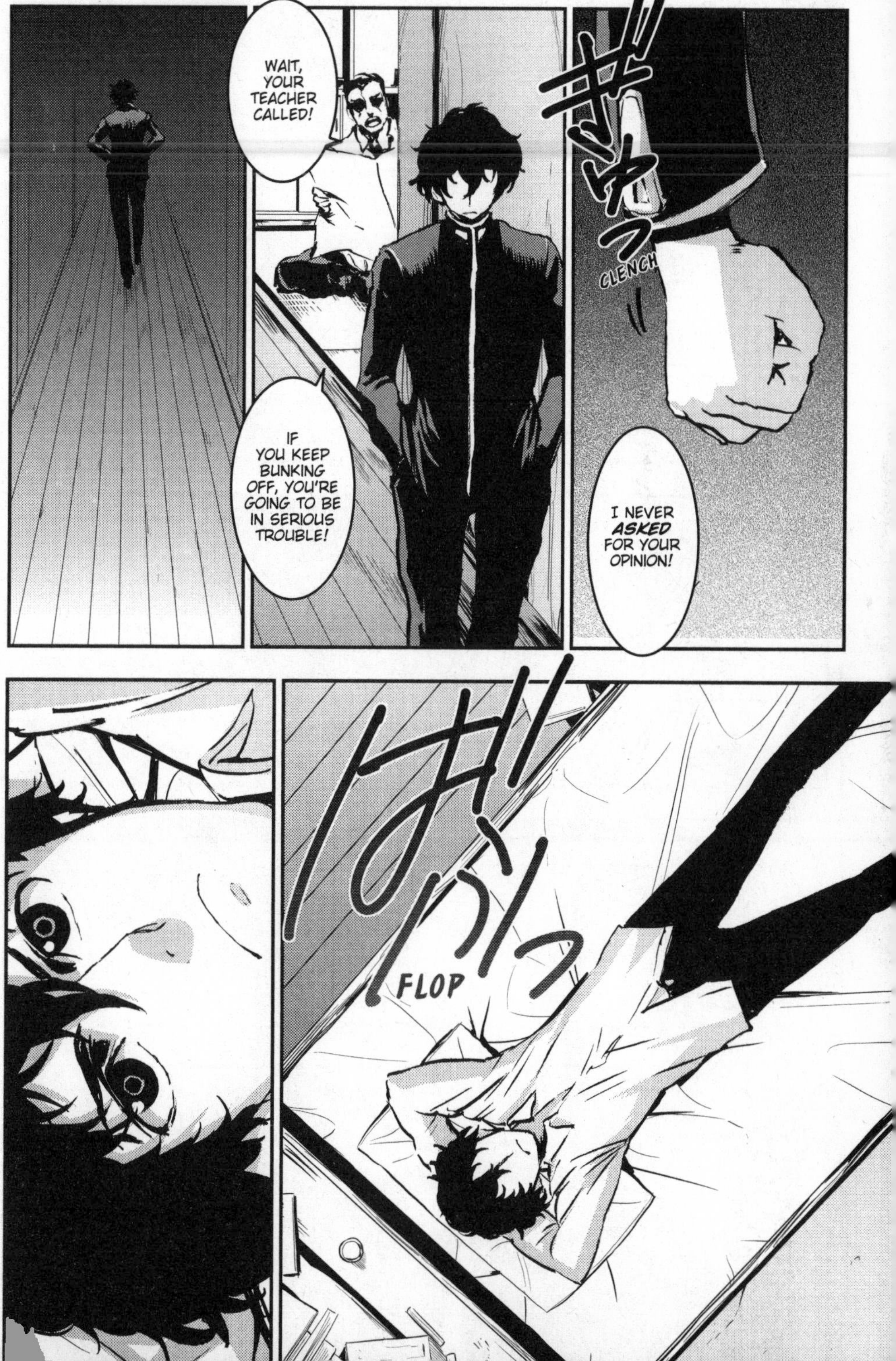
ぎゅっ
CLENCH
I NEVER ASKED FOR YOUR OPINION!
WAIT, YOUR TEACHER CALLED!
IF YOU KEEP BUNKING OFF, YOU'RE GOING TO BE IN SERIOUS TROUBLE!
ばふっ
FLOP

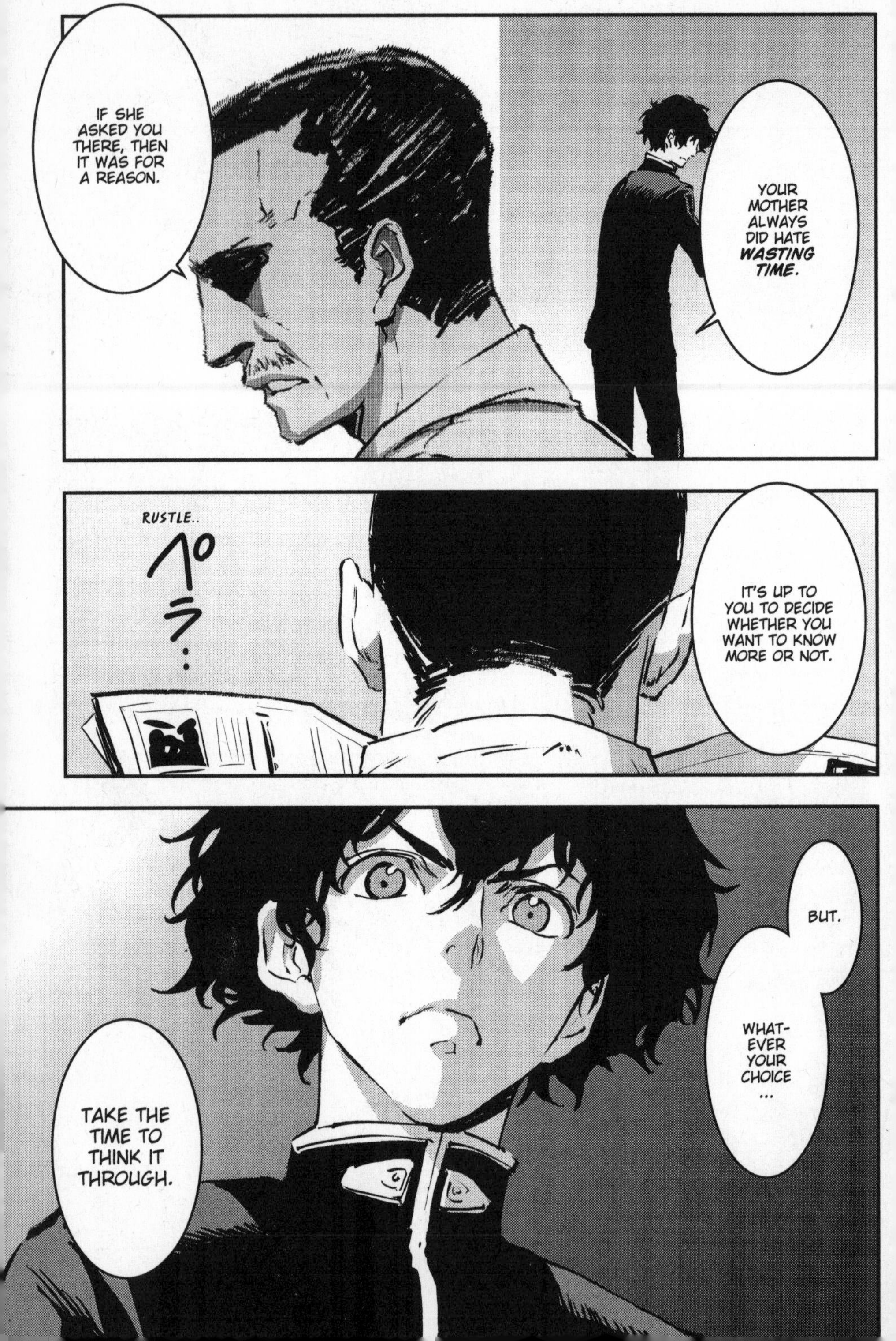
YOUR MOTHER ALWAYS DID HATE ***WASTING TIME.***
IF SHE ASKED YOU THERE, THEN IT WAS FOR A REASON.
IT'S UP TO YOU TO DECIDE WHETHER YOU WANT TO KNOW MORE OR NOT.
RUSTLE..
ペラ..
BUT.
WHAT-EVER YOUR CHOICE ...
TAKE THE TIME TO THINK IT THROUGH.

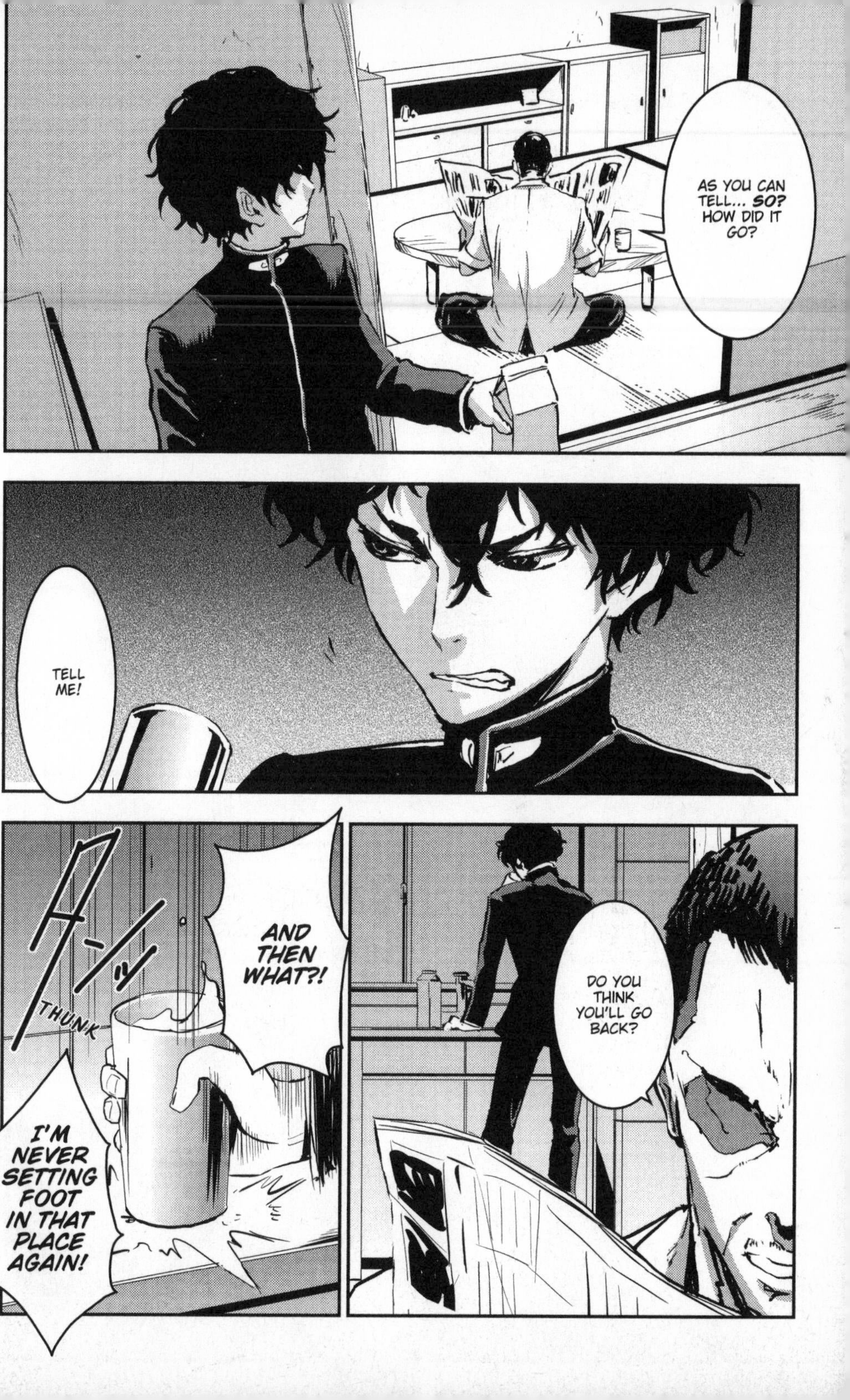
AS YOU CAN TELL... SO? HOW DID IT GO?
TELL ME!
DO YOU THINK YOU'LL GO BACK?
AND THEN WHAT?!
THUNK
I'M NEVER SETTING FOOT IN THAT PLACE AGAIN!

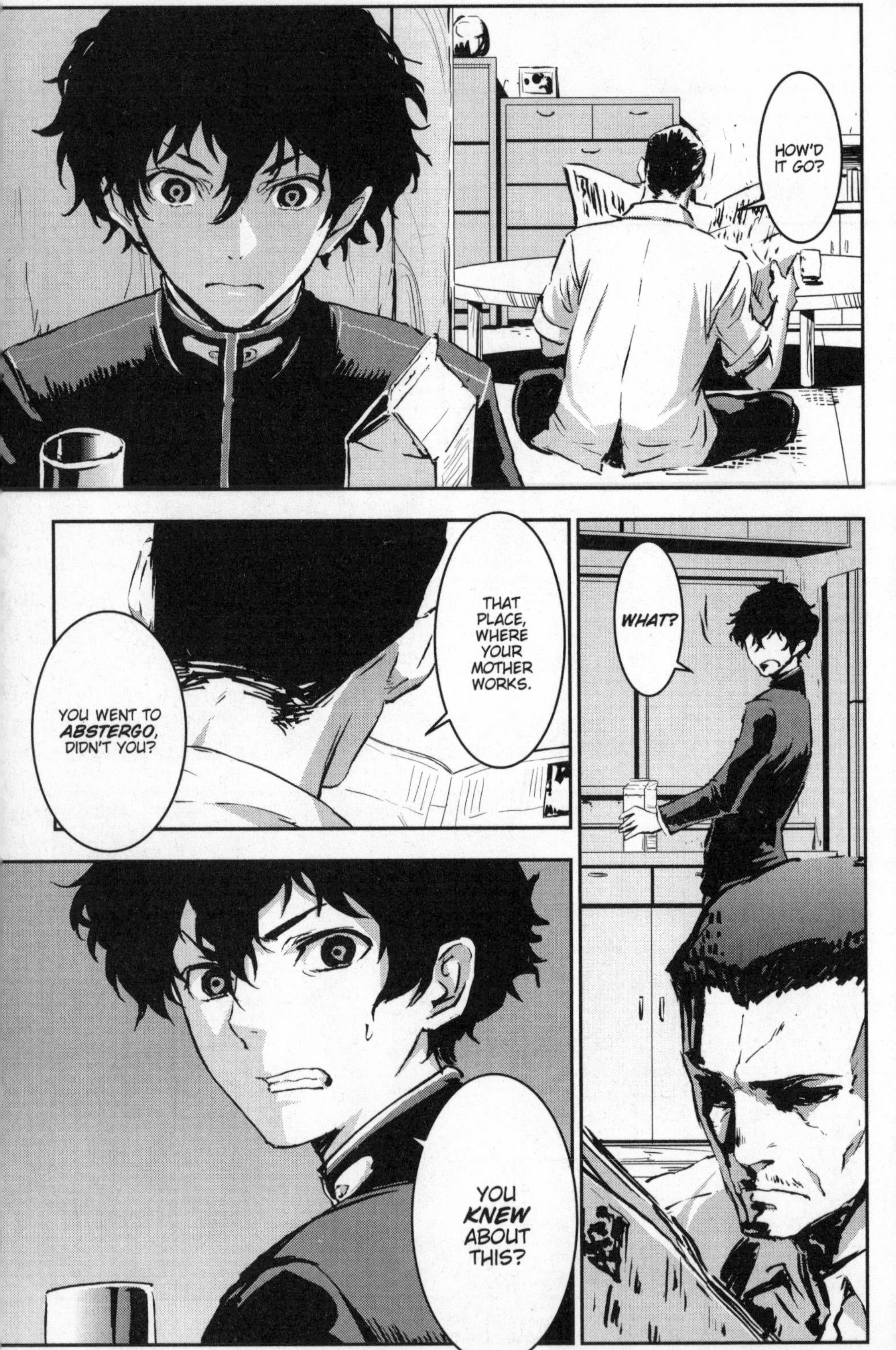
HOW'D IT GO?
WHAT?
THAT PLACE, WHERE YOUR MOTHER WORKS.
YOU WENT TO **ABSTERGO**, DIDN'T YOU?
YOU **KNEW** ABOUT THIS?

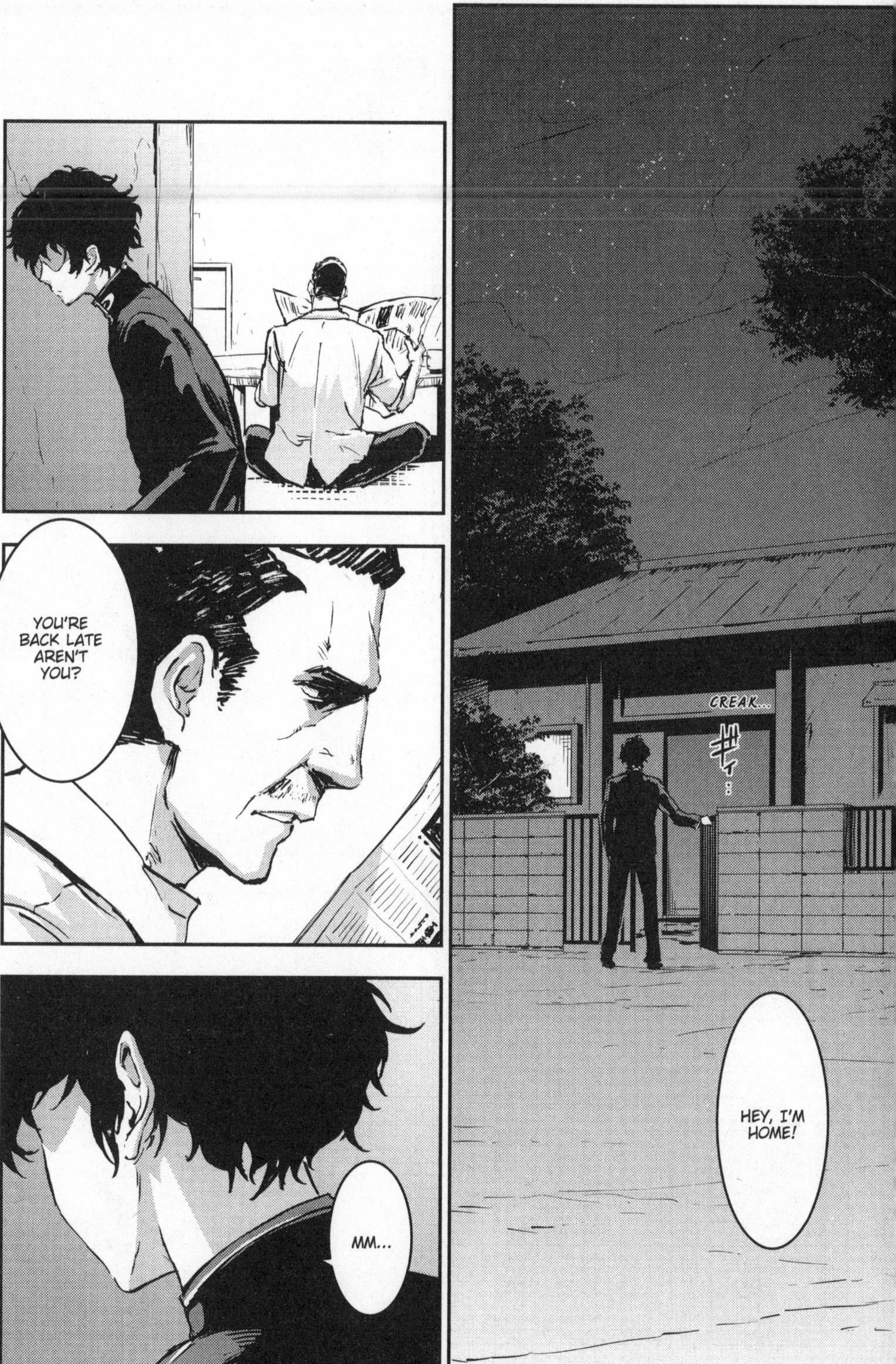
CREAK...
ギィ…
HEY, I'M HOME!
YOU'RE BACK LATE AREN'T YOU?
MM...

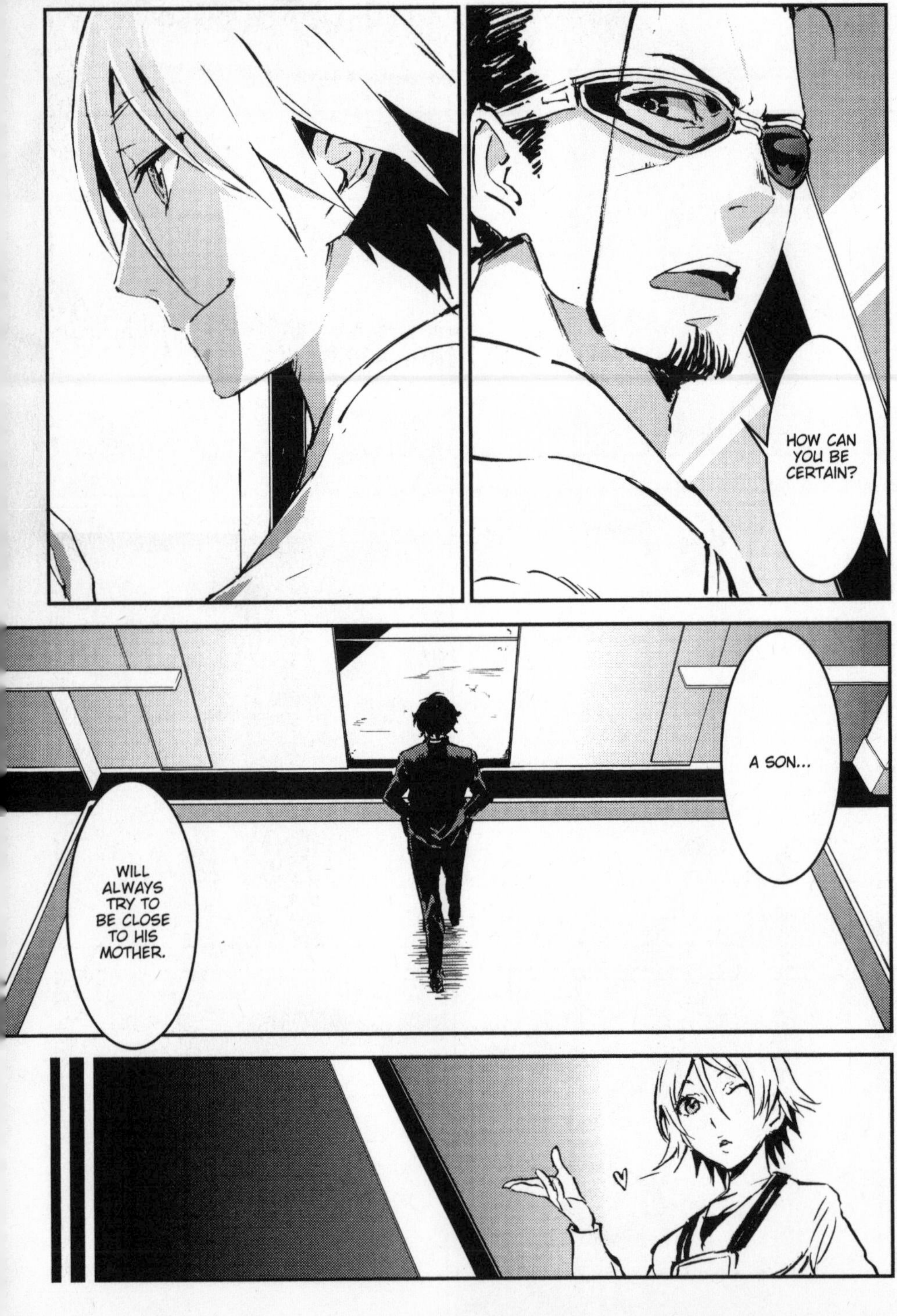
HOW CAN YOU BE CERTAIN?
A SON...
WILL ALWAYS TRY TO BE CLOSE TO HIS MOTHER.

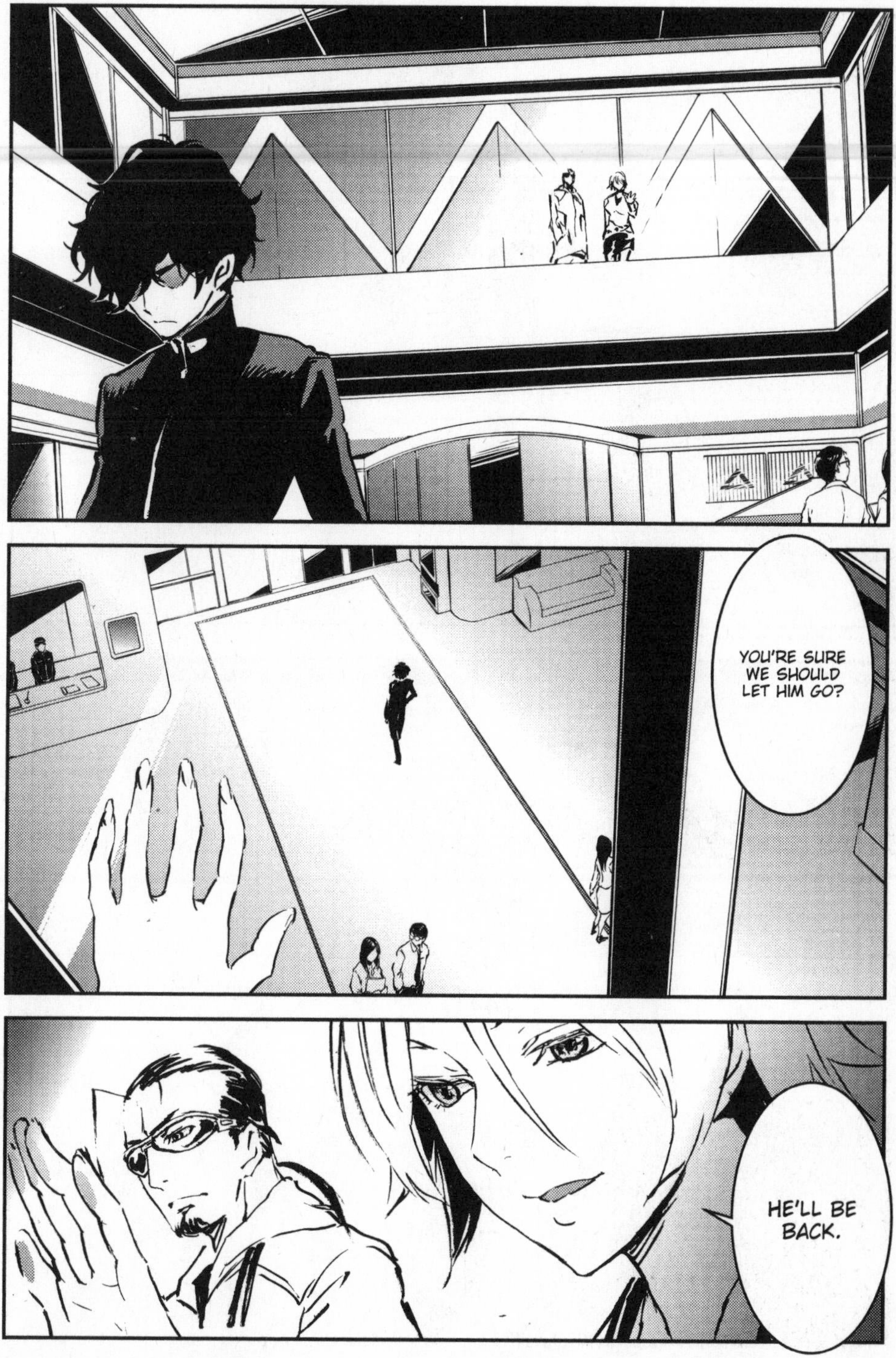
YOU'RE SURE WE SHOULD LET HIM GO?
HE'LL BE BACK.

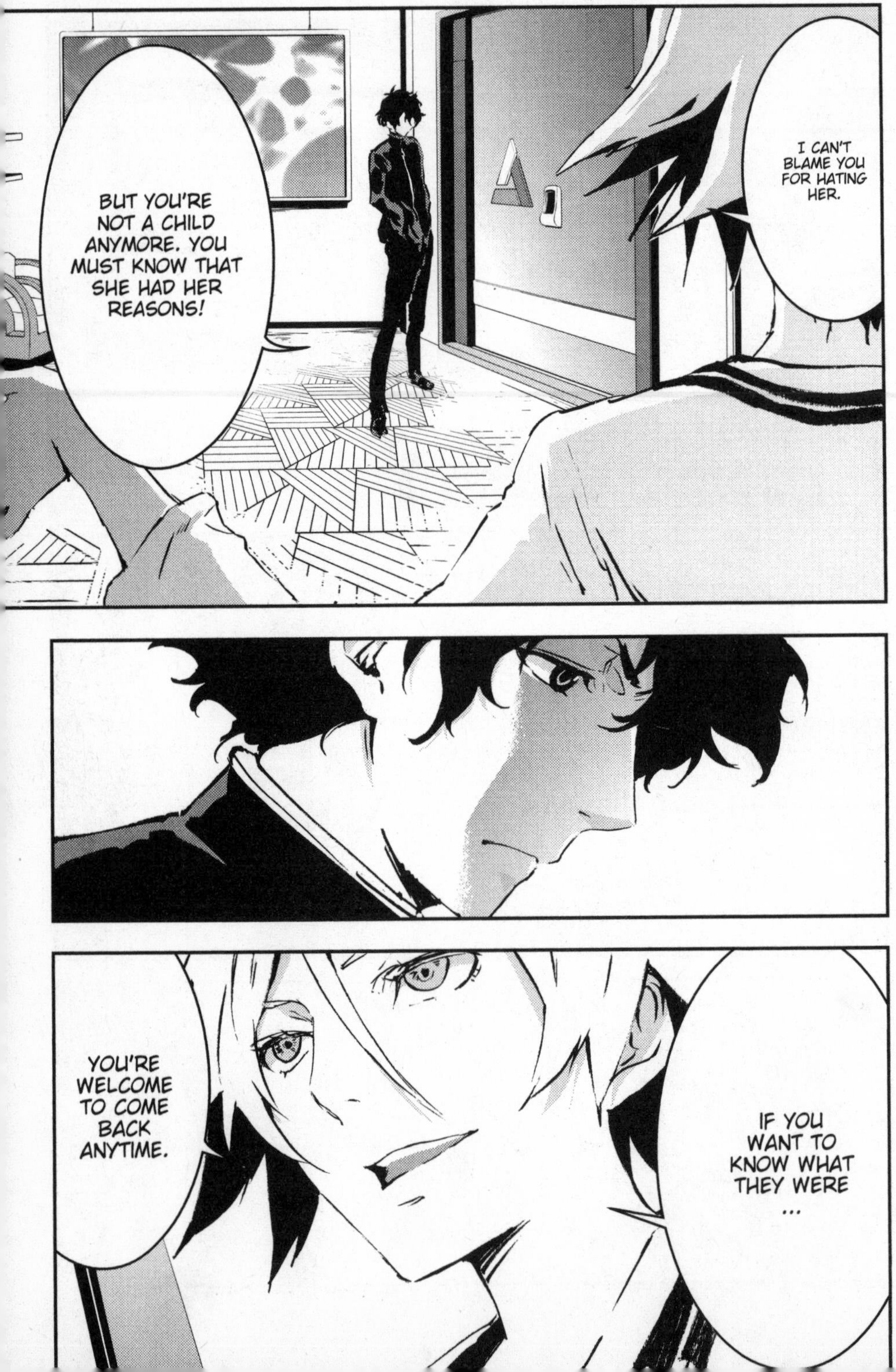
I CAN'T BLAME YOU FOR HATING HER.
BUT YOU'RE NOT A CHILD ANYMORE. YOU MUST KNOW THAT SHE HAD HER REASONS!
IF YOU WANT TO KNOW WHAT THEY WERE ...
YOU'RE WELCOME TO COME BACK ANYTIME.

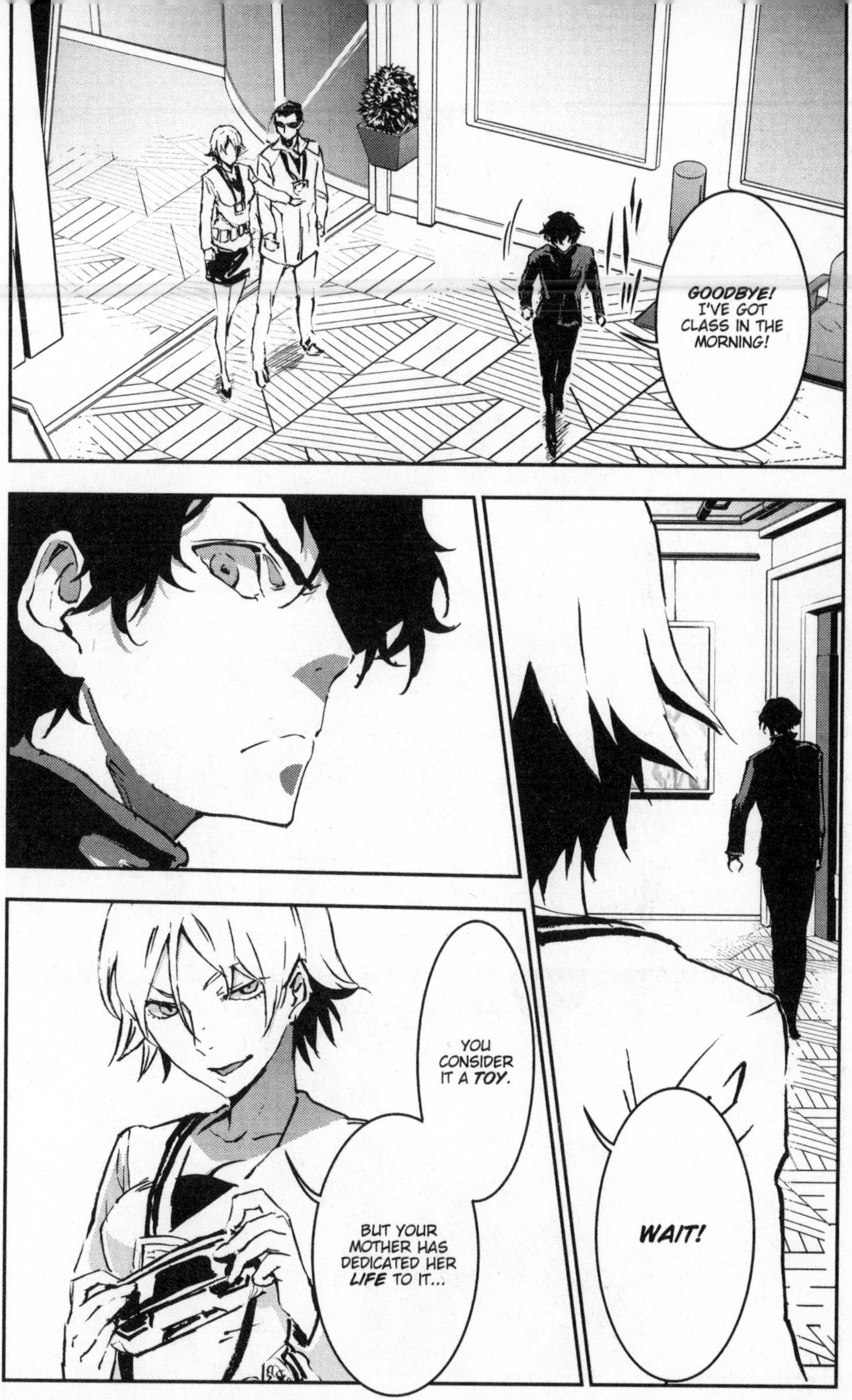
GOODBYE! I'VE GOT CLASS IN THE MORNING!
WAIT!
YOU CONSIDER IT A *TOY*.
BUT YOUR MOTHER HAS DEDICATED HER *LIFE* TO IT...

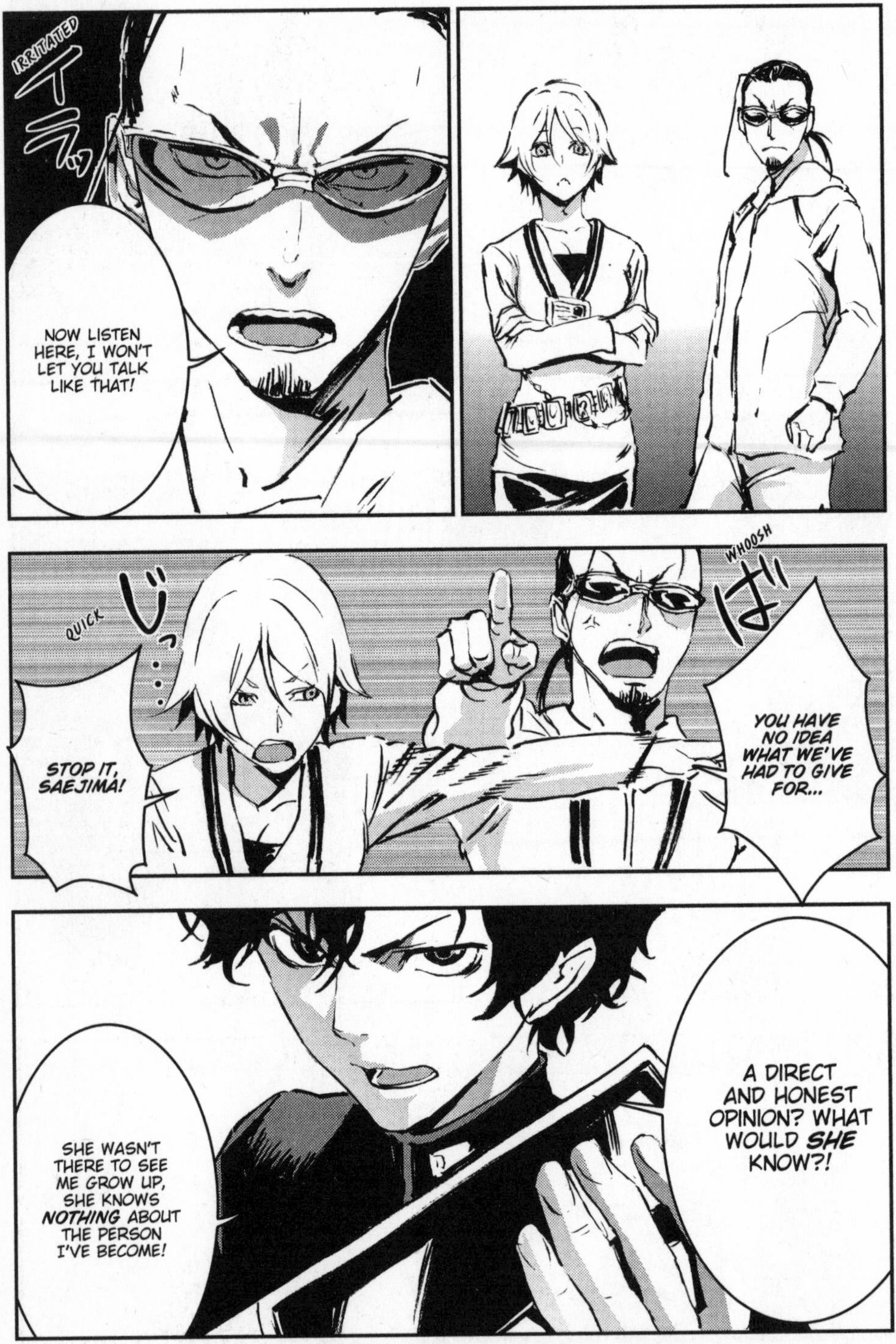
IRRITATED
NOW LISTEN HERE, I WON'T LET YOU TALK LIKE THAT!
WHOOSH
YOU HAVE NO IDEA WHAT WE'VE HAD TO GIVE FOR...
QUICK
STOP IT, SAEJIMA!
A DIRECT AND HONEST OPINION? WHAT WOULD *SHE* KNOW?!
SHE WASN'T THERE TO SEE ME GROW UP, SHE KNOWS *NOTHING* ABOUT THE PERSON I'VE BECOME!

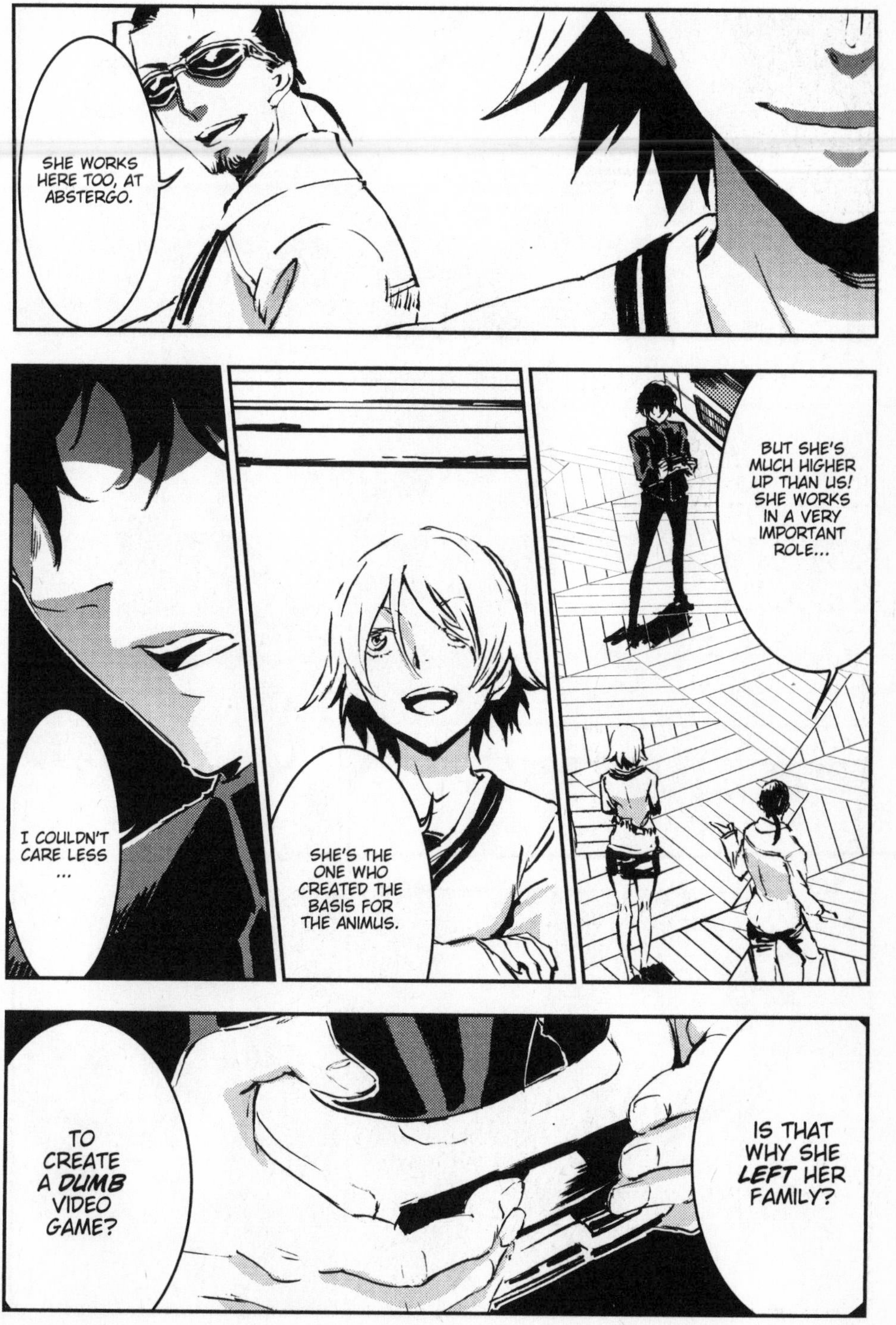
SHE WORKS HERE TOO, AT ABSTERGO.
BUT SHE'S MUCH HIGHER UP THAN US! SHE WORKS IN A VERY IMPORTANT ROLE...
SHE'S THE ONE WHO CREATED THE BASIS FOR THE ANIMUS.
I COULDN'T CARE LESS ...
IS THAT WHY SHE *LEFT* HER FAMILY?
TO CREATE A *DUMB* VIDEO GAME?

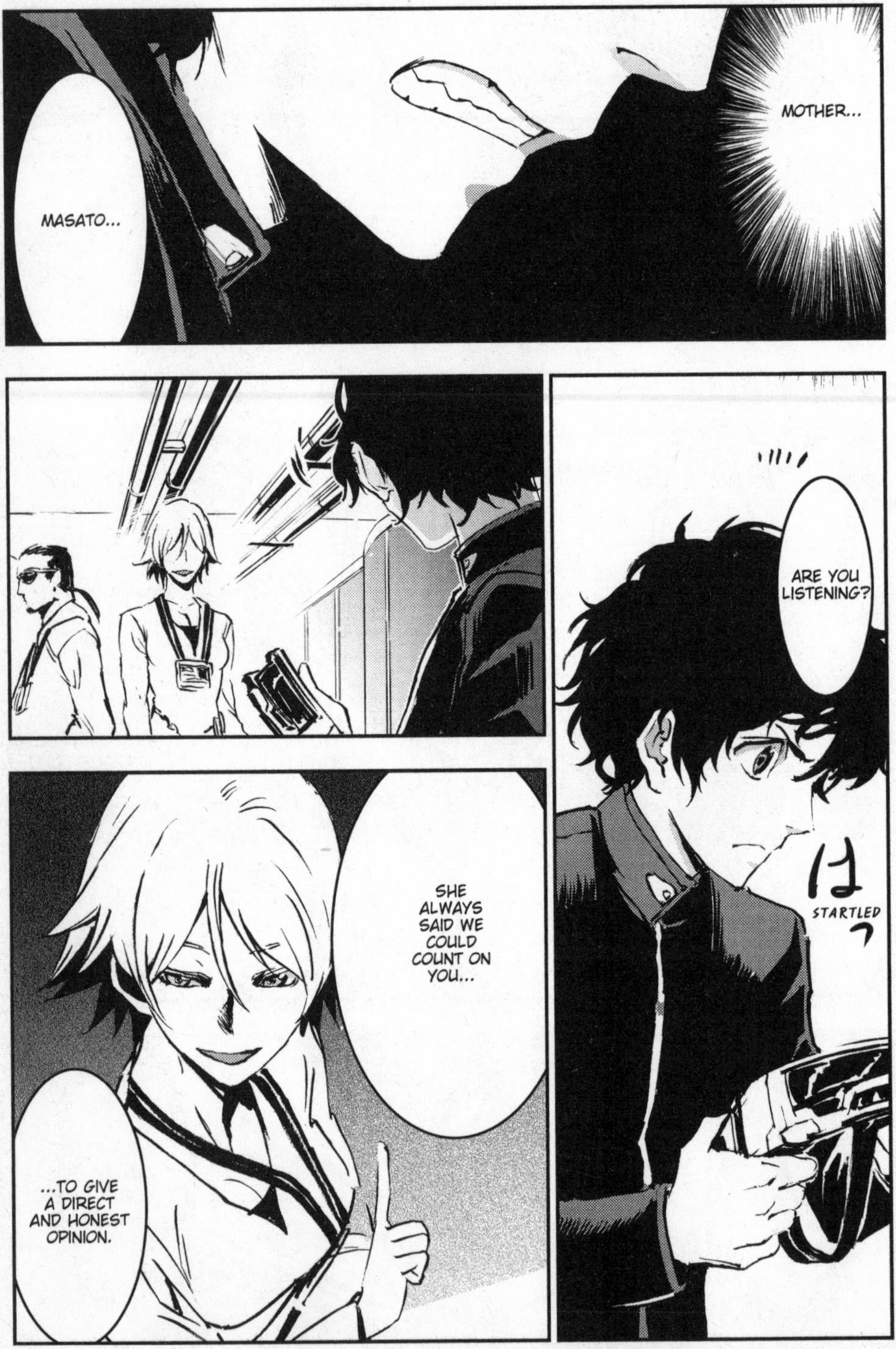
MOTHER...
MASATO...
ARE YOU LISTENING?
は
STARTLED
SHE ALWAYS SAID WE COULD COUNT ON YOU...
...TO GIVE A DIRECT AND HONEST OPINION.

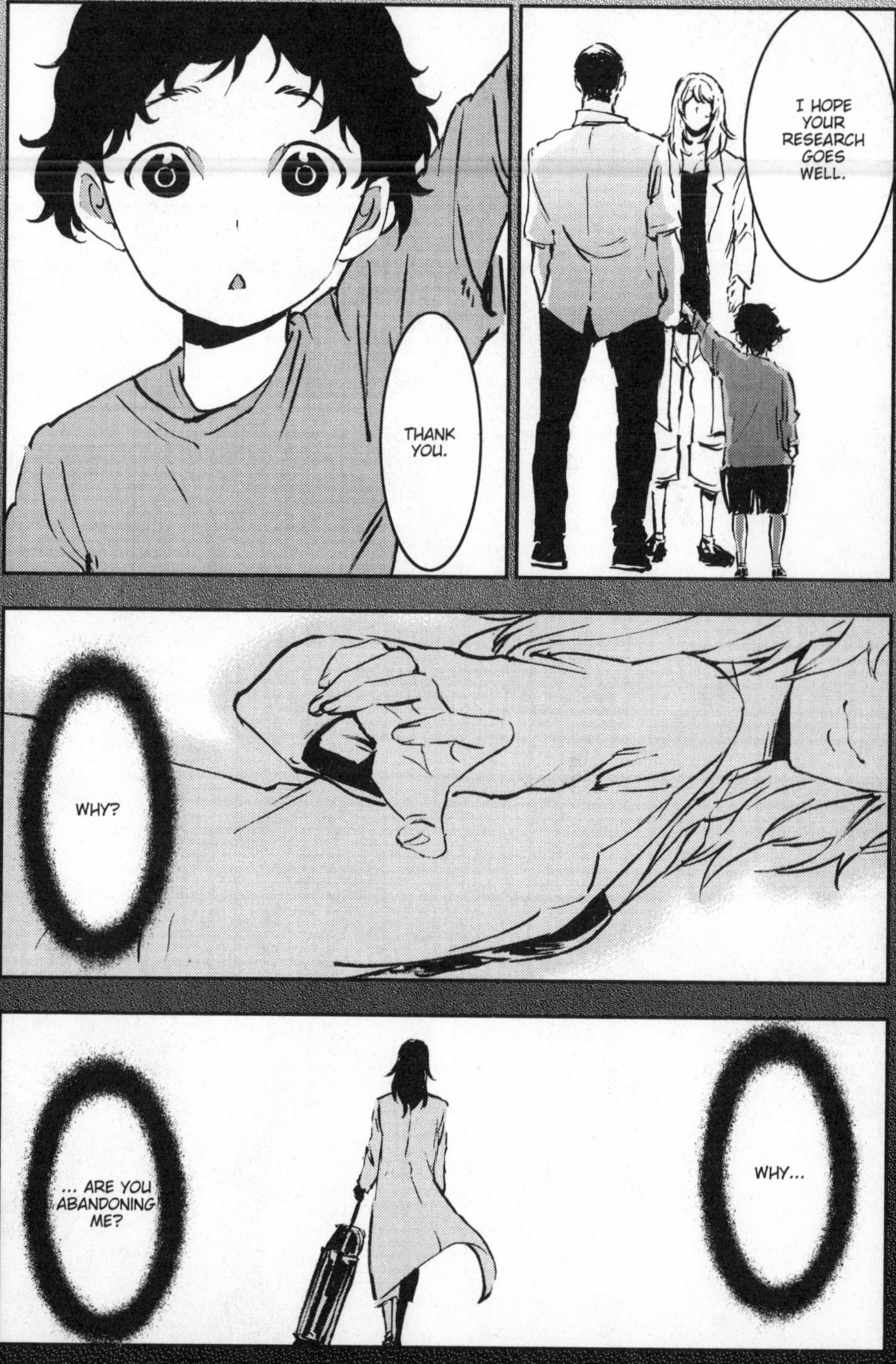
I HOPE YOUR RESEARCH GOES WELL.
THANK YOU.
WHY?
WHY...
... ARE YOU ABANDONING ME?

IT WAS YOUR *MOTHER* WHO RECOMMENDED YOU.

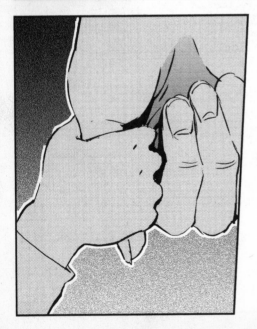

GOODBYE, MASATO!

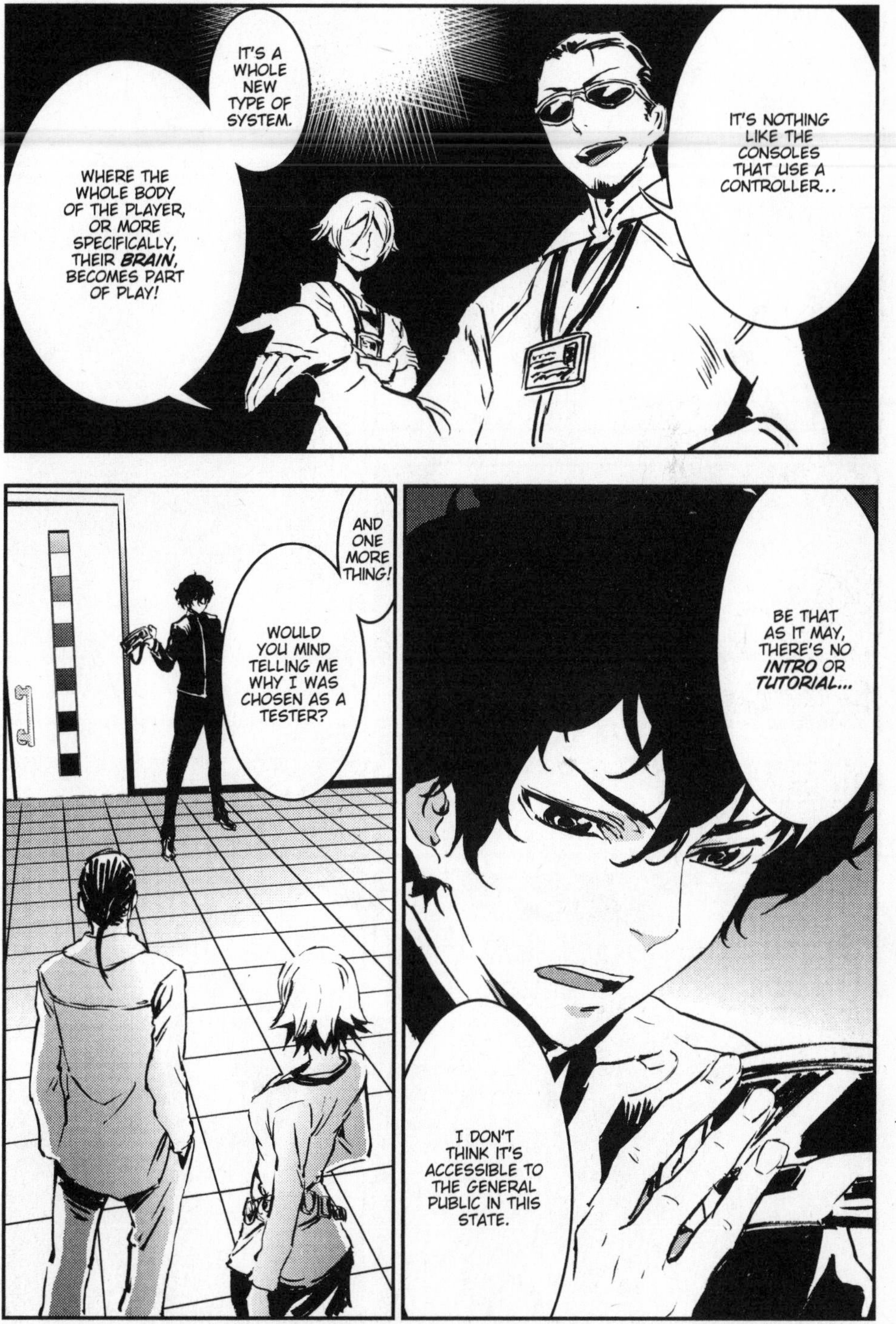
IT'S NOTHING LIKE THE CONSOLES THAT USE A CONTROLLER...
IT'S A WHOLE NEW TYPE OF SYSTEM.
WHERE THE WHOLE BODY OF THE PLAYER, OR MORE SPECIFICALLY, THEIR ***BRAIN***, BECOMES PART OF PLAY!
BE THAT AS IT MAY, THERE'S NO ***INTRO*** OR ***TUTORIAL...***
I DON'T THINK IT'S ACCESSIBLE TO THE GENERAL PUBLIC IN THIS STATE.
AND ONE MORE THING!
WOULD YOU MIND TELLING ME WHY I WAS CHOSEN AS A TESTER?

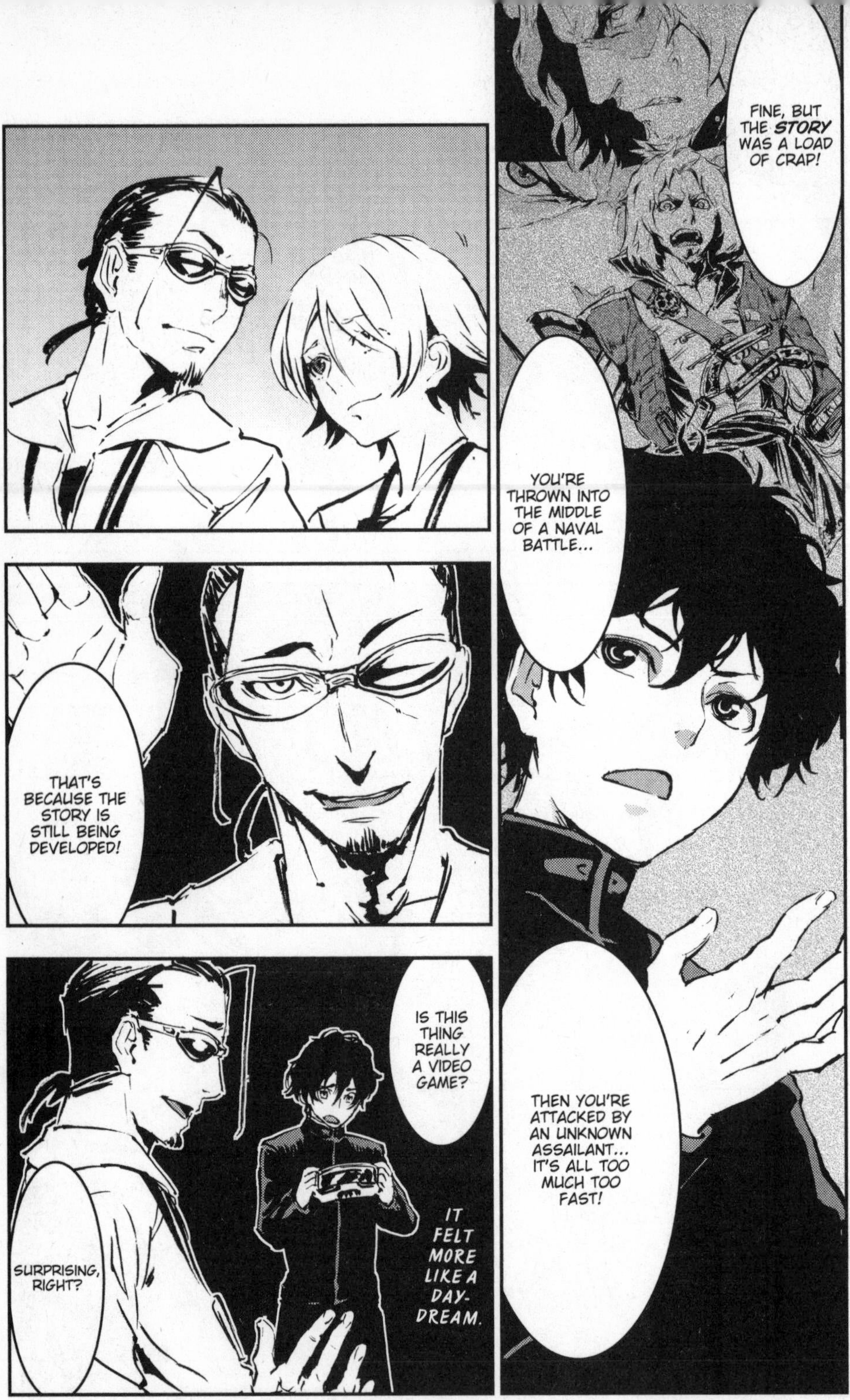
FINE, BUT THE ***STORY*** WAS A LOAD OF CRAP!
YOU'RE THROWN INTO THE MIDDLE OF A NAVAL BATTLE...
THEN YOU'RE ATTACKED BY AN UNKNOWN ASSAILANT... IT'S ALL TOO MUCH TOO FAST!
THAT'S BECAUSE THE STORY IS STILL BEING DEVELOPED!
IS THIS THING REALLY A VIDEO GAME?
IT FELT MORE LIKE A DAY-DREAM.
SURPRISING, RIGHT?

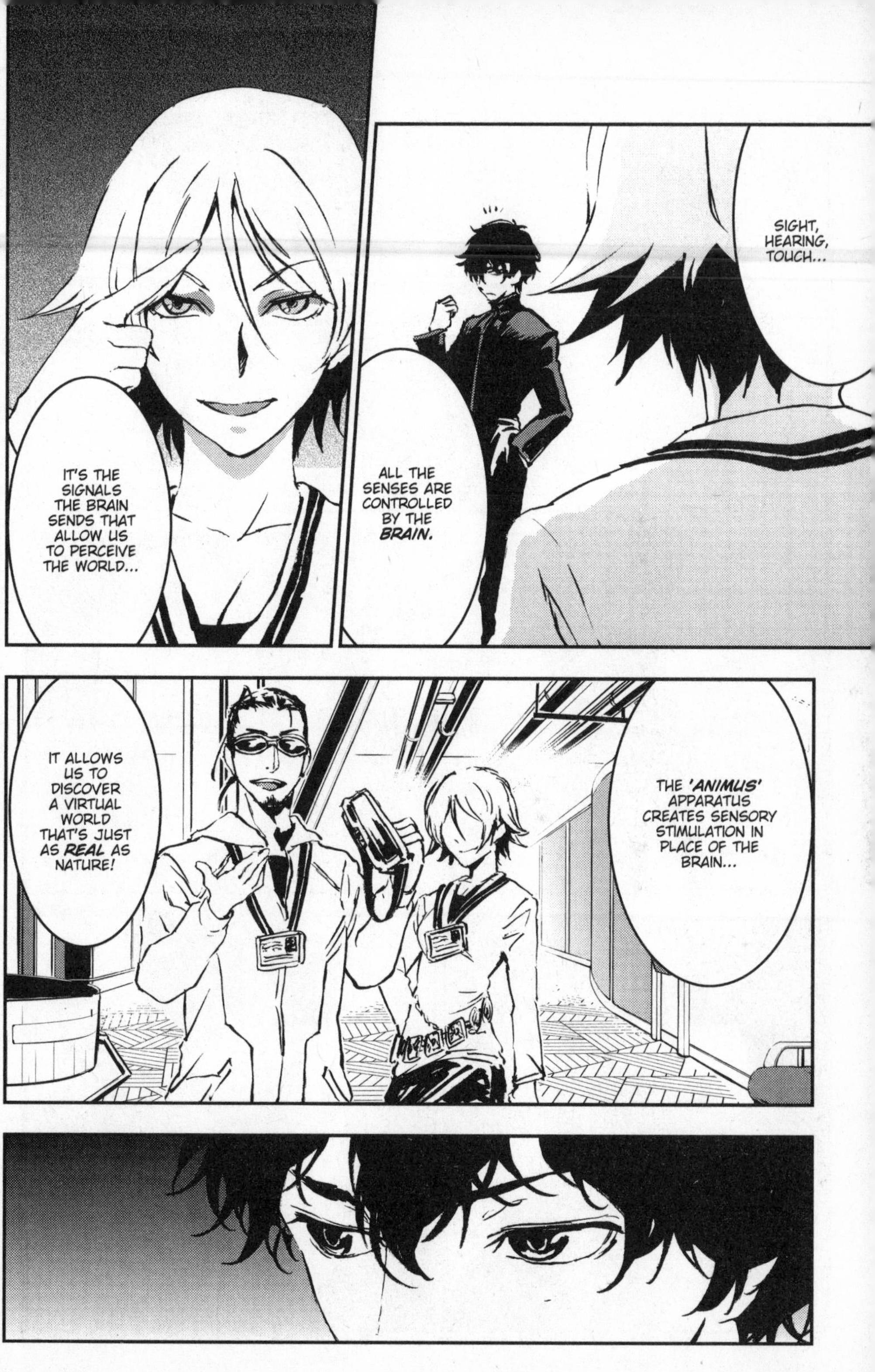
SIGHT, HEARING, TOUCH...
ALL THE SENSES ARE CONTROLLED BY THE BRAIN.
IT'S THE SIGNALS THE BRAIN SENDS THAT ALLOW US TO PERCEIVE THE WORLD...
THE 'ANIMUS' APPARATUS CREATES SENSORY STIMULATION IN PLACE OF THE BRAIN...
IT ALLOWS US TO DISCOVER A VIRTUAL WORLD THAT'S JUST AS REAL AS NATURE!

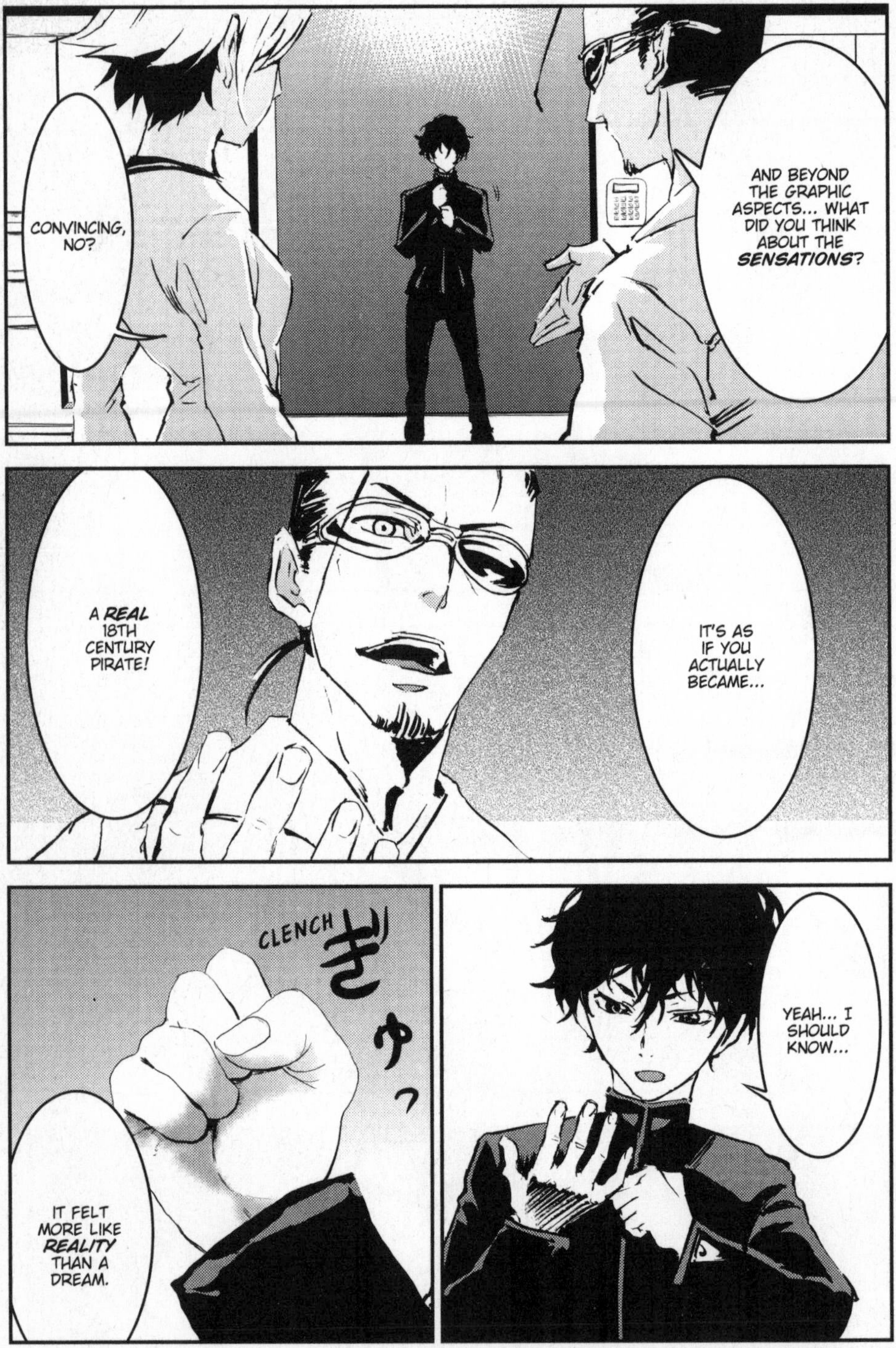
AND BEYOND THE GRAPHIC ASPECTS... WHAT DID YOU THINK ABOUT THE **SENSATIONS**?
CONVINCING, NO?
IT'S AS IF YOU ACTUALLY BECAME...
A **REAL** 18TH CENTURY PIRATE!
YEAH... I SHOULD KNOW...
CLENCH
ぎゅっ
IT FELT MORE LIKE **REALITY** THAN A DREAM.

CHAPTER II

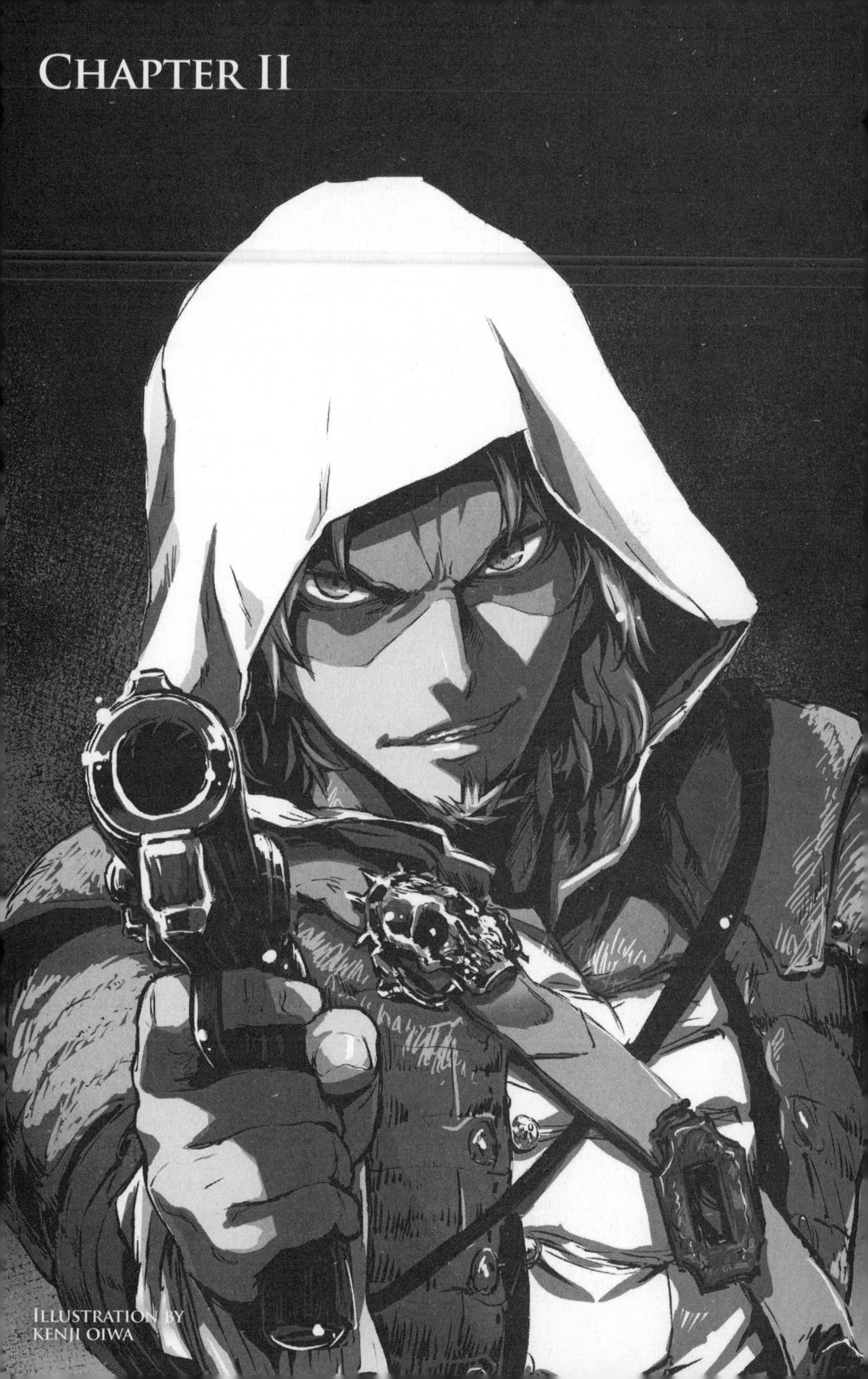

ILLUSTRATION BY
KENJI OIWA

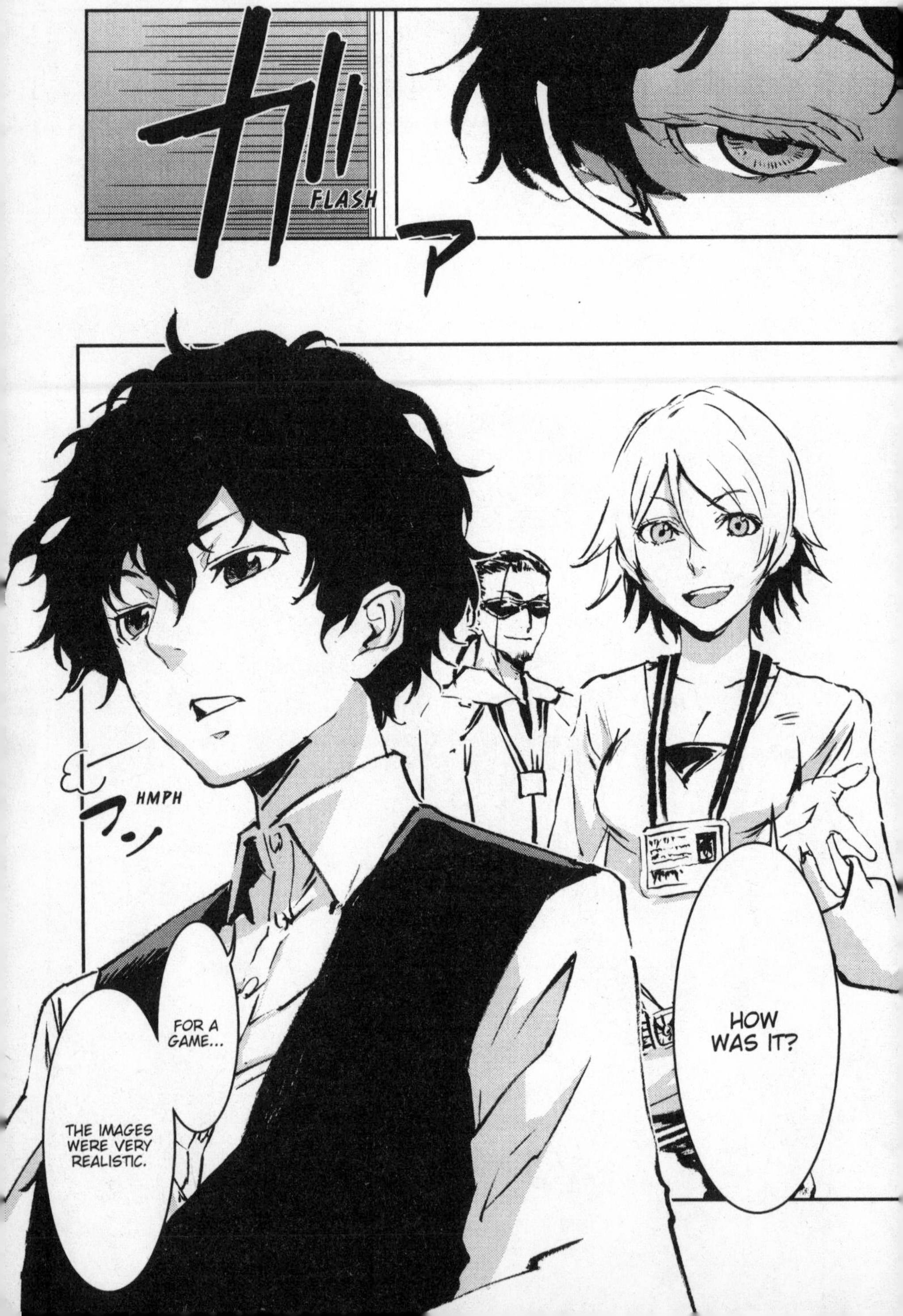

FLASH
HOW WAS IT?
HMPH
FOR A GAME...
THE IMAGES WERE VERY REALISTIC.

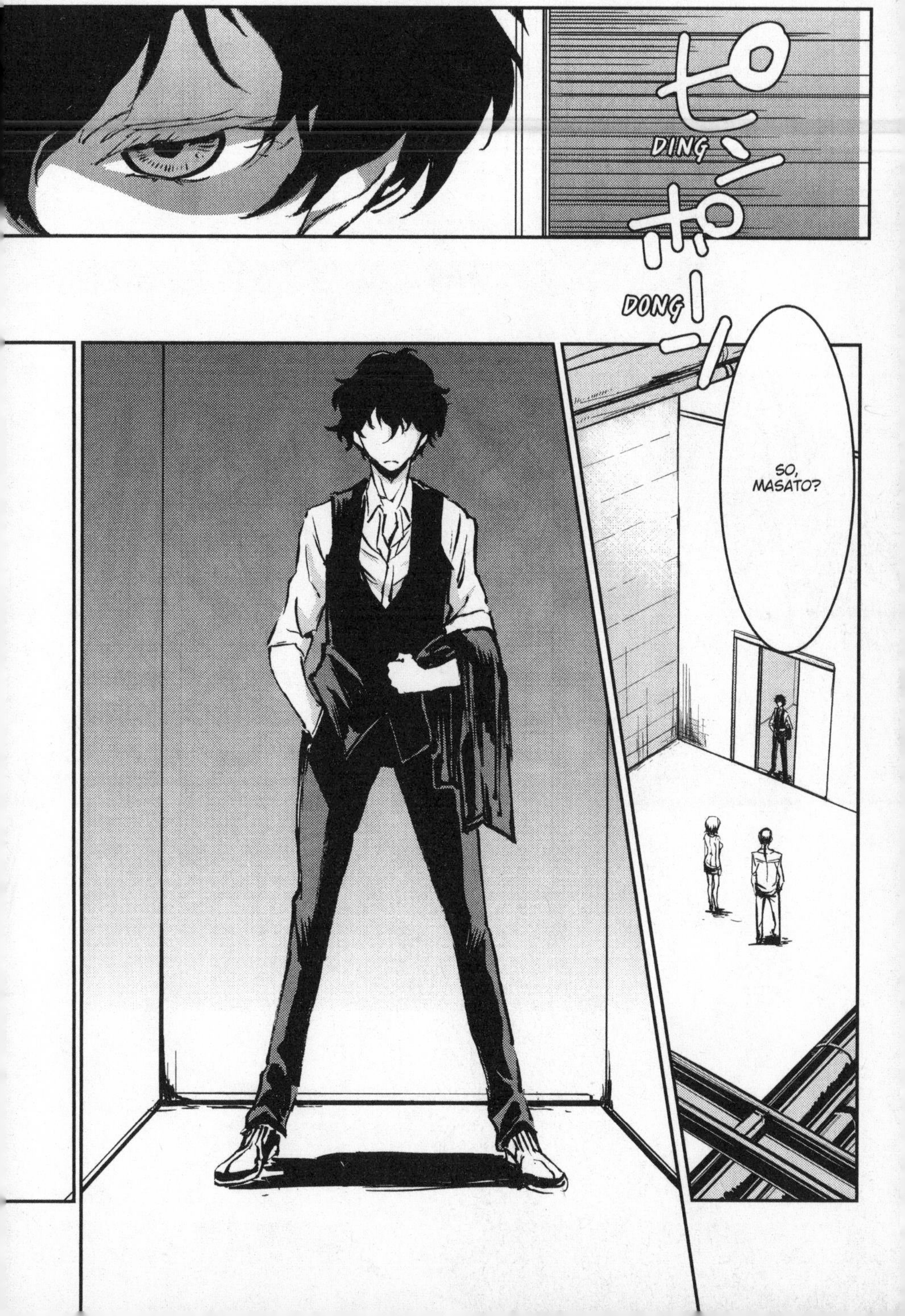
ピンポーン
DING
DONG
SO, MASATO?

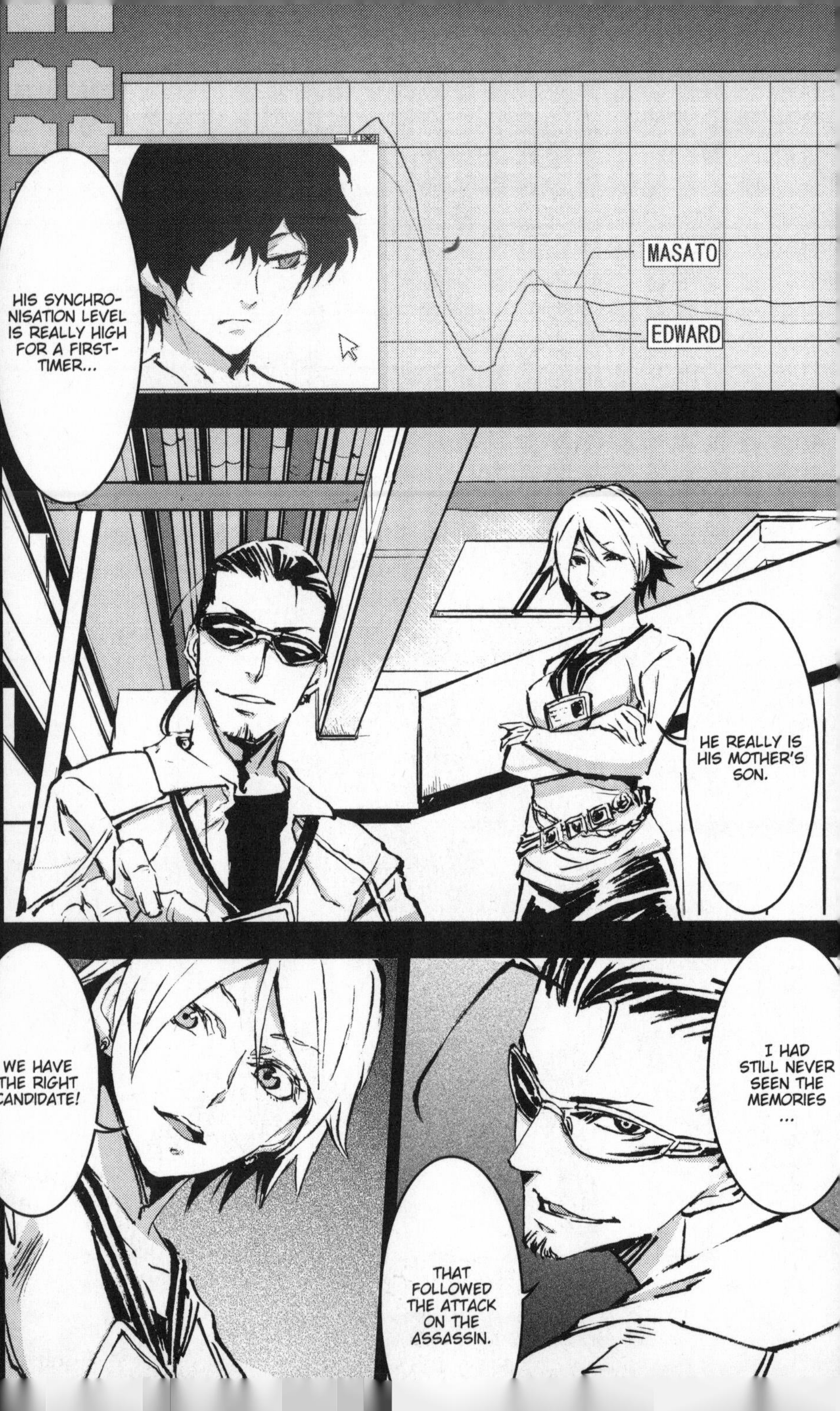
MASATO
EDWARD
HIS SYNCHRONISATION LEVEL IS REALLY HIGH FOR A FIRST-TIMER...
HE REALLY IS HIS MOTHER'S SON.
I HAD STILL NEVER SEEN THE MEMORIES ...
THAT FOLLOWED THE ATTACK ON THE ASSASSIN.
WE HAVE THE RIGHT CANDIDATE!

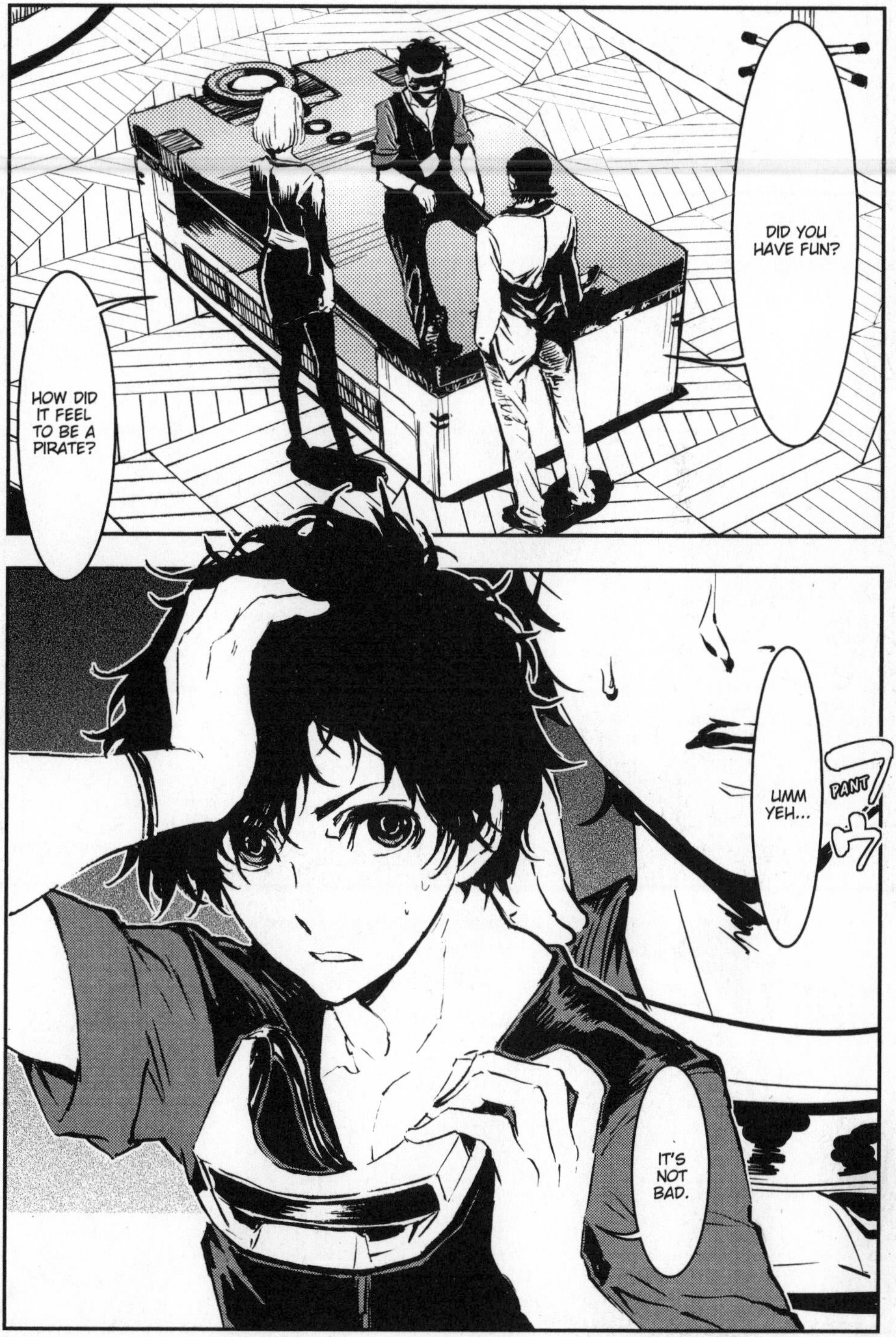
DID YOU HAVE FUN?
HOW DID IT FEEL TO BE A PIRATE?
UMM YEH...
PANT
IT'S NOT BAD.

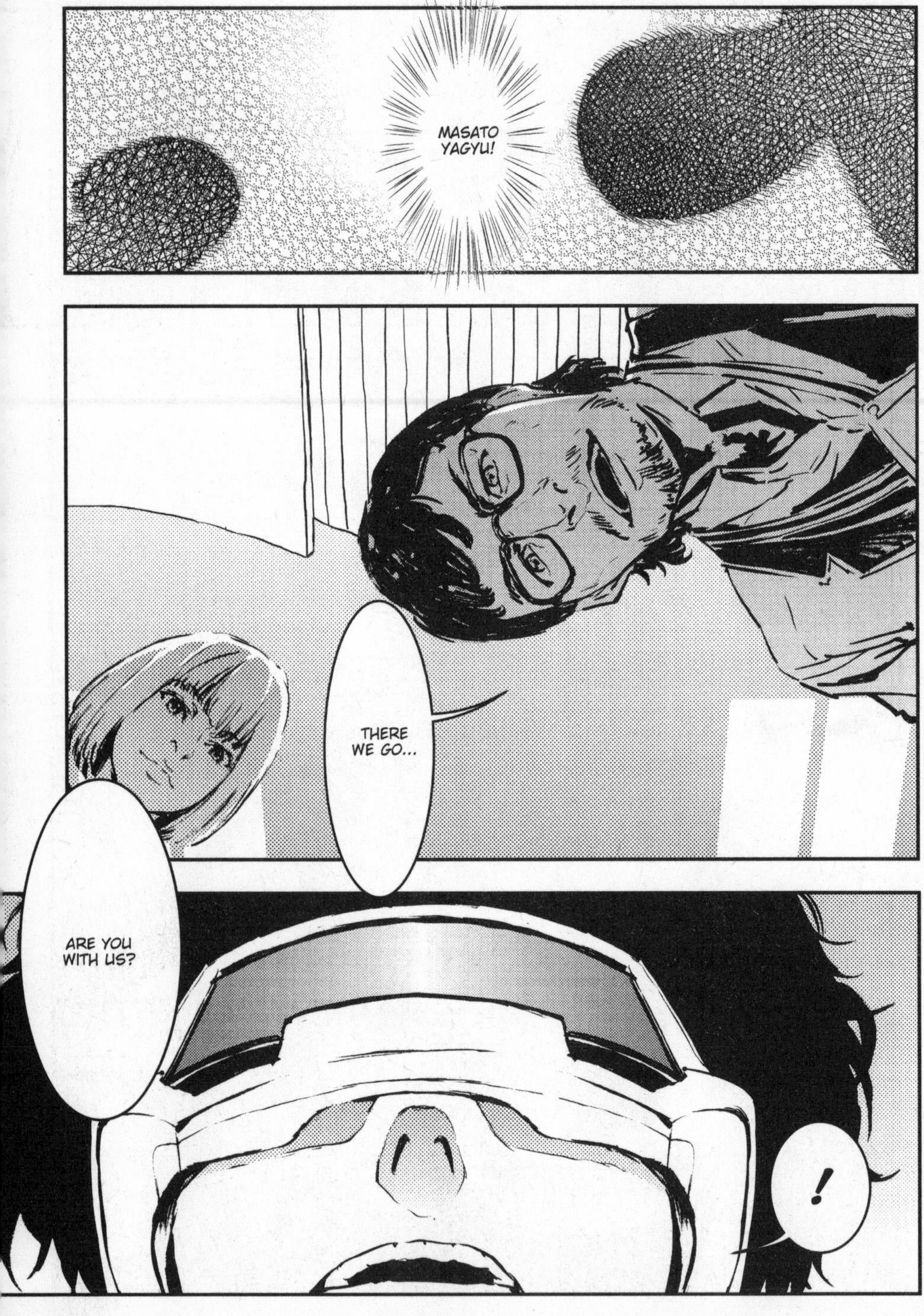
MASATO YAGYU!
THERE WE GO...
ARE YOU WITH US?
!

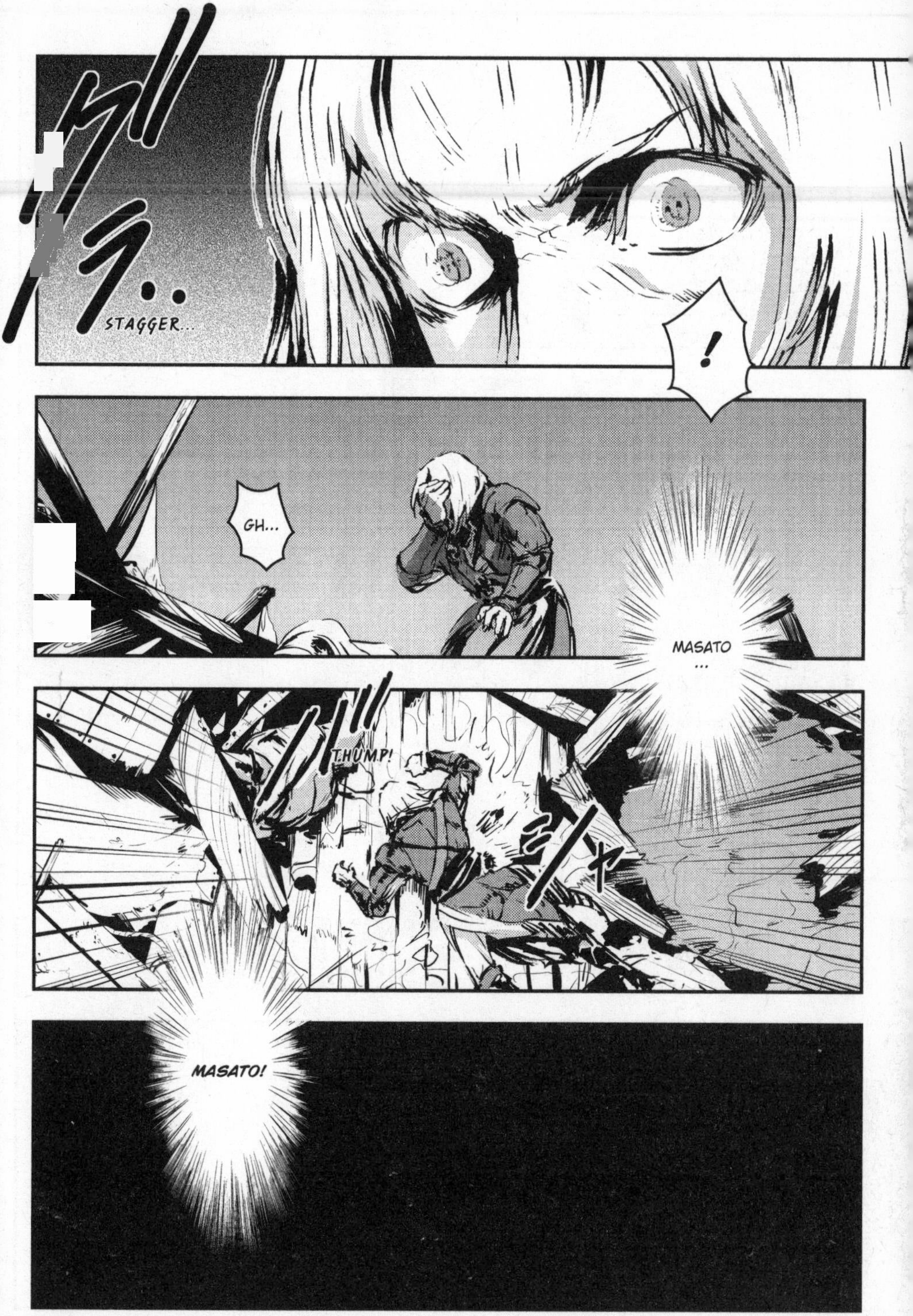
!
STAGGER...
MASATO
...
GH...
THUMP!
MASATO!

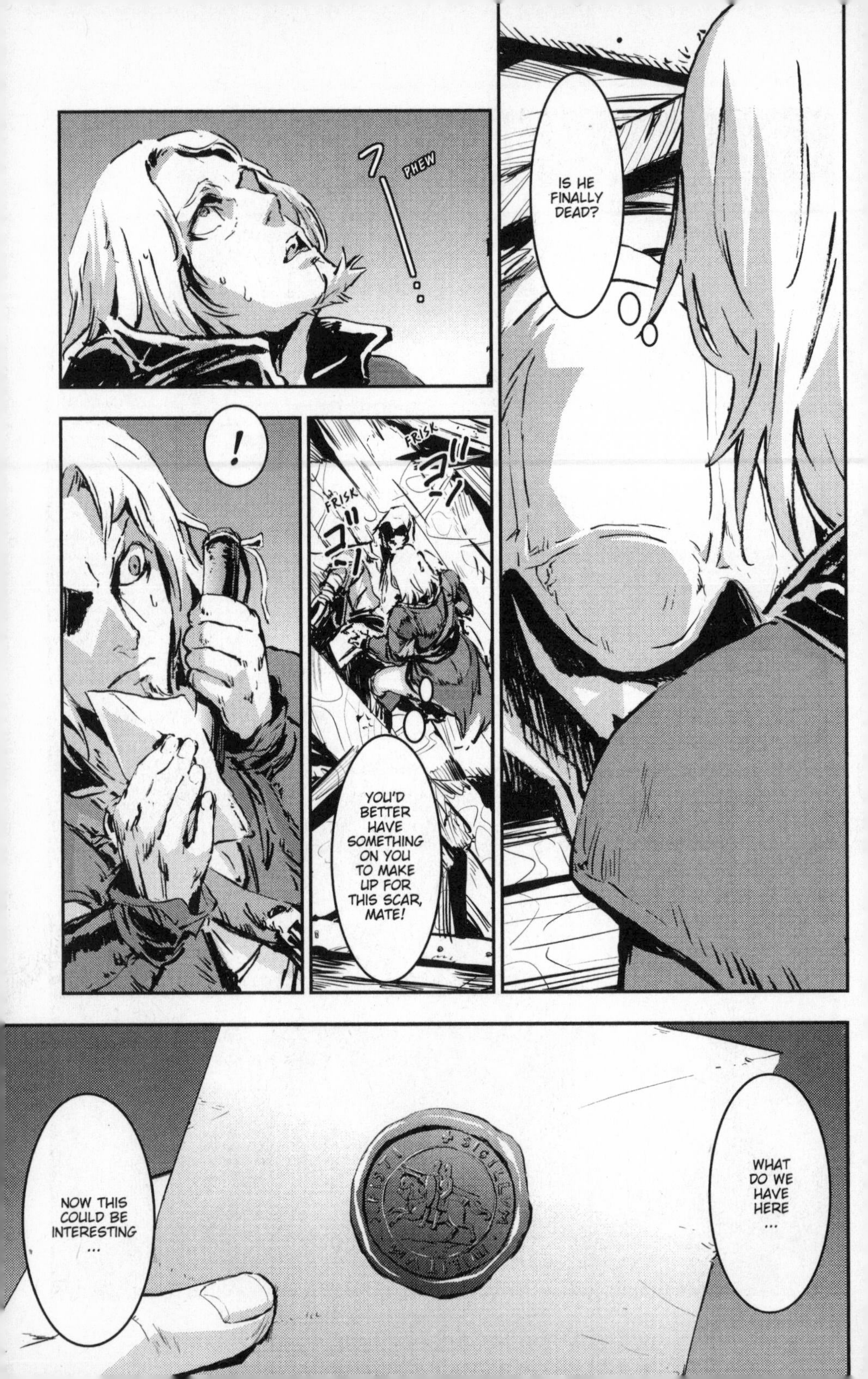
IS HE FINALLY DEAD?
PHEW
FRISK
FRISK
YOU'D BETTER HAVE SOMETHING ON YOU TO MAKE UP FOR THIS SCAR, MATE!
!
WHAT DO WE HAVE HERE ...
NOW THIS COULD BE INTERESTING ...

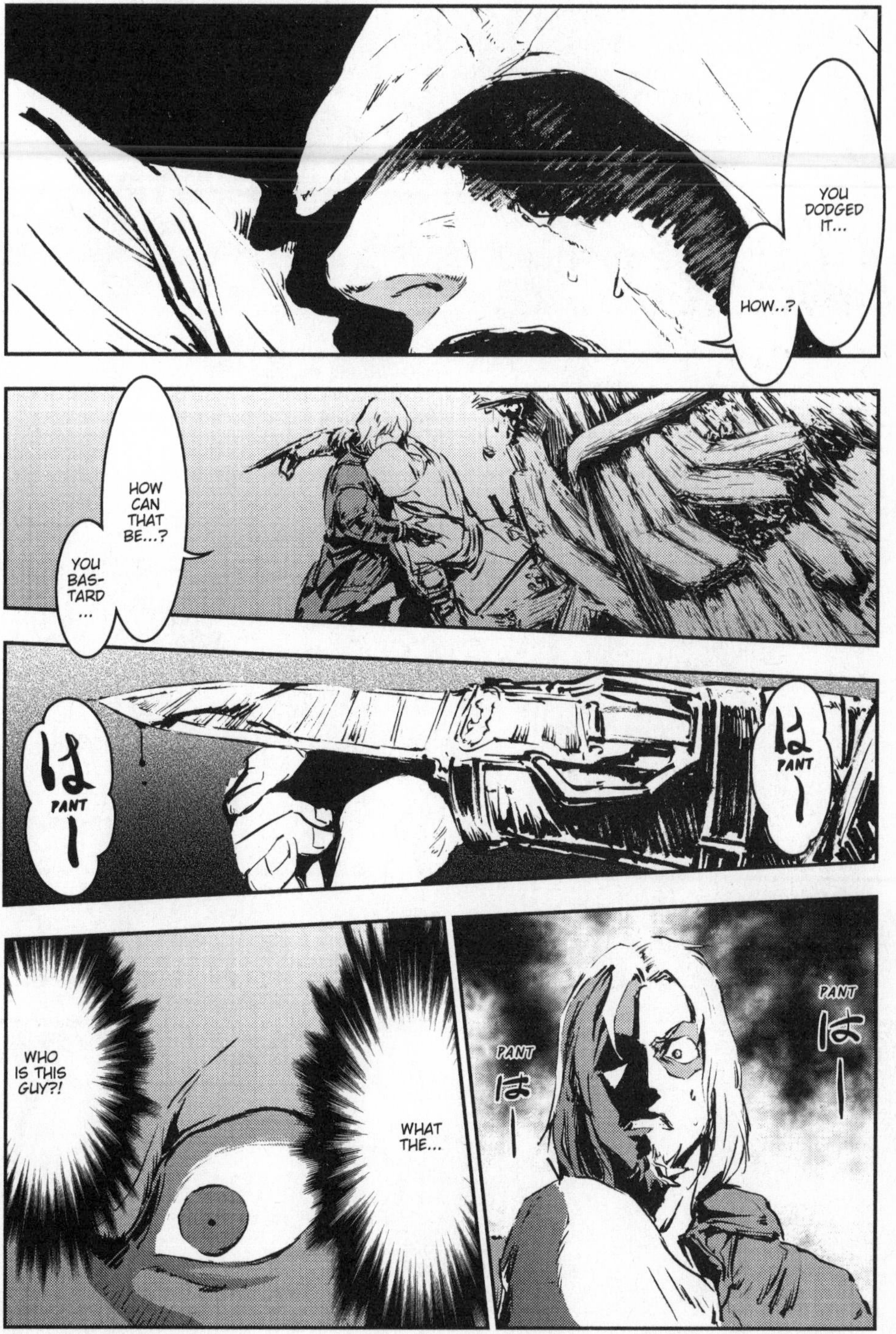
YOU DODGED IT…
HOW..?
HOW CAN THAT BE…?
YOU BAS-TARD …
はー PANT
はー PANT
PANT はー
PANT はー
WHAT THE…
WHO IS THIS GUY?!

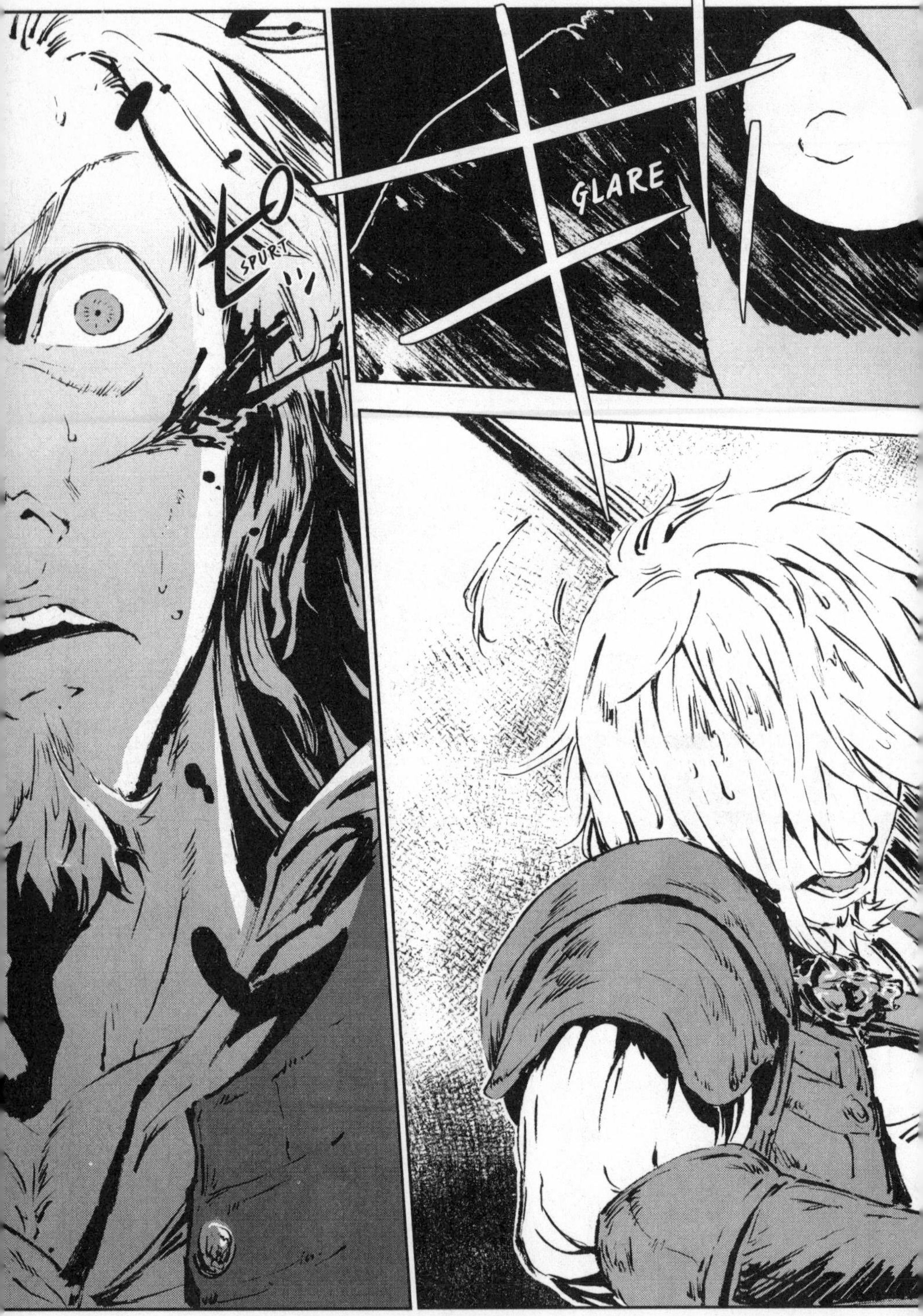
GLARE
SPURT

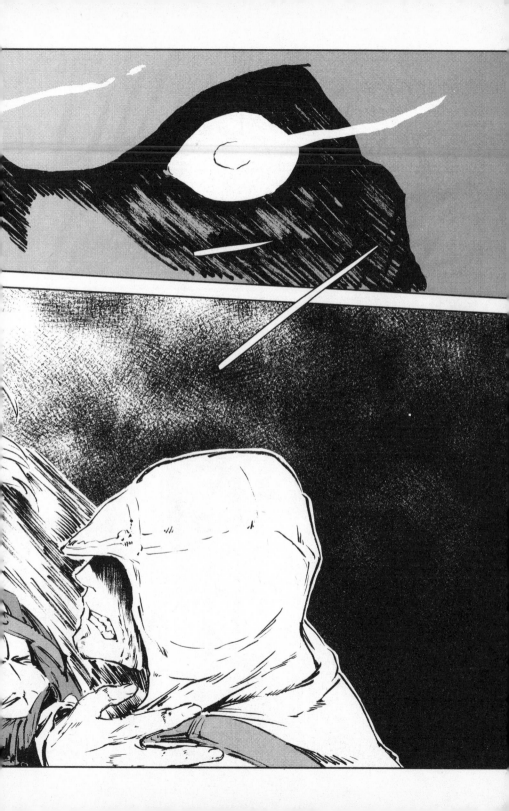

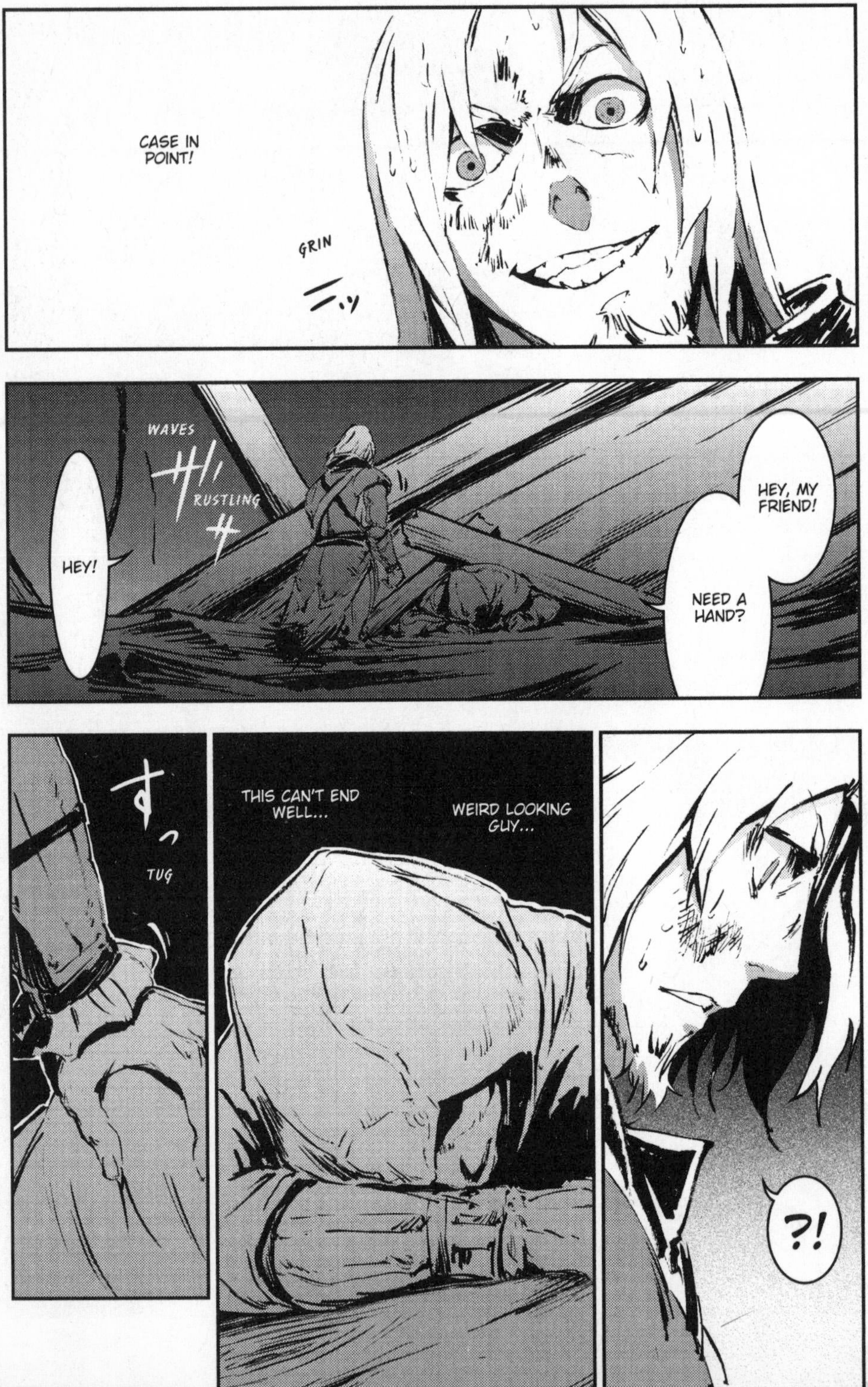
CASE IN POINT!
GRIN
ニッ
HEY, MY FRIEND!
NEED A HAND?
WAVES
RUSTLING
HEY!
?!
WEIRD LOOKING GUY...
THIS CAN'T END WELL...
すっ
TUG

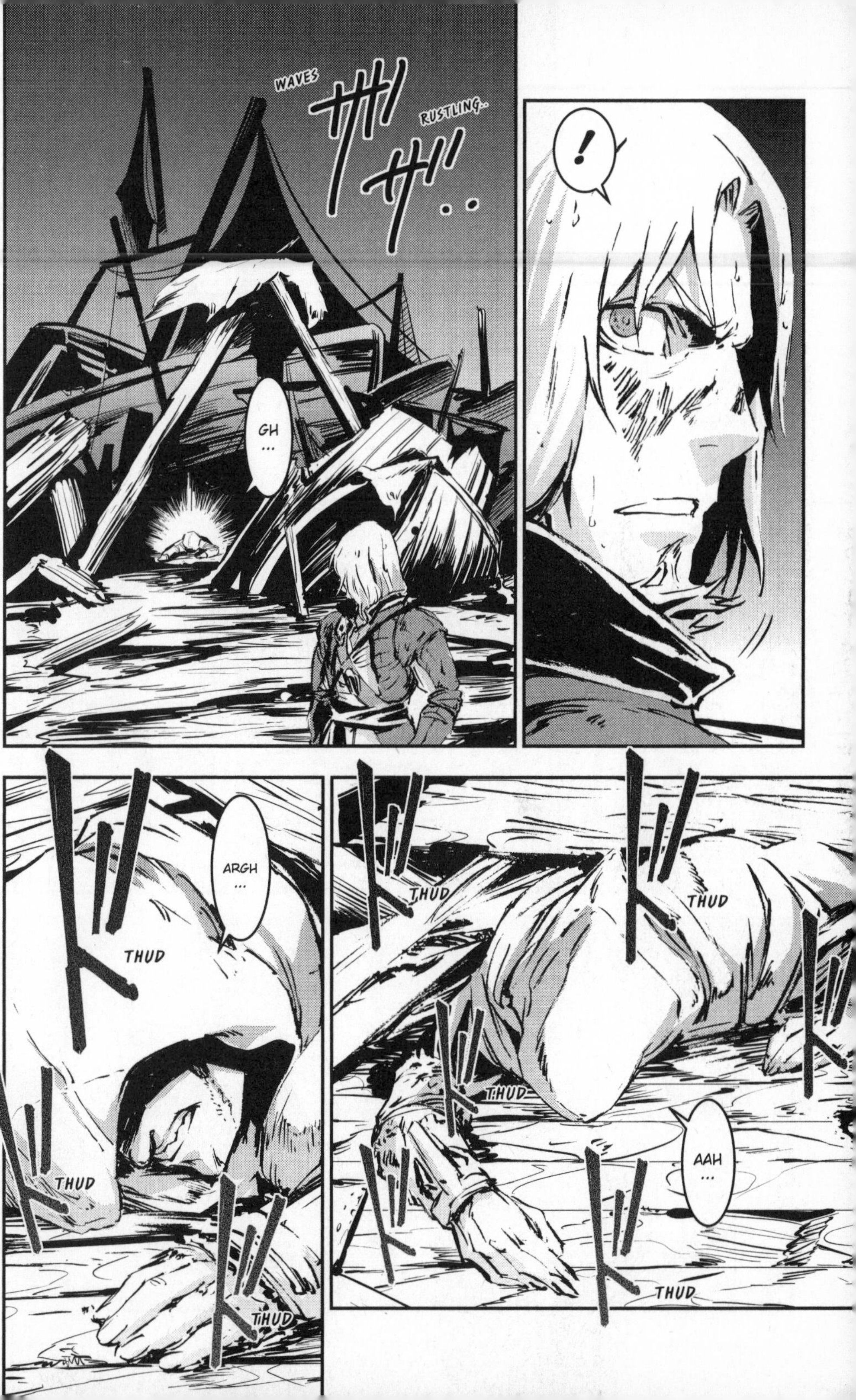
!
WAVES
RUSTLING..
GH ...
THUD
THUD
THUD
AAH ...
THUD
ARGH ...
THUD
THUD
THUD

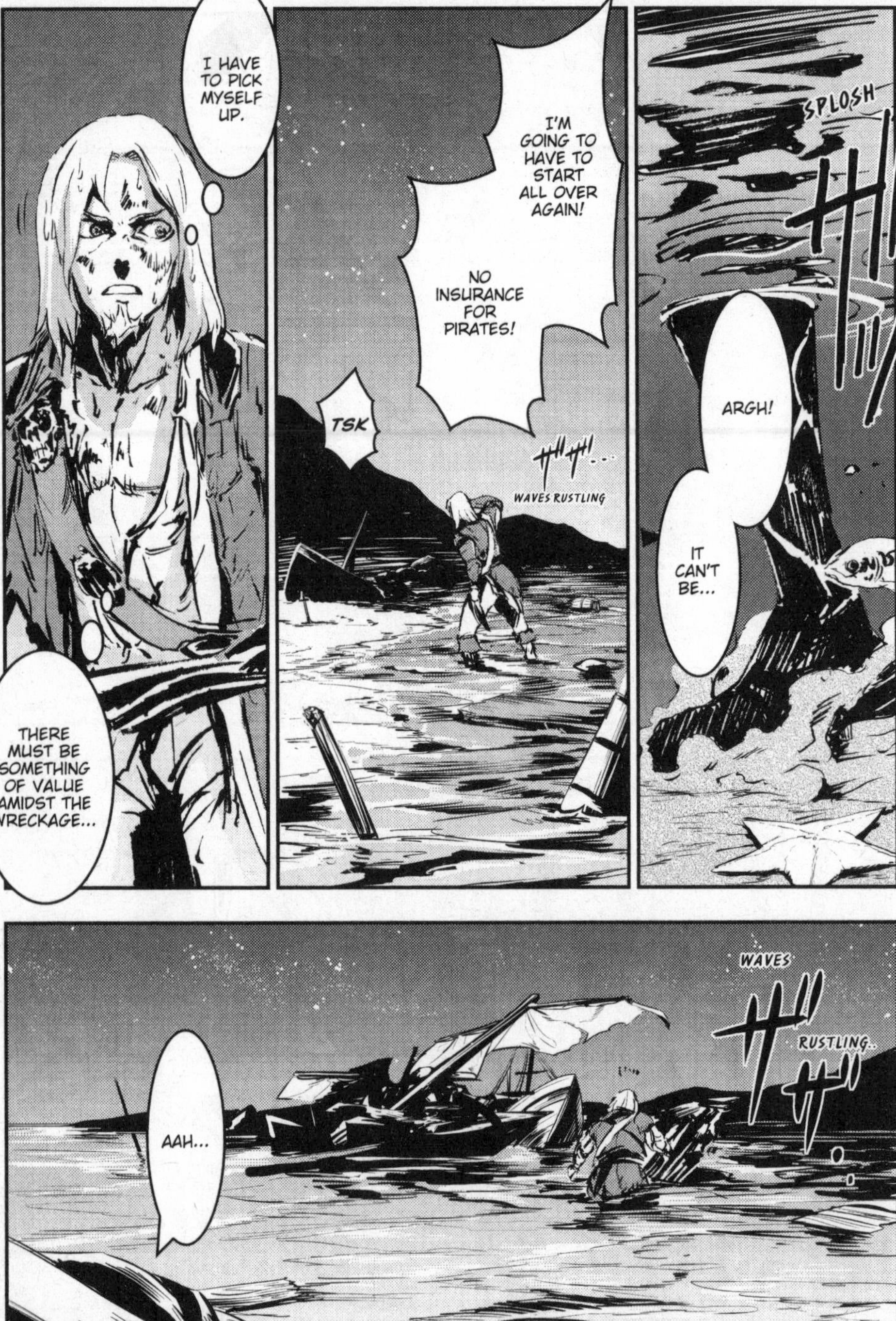
SPLOSH
ARGH!
IT CAN'T BE...
I'M GOING TO HAVE TO START ALL OVER AGAIN!
NO INSURANCE FOR PIRATES!
TSK
WAVES RUSTLING
I HAVE TO PICK MYSELF UP.
THERE MUST BE SOMETHING OF VALUE AMIDST THE WRECKAGE...
WAVES RUSTLING..
AAH...

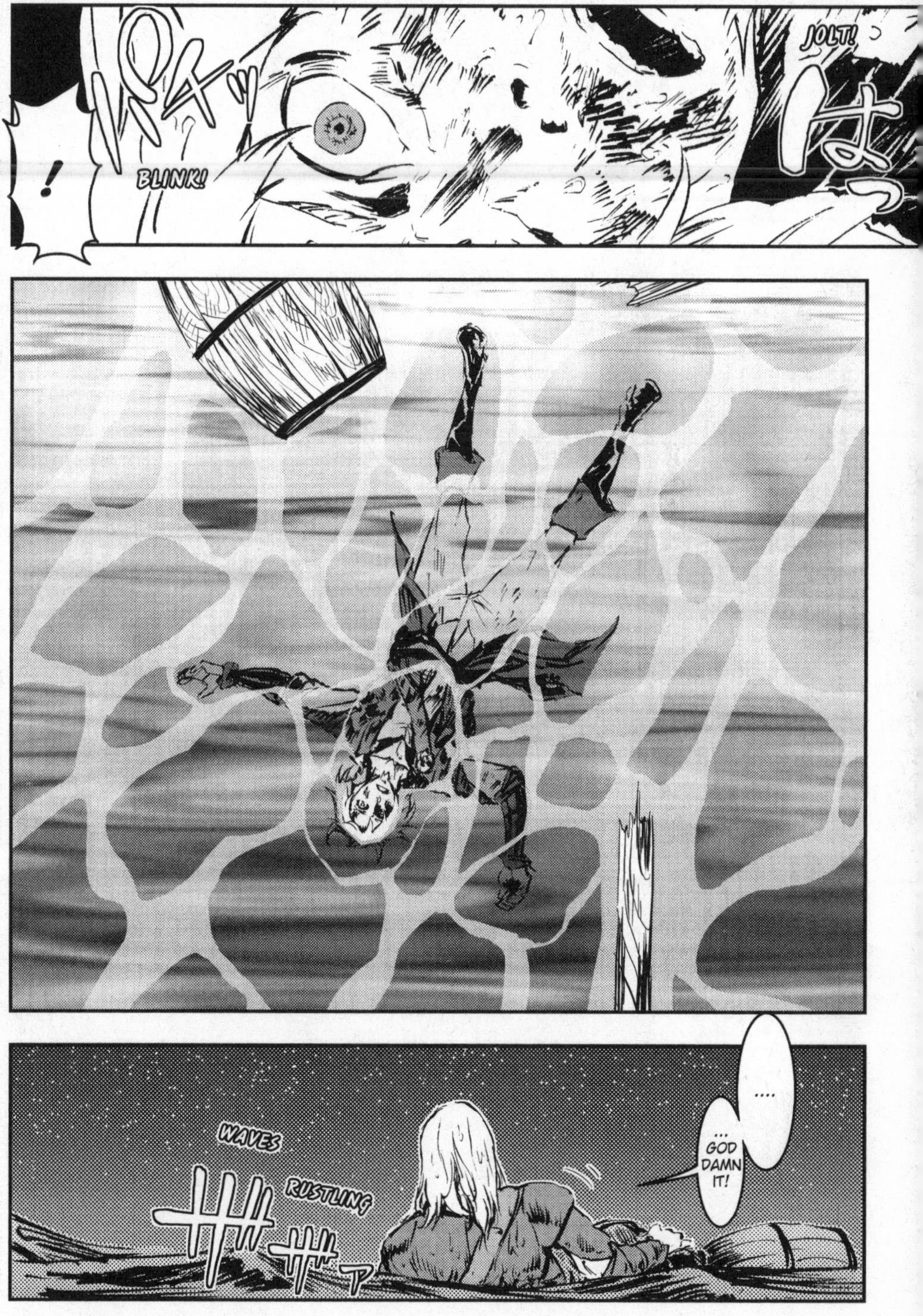

JOLT!
はっ
パチッ!
BLINK!
!
....
... GOD DAMN IT!
WAVES
ザザ
RUSTLING
ザザァ

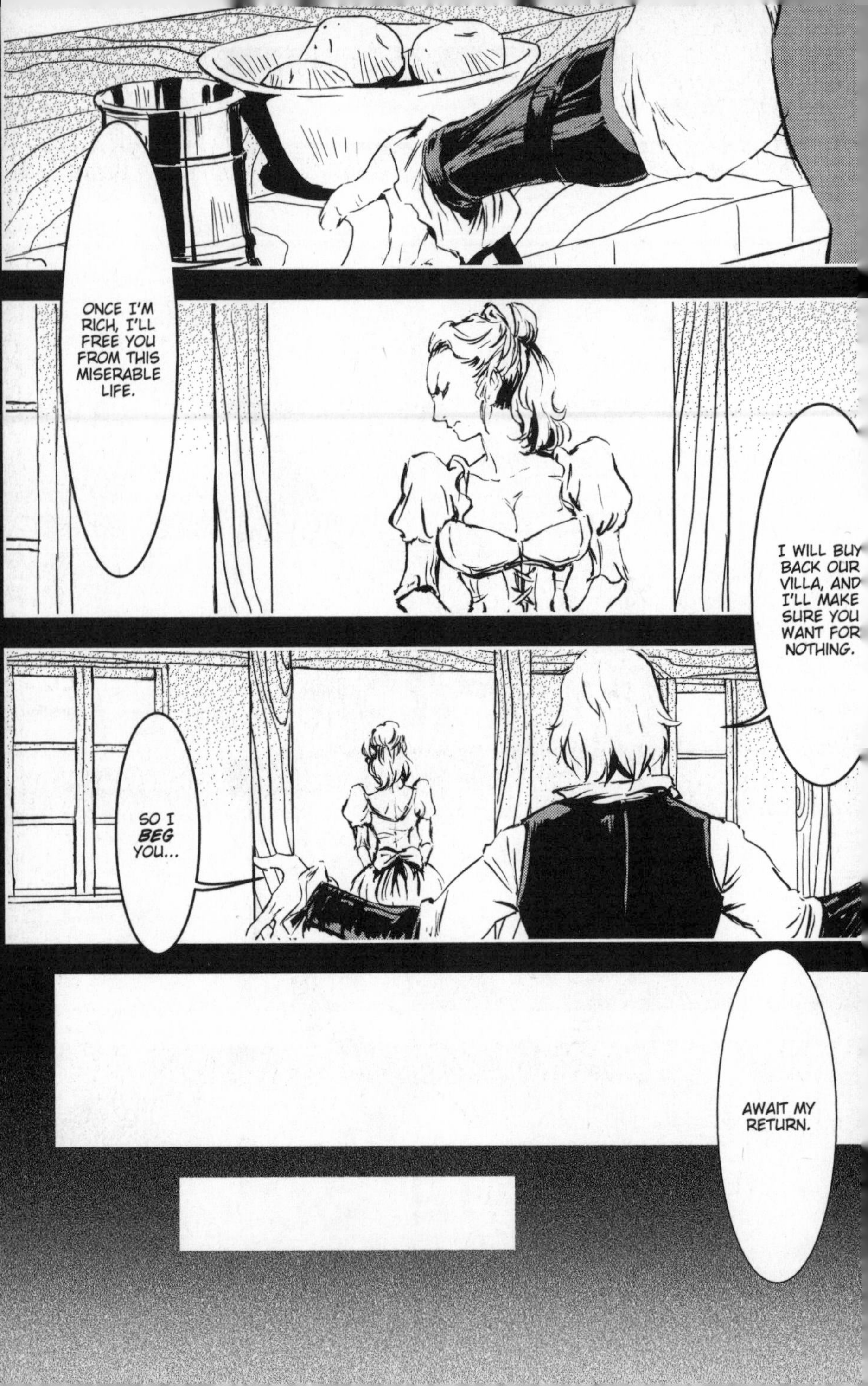
ONCE I'M RICH, I'LL FREE YOU FROM THIS MISERABLE LIFE.
I WILL BUY BACK OUR VILLA, AND I'LL MAKE SURE YOU WANT FOR NOTHING.
SO I *BEG* YOU...
AWAIT MY RETURN.

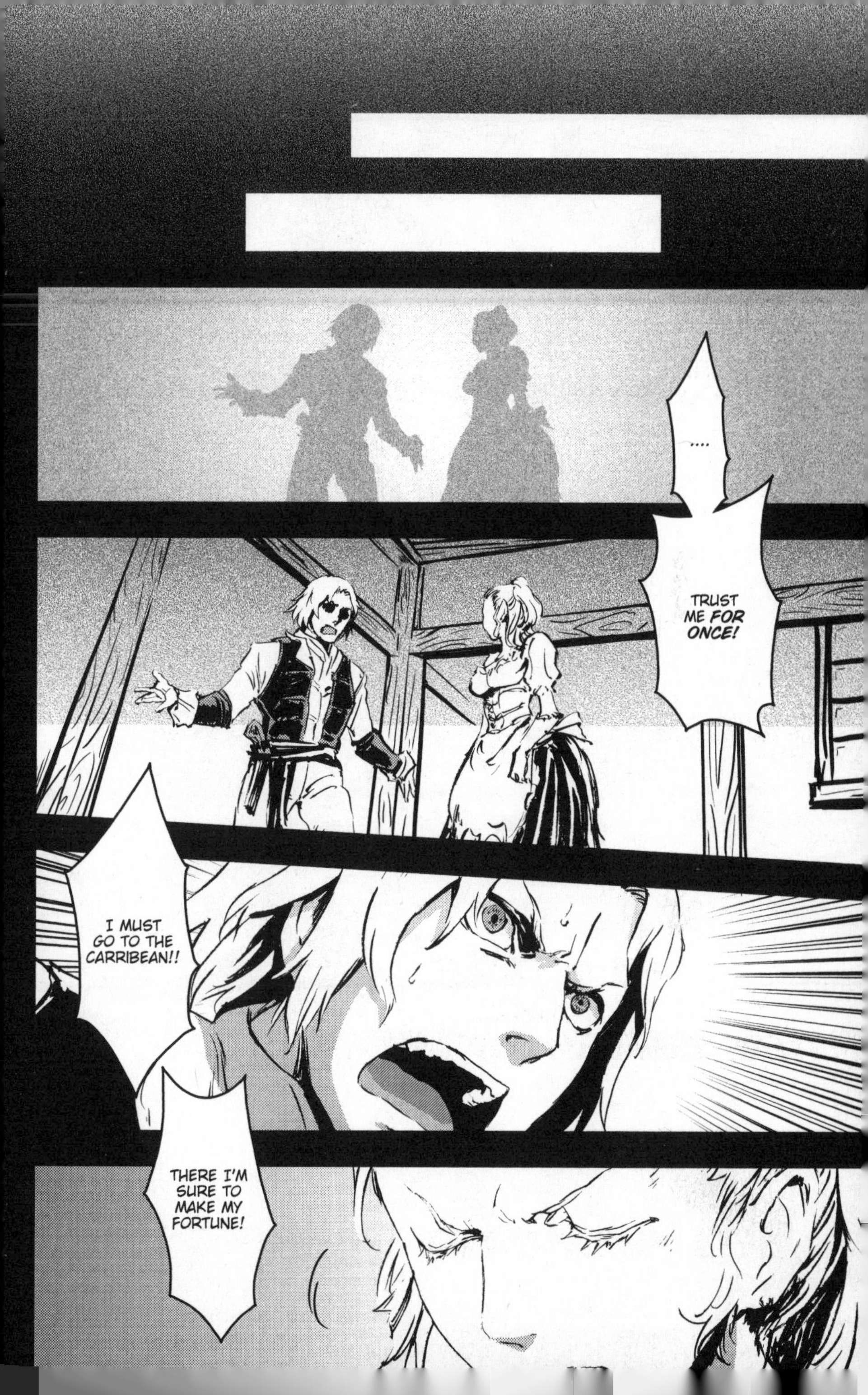
....
TRUST ME FOR ONCE!
I MUST GO TO THE CARRIBEAN!!
THERE I'M SURE TO MAKE MY FORTUNE!

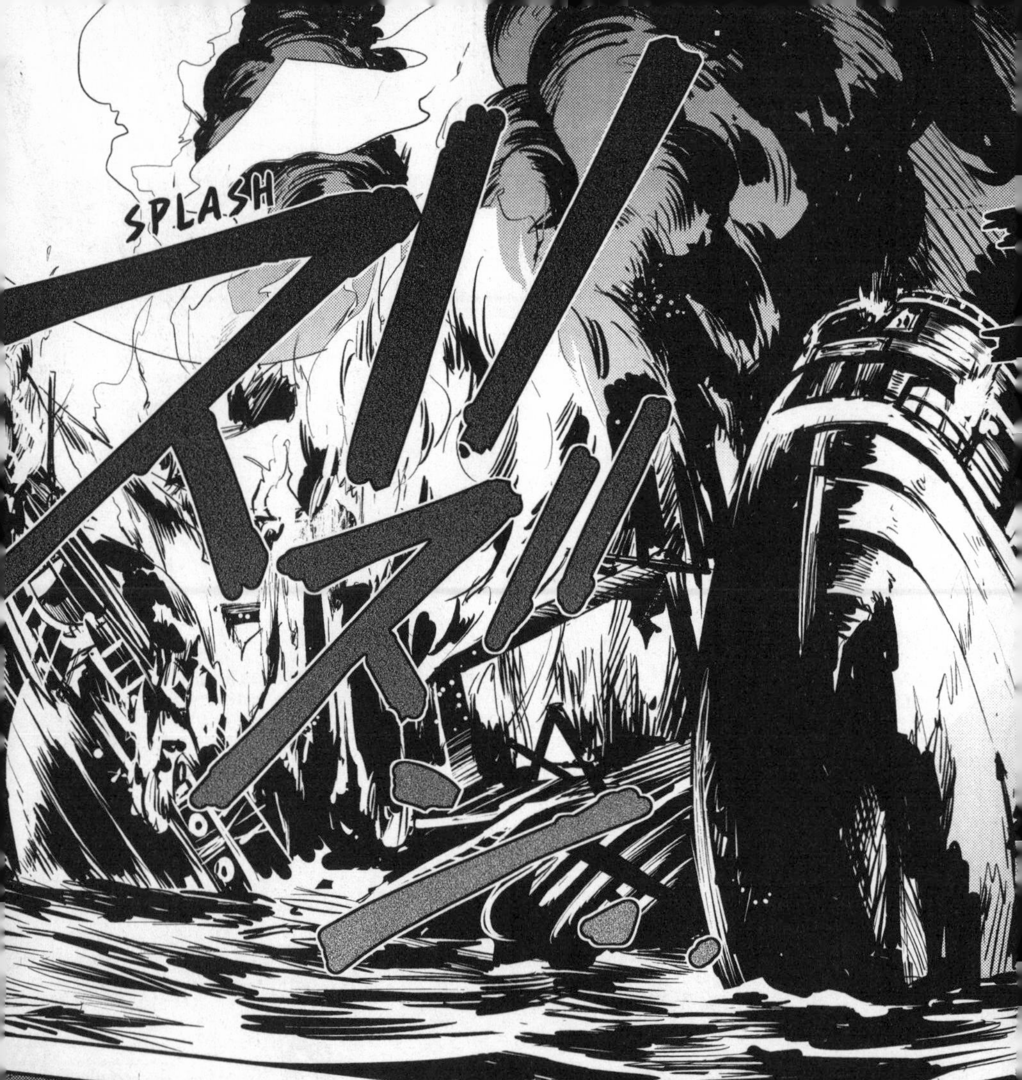
SPLASH

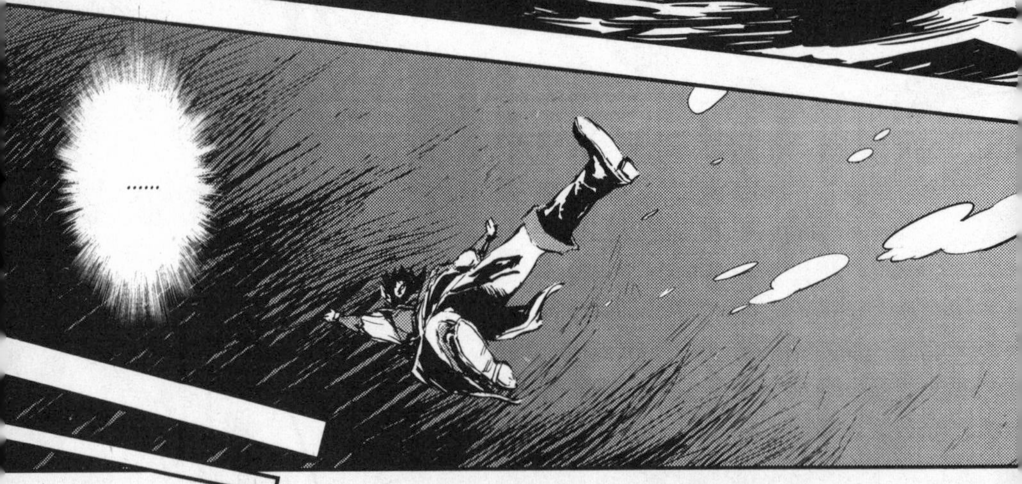
……

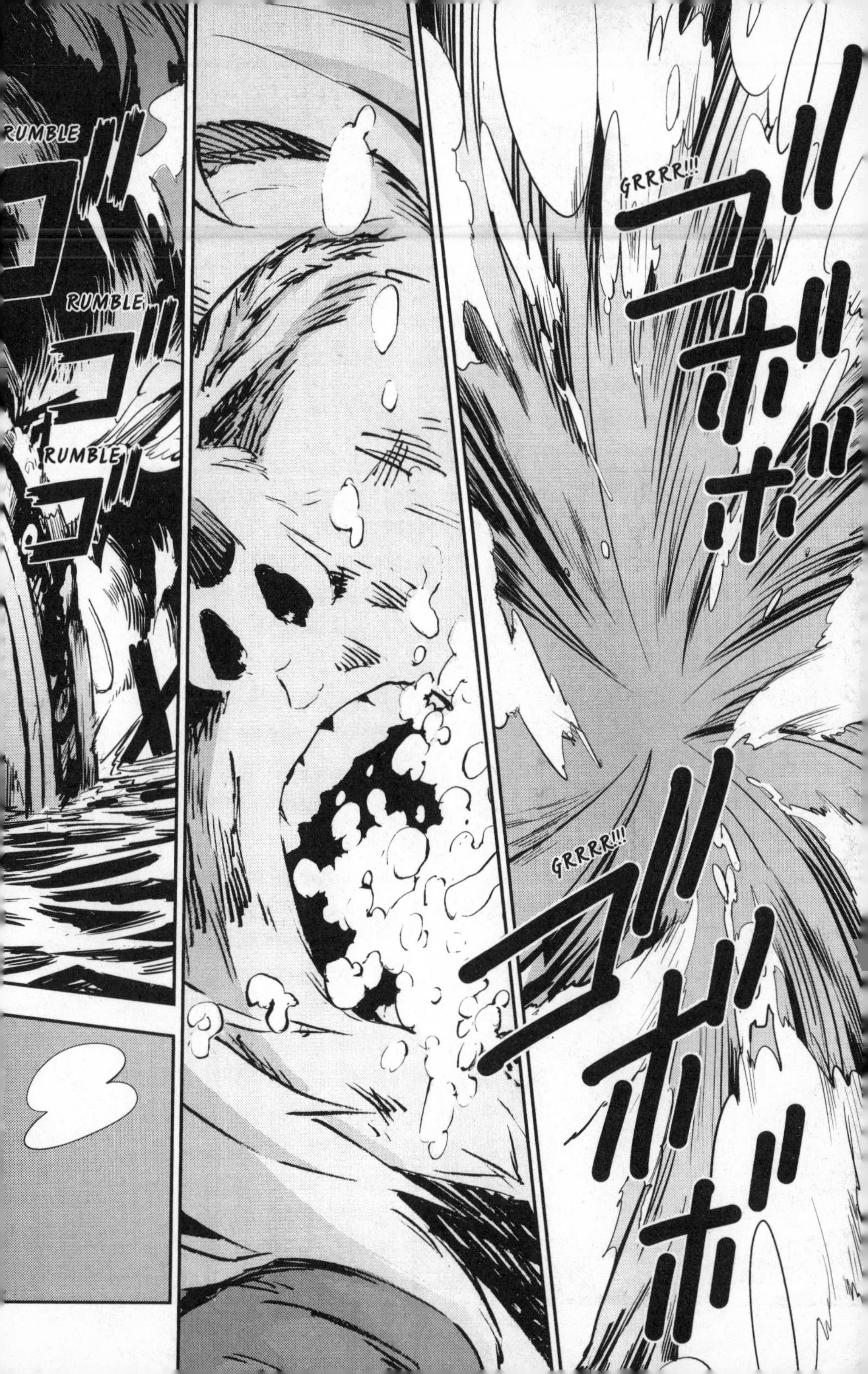
GRRRR!!!
GRRRR!!!
RUMBLE
RUMBLE
RUMBLE

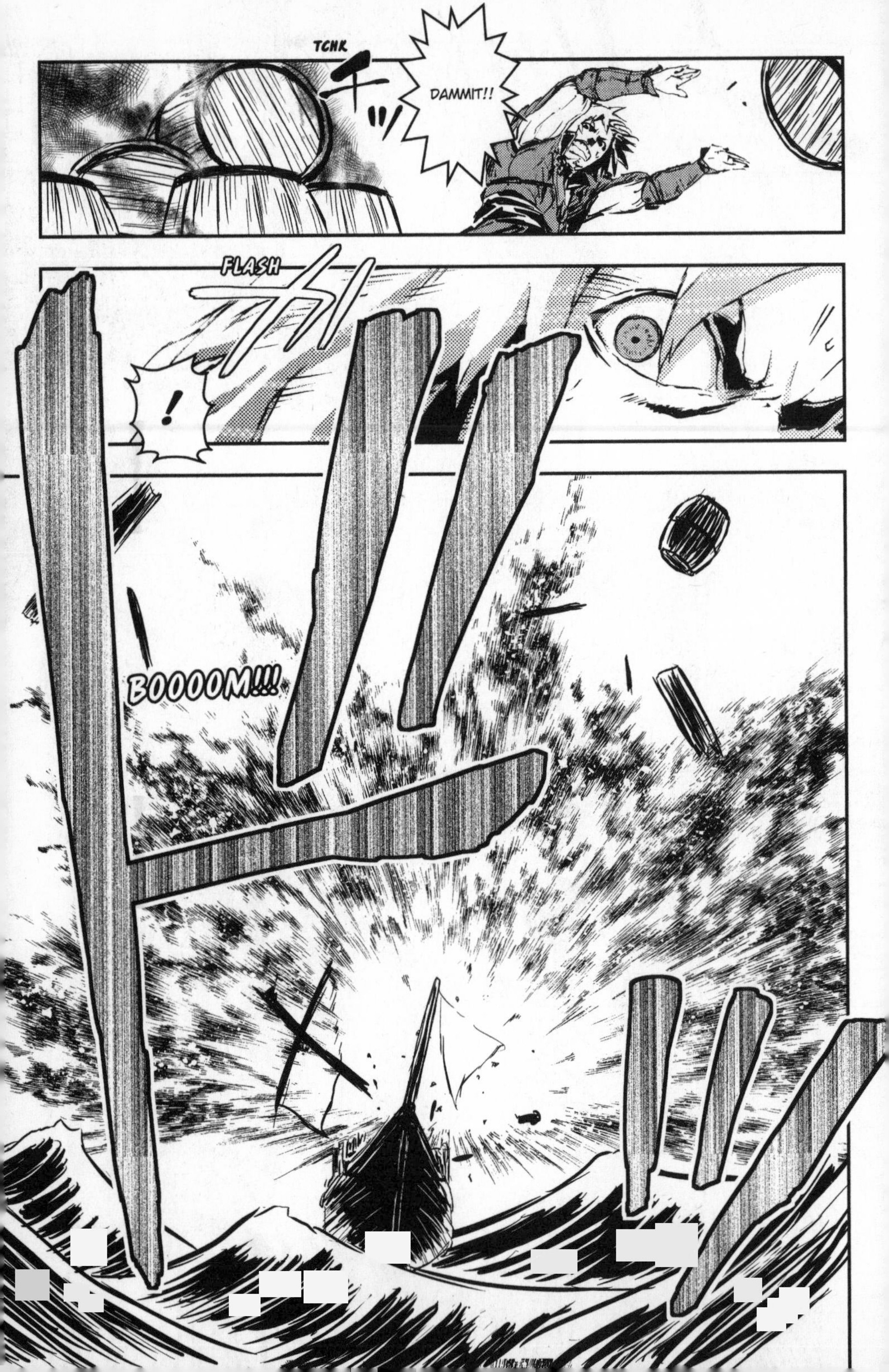
DAMMIT!!
TCHK
FLASH
!
BOOOOM!!!

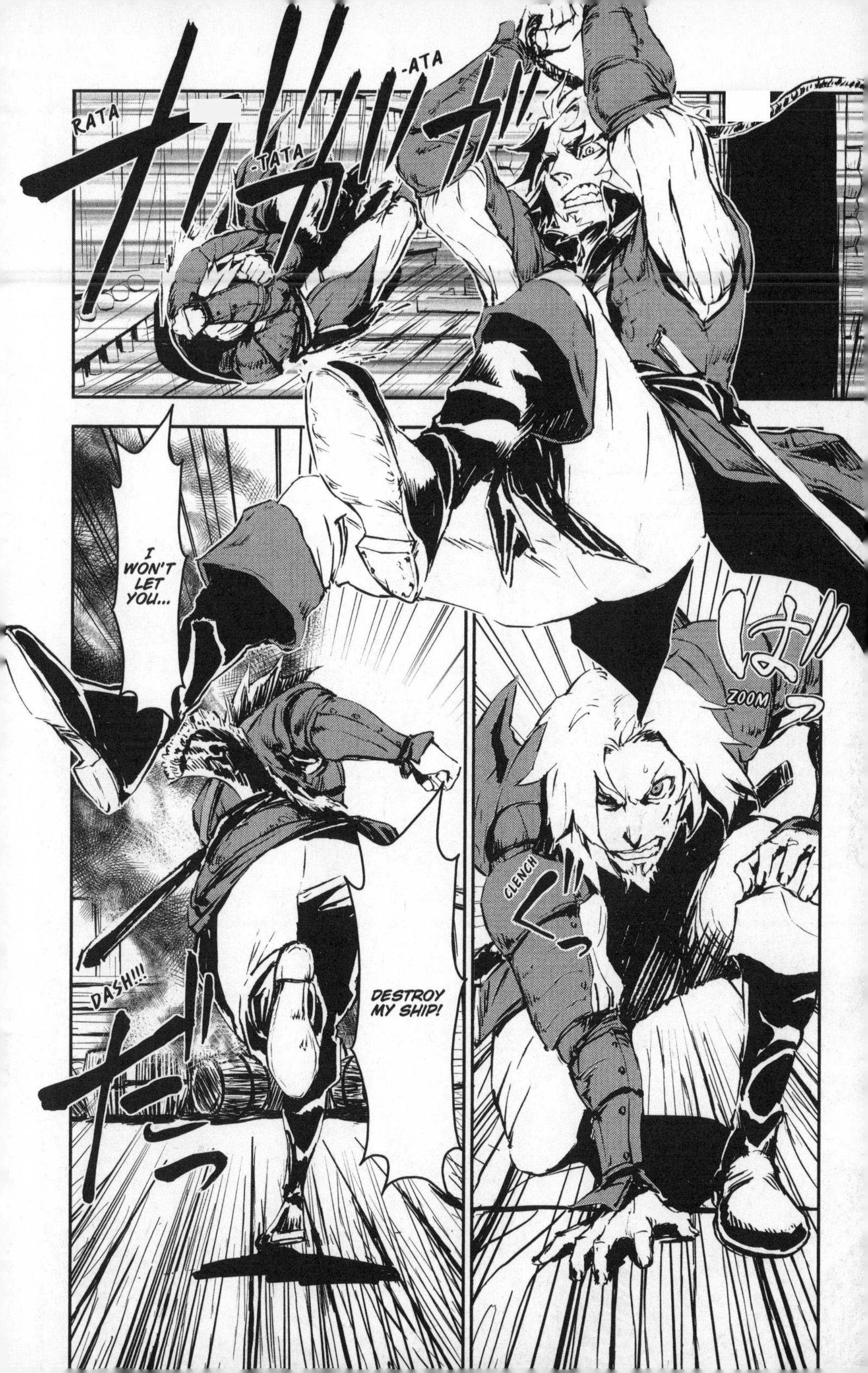
RATA
-TATA
-ATA
ZOOM
CLENCH
I WON'T LET YOU...
DESTROY MY SHIP!
DASH!!!

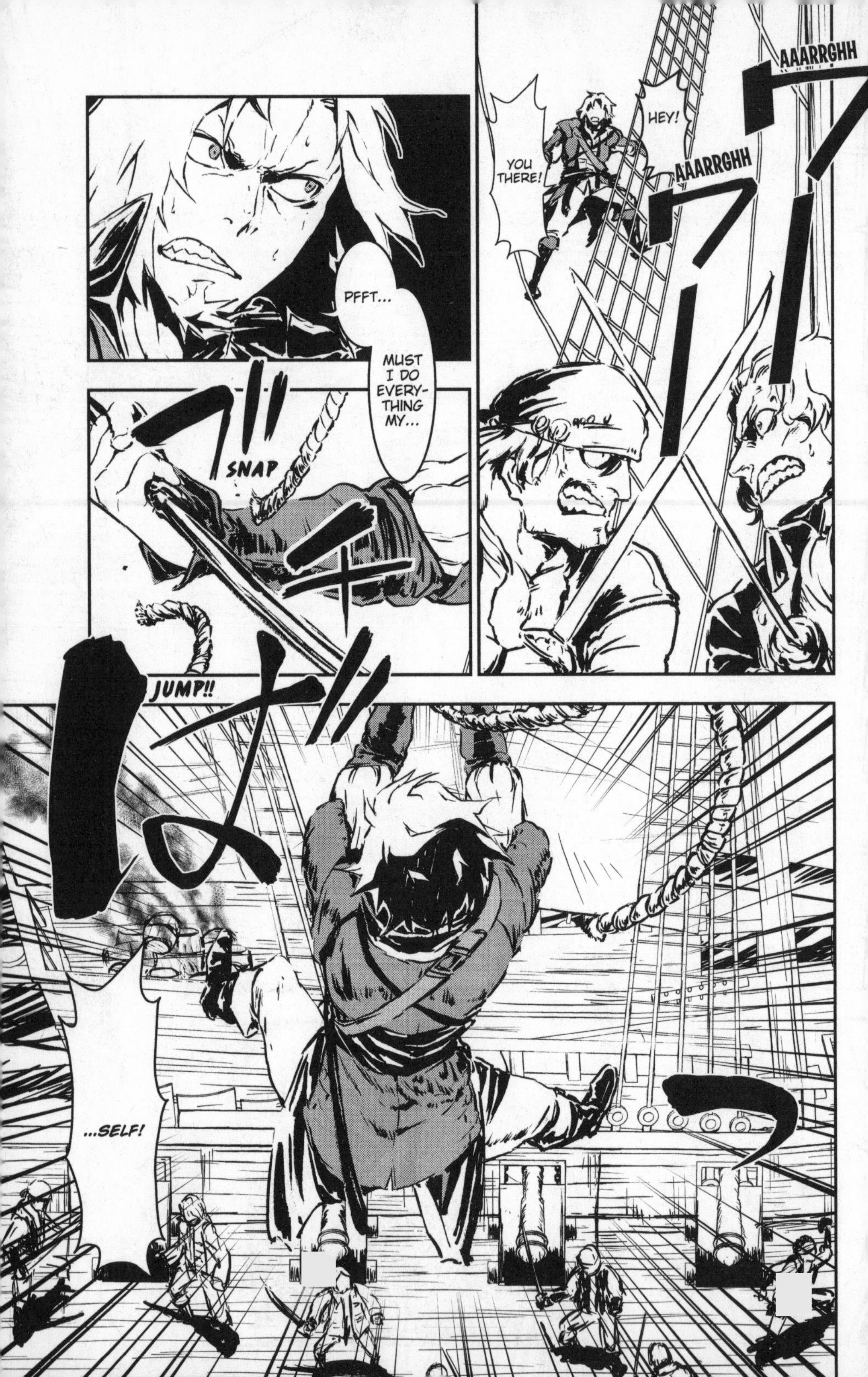
AAARRGHH
AAARRGHH
HEY!
YOU THERE!
PFFT...
MUST I DO EVERY-THING MY...
SNAP
JUMP!!
...SELF!

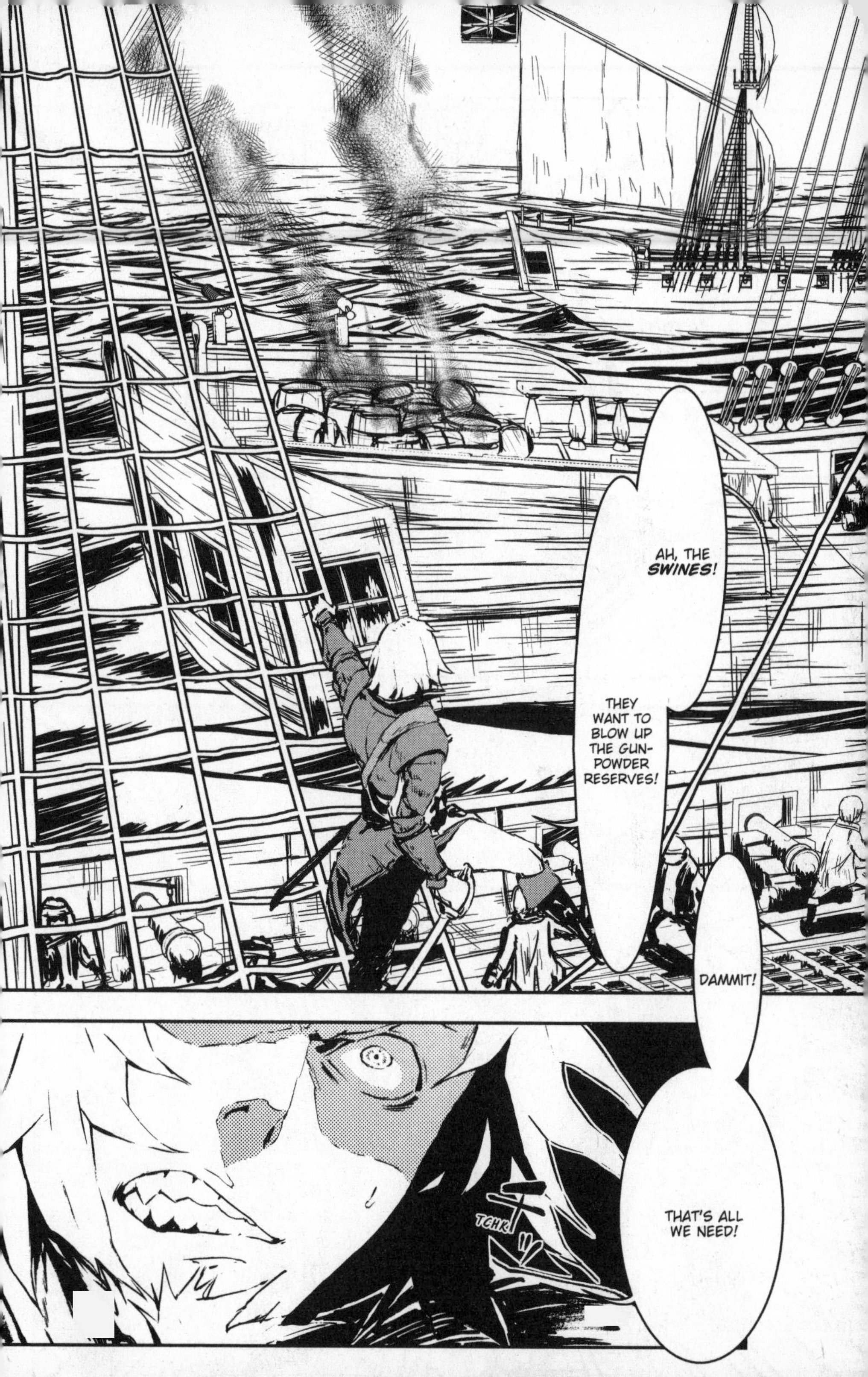
AH, THE *SWINES!*
THEY WANT TO BLOW UP THE GUN-POWDER RESERVES!
DAMMIT!
THAT'S ALL WE NEED!
TCHK!

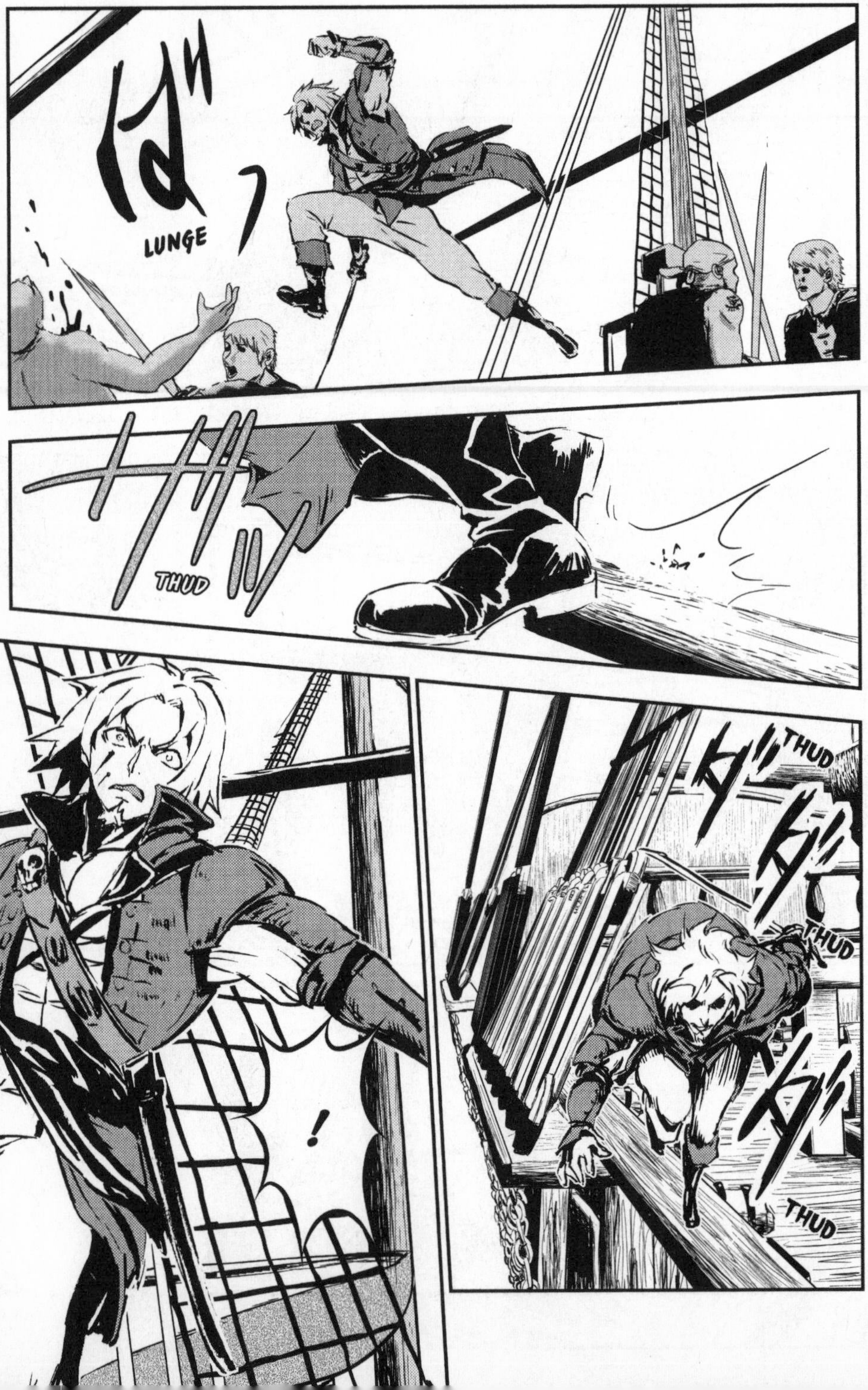
LUNGE
THUD
THUD
THUD
THUD
!

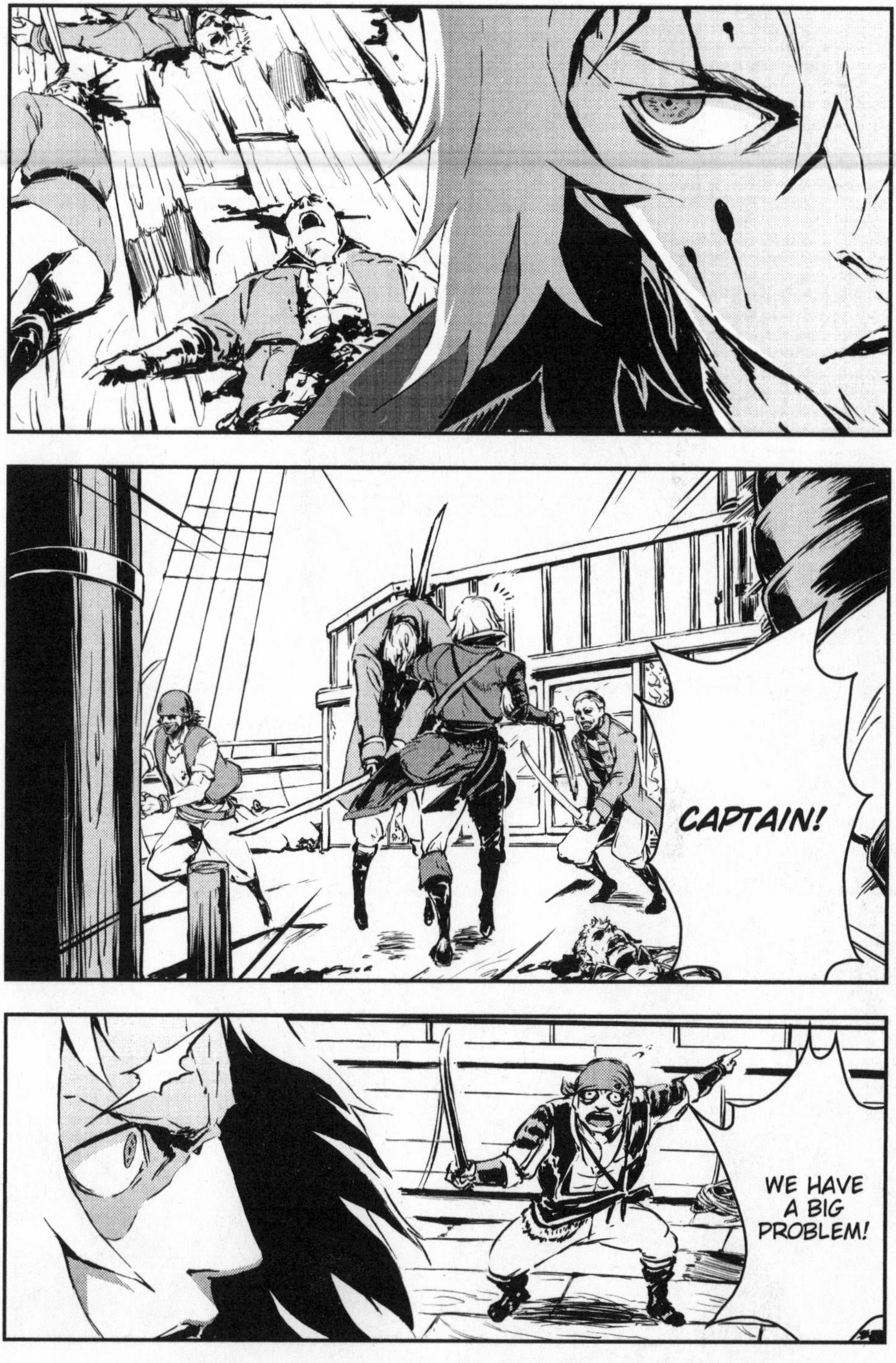
CAPTAIN!
WE HAVE A BIG PROBLEM!

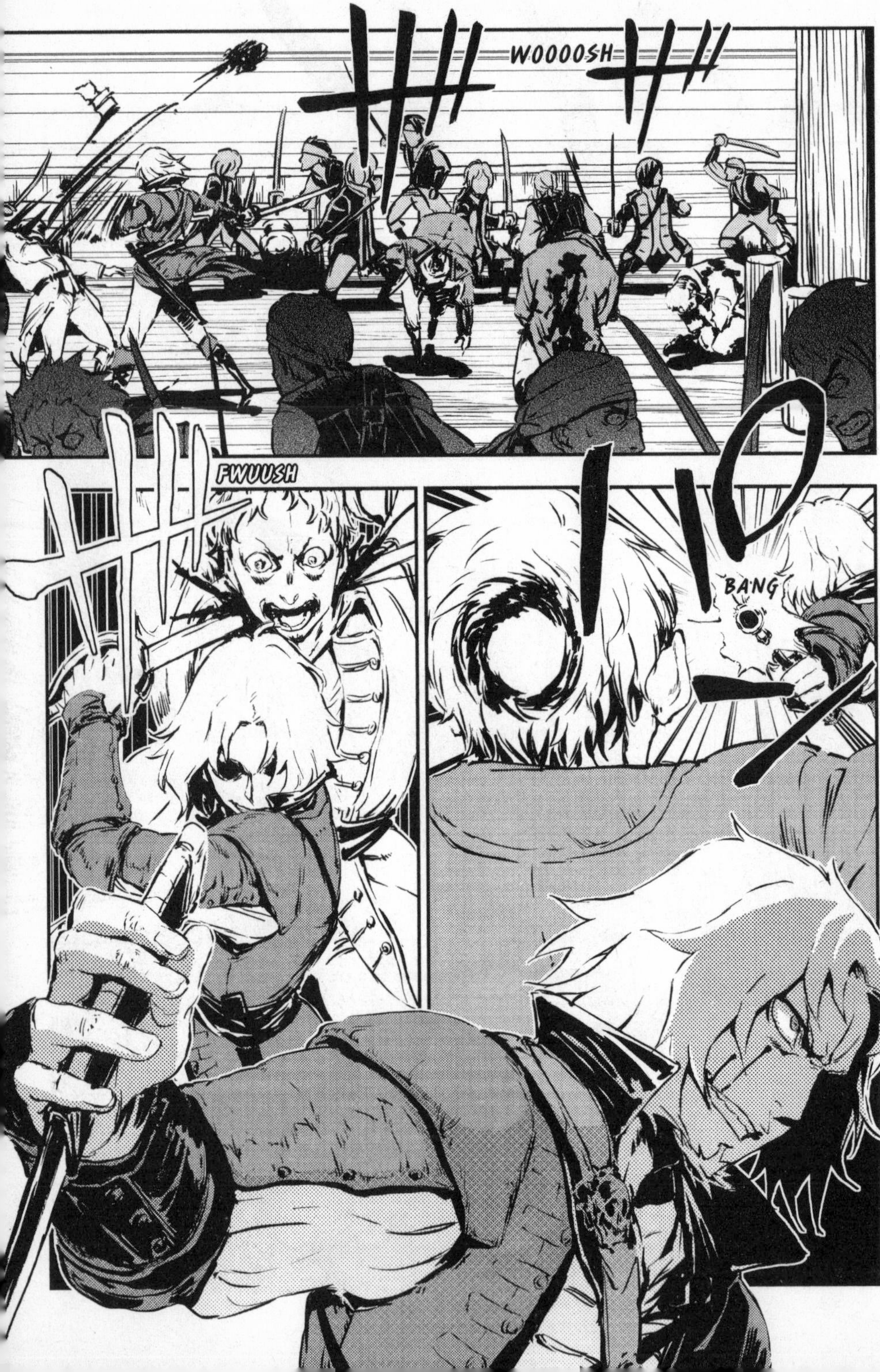
WOOOOSH
BANG
FWUUSH

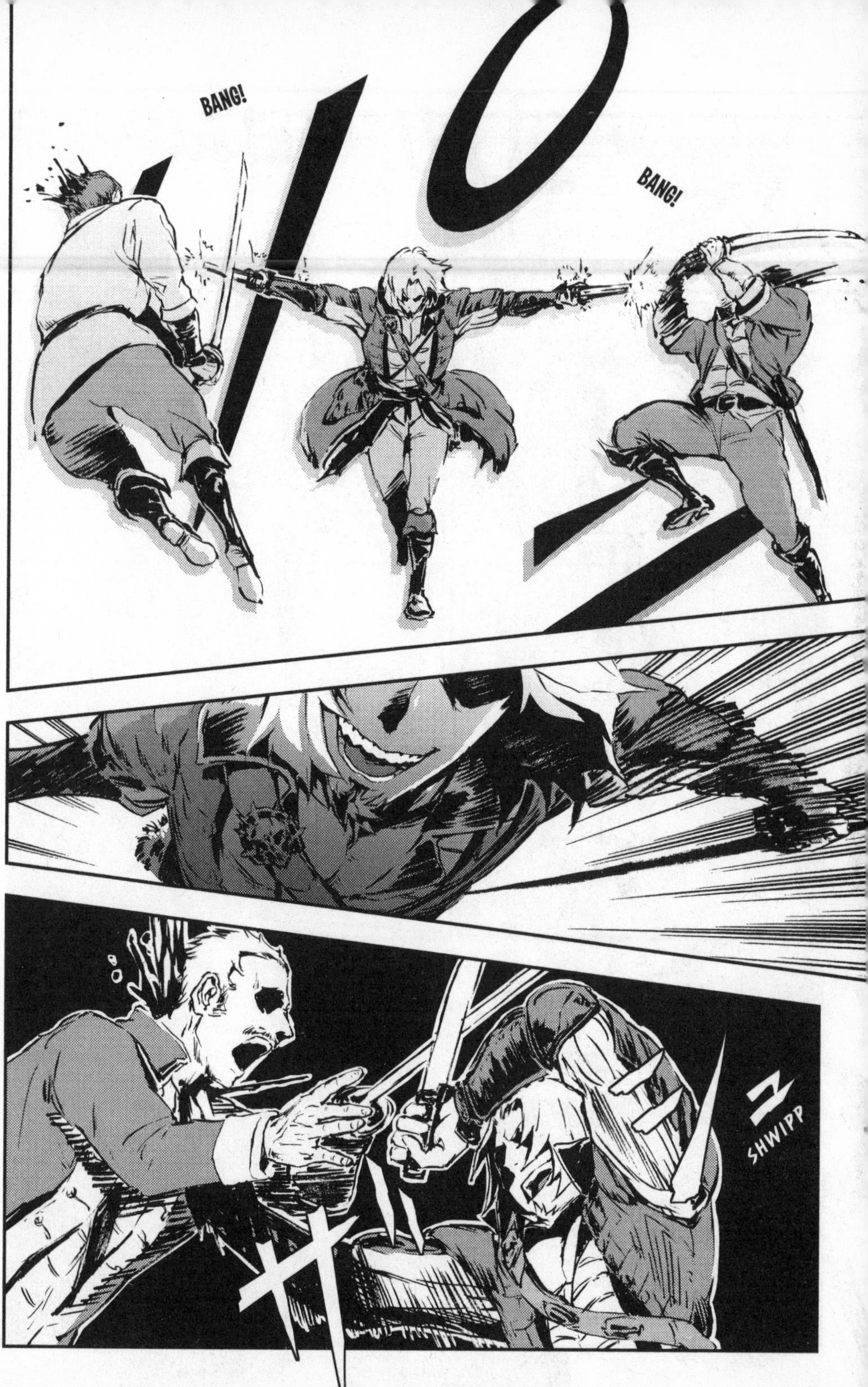
BANG!
BANG!
SHWIPP

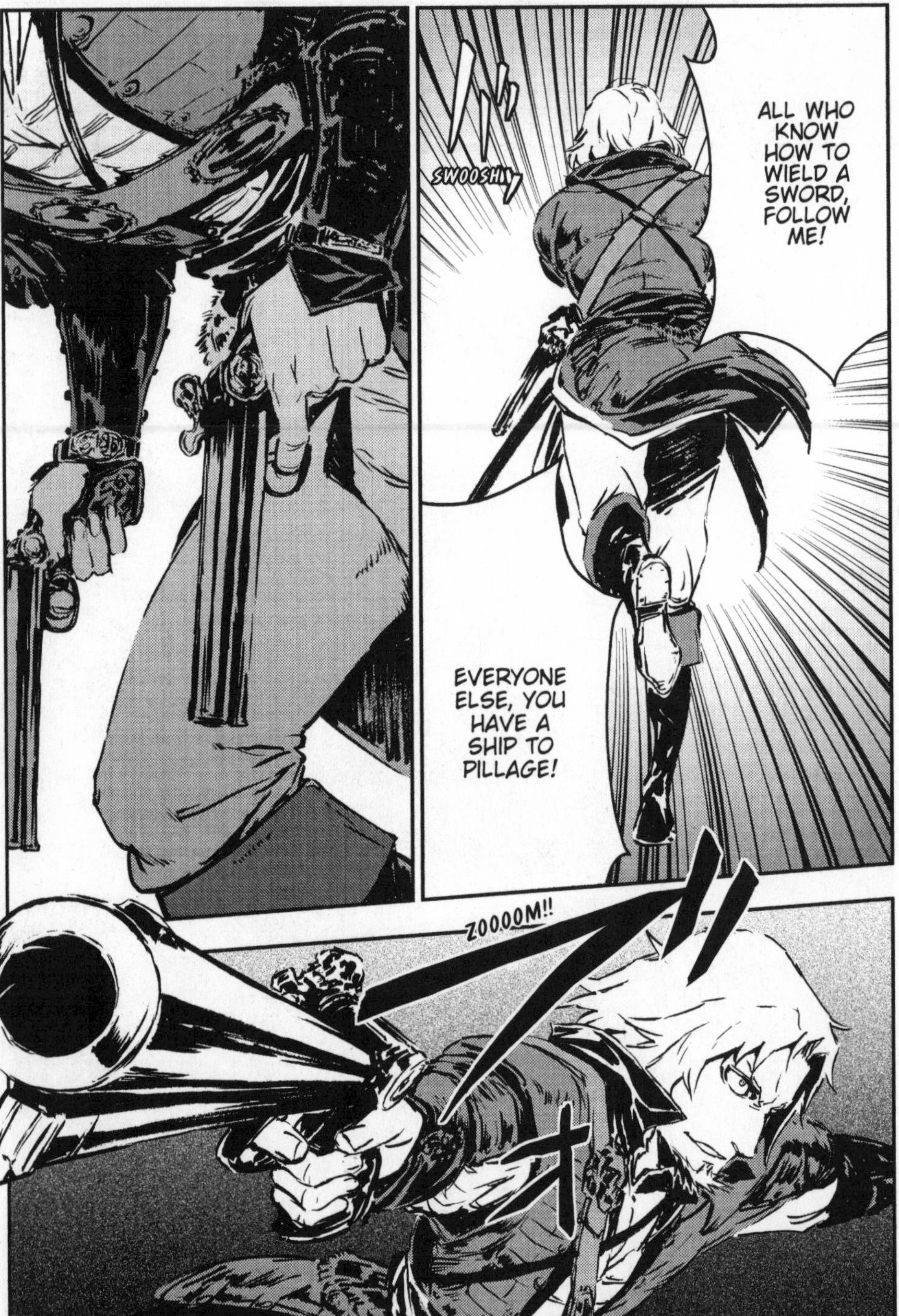
ALL WHO KNOW HOW TO WIELD A SWORD, FOLLOW ME!
SWOOSHH
EVERYONE ELSE, YOU HAVE A SHIP TO PILLAGE!
ZOOOOM!!

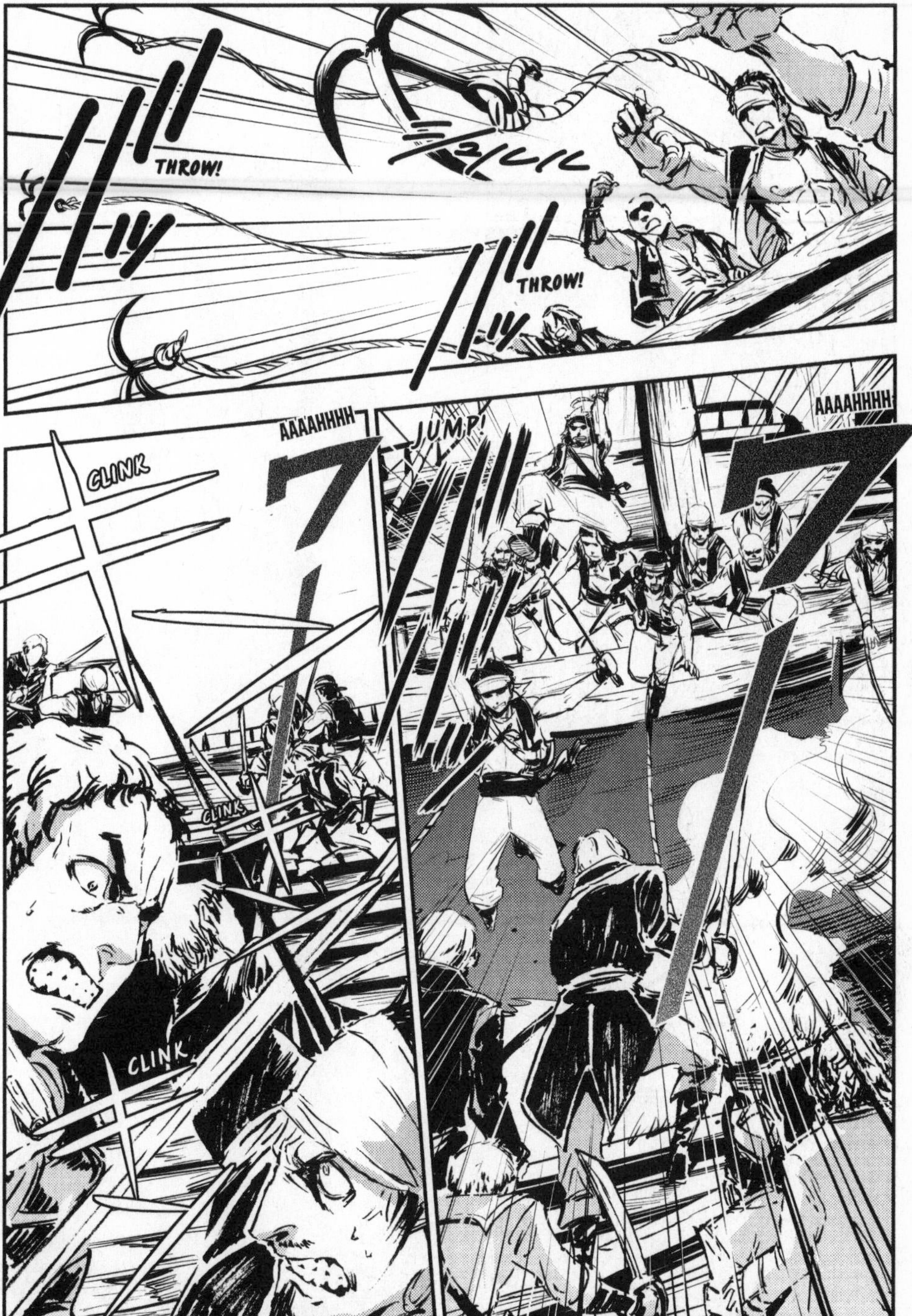
THROW!
THROW!
AAAAHHHH
JUMP!
AAAAHHHH
CLINK
CLINK
CLINK

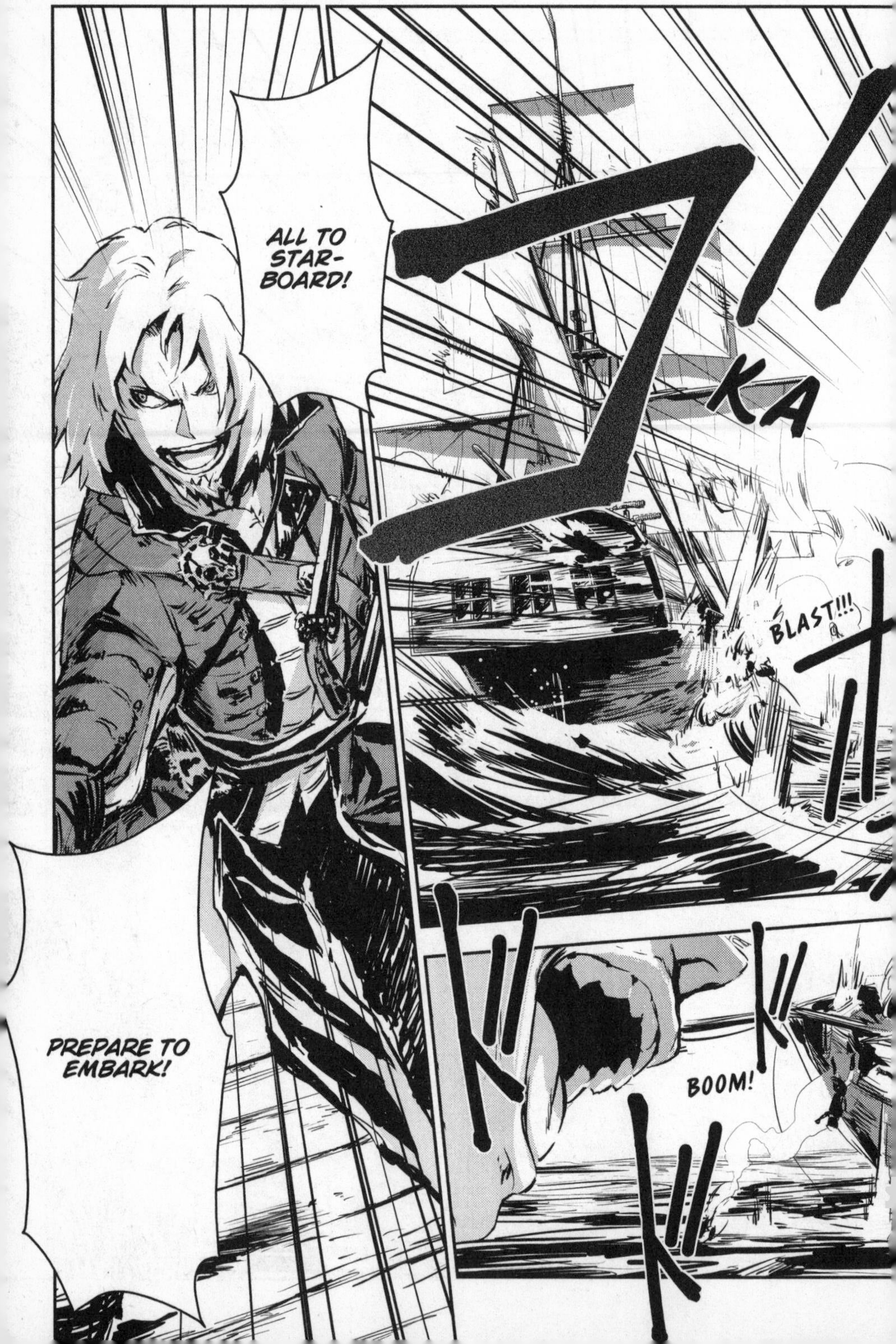
KA
BLAST!!!
BOOM!
ALL TO STAR-BOARD!
PREPARE TO EMBARK!

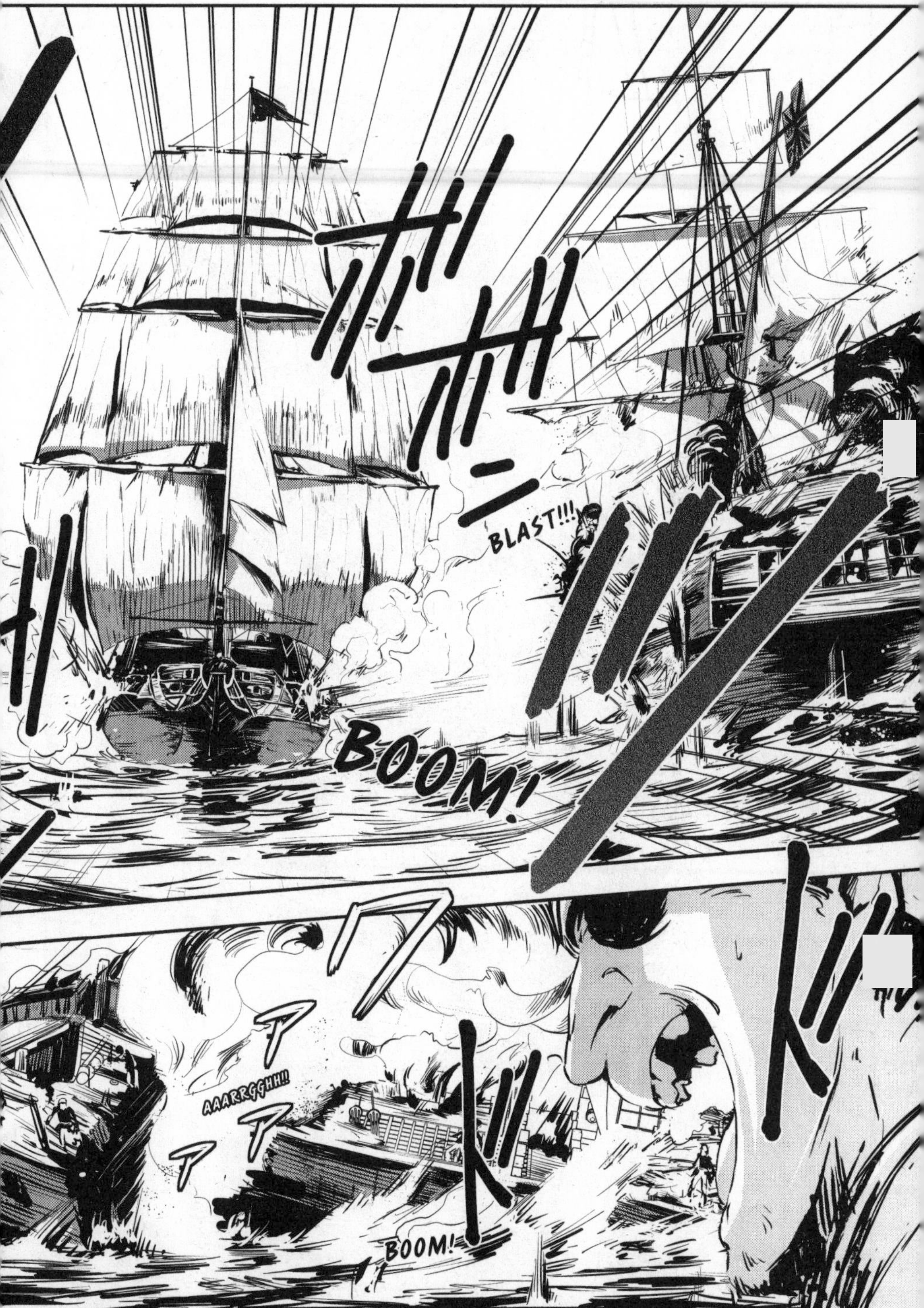
BLAST!!!
BOOM!
AAARRGGHH!!
BOOM!

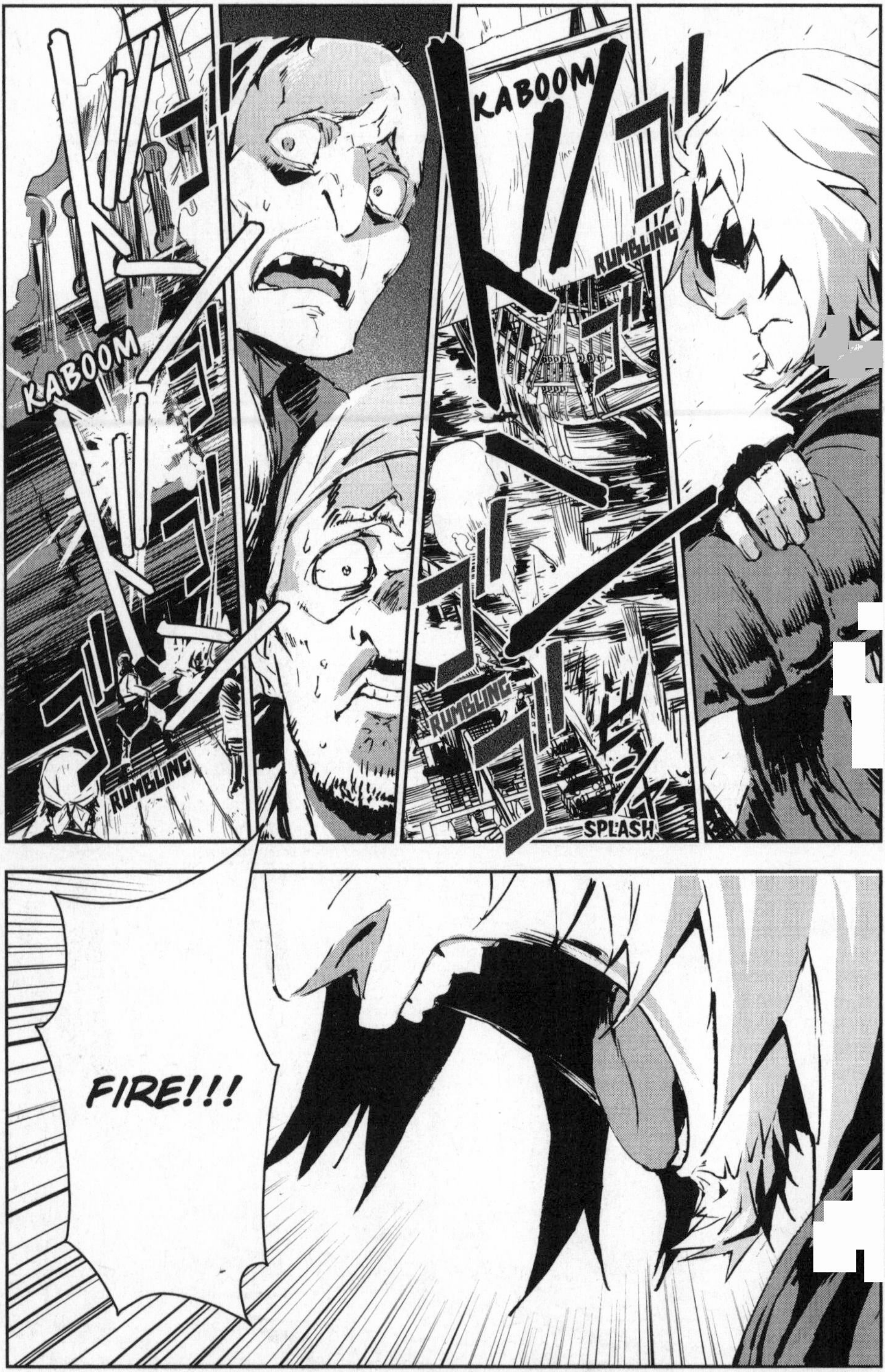
KABOOM
RUMBLING
RUMBLING
SPLASH
KABOOM
RUMBLING
FIRE!!!

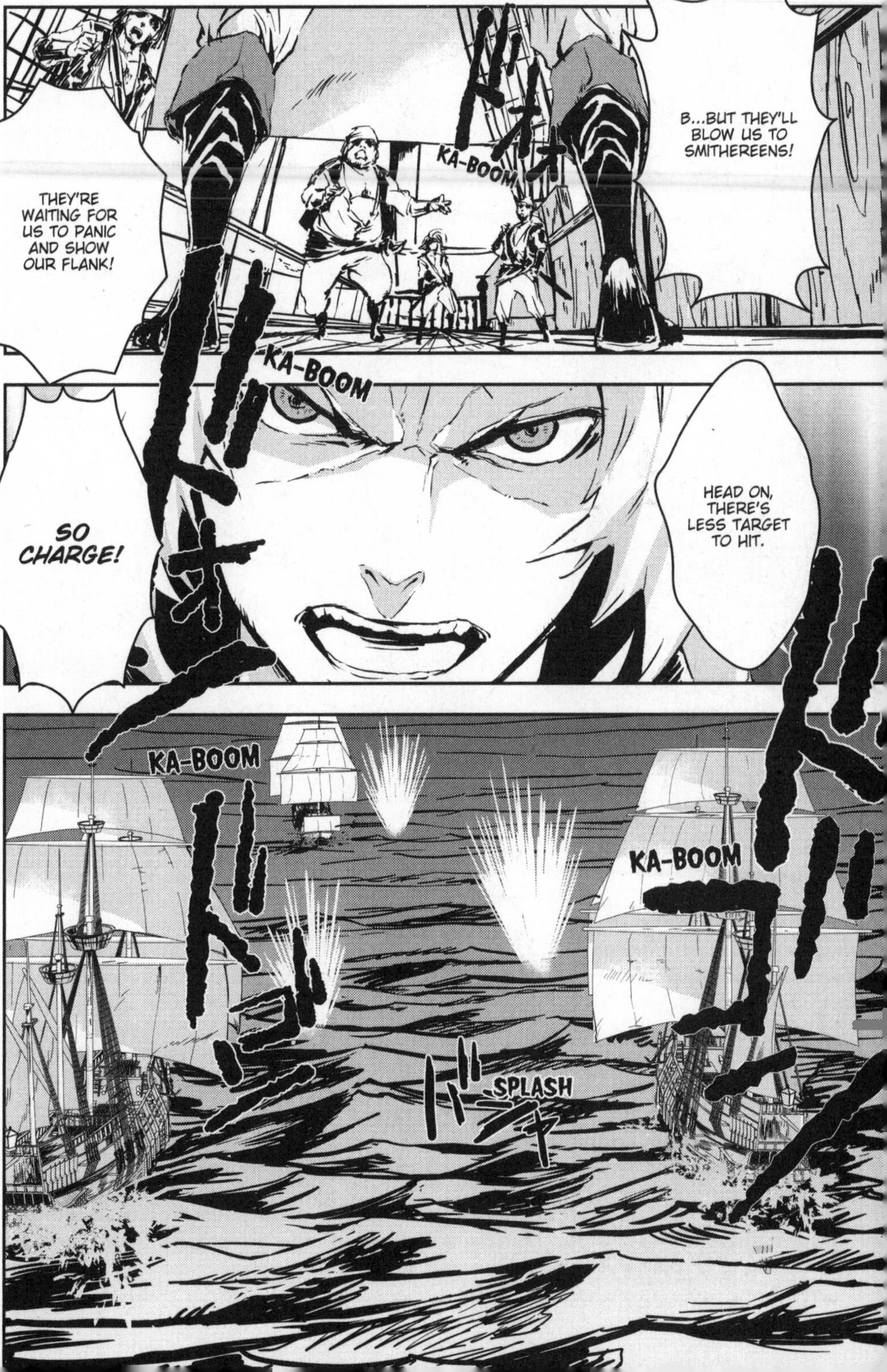
B...BUT THEY'LL BLOW US TO SMITHEREENS!
KA-BOOM
THEY'RE WAITING FOR US TO PANIC AND SHOW OUR FLANK!
KA-BOOM
HEAD ON, THERE'S LESS TARGET TO HIT.
SO CHARGE!
KA-BOOM
KA-BOOM
SPLASH

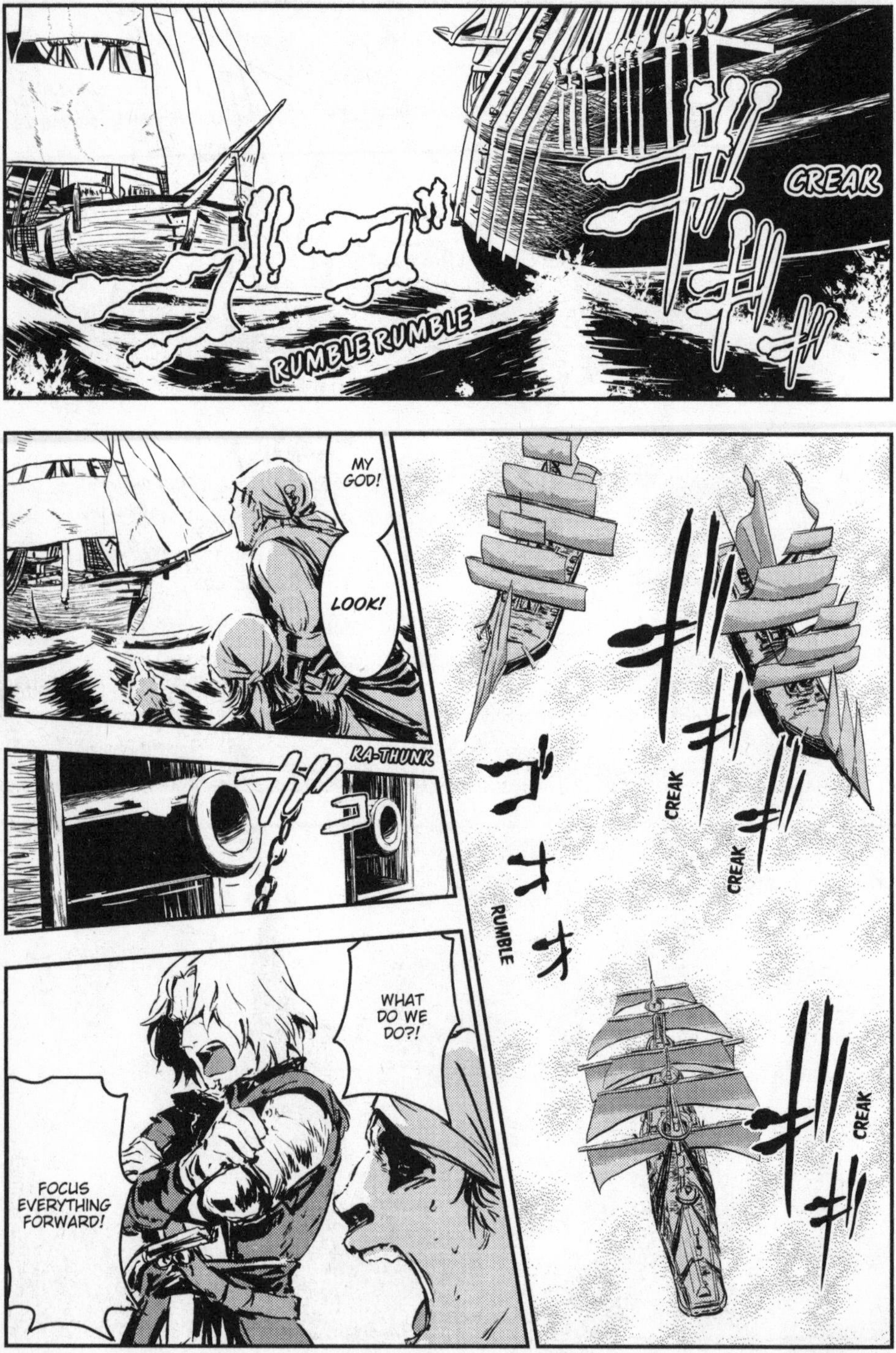
CREAK
RUMBLE RUMBLE
CREAK
CREAK
RUMBLE
CREAK
MY GOD!
LOOK!
KA-THUNK
WHAT DO WE DO?!
FOCUS EVERYTHING FORWARD!

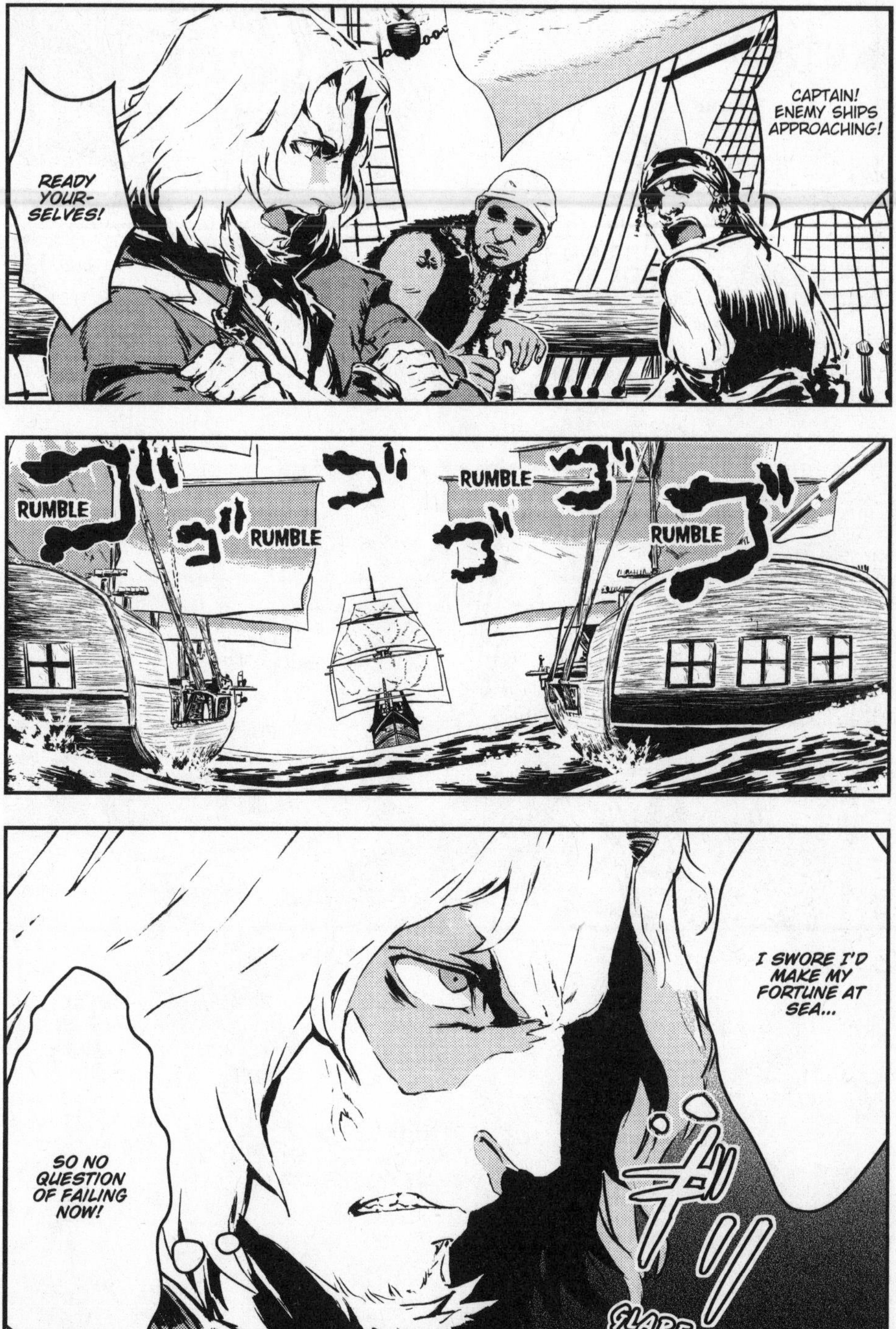
CAPTAIN! ENEMY SHIPS APPROACHING!
READY YOUR-SELVES!
RUMBLE
RUMBLE
RUMBLE
RUMBLE
I SWORE I'D MAKE MY FORTUNE AT SEA...
SO NO QUESTION OF FAILING NOW!
GLARE

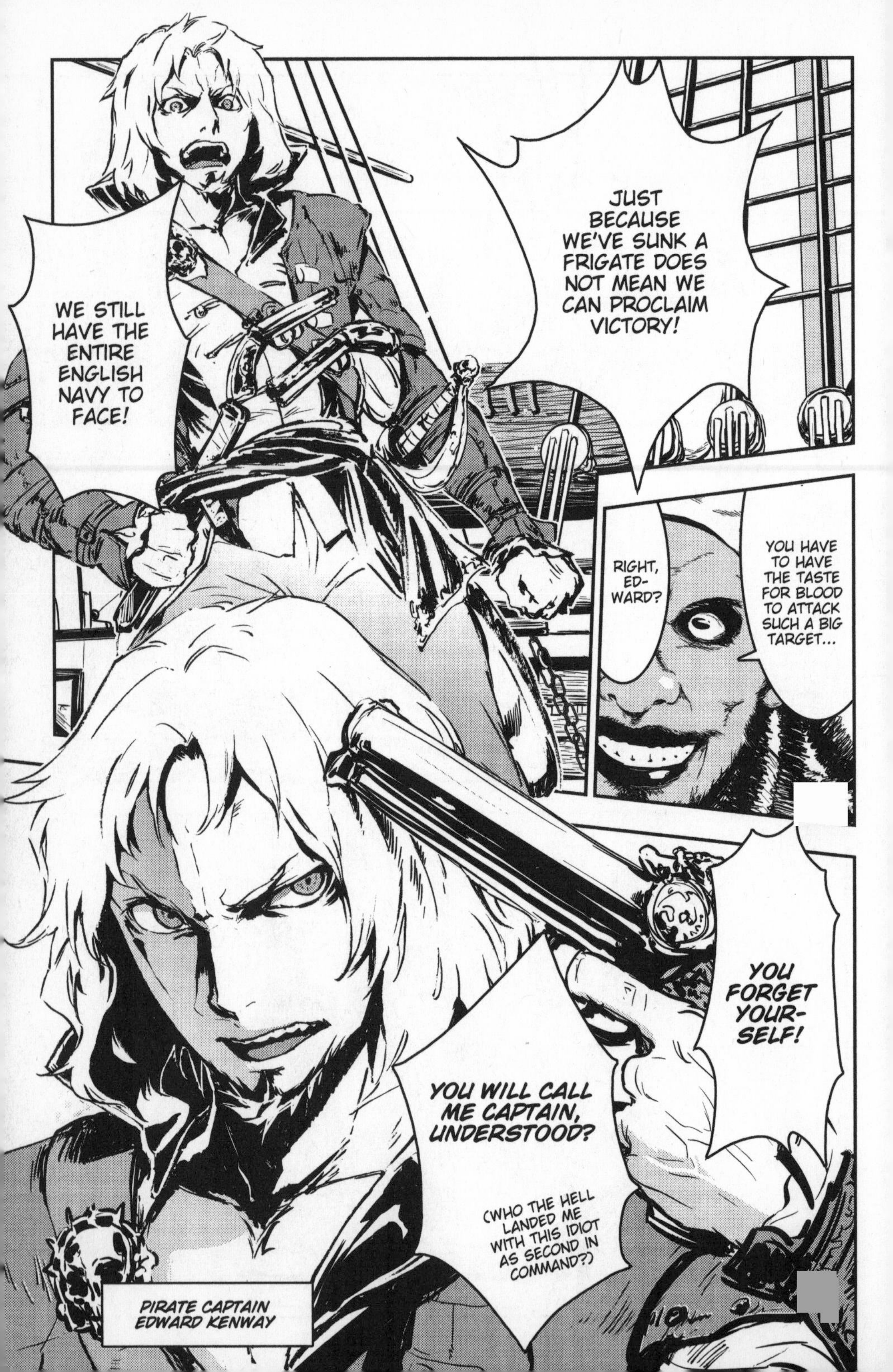
JUST BECAUSE WE'VE SUNK A FRIGATE DOES NOT MEAN WE CAN PROCLAIM VICTORY!
WE STILL HAVE THE ENTIRE ENGLISH NAVY TO FACE!
YOU HAVE TO HAVE THE TASTE FOR BLOOD TO ATTACK SUCH A BIG TARGET...
RIGHT, ED-WARD?
YOU FORGET YOUR-SELF!
YOU WILL CALL ME CAPTAIN, UNDERSTOOD?
(WHO THE HELL LANDED ME WITH THIS IDIOT AS SECOND IN COMMAND?)
PIRATE CAPTAIN EDWARD KENWAY

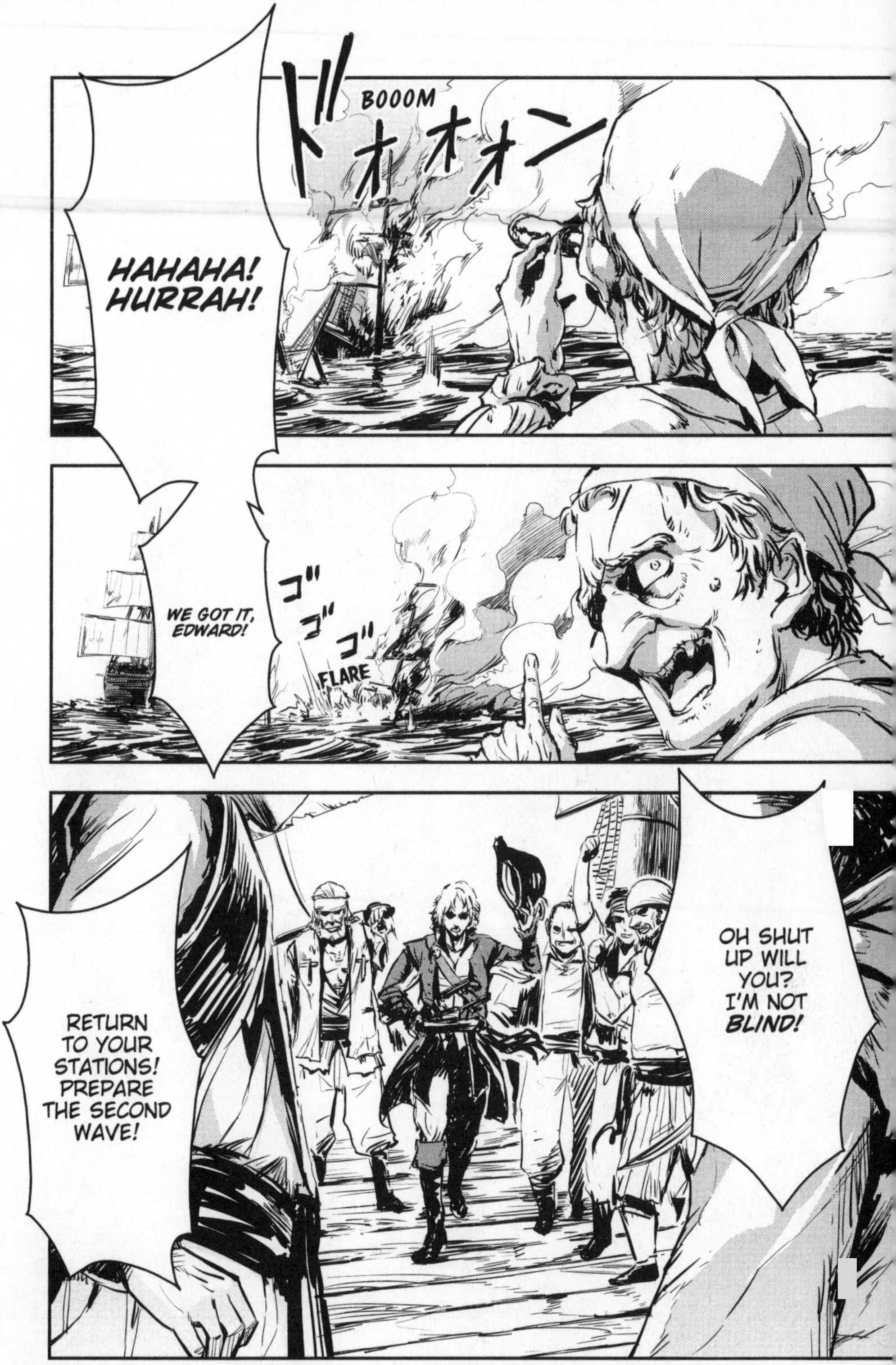
ドオオオン
BOOM
HAHAHA! HURRAH!
ゴゴゴ
FLARE
WE GOT IT, EDWARD!
OH SHUT UP WILL YOU? I'M NOT BLIND!
RETURN TO YOUR STATIONS! PREPARE THE SECOND WAVE!

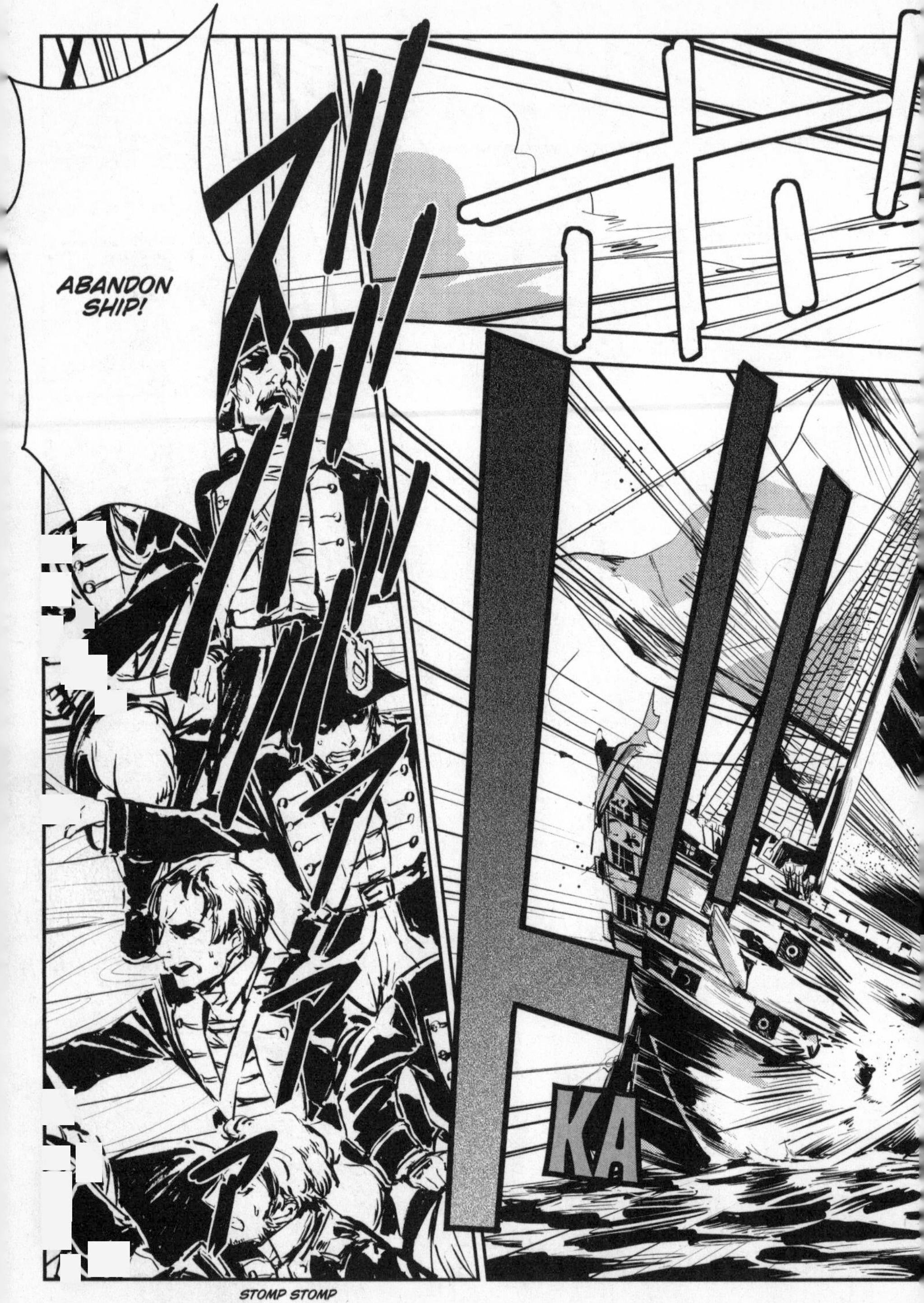
KA
ABANDON SHIP!

STOMP STOMP

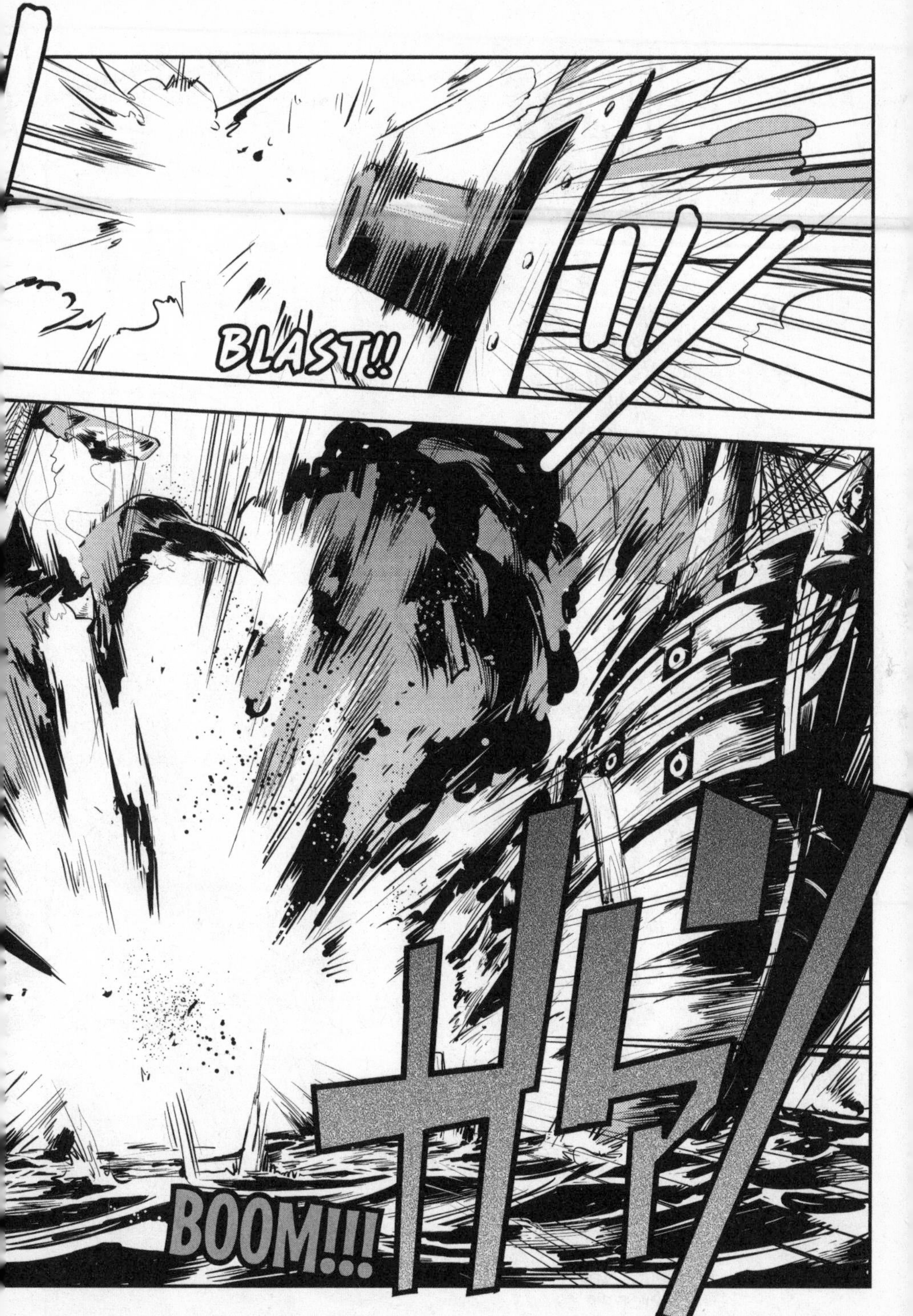
BLAST!!
BOOM!!!

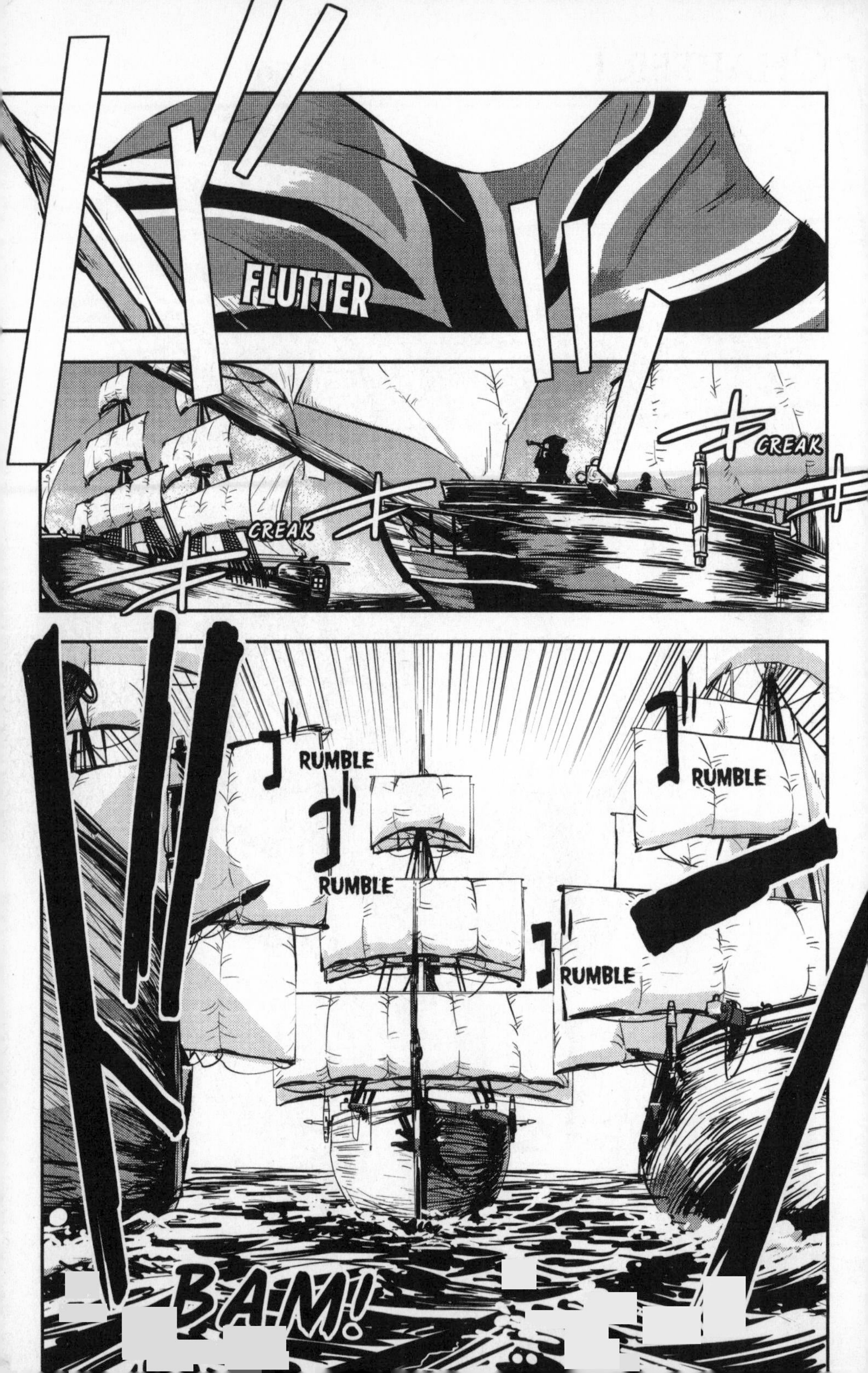
FLUTTER
CREAK
CREAK
RUMBLE
RUMBLE
RUMBLE
RUMBLE
BAM!

CHAPTER I

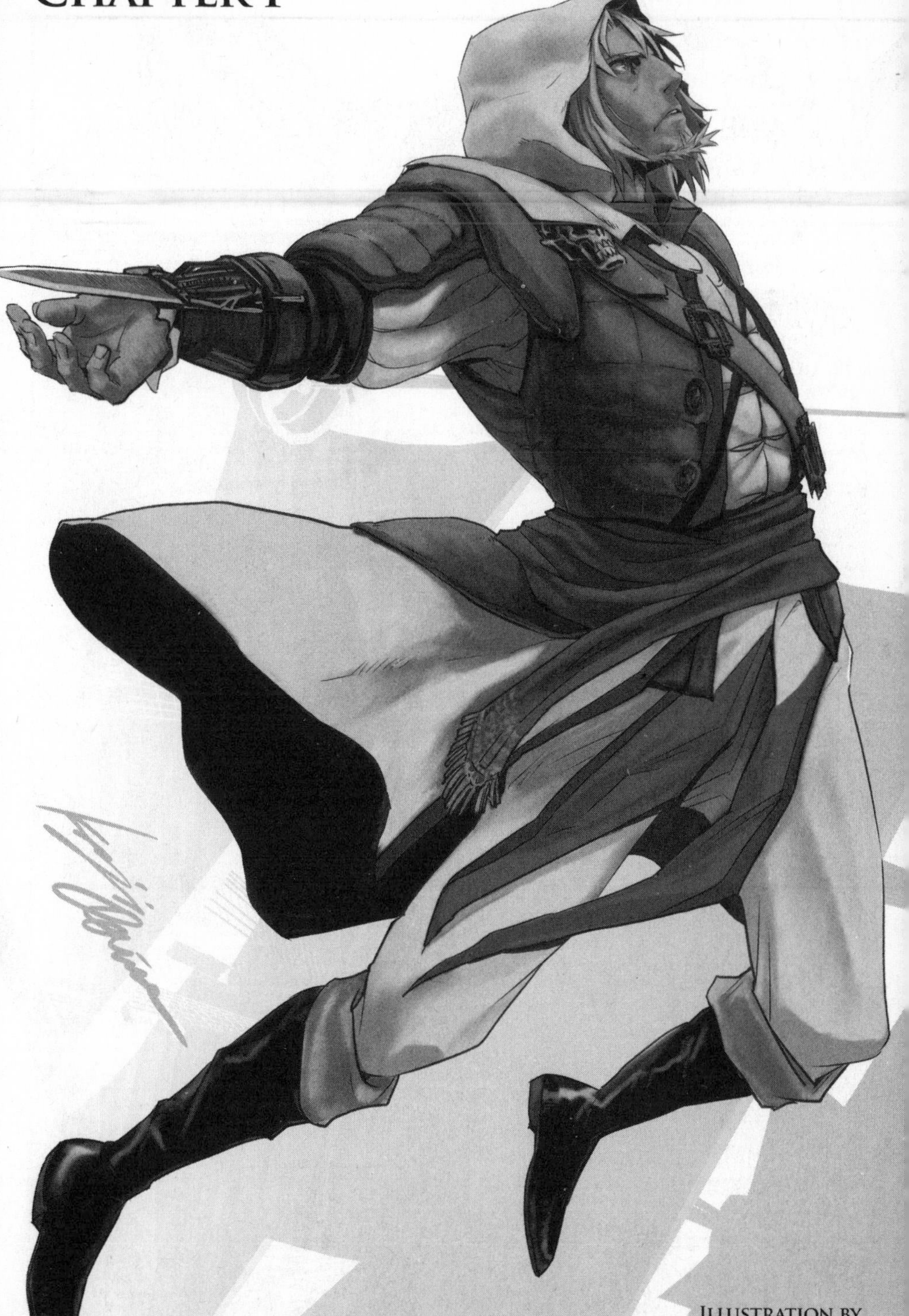

ILLUSTRATION BY
KENJI OIWA

TITAN COMICS

SENIOR EDITOR
MARTIN EDEN
ASSISTANT EDITOR
AMOONA SAOHIN
SENIOR DESIGNER
ANDREW LEUNG

PRODUCTION CONTROLLER
PETER JAMES
PRODUCTION SUPERVISOR
MARIA PEARSON
SENIOR PRODUCTION CONTROLLER
JACKIE FLOOK
ART DIRECTOR
OZ BROWNE
SENIOR SALES MANAGER
STEVE TOTHILL
PRESS OFFICER
WILL O'MULLANE
COMICS BRAND MANAGER
LUCY RIPPER
DIRECT SALES & MARKETING MANAGER
RICKY CLAYDON
COMMERCIAL MANAGER
MICHELLE FAIRLAMB
PUBLISHING MANAGER
DARRYL TOTHILL
PUBLISHING DIRECTOR
CHRIS TEATHER
OPERATIONS DIRECTOR
LEIGH BAULCH
EXECUTIVE DIRECTOR
VIVIAN CHEUNG
PUBLISHER
NICK LANDAU

SPECIAL THANKS TO:
CLEMENCE DELEUZE AND ALL AT UBISOFT.

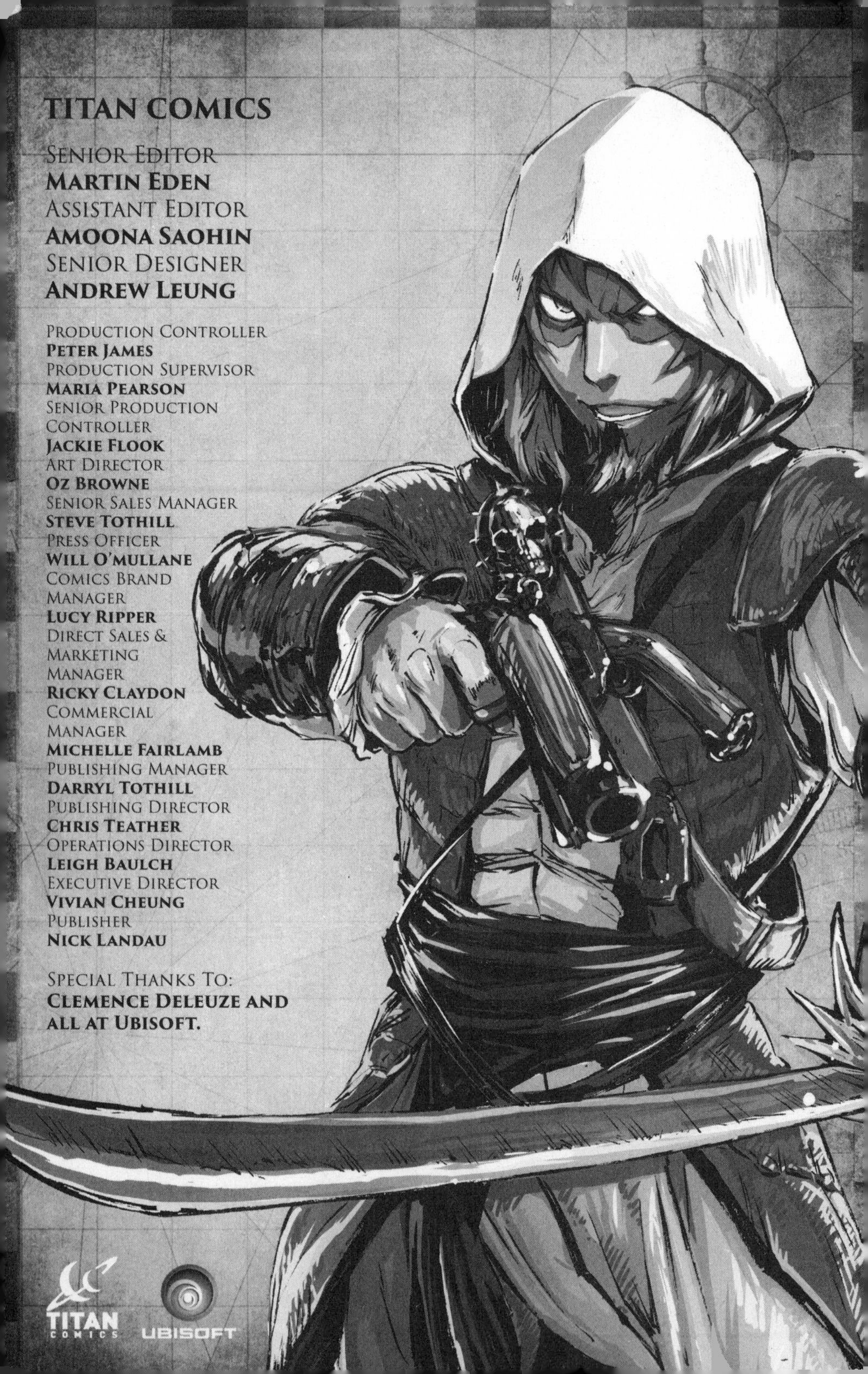

TITAN COMICS UBISOFT

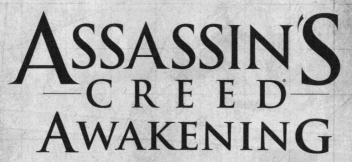

ASSASSIN'S
—CREED—
AWAKENING

ORIGINAL STORY **UBISOFT**
SCRIPT **TAKASHI YANO**
ART **KENJI OIWA**
LETTERING **AMOONA SAOHIN**

ORIGINALLY PUBLISHED IN JAPANESE BY
SHUEISHA.
**THIS MANGA IS PRESENTED IN ITS
ORIGINAL RIGHT-TO-LEFT READING
FORMAT.**

Assassin's Creed Awakening Volume One
© 2017 Ubisoft Entertainment. All rights reserved. Assassin's Creed, Ubisoft and the Ubisoft logo are trademarks of
Ubisoft Entertainment in the U.S. and/or other countries. Printed in the USA.
Published by Titan Comics, a division of Titan Publishing Group, Ltd, 144 Southwark Street, SE1 0UP, London, UK.
No part of this publication may be reproduced, stored in a retrieval system or transmitted, in any form or by any means,
without the prior written permission of the publisher. Names, characters, places and incidents featured in this publication
are the product of the author's imagination or used fictitiously. Any resemblance to persons either living or dead (except
for satirical purposes) is entirely coincidental.
10 9 8 7 6 5 4 3 2 1
First printed in the US in September 2017. ISBN: 9781785858581
A CIP catalogue record for this title is available from the British Library.
www.titan-comics.com

ASSASSIN'S
C R E E D
AWAKENING
VOLUME ONE